TEACHING STRATEGIC PROCESSES IN READING

SOLVING PROBLEMS IN THE TEACHING OF LITERACY
Cathy Collins Block, *Series Editor*

Teaching
Strategic Processes
in
Reading

Janice F. Almasi

Foreword by
Michael Pressley

THE GUILFORD PRESS
New York   London

KH

Library of Congress Cataloging-in-Publication Data

Almasi, Janice F.
  Teaching strategic processes in reading / by Janice F. Almasi; foreword by Michael Pressley.
    p.   cm. — (Solving problems in the teaching of literacy)
  ISBN 1-57230-807-9 (hardcover) — ISBN 1-57230-806-0 (paberback)
  1. Reading. 2. Reading comprehension. 3. Word recognition. I. Title. II. Series.
LB1050.42.A44 2003
372.41—dc21

                                              2002015630

10/25/04

*To my graduate students
and the children you teach.*

*Your persistence and dedication to learning
inspire me daily.*

About the Author

Janice F. Almasi, PhD, is currently Associate Professor in the Department of Learning and Instruction at the State University of New York at Buffalo, where she teaches courses in childhood literacy methods, strategic reading processes, reading theory, and research methodology. After earning her BS in Education from Edinboro State University of Pennsylvania, she began teaching fourth graders on the Eastern Shore of Maryland. While teaching, she earned her MEd in Reading Education from the University of Maryland. She then pursued her research interests, earning a PhD in Curriculum and Instruction from the University of Maryland. Prior to coming to Buffalo, she was also a postdoctoral fellow at the Learning Research and Development Center at the University of Pittsburgh. Dr. Almasi's pedagogical and research endeavors have examined critically the contexts in which children learn from text. Her research focuses on patterns of social interaction, discourse, engagement, and cognitive processing during peer discussions of literature. She earned the National Reading Conference's Outstanding Student Research Award in 1993 and the International Reading Association's Outstanding Dissertation of the Year Award in 1994. She is currently working on a developmental model of peer discussion. Her work has been published in *Reading Research Quarterly*, the *Journal of Literacy Research*, *Educational Psychologist*, and *Race, Ethnicity, and Education*.

Foreword

When I first started studying strategic processes in reading, the question often posed to me was, "Why? . . . Why would anyone study strategic processes in reading?" A quarter of a century later, it is much more well understood how "strategic" skilled reading really is. Good beginning readers use strategies to recognize words, for example; adults who read well are strategically active as they try to understand text.

As the study of reading strategies has progressed, many questions have been asked. In this volume, Janice F. Almasi answers many of those questions and summarizes what has emerged as reading strategies have been documented and analyzed.

She begins with the definition of strategic processes, a definition that has not been worked out without some huge disagreements among investigators over the years. She does a great job of summarizing how researchers know when readers are strategic, and how reading strategies are assessed. Her coverage makes very clear, however, that assessment is never certain, with strategic reading remaining an elusive cognitive activity, one only studied indirectly.

Much of my own work has been about strategies instruction, so the breadth and depth of what Almasi has to say on the topic is what especially attracted me to this book. She covers all the important models of teaching and fostering strategic reading instruction, providing balanced coverage of competing perspectives. In doing so, she clarifies important distinctions that must be understood by those who seek professional-level knowledge about strategic reading. Almasi's book is notable in that there is strong coverage of both word recognition and comprehension strategies, in contrast to many books that treat one or the other.

Almasi's coverage of strategy instruction is realistic—this is crucial. Strategy instruction is not easy. Most teachers need considerable experience before they can do it in an assured manner. Almasi does a good job of walking through the process whereby teachers can develop into strategy instructors. Anyone reading this volume will emerge with an understanding of why too few teachers try to become strategies instructors, and why many give up before they fully complete the task.

I am hopeful that this book will convince many more teachers to take up the challenge, for there is a good reason for strategies instruction: So many readers, young and old, are less strategic than they might be, or should be. Almasi does a good job of making this clear and analyzing why strategic reading is not more common. Probably the only way to make it more common would be to make the teaching of strategic processes more common. I think Almasi will have done a great service by moving us more in that direction with this book.

I close by pointing out that when I have seen effective strategies instruction, such teaching is at the center of the curriculum, and such teaching goes on every day—indeed, often every hour—for semesters and even years. Strategies instruction is a long-term approach to the development of effective readers, not a quick fix. It is high-quality teaching, and this is a high-quality volume by an author who knows the topic well, who has acquired her expertise through knowledge of the academic research, by teaching strategies teachers, and by being a strategies teacher herself.

MICHAEL PRESSLEY, PHD
University of Notre Dame

Preface

This volume came about at the request of my graduate students. Many of these students are or are striving to become practicing teachers. All are enrolled in reading education courses; however, the course from which this text evolved is an elective in the program. This is meaningful primarily because, as professors and students are aware, electives are often selected based on their ease relative to required courses. This was not an easy elective, however. There were many other courses in which to enroll that would have been easier. These students chose a more difficult route. Becoming a teacher of strategic reading processes is extremely difficult. It is harder than becoming a teacher of other subjects because it permeates all subjects. It is a way of thinking, a state of mind that must occur at every opportunity throughout the school day. Recognizing these opportunities as they occur in relation to a classroom of children with very different motivations, abilities, and interests is what makes teaching strategic processes complex. The amount of reflection and self-awareness that must accompany strategies instruction is what makes it difficult. Becoming a proficient strategies teacher is a personal journey that requires a teacher who is willing to open him- or herself up entirely for critical examination, and who is willing to adapt to the ever changing needs of students. Few are willing to take on this challenge, which is why it is important to know that the graduate students, who are the life of this book, willingly undertook it. They are tremendous individuals who gave entirely of themselves—often overlooking their own personal needs to selflessly teach struggling readers. I admire each and every one of them. I would even encourage readers to read the final chapter (Chapter 7) first, because it describes the journeys on which these incredible teachers embarked. Through journal entries and portfolios, it tells the tales of my students as they learned about becoming teachers of strategic processes. These are poignant and, at times, painful tales of reflection and self-discovery.

Chapter 1 sets the groundwork for the volume by explaining what is involved in strategic processing and distinguishes between strategies and skills—a common misunderstanding. The chapter also describes the characteristics of strategic and nonstrategic readers.

Chapter 2 describes a multitude of methods for assessing strategic processing. The premise of the chapter is that assessment must be ongoing and integrally related to instruction. Assessment cannot be an end product, for strategic processing is active and dynamic and must be assessed while it occurs. The assessments described are process-oriented assessments. Assessments must also be used to individualize instruction. Teachers are encouraged to generate and continually refine hypotheses about individual students' strengths and needs as strategic readers based on the recursive cycle of ongoing assessment and instruction.

Chapter 3 provides a model of strategy instruction grounded in research and clinical practice. A number of strategy instruction models are compared to situate the present model. From there, the key components of the strategy instruction model used by my students are described, accompanied by examples from the authentic teaching contexts my graduate students created: providing a safe environment, providing explicit instruction, reducing processing demands, and creating opportunities for verbalization.

Chapter 4 describes theoretical explanations for students' struggles with comprehension. It also describes the types of cognitive strategies that will assist readers who have various comprehension difficulties and provides background material for Chapter 5, in which the research supporting various comprehension strategies is reviewed. Text anticipation strategies, text maintenance strategies, and fix-up strategies are discussed in detail, and lesson plans and instructional materials for each strategy are provided. Each lesson shared was created and implemented by teachers in my graduate course. The teachers' reactions to, and reflections on, the lessons provide readers with an idea of the success of the lessons and how children reacted to them.

Chapter 6 describes the relevant theory underlying word recognition strategies, and provides sample lessons and guidelines for instruction. It also provides lists of children's literature that is well suited for use in instruction focusing on word recognition.

Chapter 7, as noted above, describes the teachers' growth and development as they learned about teaching strategic processes. The chapter should be read—and reread—because it is the heart and soul of the book. As you begin to understand the personal journeys that these teachers undertook, you will begin to understand what strategy instruction is really about. It is not about individual strategies, lesson plans, activities, or texts—it is about people learning from one another and with one another. It is about the feeling one has when one looks into the eyes of a child and truly feels his or her frustration. It is about knowing and, more importantly, realizing that you may have caused that frustration. It is about being driven to understand complex theories because you want to make the difference in the literate life of that frustrated child. It is about learning how to inspire and create a safe space in which to learn, and it is about the feeling one has when a child with fragile self-esteem takes a risk as a reader because you have gently nurtured him or her into the world of literacy. I encourage you to take the challenge of becoming a teacher of strategic processes. It is a difficult but obviously most rewarding journey.

Acknowledgments

I am most graciously indebted to my graduate students, who have taught me so much. Without your help and inspiration this book would not have become a reality—you are its heart and soul. I admire and respect each and every one of you: Angela Bies, Anita Brocker, Erin David, Renee Danielewicz, Sheila Ewing, AnnaMaria Figliomeni, Chastity Flynn, Keli Garas, Patty DiLaura George, Liz Graffeo, Renee Guzak, Jill Hatfield, Bob Hirsch, Jennifer Izzo, Krista Jaekle, Eileen Ludwig, Jaime Quackenbush, Jody Rabinowitz, Mike Rock, Kathy Sadowski, Summer Sciandra, Donna Von Hendy, and Kristin Zahn. Please continue to challenge yourself.

I would also like to acknowledge those who were my mentors while I studied at the University of Maryland. The connections I make to theoretical work throughout the book were informed by their research and insights: Linda B. Gambrell, Michael Pressley, Peter Afflerbach, John Guthrie, John O'Flahavan, Jean Dreher, Beth Davey, and Ruth Garner.

I am also indebted to The Guilford Press's Chris Jennison, for his vision and editorial expertise throughout the writing of this book. I would also like to acknowledge and thank William Meyer and Guilford's talented editorial and production staff for bringing the book to reality. I am very appreciative of the constructive and critical feedback provided by Diane Tracey, Beth Roberts, and anonymous reviewers who saw the book at various stages.

I knew that I would have to go to another place (both literally and figuratively) to write this book. Therefore, I chose to spend 6 months in Newfoundland, Canada, where my mother was raised. Based on stories I had heard throughout my life, and the few times I visited before, I knew that the natural splendors of the rocky and rugged landscape, the untainted waters, and the sparse population would provide a peaceful and tranquil environment in which to write. In the dead of winter, surrounded by 200 inches of snow, and ice 3-feet thick on the water, it was peaceful, to say the least. I had never visited Newfoundland alone, nor in the winter, but I was desperate to live in the place that spawned my mother's incredible stories of human triumph and tragedy. Those stories are another book, but they are stories of ingeniously *strategic* individuals who struggled each day to survive in a savagely harsh environment. The Newfoundland in which I lived is not the

Newfoundland in which my mother lived. That Newfoundland no longer exists. But I could not have written a book about strategies without having experienced the winters the Newfoundlanders experienced, and having lived with, and among, these honest, hardworking, and strategically resourceful people. Though times have changed a great deal in Newfoundland, the people there continue to face incredible political, economic, and social challenges. In this sense, Newfoundland is the same as in my mother's stories. It is an island of profoundly genuine and giving people who can make something out of nothing, and who can make you feel warm, in spite of what the world outside brings.

I am grateful to my relatives in Newfoundland who selflessly became my tour guides, translators, historians, and cultural brokers. On a daily basis they shared their hospitality and their culinary expertise, and I am highly appreciative. I am especially grateful to my aunt Susie (Spencer) Barbour; my uncle, George Spencer; and my aunt Maisie (Hodder) Spencer who gave so much of themselves. Thank you for sharing your life and your love with me. I will always cherish the special times that we shared. I would also like to thank my cousins Maisie and Dick Hardy, Don and Roberta Hogan, Paulette Spencer and Ken Andrews, Chris and MD Spencer, Stephen Spencer, Eileen (Spencer) Staples, Sheila and Fabian O'Brien, and Tina and Doug.

I am also indebted to the wonderful friends I met in Victoria Cove and Gander Bay, Newfoundland, who welcomed me into their community and their lives, and who often provided me with a safe haven. Thanks especially to my neighbors Lynn, Barry, and Nick Torraville and Joy Hodder, who provided sunshine on even the darkest and coldest winter days. Thanks also to Don and Margaret Elliott, Netta French, Bill and Annie Harbin, Marvin and Dianne Hodder, Melvin and Gertie Hodder, Harry and Susie Thompson, Flo Torraville, and Les and Marjorie Vivian, who entertained and taught me so much about life in Newfoundland. I am also indebted to Reverend Yvonne Thistle, who provided spiritual guidance throughout my stay. I would also like to thank the boys of Victoria Cove for teaching me about their very special community: David Collins, Johnny Collins, Josh Downer, Dylan Elliott, Thomas Newman, Nick Torraville, and Donovan Vivian.

As always, however, I am indebted to my first teachers and mentors, my mother, Jessie Spencer Almasi, and my father, John Almasi. The warmth of a home filled with unconditional love is the greatest gift a child could ever receive. Thank you for that most special gift. Thank you for listening. Thank you for your patience. Thank you for your understanding. Thank you for renewing each and every one of these gifts every day, and sometimes twice a day while I was writing this book. I love you.

I am also grateful to my sisters, Judy L. Downing and JoAnn M. Suchko. You are my first and forever friends. Thank you for always being there. I love you.

Contents

CHAPTER ONE

What Does It Mean to Be Strategic?

Cognitive strategies are actions an individual selects deliberately to attain a particular goal. Thus, strategic actions require intentionality (Paris, Wasik, & Turner, 1991; Pressley, Borkowski, & Schneider, 1989). To understand fully what it means to be strategic *while reading*, it is helpful to examine the many strategic behaviors we employ in our everyday lives. Consider the daily task of driving home from work. At times we accomplish this task in such an automated mode that we arrive home and wonder whether we really stopped at a particular stop sign or drove by certain landmarks. Driving a familiar route becomes a highly routinized process that requires little cognitive effort. In effect, we are operating on automatic pilot (Garner, 1987).

Now consider the same task—driving home from work—having heard, before, about a terrible traffic accident that is tying up the main artery leading home. Now we begin to think and act strategically, processing a multitude of thoughts and plans in just a few milliseconds: "How long will it be tied up? Should I just go forward and wait in the traffic? What alternate routes can I take? Should I just stay at work a little while, until the traffic clears?" At this point each of these plans is possible, until we begin to consider the conditions in which this event occurred: "When there's an accident on that road, it can take hours before the traffic clears. I have a meeting at 7:00 and I can't be late, and I have to stop at the store and pick up groceries for dinner." Given these conditions, we might decide not to waste any time and choose to take an alternate, less direct route around the accident. This entire process often takes less than a second. We enact thousands of these tiny strategic processing sequences throughout the course of a day. Sometimes the planning is for a much larger or complex event (e.g., a wedding) that requires much more thought and preparation. For such complex events a sequence of strategies, rather than a single strategy, is enacted (Pressley, Borkowski, et al., 1989), but for the most part we enact these strategic sequences so quickly that we hardly notice they are taking place.

WHAT IS INVOLVED IN STRATEGIC PROCESSING?

Strategic processing occurs when an individual plans, evaluates, and regulates his or her own behavior (Paris, Lipson, & Wixson, 1983; Paris et al., 1991; Pressley, Borkowski, et al., 1989). In the first driving scenario, on automatic pilot, little strategic processing occurred because it was not necessary for a routine drive home from work. However, the second scenario was quite different. Figure 1.1 depicts the strategic processing that occurred during this scenario. The process began with an attainable goal of arriving home. The moment we heard that an accident had occurred on the major highway leading home, we became aware of a problem. This "metacognitive awareness" activated a planning phase. Metacognition is a key aspect of strategic planning that occurs whenever we realize that something has gone wrong or that a change is warranted in a usual procedure. In this instance, had there been no metacognitive realization of a problem, we probably would have driven home on the usual route. Without a strategic intervention, we would have wound up in traffic. However, with awareness of the problem, we begin to evaluate ways to attain our goal by considering various alternatives; waiting in the traffic; staying at work until the traffic clears; or taking an alternate route. With these alternatives in mind, we begin to weigh each in terms of its costs and benefits in relation to the context, or conditions, surrounding this circumstance. Given the 7:00 PM meeting and the need to stop for groceries on the way home, there clearly is no time to wait. The decision crystallizes: Take an alternate route home. This evaluative thinking helped us make a

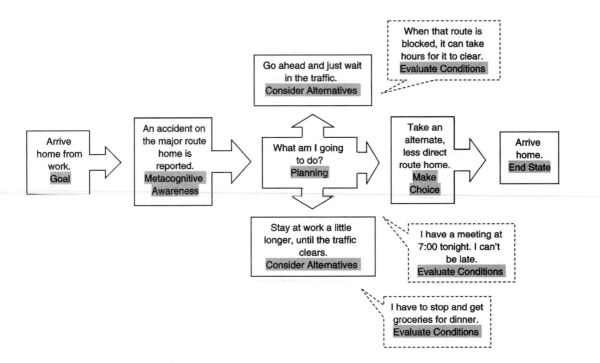

FIGURE 1.1. Diagram of strategic processing.

decision about which plan to enact to attain our goal of arriving home. It is our intentional self-selection of a means to an end that makes our behavior *strategic*.

Goals that are attained by accident or chance do not involve strategic behavior (Paris et al., 1983). Consider a variation of the previous example in which it is our first week on the job in a new city. We do not hear about the traffic accident prior to leaving work. Not knowing the area very well, we inadvertently make a wrong turn onto a less direct, alternate route, and it steers us around the traffic accident. Unknowingly, we have avoided the congested route and attained our desired goal. In this example we are not acting strategically. Taking the alternate route was an accident involving no planful thinking, evaluation of the situation, or intentional decision making.

Likewise obedient responses undertaken because of an external suggestion or demand are not strategic (Paris et al., 1983). For example, let's say that just prior to leaving work, the boss told us about the accident on the highway and suggested that we take an alternate route home in order to be able to arrive back at work in time for the meeting at 7:00 PM. We take the alternate route not because of a deliberate, well thought-out plan but because it was suggested to us as the best solution.

WHY IS STRATEGIC PROCESSING IMPORTANT?

We have known for decades that teaching the type of higher-level thinking required for strategic processing is not a regular part of the school curriculum (e.g., Durkin, 1978–1979). Perhaps instruction related to strategic processing is not included in schools because it is difficult to do well (it takes at least 3 years to become a proficient teacher of strategic processing [Brown & Coy-Ogan, 1993; Duffy, 1993a, 1993b; Pressley, Goodchild, Fleet, Zajchowski, & Evans, 1989]). Nevertheless, the value of teaching learners how to process text strategically is grounded in a wealth of sound research and theory demonstrating enhanced learning (Pressley, Goodchild, et al., 1989).

Paris et al. (1991) highlighted six reasons for teaching students how to become strategic readers: First, strategies enable readers to elaborate, organize, and evaluate information contained in text. Second, teaching students to read strategically can coincide with their cognitive development in other areas. That is, as children learn to become strategic readers, they become familiar with the use of strategies for enhancing attention, memory, communication, and learning. Third, because strategies are self-selected and can be used flexibly, readers take control of their own learning as they acquire a larger repertoire of strategies. Fourth, strategic processing requires, and therefore fosters, metacognitive development and motivation. Fifth, strategic processing is valuable simply because, as research shows, it can be taught to children. Sixth, teaching students to become strategic readers promotes their growth and development in all areas of the curriculum.

WHAT ARE COGNITIVE STRATEGIES?

According to Prawat (1989), strategic behaviors involve a range of techniques from heuristics to general control strategies. Heuristic techniques, which access relevant information during problem solving, do not require much cognitive processing and are considered to be at the lower end of the executive control continuum. Heuristics are considered "tricks of the trade" that are less connected to specific goal contexts than general control strategies. Examples of heuristics include teaching students to look at headings or introductions before reading, or teaching them a mnemonic to help them remember certain information (e.g., HOMES to help remember the names of the Great Lakes in the United States). Heuristics do not necessarily transfer to new, possibly relevant situations.

General control strategies involve the higher end of the executive control continuum and are more generalizable (Prawat, 1989). That is, general strategies such as planning, monitoring, and checking retain their essential properties in any domain (e.g., reading, writing, mathematics). For example, the process of planning—of carefully considering possible alternatives prior to embarking upon a task—is essentially the same in any domain. Planning was involved in the driving scenario described earlier; it would also be used if one were planning to study for a test. No matter what domain, planning always involves considering the possible, specific actions needed to attain a goal. Such general strategies require more cognitive processing than domain-specific ones, thereby requiring greater executive control, or management, on the thinker's part. A domain-specific strategy, such as using letter–sound cues to recognize unfamiliar words, is obviously specific to reading. Because domain-specific strategies are less generalizable and require less cognitive processing to apply, they are considered to lie at the lower end of the executive control continuum.

As noted, cognitive strategies of any form require intentionality, and intentionality means that the strategic process is available for introspection—it can be examined, discussed, and analyzed publicly or privately. In contrast, acquired *skills* are executed automatically and applied unconsciously (Paris et al., 1991). The first driving scenario is an example of a skilled response. Arriving home and realizing that we were not aware of whether we stopped at signals or stop signs is an indication that we were using an automatic skill that had been acquired and perfected through repeated practice. Paris et al. (1991) noted that, for novices, emerging skills may be used as a strategy if they are applied deliberately. Likewise, strategic processing can become automatic if practiced and repeated frequently (Pressley, Borkowski, et al., 1989; Pressley, Woloshyn, & Associates, 1995).

Many incorrectly refer to teaching tools such as graphic organizers (K-W-L charts, story maps, character maps) and teaching activities/techniques (e.g., Language Experience Approach, Making Words) as strategies. Inanimate objects, such as a graphic organizer, or activities, such as Making Words, are incapable of deliberately planning, selecting, evaluating, monitoring, and regulating behavior. Only people are capable of strategic thinking and processing. In this text, then, the term *strategy* refers to the deliberate cognitive process of selecting, enacting, and monitoring a plan to attain a goal; the distinctions between *strategies*, *skills*, and *teaching activities* are made clearer as they pertain to reading strategies and strategy instruction.

WHAT ARE THE CHARACTERISTICS OF GOOD STRATEGY USERS?

To identify the characteristics that good strategy users possess, begin by thinking about a topic at which you consider yourself to be an expert (Koskinen & Blum, 2002). Think about the qualities you possess that make you an expert in that area.

Consider, as an example, my own expertise in waxing cars. I have a fair amount of knowledge about waxing cars by hand. I know that there are many different types of waxes, most of which do generally the same job. Some give a glossier shine but do not last as long or hold up as well when exposed to various weather conditions; others do not provide as glossy a shine but hold up better. I know the procedures for waxing a car by hand. I know when and where it is best to wax cars—away from direct afternoon sun—and I also know why it is important to wax a car. This information shows that, as an expert car waxer, I have an *extensive knowledge base.*

I also am *motivated* to wax cars. I enjoy the mindlessness of the task, and I enjoy the results that can be obtained in just a few hours. I am motivated because I know that my effort pays off in the end. Thus motivation plays a key role in my becoming an expert car waxer. If I were not motivated by the task, I might not engage in it nearly as often as I do.

While I am waxing my car, I am also very aware of how the whole procedure is progressing. I am able to look critically at the way I am performing the task and know when something is going wrong. In this sense, I am *metacognitive*—I am able to monitor my performance and determine whether I should continue the task in the same manner, abandon the task, or use a more effective approach.

When I recognize that something is not going well (e.g., I am applying the wax too thickly or that it is about to rain), I am able to *analyze the task* to know how to make adjustments to my procedure. For example, if I am applying the wax too thickly, I know why it is occurring, and I know what to do to correct the problem. Thus, I also *possess a variety of strategies* for accomplishing the desired goal. To apply the wax more thinly, I need to moisten the applicator a bit and spread the wax over a larger portion of the car. Through my metacognitive awareness of a problem, my ability to analyze the task, and my selection of an appropriate alternate strategy from my available repertoire, I am able to solve the dilemma and attain my goal.

These five characteristics—possessing an extensive knowledge base, being motivated to use strategies, being metacognitively aware, possessing an ability to analyze the task, and possessing a variety of strategies for accomplishing the desired goal—comprise the qualities of experts in nearly any domain, whether it is car waxing, sewing, reading, or writing (Meichenbaum, 1977). Michael Pressley and his colleagues identify similar characteristics in their Good Strategy User Model (e.g., Pressley, 1986; Pressley, Borkowski, et al., 1989; Pressley, Symons, Snyder, & Cariglia-Bull, 1989; Pressley et al., 1995). These characteristics were derived from a host of expert/novice research studies conducted in the 1980s (e.g., August, Flavell, & Clift, 1984; Davey, 1988; Gambrell, Wilson, & Gantt, 1981; Garner & Kraus, 1981; Garner & Reis, 1981; Recht & Leslie, 1988). These studies revealed that novice readers (1) focus on decoding individual words, (2) cannot adjust their reading rate, (3) are not aware of alternative strategies for enhancing comprehension and memory of text, and (4) are not adept at monitoring their own comprehension. In their synthesis of strategy research, Paris et al. (1991) noted that expert readers have (1) rapid decoding skills, (2) large vocabularies, (3) phonemic awareness, (4) knowledge of text features, and (5) knowledge of a variety of strategies to enhance comprehension and memory of text. From an instructional standpoint, our goal must include providing instruction, modeling, and guided practice so that less proficient readers begin to understand how to read and process text strategically.

The Good Strategy User Model is depicted in Figure 1.2. Each aspect of the model is explained further as it relates to reading; however, it is important to recognize that al-

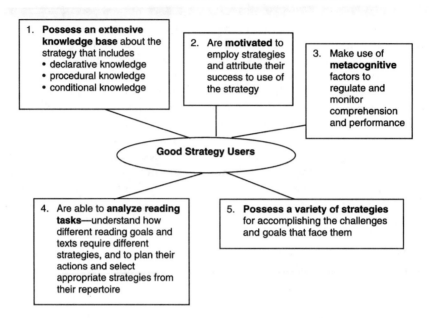

FIGURE 1.2. Good Strategy User Model. *Sources:* Pressley (1986) and Pressley, Symons, Snyder, and Cariglia-Bull (1989).

though each component is discussed separately, the components do not work in isolation from one another. As Pressley et al. (1995) noted, each component continually interacts with the others.

Possession of an Extensive Knowledge Base

One of the primary distinctions between experts and novices is the type and extent of knowledge they acquire as they become more proficient (Paris et al., 1983). Like experts, good strategy users possess a great deal of knowledge that they use to inform strategy selection and use.

Cognitive and developmental psychologists have emphasized two types of knowledge: declarative and procedural. Paris et al. (1983) add to that a third type: conditional.

Declarative Knowledge

Declarative knowledge is information about the structure of a task and the goal (Paris et al., 1983); it is sometimes referred to as "knowledge *that*." In the car-waxing example above, I had knowledge *that* some waxes provide a glossier shine but do not hold up well under various weather conditions. If my goal for the car is to have a high gloss shine, then I will use one type of wax; if my goal is to have a durable coat of wax, then I will use a different type of wax. Declarative knowledge was also involved in the opening driving scenario. Knowing *that* a particular blocked route would take hours to clear helped you to self-select a strategy from the three alternatives. If you had not had that declarative knowledge, you may have made a different choice and wound up in traffic. In reading, declarative knowledge includes information about how particular reading tasks are structured. For example, expert readers know *that* stories have a particular narrative structure *that* includes setting, characters, problems or goals, attempts to solve the problem or attain the goal, and a resolution. Expert readers also know *that* they read differently when studying for a test than when reading for pleasure.

Declarative knowledge also refers to one's beliefs about the task and one's abilities (Paris et al., 1983). In the car-waxing example, a relevant belief would be, "I believe that I am a good car waxer." For readers, these beliefs would reflect the specific reading task and their perceived ability to perform it. For example: "I don't like informational books" or "Informational books are hard for me to understand."

Declarative knowledge resides in long-term memory. Derry (1990) described it "as a large, tangled network" (p. 351) that is only useful if it can be recalled when needed. The result of activating declarative knowledge is simple recall. It is important to help learners organize this level of information and establish connections that enable them to access this reservoir of declarative knowledge. For those learners who do not possess an extensive amount of declarative knowledge about reading, it is important to help them make connections between new information and their prior knowledge. New ideas and knowledge are more likely to be remembered if they are associated with prior knowledge. The role of declarative knowledge in strategic processing is that it enables such knowledge about a given strategy to be accessed quickly.

Procedural Knowledge

Whereas declarative knowledge involves information about a task's structure, procedural knowledge involves knowing *how* (Paris et al., 1983) to do something—how to execute or perform a given task. In contrast to declarative knowledge, the result of procedural knowledge involves transforming information into action (Derry, 1990) rather than simple recall.

Using the car-waxing task, knowing *how* to wax a car by hand is an example of procedural knowledge. The step-by-step procedures involved in performing the task are part of this knowledge. For car waxing those steps might include: (1) start with a clean car; (2) obtain relevant materials (appropriate car wax, an applicator, and a soft dry cloth); (3) moisten the applicator lightly; (4) dip the applicator into the wax; (5) spread the wax onto the surface of the car, using smooth, circular motions; (6) apply wax to the entire surface of the car in this manner; (7) wait for the wax to dry; and (8) using a soft, dry cloth, wipe off the residue from the car's surface. Procedural knowledge in the context of reading includes the step-by-step procedures for how to make predictions about a story outcome or how to set a purpose for reading. Without procedural knowledge, readers are unable to execute a given strategy. How often have we asked students to summarize a given passage without having taught them *how* to summarize in a step-by-step fashion? How often have we asked students to make predictions about what will happen in stories without first teaching them prediction procedures? For those students who struggle with learning to read, it is essential to teach procedural knowledge related to reading strategies.

Conditional Knowledge

Paris et al. (1983) have aptly noted that declarative and procedural knowledge are not sufficient to enable readers to process text strategically. The ability to understand *when* and *why* to use a given strategy is also essential. They termed this type of understanding "conditional knowledge."

In the car-waxing example, it does me no good to have the declarative knowledge about different types of car wax or the procedural knowledge about how to wax a car by hand if I do not know when I should wax a car or why I should wax a car. Conditional knowledge explains the circumstances under which a strategy should be employed, and it provides a rationale for employing the strategy. Without knowing about the utility and value of a given procedure, an individual is not likely to expend the time and effort needed to execute a strategy. Waxing a car by hand is tediously hard work. Why should I do it? If I do not see value in the activity, then I am not going to perform it. When we know that at least two coats of wax a year protect the exterior paint and prevent body rust on this valuable investment, then maybe we would be convinced to wax our car. However, if we leased a car, do not care about body rust, or do not live in a climate where body rust is a problem, then this rationale may not convince us to expend the effort to wax the car. An example of conditional knowledge in the context of reading is knowing *when* we should make predictions and *why* it is important to make predictions while reading. Even if a child knows how to predict, he will not expend the effort to employ the strategy if he does not know when to do it or why it is important.

Conditional knowledge plays a critical role in strategic processing. In fact, without knowledge of when and why to use a given strategy, it is most probable that a student will not employ the strategy on her own unless she is prompted or forced to do so. In this case, the student is not independently employing the strategy; she is doing so out of compliance, which means that it is highly unlikely that she will elect to use the strategy on her own.

Motivation

Students must be motivated to employ strategies, and their personal attributions must support this usage. Using strategies is hard work and requires a great deal of effort; students will expend energy only on strategies that are meaningful, worthwhile, and rewarding to them (Paris et al., 1983). The key to this goal is ensuring that students see that strategic procedures enhance their performance (Pressley et al., 1995), and that their efforts are rewarded (Pressley, Symons, et al., 1989).

In the car-waxing example, my motivation for waxing my car was twofold: I enjoy the mindless physical activity (as well as being outside), and I like the fact that when I am done, I can see the results immediately. Although waxing a car by hand is tedious, I see a payoff in expending that effort, and I value the end result.

Attribution theory helps explain why individuals are motivated in this manner (Weiner, 1979). Four attributes are relevant to achievement-related behavior: ability (one's innate cognitive ability), effort (level of effort exerted), task difficulty (a general perspective on the intricacy of a particular task at a given moment), and luck (chance occurrences). Each of these four attributes has three characteristics: (1) stability, (2) locus of causality, and (3) controllability. Table 1.1 depicts the four attributes and their characteristic features.

A *stable characteristic* is one that does not change. One's innate cognitive ability does not change, nor does the difficulty of a task at a particular moment. If the task were hard when first encountered, it would not suddenly change and become easier on its own.

TABLE 1.1. Attributions for Achievement-Related Behavior. Adapted from Weiner (1979).

Attribution	Stability		Locus of Causality		Controllability	
	Stable	Unstable	Internal	External	Controllable	Uncontrollable
Ability	■		■			■
Effort		■	■		■	
Task difficulty	■			■		■
Luck		■		■		■

The task of hand-waxing a car remains the same task. Assessment of stable attributes leads to consistent expectations (Diener & Dweck, 1980). If a student attributes his success to his own ability or to the difficulty of the task, which are both stable attributes, then he will expect to succeed again with the same task. Likewise, if a student attributes his failure on a give task to his ability, then he will expect to fail again. Effort and luck are unstable attributes; one can expend more or less effort on the same task, if one desires. Likewise luck is not an attribute that produces consistent results because it is based on chance.

Locus of causality refers to where the source of the attribute lies. The source could be within you (i.e., internal), or it could be external. As Table 1.1 shows, ability and effort are internal attributes. One's ability and the effort one exerts are within oneself. However, the difficulty of the task and luck are external attributes. One's affect (i.e., disposition or attitude) is related to locus of causality. Butkowsky and Willows (1980) found that students who attributed success to internal sources, such as ability or effort (e.g., "I'm smart" or "I tried hard"), experienced increased pride and self-esteem. When students attributed success to external factors (e.g., "I only did well because the test was easy" or "I was lucky"), lowered self-esteem occurred. If we fail at something, and attribute this failure to an internal source such as ability (i.e., "I'm dumb"), this serves to lower self-esteem. However, if we attribute the failure to an external source (i.e., "The test was too hard") this preserves self-esteem.

Controllability refers to whether the attribute is managed by us or not. The only attribute that we have conscious control over is effort. Only I can decide whether to exert more or less effort on a task. All other attributes are outside our range of control. We cannot control the innate ability with which we were born, we cannot control the difficulty of a task, and we cannot control luck. Unsuccessful students tend to attribute their failure to uncontrollable factors (Diener & Dweck, 1978, 1980), which means that they blame their failure on factors outside their control. Successful students tend to attribute their success to the controllable attribute—effort (Butkowsky & Willows, 1980).

How is this theory relevant for strategic readers? Expert readers attribute successful reading to deliberate, effortful execution of strategies. Strategic processing is contingent on self-selected and self-regulated behavior. The *individual* is key to successful strategy use. The only attribute that an individual has control over is effort. The internal locus of this attribute means that it has the potential to impact self-esteem. It also is an unstable attribute, meaning that how much effort is exerted on any given task varies.

Struggling readers often present motivational problems for classroom instructors. Johnston and Winograd (1985) suggested that many of these problems are related to the fact that "they are passive, helpless participants in what is fundamentally an interactive process—reading" (p. 279). Many struggling readers have low self-esteem and exhibit characteristics of "learned helplessness" (Seligman & Maier, 1967, p. 1). These characteristics are seeded in struggling readers when they begin trying to learn how to read, using the limited knowledge and strategies they possess, and are unsuccessful. After repeated exposure to such failure, they give up and passively accept the fact that they cannot learn to read. They believe that inability, not lack of effort, is the cause of their failure—and they refuse to exert effort because they think it is futile to do so (Borkowski, Carr, Rellinger, & Pressley, 1990). Because they attribute their failure to an internal, stable attribute that is out of their control (i.e., ability), struggling readers tend to have low self-esteem (Hiebert, Winograd, & Danner, 1984). Simply put, they believe that they cannot learn to read because they are "dumb."

Given that effort is the only attribute that is both controllable and internal, it is the only attribute that can actually make a difference in reversing the debilitating effects of learned helplessness. Thus strategy instruction begins by focusing on teaching students that it is their effort that determines their success. If they put forth the effort to employ a strategy, it *will* improve their reading—on the condition that the sociocultural context of the classroom affords students the opportunity to experience first-hand how their efforts pay off in the dividend of success (Borkowski et al., 1990). Strategy instruction also must include explicit instruction about the utility of a given strategy (i.e., fostering conditional knowledge) so that students see its value, and students must be given feedback about their performance after using the strategy (Pressley et al., 1995). Developmentally appropriate materials must be used, and the environment should foster risk taking. Students also should chart their progress as they use new strategies so that they can see their own progress. This will serve to enhance motivated strategy use. Table 1.2 lists guidelines for motivating students' use of strategies.

Metacognition

Metacognition is the key to strategic processing because it enables us to monitor the progress made toward achieving our goal (Flavell, 1979). It also involves the control we have over our learning and thinking (Baker & Brown, 1984).

In the car-waxing example, my metacognitive awareness informed me about how the job was proceeding. When I noticed that I was applying the wax too thickly, I was mak-

---

TABLE 1.2. Guidelines for Motivating Students to Use Strategies. *Source:* **Borkowski, Carr, Rellinger, and Pressley (1990).**

---

1. Teach strategies that provide appropriate challenges (not too hard, yet not too easy).
2. Choose strategies that are clearly worth learning, and help students recognize their value.
3. Create conditions that foster students' experience of success.
4. Reinforce progress steadily and consistently.
5. Set clear goals.
6. Give specific, detailed, and constructive feedback.
7. Teach students how to self-reinforce for achieving success.

---

ing an evaluation or judgment about my performance on a metacognitive level. This type of awareness may be very brief, involving only that instant recognition that things are, or are not, going well. In response to that metacognitive awareness, I began to think and act strategically about what to do to resolve the problem. Hearing about the traffic accident was a moment of metacognitive awareness that prompted a consideration of various strategic actions. The metacognitive moment is an "aha" experience (Garner, 1987, p. 19), or, as Anderson (1980) described it, it is a "clunk" (p. 490) that vaults us into strategic processing in which we begin to enact cognitive strategies to resolve a problem. Without that experience we would muddle along, not realizing that a problem had even occurred.

Unfortunately, this lack of metacognition is precisely the problem that younger and less proficient readers have: They are less able to monitor and regulate their performance (Baker & Brown, 1984; Garner, 1980; Garner & Reis, 1981; Markman, 1977; Myers & Paris, 1978; Paris & Myers, 1981) than are older and more proficient readers (Baker, 1984; Baker & Anderson, 1982; Winograd & Johnston, 1982). While reading, these students would not recognize when something did not make sense or when the text was confusing. They would continue reading words, turning pages, completely unaware that their comprehension was obstructed. Therefore, fix-up strategies such as rereading, reading ahead, or talking about the materials with someone would not be used. After they finished "reading," their comprehension, recall, and memory of text would be seriously impaired by their inability to monitor or detect a situation in which comprehension might be difficult..

Ability to Analyze the Task

Good strategy users are aware of the processes involved in successfully performing a given task or strategy (Pressley et al., 1995). Such awareness goes beyond the procedural knowledge of how to perform a strategy and it is inherently linked to metacognition in that it involves being able to recognize, in the midst of performing a task, what to do next. If something goes wrong, a successful strategy user immediately knows how to rectify the problem and redirect efforts efficiently to attain the goal. The ultimate goal of task analysis is to assess the situation and flexibly make adjustments based on the parameters of the task (Pressley et al., 1995).

In the driving event, the metacognitive awareness about the traffic accident led to an analysis of the task involving a consideration of the conditions in relation to the goal of arriving home. In reading, specific strategies (e.g., summarizing, comprehension monitoring) have been analyzed to determine what steps are necessary to employ the strategies successfully (Garner, 1987). These task analyses are presented in Chapters 5 and 6.

Possession of a Variety of Strategies

Good strategy users possess a large repertoire of strategies (see Table 1.3) (Pressley, Symons, et al., 1989). This repertoire may be likened to a "cognitive toolbox." When a reader has a metacognitive realization that something has gone wrong, she can reach into her cognitive toolbox to select a strategy or tool that will help resolve the difficulty. The proficient reader possesses strategies for decoding, comprehending, interpreting, and studying text. Although strategies for interpreting and studying text are essential to profi-

TABLE 1.3. A Variety of Strategies Employed by Good Strategy Users

Word Recognition	Comprehension	Fix-up Strategies
Know words by sight	Look at pictures, titles, headings	Reread text
Use phoneme–grapheme correspondences (phonics)	Activate prior knowledge	Read ahead for clarification
Analogize to known words	Set purposes for reading	Question one's understanding
Use orthographic patterns in words	Make predictions	Ask or discuss with others
Use context cues	Verify/revise predictions	
	Relate new knowledge to prior knowledge	
	Identify structure of text	
	Summarize text while reading	
	Create mental images while reading	
	Question one's understanding while reading	
	Highlight or make marginal notes about important aspects	
	Make inferences that enhance comprehension	
	Skim text	

cient reading, this book deals only with strategies for decoding and comprehending text. Table 1.3 depicts the range of cognitive strategies available to readers for comprehending and decoding text. Successful readers integrate these specific strategies into higher-order sequences to accomplish the more complex goal of reading (Pressley, Symons, et al., 1989). Again, these strategies are *not* used in isolation. A good reader may begin by looking at the title and pictures for clues about the text, which triggers initial predictions, which leads to a purpose for reading. As the reader begins to process the text he monitors his comprehension and realizes that one of his predictions was accurate. He reads on and makes another prediction about what will happen next to the character. Thus, the reading process involves a multitude of strategic sequences enacted differently by individual readers. Those who possess a variety of strategies approach this complex cognitive task with an array of tools that prepares them for any difficulties they may encounter.

If an individual has a limited number of strategies available, she will struggle to make do with what she has. If her goal is to drive a nail into a wall, for example, and her toolbox contains only a screwdriver, she will employ it in a less than efficient effort to accomplish the task. It is not the best or most efficient tool, but it is the only one she has until she can acquire new, more effective tools. Comparably, in reading, a reader recognizing that the text does not make sense can stop and employ a strategy to repair her comprehension. If the only tool she possesses is to go back and reread, then she uses that strategy. If the comprehension failure occurred in the beginning of the text, for example, then this strategy will not work very well. Thus having a wide range of strategies available in one's cognitive toolbox is essential for enhancing success. Possessing the conditional knowledge associated with each strategy is an integral part of the cognitive toolbox, for it equips strategy users with the ability to determine which strategies are best suited to various textual conditions.

In sum, the five characteristics of good strategy users are essential for proficient reading. Successful readers must (1) possess an extensive knowledge base, (2) be motivated to employ strategies, (3) be metacognitive, (4) analyze the reading task, and (5) possess a variety of strategies. These characteristics work in unison as a coherent whole, rather than in isolation, to produce efficient strategy use in only a matter of seconds. The challenge, however, is teaching struggling readers the value of strategy use. Once students experience the value of using strategies, they will be more inclined to use them.

WHY STUDENTS DO NOT USE STRATEGIES

When thinking about why students may not use strategies it is helpful to do the inverse of what we did when we thought about strategic, or expert, readers. Think about something that you do *not* do well. Think about why you are not good at that particular task and how you feel when you are doing it. Although I am excellent at waxing cars, I am not good at many things—bowling, knitting, and dancing are but a few. When I even think about doing these activities, I become dismayed. I do not like doing these activities, I do not understand how to do them well, and I really do not care if I ever know how to do them to any degree of proficiency. I know many who are good at each of these activities, and I admire their talents greatly, but ultimately I have no use for those activities. I am unsuccessful at them and when I engage in these activities I feel foolish and inept. This is the same way that struggling readers feel about reading. They may know that it is an important task to learn, but they really do not like doing it, they are not good at it, and they feel foolish and inept. They experience these feelings every day, sometimes for hours each day, while they are in school. Sometimes we even ask them to perform this task that they are so inept at, and that they dislike so much, in public, in front of their peers. Imagine if you had to perform the task or activity that you are terrible at in public and in front of your colleagues! It is a dreadful thought. Yet, poor readers face this dreaded possibility every day, sometimes for hours each day, over the course of many years.

Garner's (1990) review of strategy research analyzed the reasons why many readers do not use strategies. Five reasons, which are nearly the inverse of the good strategy user model, emerged from her synthesis: Poor readers possess (1) a meager knowledge base, (2) personal attributes that do not support strategy use, (3) poor cognitive monitoring (in our terms, poor use of metacognition), (4) primitive routines, and (5) minimal ability transfer knowledge to new settings.

Meager Knowledge Base

Nonstrategic readers do not have a sufficient knowledge base about the reading process to support strategy use. They may lack declarative knowledge about the structure of the task, procedural knowledge about how to perform the strategy, conditional knowledge about when and why they should use a given strategy, or they may lack some combination of all three. In the example above, I noted that I am not good at knitting. In fact, I really know very little about it. I know that you need knitting needles and yarn (declarative knowledge), but I don't know what kind of needles. Are they all the same? I don't think so, but I'm not sure. I have no idea at all about *how* to knit (procedural knowledge). I have heard the phrase "knit one, purl two," but I have no idea what it means or how it is pertinent. I certainly do not have any conditional knowledge of when I should enact a strategy because I do not possess a single knitting strategy. Thus, I bring no knowledge about knitting to the task.

Struggling readers are no different. They have a limited knowledge base about many reading strategies (Baker & Brown, 1984; Garner, 1987, 1990). For example, struggling readers may have some declarative knowledge about a given strategy, such as prediction. They may know *that* a prediction is a guess about what might happen in the story, but they may not know *that* good readers continually revise and update their predictions throughout their reading of the text. Thus the knowledge base is limited. They may have a general idea about *how* to predict (i.e., procedural knowledge), but they may not know *how* to make a textually relevant prediction. Their predictions may be completely "off the wall" or "out of the blue." Likewise, they may not know the conditions under which they should use prediction as a strategy. Thus, one of our instructional goals must be to provide explanations and experiences that *instantiate* (concretize) readers' knowledge base about strategies.

Personal Attributions Do Not Support Strategy Use

Strategy use is time consuming and requires persistence. Many readers do not believe that the time and effort it takes to employ strategies will pay off; therefore, they fail to use them (Garner, 1990). Readers with high self-esteem tend to attribute their successful and unsuccessful reading experiences to their level of effort (Borkowski et al., 1990; Butkowsky & Willows, 1980), whereas readers with lower self-esteem are not as likely to initiate or persist at strategy use because they attribute their difficulties to lack of ability (Garner, 1990). These readers often have experienced years of frustration in school and rather than be embarrassed one more time, they give up. In many cases, their schools and their teachers have failed them. Rather than blaming these external sources for their failures, these readers tend to attribute their failures to internal, stable factors such as ability, and their successes to external factors such as luck or task difficulty (Hiebert et al., 1984).

Garner (1990) also noted that many of these students appear lazy or unmotivated, often engaging in defensive behaviors that emerge to guard the feelings of ineptitude that result from repeated exposure to failure. They often state that they "can't do it," refuse to engage in strategic actions, or become dependent on support from others to scaffold their every move. These readers lack persistence and confidence in much the same way that I described my own experiences with knitting, bowling, and dancing. When you are not good at something, you usually do not want to engage in it—even if someone is trying to teach you how to perform it better.

Poor Cognitive Monitoring/Metacognition

Many readers are unable to evaluate and monitor their reading process to know when something does not make sense. Instead, because they do not recognize that anything is wrong, they continue reading without stopping to employ a repair strategy. In particular, younger and less proficient readers have difficulty monitoring their reading, yet rarely do we provide instruction related to metacognition or cognitive monitoring to help them (Garner, 1990).

Sometimes the conditions of the reading task do not permit close monitoring either. Garner (1990) has noted that when memory resources are strained, it is difficult to monitor. That is, if the text is too difficult to read, or if there are interruptions, the additional load placed on memory to overcome these difficulties makes it impossible to monitor cognitive processing as well. Likewise, if readers do not see the task as important, it is unlikely they will attend to the task enough to monitor their progress with it. It is similar to my experiences with knitting or bowling: If I am spending so much energy and effort to just get the procedures down, I may not have enough cognitive resources left over to monitor my progress. I also may not care enough about my performance to expend the extra energy to monitor how well I am doing.

Routines Used Are Primitive

Garner (1990) has also noted that readers who do not use strategies often do not do so because they use a primitive routine. In effect, because these readers may not have a large repertoire of available strategies to use, or because they may not have the conditional knowledge of when and why they should use a given strategy, they rely on the strategy they know. As an example, I use my own experiences when I first moved to Buffalo, New York. At first I knew only three streets: Main Street, Youngs Road, and Maple Road. Because they were the only three streets with which I was familiar, I planned all of my travels using them—even if it took longer. To drive from my home to downtown Buffalo, there are several major highways that I could have used; however, I always took Main Street (with all of its traffic lights) to travel the 15 miles downtown. Certainly this was not the easiest or most efficient route downtown, as I have come to learn, but I did not care. It was the only route I knew. I felt safe using my few, carefully chosen routes. Similarly, in using their cognitive toolboxes, nonstrategic readers use the tools that are available to them even if they are an inappropriate or less effective means of accomplishing the task.

Transfer of Strategies Is Minimal

Teaching students how to transfer strategy use to new situations is one of the most difficult aspects of strategy instruction. Even if we provide the best and most thorough instruction related to strategy use, there is no guarantee that readers will use a given strategy independently when the time comes. Readers tend to learn and use strategies in the contexts in which they were originally taught. That is, they become somewhat "context bound" (Perkins & Salomon, 1989) and have a difficult time transferring this knowledge to other contexts (Garner, 1990). During reading instruction, the context includes the instructional setting (e.g., type of text, type of task, level of scaffolded support) in which the strategies were taught. When the student reads a different type of genre, engages in a different task, or engages in an activity that has a different level of instructional support (i.e., whole class lecture, one-on-one tutoring, paired activity, group activity) the context is different, which makes it difficult to generalize the use of a strategy learned in the prior context. Chapter 4 discusses ways to facilitate transfer of strategy use to new contexts.

SUMMARY

Cognitive strategies are plans that are self-selected, evaluated, and regulated by an individual to attain a goal. Using strategies is important because they enhance learning and permit students to take control of their own learning. Good strategy users have an extensive knowledge base that includes declarative, procedural, and conditional knowledge related to strategic processes. They also see the value in using strategies and are motivated to use them. Good strategy users are metacognitively aware of how the process is going, are able to analyze the task to see what adjustments may be needed, and possess a variety of strategies for accomplishing the desired goal. Those who do not use strategies do not possess an extensive knowledge base about strategic processing. Furthermore, their personal attributions do not support strategy use, and they have poor cognitive monitoring, use primitive routines to accomplish the task, and are unable to use strategies in multiple contexts.

REFERENCES

Anderson, T. H. (1980). Study strategies and adjunct aids. In R. J. Spiro, B. C. Bruce, & W. F. Brewer (Eds.), *Theoretical issues in reading comprehension* (pp. 483–502). Hillsdale, NJ: Erlbaum.

August, D. L., Flavell, J. H., & Clift, R. (1984). Comparison of comprehension monitoring of skilled and less skilled readers. *Reading Research Quarterly, 20,* 39–53.

Baker, L. (1984). Spontaneous vs. instructed use of multiple standards for evaluating comprehension: Effects of age, reading proficiency, and type of standard. *Journal of Experimental Psychology, 38,* 289–311.

Baker, L., & Anderson, R. I. (1982). Effects of inconsistent information on text processing: Evidence for comprehension monitoring. *Reading Research Quarterly, 17,* 281–294.

Baker, L., & Brown, A. L. (1984). Metacognitive skills and reading. In P. D. Pearson, R. Barr, M. L. Kamil, and P. B. Mosenthal (Eds.), *Handbook of reading research* (vol. 1, pp. 353–394). New York: Longman.

Borkowski, J. G., Carr, M., Rellinger, E., & Pressley, M. (1990). Self-regulated cognition: Interdependence of metacognition, attributions, and self-esteem. In B. F. Jones & L. Idol (Eds.), *Dimensions of thinking and cognitive instruction* (pp. 53–92). Hillsdale, NJ: Erlbaum.

Brown, R., & Coy-Ogan, L. (1993). The evolution of transactional strategies instruction in one teacher's classroom. *The Elementary School Journal, 94*(2), 221–233.

Butkowsky, I. S., & Willows, D. M. (1980). Cognitive–motivational characteristics of children varying in reading ability: Evidence for learned helplessness in poor readers. *Journal of Educational Psychology, 72*(3), 408–422.

Davey, B. (1988). The nature of response error for good and poor readers when permitted to reinspect text during question-answering. *American Educational Research Journal, 25*(3), 399–414.

Derry, S. J. (1990). Learning strategies for acquiring useful knowledge. In B. F. Jones and L. Idol (Eds.), *Dimensions of thinking and cognitive instruction* (pp. 347–379). Hillsdale, NJ: Erlbaum.

Diener, C. I., & Dweck, C. S. (1978). An analysis of learned helplessness: I. Continuous changes in performance, strategy, and achievement cognitions following failure. *Journal of Personality and Social Psychology, 36*(5), 451–462.

Diener, C. I., & Dweck, C. S. (1980). An analysis of learned helplessness: II. The processing of success. *Journal of Personality and Social Psychology, 39*(5), 940–952.

Duffy, G. G. (1993a). Rethinking strategy instruction: Four teachers' development and their low achievers' understandings. *The Elementary School Journal, 93*(3), 231–247.

Duffy, G. G. (1993b). Teachers' progress toward becoming expert strategy teachers. *The Elementary School Journal, 94*(2), 109–120.

Durkin, D. (1978/1979). What classroom observations reveal about reading comprehension instruction. *Reading Research Quarterly, 14,* 481–538.

Flavell, J. H. (1979). Metacognition and cognitive monitoring: A new area of cognitive-developmental inquiry. *American Psychologist, 34,* 906–911.

Gambrell, L. B., Wilson, R. M., & Gantt, W. N. (1981). Classroom observations of task-attending behaviors of good and poor readers. *Journal of Educational Research, 74*(6), 400–404.

Garner, R. (1980). Monitoring of understanding: An investigation of good and poor readers' awareness of induced miscomprehension of text. *Journal of Reading Behavior, 12,* 55–63.

Garner, R. (1987). *Metacognition and reading comprehension.* Norwood, NJ: Ablex.

Garner, R. (1990). When children and adults do not use learning strategies: Toward a theory of settings. *Review of Educational Research, 60*(4), 517–529.

Garner, R., & Kraus, C. (1981). Good and poor comprehender differences in knowing and regulating reading behaviors. *Educational Research Quarterly, 6*(4), 5–12.

Garner, R., & Reis, R. (1981). Monitoring and resolving comprehension obstacles: An investigation of spontaneous text lookbacks among upper-grade good and poor comprehenders. *Reading Research Quarterly, 16,* 569–582.

Hiebert, E. H., Winograd, P. N., & Danner, F. W. (1984). Children's attributions of failure and success in different aspects of reading. *Journal of Educational Psychology, 76*(6), 1139–1148.

Johnston, P. H., & Winograd, P. N. (1985). Passive failure in reading. *Journal of Reading Behavior, 17*(4), 279–301.

Koskinen, P., & Blum, I. (2002, August). *Supporting the comprehension development of diverse learners: Book access, shared reading, and audio models.* Paper presented at the 19th World Congress on Reading, Edinburgh, Scotland.

Markman, E. M. (1977). Realizing that you don't understand: A preliminary investigation. *Child Development, 48,* 986–999.

Meichenbaum, D. (1977). *Cognitive behavior modification.* New York: Plenum.

Myers, M., & Paris, S. G. (1978). Children's metacognitive knowledge about reading. *Journal of Educational Psychology, 70,* 680–690.

Paris, S. G., Lipson, M. Y., & Wixson, K. K. (1983). Becoming a strategic reader. *Contemporary Educational Psychology, 8,* 293–316.

Paris, S. G., & Myers, M. (1981). Comprehension monitoring, memory, and study strategies of good and poor readers. *Journal of Reading Behavior, 13,* 5–22.

Paris, S. G., Wasik, B. A., & Turner, J. C. (1991). The development of strategic readers. In R. Barr, M. L. Kamil, P. Mosenthal, and P. D. Pearson (Eds.), *Handbook of reading* research (vol. 2, pp. 609–640). New York: Longman.

Perkins, D. N., & Salomon, G. (1989). Are cognitive skills context-bound? *Educational Researcher, 18,* 16–25.

Prawat, R. S. (1989). Promoting access to knowledge, strategy, and disposition in students: A research synthesis. *Review of Educational Research, 59*(1), 1–41.

Pressley, M. (1986). The relevance of the good strategy user model to the teaching of mathematics. *Educational Psychologist, 21,* 139–161.

Pressley, M., Borkowski, J. G., & Schneider, W. (1989). Good information processing: What it is and how education can promote it. *International Journal of Educational Research, 13,* 857–867.

Pressley, M., Goodchild, F., Fleet, J., Zajchowski, R., & Evans, E. D. (1989). The challenges of classroom strategy instruction. *The Elementary School Journal, 89,* 301–342.

Pressley, M., Symons, S., Snyder, B. L., & Cariglia-Bull, T. (1989). Strategy instruction comes of age. *Learning Disability Quarterly, 12,* 16–30.

Pressley, M., Woloshyn, V., & Associates. (1995). *Cognitive strategy instruction that really* improves children's academic performance (2nd ed.). Cambridge, MA: Brookline Books.

Recht, D. R., & Leslie, L. (1988). Effect of prior knowledge on good and poor readers' memory of text. *Journal of Educational Psychology, 80*(1), 16–20.

Seligman, M. E. P., & Maier, S. F. (1967). Failure to escape traumatic shock. *Journal of Experimental Psychology, 74*(1), 1–9.

Weiner, B. (1979). A theory of motivation for some classroom experiences. *Journal of Educational Psychology, 71,* 3–25.

Winograd, P., & Johnston, P. (1982). Comprehension monitoring and the error-detection paradigm. *Journal of Reading Behavior, 14,* 61–74.

CHAPTER TWO

Assessing
Strategic Processing

One of the greatest difficulties of assessment is determining the validity of the assessment process itself. That is, how can we be sure that we are really assessing what we think we are assessing? When assessing strategic processing, the goal is to determine how proficiently the reader is using strategies as he processes text. But strategic processing occurs internally, mentally, and is not available for public observation. Thus it is difficult to determine what strategies readers are using, when they are using them, and how they are using them. The goal of this chapter is to introduce several forms of informal assessment that can be used collaboratively to provide an overall picture of how a reader processes text strategically.

WHAT IS IMPORTANT TO ASSESS IN STRATEGIC PROCESSING?

Consider the following scenario. Two fifth graders, Dylan and Sam, are given the same reading assignment by their language arts teacher:

> Read *Sarah, Plain and Tall* by Patricia MacLachlan. Prepare an essay on the following topic related to your reading of this story. Select one of the main characters (e.g., Sarah, Pa, Caleb) and describe that character's development from the beginning of the novel to the end. Be sure to explain how the character's traits evolved over time, why you think the character evolved in this manner, and, using support from the text, show that the character's appearance, dialogue, actions, or thoughts revealed that the character possessed a given trait.

Dylan is unhappy with the essay assignment. He would much rather take a multiple-choice test about the book. As he is reading the book, he remembers that when he takes a multiple-choice test about books, it always helps him to read for details. While he is reading, he decides to use a story map to take notes on the basic story elements: setting, character, problem, attempts to solve the problem, and the resolution. He reads the book in its entirety and then begins the essay assignment. He selects Sarah as the character about whom he will write his essay and uses his notes to help him as he writes.

Sam is also unhappy with the essay assignment because he also prefers multiple-choice tests. He decides that he will prepare for the assignment as he reads. He decides that he will focus his essay on Sarah, since she is the main character. As he reads, he decides that he will use three character maps to help record information related to Sarah's appearance, how she talks, her actions, and her thoughts. He will use one character map to track her traits at the beginning of the story, one for the middle, and one for the end. He marks the page numbers where he located his supporting evidence on his character map, and he thinks about what type of trait Sarah is exhibiting, based on that evidence. When he finishes reading the book, he compares the three character maps to see how Sarah's traits evolved over the course of the book. He uses those notes to help him as he writes his essay.

Both students were given the same task but used different strategies for accomplishing the same goal. Which student approached the task more strategically? To consider this question more formally, recall each of the five characteristics of a good strategy user introduced in Chapter 1 and think about which of those characteristics Dylan and Sam exhibited in the descriptions above (see Figure 2.1). In each cell describe how Dylan and Sam exhibited strategic characteristics and use the figure to compare.

What kind of declarative knowledge about the task might these boys need to be able to perform it successfully? They would need to know *that* essays require a different type of preparation than other assessments. One would need to know *that* it helps to organize their thoughts before writing the essay; they would need to know *that* all directions in the assignment must be attended to; and they would need to know *that* essays require them to think across the entire text and use evidence from the text to support their claims. In this example, Dylan knew *that* the essay required some form of organization before writing it, but he chose to organize his ideas by thinking about all story elements rather than focusing exclusively on character development, as directed in the assignment. Sam also knew *that* he needed to organize his thoughts, but he chose to do his organization while he read because he knew that he needed to see how the character developed over the course of the entire book. He also elected to organize his ideas by using a character map, in which he could take notes about the character's dialogue, actions, and thoughts. Both boys were aware *that* they needed to do something to help them organize their thoughts about the reading, and each chose to organize their thoughts in different ways.

The two boys also differed in the procedures they used to accomplish the task. Dylan elected to read for details, take notes on story elements, select a character, and then use his notes to organize his thoughts before writing. Sam decided which character he would write about before he started and took notes while he was reading. He then used his notes to help him see how the character developed over time. Although the boys used different procedures, they were both able to accomplish the task—with different degrees of success, most assuredly.

Conditional knowledge informs us about *when* and *why* to use a given strategy. In this example, Dylan knows that he must take some notes to help organize his ideas before writing, but he fails to think about the conditions. He prepares for an essay in the same manner that he would prepare for a multiple-choice quiz. We do not know *why* he

Characteristic	Dylan	Sam
Extent of Knowledge Base: Declarative Knowledge (knowing that . . .)		
Procedural Knowledge (knowing how to . . .)		
Conditional Knowledge (knowing when and why . . .)		
Motivation		
Metacognition		
Ability to Analyze the Task		
Possession of a Variety of Strategies		

FIGURE 2.1. Comparison of Dylan's and Sam's strategic processing.

chooses to prepare in the same manner as for a multiple-choice quiz. Alternatively, Sam recognizes that *when* preparing for an essay, he must think in a particular style. He must gather evidence and then think across that evidence to see development in the character's behavior.

In terms of motivation, both boys note they do not enjoy essay assignments, but they both put forth effort to accomplish the task—though Dylan does not appear to put forth the same degree of effort as Sam. Had they been totally unmotivated, they would not have attempted to complete the task.

Metacognitive awareness would indicate that the boys were able to monitor their progress as they attempted to achieve their goal. It seems that Dylan may not be quite as metacognitively aware as Sam, in that he was not able to recognize that extensive note taking was a prerequisite to writing. Sam seemed to show that he was aware of his process and was able to monitor it by taking notes throughout the reading of the text.

Dylan's inability to analyze the task is his greatest weakness. He was completely unaware that writing an essay about character development would require more elaborative thinking. He did nothing to attend to the essay's requirement that he use evidence from the character's appearance, dialogue, actions, and thoughts to support his writing. Instead, he applied the strategy he used in another context—multiple-choice tests. Sam, on the other hand, showed that he was keenly aware of the requirements of the task and used appropriate strategies to help him achieve the goal.

We are unsure what other types of strategies the boys possess. We do not know whether Dylan chose to take notes on story elements because he did not know any other strategies, or whether he knew of other strategies but chose not to use them because they were too time consuming (which would be a motivation problem). The problem could also be that Dylan knows about the appropriate strategy but is not able to analyze the task and does not know the conditions under which he should employ the appropriate strategy. This confusion would indicate that he is having trouble transferring strategy use to different contexts. Since Sam used a successful strategy, we do not know whether he possesses a variety of strategies or not.

When we assess students' strategic processing, it is essential to frame the assessment in terms of the five characteristics of good strategy users so that we gain insight into them as self-regulated, independent strategy users. This assessment tool enables us to examine the complete context in which strategic processing occurs. The next section describes a variety of informal assessments. These assessments are described in terms of which aspect of the Good Strategy User Model each informs. Unfortunately, no single assessment tool provides all of this information. We must use an assortment of authentic assessment tools and continuously collect information to gain insight into the whole process (Lipson, 1996).

INDIVIDUAL INFORMAL ASSESSMENTS OF STRATEGIC PROCESSING

Calfee and Hiebert (1991) described assessment as consisting of two tiers: assessment designed for instruction (i.e., informal assessment), and assessment designed for external accountability (i.e., formal assessment). Assessments designed for external accountability use a single index of student achievement that stands apart from curriculum and instruction. These assessments are often objective, standardized measures that provide comparison of an individual student's score to a normed sample (e.g., California Achievement Test, Terra Nova, Woodcock–Johnson Reading Mastery test). Such tests typically utilize a multiple-choice format and include subtests related to word attack, comprehension, and vocabulary. Formal assessments of reading are primarily concerned with the products of reading—that is, with how well a student performs in relation to others of the same age.

Assessment designed for instruction is developed by classroom teachers, is strongly linked to curriculum and instruction, and is intended to be used in the classroom. These assessments include performance-based and authentic assessments of literacy via observations, interviews, informal reading inventories, miscue analyses, and discussion. These assessments are used in conjunction with instruction so that assessment and instruction inform one another. Rather than comparing students' scores, the goal of informal assessments is to inform instruction so that students attain higher levels of literacy (Calfee & Hiebert, 1991). Although informal assessments can be used to evaluate the products of students' thinking (e.g., responses to comprehension questions), in this chapter we are concerned with those tools that inform teachers about the *processes* students engage in while they read. By using these assessments, we are able to gain insight into those covert thought processes that occur while students read, thereby identifying the types of strategic processing students do, or do not, employ.

Assessment of this nature must be a discursive practice that is intimately connected to instruction. Klenk and Almasi (1997) developed a model of ongoing assessment based on the work of Gillett and Temple (1994). A simplified version of this model is depicted in Figure 2.2. In this model, observing and assessing students, planning and implementing instruction with students, and generating hypotheses about students are the three primary components of ongoing assessment. The process can begin at any point in the cycle. Information gained from an assessment helps the teacher (1) generate an initial hypothesis about the student's strengths and weaknesses as a reader, and (2) plan and implement instruction to help that student further. Assessing the results of instruction can also generate hypotheses about the student. Thus the model depicts a recursive process in which all components are integral to one another. The remainder of this chapter describes informal assessments of strategic processing, as depicted in Figure 2.2, and describes the process of generating hypotheses about students' strategic processing.

Observation and Conversation

Lipson (1996) noted that teachers rarely use classroom conversations to gain insight into students' reading performance. Obviously, it is easier and more efficient to administer a test to the entire class than to take time out to chat with each individual student. However, the type of information that one gains from talking with students helps us understand *why* they are reading as they do. Think about the information provided in the example with Dylan and Sam. How did the teacher gather this information? It is possible that the teacher asked the students to explain in writing how they went about preparing

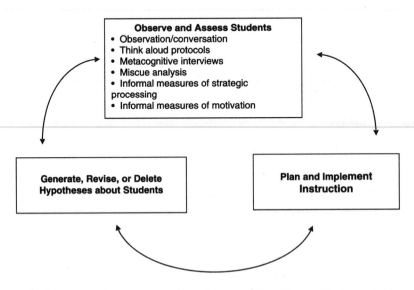

FIGURE 2.2. Model of ongoing assessment and instruction. From Klenk and Almasi (1997). Copyright 1997 by the New York State Reading Association. Adapted by permission.

for the essay—an excellent means of gathering information about strategic processing from a large group. However, the same information may have been gathered by simply chatting with each boy some time during the day and jotting down a few quick notes (i.e., anecdotal records). Knowing how each boy prepared for the essay provides insight that helps the teacher understand the resulting product—the essay itself. It is likely that Dylan's essay would not be as well organized or address all of the required points that Sam's essay did. Sam's performance would earn him a higher grade on the essay than Dylan. However, without the knowledge about strategic processing, the teacher does not know why Dylan performed as he did and cannot adjust her instruction to meet his needs adequately. Responsive teaching requires teachers to identify the specific needs of individual students as well as the contexts surrounding their performance (Pressley & Afflerbach, 1995).

As we engage in our daily instruction, it is essential that we jot down anecdotal notes based on our observations and informal conversations with our students. One method that some teachers find helpful is to carry a clipboard with 3″ × 5″ index cards, arrayed for her students, taped to it (see Figure 2.3). As an observation is made about a child, the teacher flips to that child's card and jots the note directly on it. Another method, perhaps easier, is to clip a sheet of white mailing labels to the clipboard and jot down observational notes for each student on an individual label. At the end of the day the labels are peeled off and placed in each child's folder. Team teaching with other grade-level teachers, reading specialists, or special education teachers provides an ideal opportunity for one of the teachers to observe and make anecdotal notes about the students while the other teacher provides instruction (Klenk & Almasi, 1997).

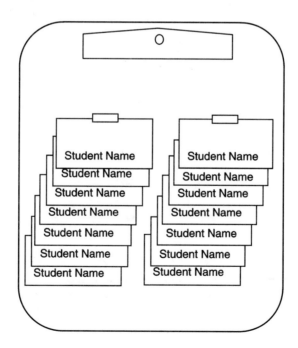

FIGURE 2.3. Using a clipboard to take anecdotal notes of student performance.

For example, while one of my graduate students, Angela, was observing one of her students select a book to read for pleasure, she made the following anecdotal note: "[The student] fumbles through pile [of texts] not looking at back cover or opening them [the texts] up to see text, but just glancing at the covers of a few, then grabs Teen magazine." Angela then asked the student why she selected that particular text. The student replied, " 'Cause I like reading about famous people."

As Lipson (1996) noted, these informal observations, chats, and notes take on diagnostic value. When reflecting on observations and conversations, it is important to consider which aspect of strategic processing is being revealed. That is, which of the five characteristics from the Good Strategy User Model does this behavior inform? From Angela's observation she was able to learn a bit more about her student's motivation for reading and her procedural knowledge about selecting texts to read for pleasure. She knows that her student enjoys reading biographical information and news about famous people of interest to teenagers. She also knows that the student does not appear to have a strategy for choosing texts, since she did not look at anything other than the front cover before selecting one. Although these hypotheses are based on a very limited amount of information, they do provide a beginning foundation for ongoing assessment. Angela can now test her hypotheses under a variety of conditions to see if they legitimately depict her student's motivation and procedural knowledge for selecting texts. Without such information, she does not know how her student is selecting texts or why she is selecting them. She only knows which text has been selected.

Observation and informal conversation are potentially illuminating sources of information about the ways our students process text. As noted in Table 2.1, observation and conversation can inform every aspect of the Good Strategy User Model. In addition to

TABLE 2.1. Using Classroom-Based Assessments to Evaluate Students' Strategic Processing

	Strategic Processing Constructs (Good Strategy User Model)						
	Extent of Knowledge Base			Motivation	Metacognition	Ability to Analyze Task	Variety of Strategies
Type of Assessment	Declarative Knowledge	Procedural Knowledge	Conditional Knowledge				
Observation/ conversation	■	■	■	■	■	■	■
Think aloud protocol	■	■	■	■	■	■	■
Metacognitive interview/ text interview	■	■	■	■	■	■	■
Miscue analysis		■	■		■		■
Index of reading awareness	■		■		■		
Metacomprehension Strategy Index	■		■		■		
Motivation to Read Profile				■			

this methodology, Table 2.1 displays six other types of assessments and how each is useful in relation to the Good Strategy User Model. These assessment approaches are explained further in the remaining portion of the chapter.

Verbal Report Data

Another way of gathering similar information about a reader's strategic processing is to develop a more planned conversation. Such information is often referred to as "verbal report" or "self-report" data. Think alouds, metacognitive interviews, and text interviews are primary ways of attaining such information. First the benefits and limitations of verbal report data are presented, followed by detailed explanation and examples of each type of data.

Benefits of Verbal Report Data

The benefits of using think alouds and interview data are numerous. First, verbal reports focus more on process than product (Afflerbach & Johnston, 1984; Garner, 1987). Strategy use *is* a process, not a product, so this method serves as a primary means of obtaining information about how (or if) students strategize. The higher-level cognitive processes that are usually unavailable for inspection become accessible as the user describes them (Afflerbach & Johnston, 1984).

Limitations of Verbal Report Data

The outcome of think alouds and interviews depend on readers' capacity to talk about their abilities (Lipson, 1996). Garner (1987) noted several limitations of verbal report data. First, it is difficult to observe the workings of the mind with accuracy. As a strategic process becomes automated, only the final products are left in memory to be reported. Hence, individuals either draw inferences about what they actually did, use their prior knowledge about what ideal readers would do, or provide incomplete reports (Garner, 1987). No individual has complete accessibility to, or is consciously aware of, all ongoing cognitive and metacognitive processes.

In addition, memory failure may play a role in verbal reporting (Garner, 1987). The accuracy of a verbal report is affected by the distance between the time the processing occurred and the time it is reported. This is not a problem for think alouds, but it is relevant to interviews, which should be conducted as close as possible to an actual reading event.

Another crimp in the accuracy of interviews occurs when students describe useful strategies but, in reality, do not employ them as they read (Garner, 1987). These students typically have declarative and procedural knowledge about the strategy but are not motivated to use either. For these reasons it is important to use verbal report in conjunction with performance data to validate any emerging hypotheses regarding a student's strategic processing.

We must also be aware of the possibility that students often respond in a manner they think will please adults, so that what they say may not actually reflect what they do. It is also important to note that our questions or probes may be leading, inadvertently cuing a student about more appropriate behaviors (e.g., "So, do you go back and reread

when something doesn't make sense?") (Garner, 1987). When designing interview protocols it is important to use open-ended questions and try to minimize the number of
probes (e.g., "What do you do when something doesn't make sense while you are reading?").

Finally, it is important to note that some young children have limited language skills
and may not be able to respond adequately to questions or to communicate the strategies
they are using to process text (Garner, 1987). In this case, rather than relying solely on
open-ended responses, we must reduce the verbal demands by using pictures or letting
them choose multiple-choice options.

These limitations should not deter teachers from using verbal report data. They are
discussed to help us avoid the pitfalls that can occur without proper planning. The benefits far outweigh these limitations. As indicated in Table 2.1, the information gained from
think alouds and interviews, if done well, can shed light on every aspect of strategic processing. These benefits are further discussed as each type of verbal report data is explained in more detail.

Think Alouds

Think alouds are one type of verbal report in which an individual expresses everything
that he or she is thinking as she performs a given task. Think alouds have been used as a
method of inquiry in research, a method of instruction, and as a means of examining the
cognitive processing that occurs during social interaction (Kucan & Beck, 1997). As a
method of inquiry, think aloud protocols are an effective means of assessing learning that
go beyond traditional methods of assessing the products of reading comprehension
(e.g., responses to comprehension questions, retellings, summaries). These protocols provide a glimpse of the way in which readers process text while they are reading (Kucan &
Beck, 1997). Think alouds enable teachers to see those strategies a reader employs, when
she employs them, where she employs them, and how she employs them. Conversely, the
protocols also reveal a student's failure to learn specific strategies (Bereiter & Bird,
1985).

The criticisms of think aloud procedures are well known. The amount of cognitive
processing that must occur while engaged in a think aloud is extensive, and can interfere
with the cognitive processing it takes to read a text. By asking an individual to read the
text and verbalize every thought that occurs to him while reading adds to his cognitive
processing load. This cognitive load may disrupt or slow down the reading process
(Bereiter & Bird, 1985). To reduce these limitations, Bereiter and Bird (1985) suggested
that teachers model think alouds for students in their everyday instruction and provide
opportunities to practice think alouds. Garner (1987) suggested that another way to reduce the processing load is to engage students in stimulated recalls, in which a portion of
an audio- or videotape is played back so that students can then explain the cognitive processes in which they were engaged.

Think alouds are relatively simple to employ; however, they are rarely used in classroom instruction or assessment. Any text can be used to elicit a think aloud, although the
selected text should probably not be at a child's frustration level. Garner (1987) suggested that think alouds begin with general instructions such as, " 'Tell me what you are
thinking as you complete this task' " (p. 69). Initial directions can be followed with
prompts and probes such as, " 'Don't forget to tell me what you are thinking about' " or

" 'Can you tell me more?' " (Wade, 1990, p. 444). As the individual reads the text aloud, he verbalizes the thoughts that occur to him. These thoughts can be recorded on video- or audiotape, or the teacher can write them on a copy of the text as the student reads. After the student is finished reading, the teacher categorizes the data. A good beginning is to consider the data in terms of the five characteristics of good strategy users to see whether any clues are given relative to declarative/procedural/conditional knowledge, motivation, metacognition, ability to analyze the task, and the variety of strategies possessed.

A grid can be developed to record the strategies and motivation statements made by the student during the think aloud. Table 2.2 depicts a think aloud coding scheme developed by Jody Rabinowitz, a former graduate student at the University at Buffalo. Jody broke her text into units and numbered them so that she could also identify the place in which the reader used a particular strategy or assumed a particular motivational stance. In this manner, Jody was able to map the specific strategies used by the reader, where the strategies were used, and the student's motivational stances to gain a better overall picture of how the reader was processing text.

The data in Table 2.2 depict a reader who appears to possess a variety of strategies.

TABLE 2.2. Coding Scheme for Recording Strategy Use and Motivational Stance during Think Alouds (developed by Jody Rabinowitz [1996])

Code	Description	No. of Incidents	Location (chunk #)
Comprehension Strategies			
LPTH	Looking at pictures, titles, headings	3	1, 7, 20
MP	Making predictions	2	8, 10
APK	Activating prior knowledge	3	6, 7, 10
Q	Questioning	2	12, 18
AQ	Answering questions	1	12
SUM	Summarizing	6	7, 10, 13, 15, 17, 20
ITS	Identifying text structure	0	
I/V	Imagery/visualization	0	
IMI	Identifying main ideas	1	3
Fix-up Strategies			
RR	Rereading	0	
RAC	Reading ahead for clarification	0	
ASK	Asking someone	0	
Word Identification Strategies			
PH	Using letter–sound correspondences (phonics)	2	17, 19
CC	Using context cues	0	
SW	Skipping a word	5	5, 14, 15, 17, 19
AG	Analogizing	0	
SA	Using structural analysis	0	
Motivational Stance			
PS	Personal significance	1	2
LM	Low motivation	1	6
HM	High motivation	0	
LC	Lack of confidence	4	6, 9, 10, 18
RC	Rise in confidence	1	11

The reader used summarization to facilitate comprehension as well as looking at titles/pictures/headings and activating prior knowledge. We would need to look at where and when she used the strategies to see whether her conditional knowledge was appropriate, but it is clear that summarization was used midway through the text, suggesting an appropriate grasp of strategy-useful circumstances. We can also note that her primary strategy for identifying unknown words was to skip them. Again, we would need to look at each word and her comprehension to determine whether the skipped words were detrimental to her understanding of the text, but here we have initial clues about how she processes text when she comes to unknown words. The reader's motivational stance indicated that she lacked confidence while reading and that she may have been slightly unmotivated to read this text.

Think aloud data can be unwieldy, but Jody's coding system enabled her to categorize a student's strategy use and motivation so she could analyze the reading processes used. As she continues to gather think aloud data for the student over the course of the year, she can compare the strategies used, their appropriateness for the situation, and the motivational stance over time. This information can also help Jody plan for the student's instruction. If the student was using inappropriate strategies, she can be taught how to analyze the task more carefully, and she can be taught the conditional knowledge associated with a given strategy. If skipping unknown words is impeding the student's comprehension, she can be taught more effective strategies for identifying unknown words. Likewise, Jody can begin to work on creating instructional contexts that will help bolster the student's self-esteem and confidence.

Think alouds provide valuable information about how a student reads text. Teachers are able to see how a student processes text while she is actually engaged in the task. This procedure eliminates the problems related to self-report data, because the student is sharing exactly what she is doing while she is reading. There is no opportunity for memory failure or for misreporting.

One challenge that teachers often face, however, is the quiet or less verbal student. My students at the University at Buffalo have found it helpful to practice doing think alouds with younger and less verbal students by using puzzles and mazes before asking them to perform a think aloud while reading. One graduate student, Eileen Ludwig, was working with a very quiet student, Maria. She explains her student's progress in this area as well as her own progress as a teacher of strategic processing:

> In the beginning of our sessions, Maria had an extremely hard time verbalizing. As time progressed, she became much more verbal. My goal was to get her to talk more about what she was thinking and doing as she read. Although [by the end of eight lessons] she still could not do this [successfully while reading], she was able to verbalize and tell me what she was thinking and doing as she completed puzzle mazes. I feel that using this concrete experience in the beginning of each lesson really made her open up and become more relaxed during the lessons. Since she was able to complete these puzzles, I also feel that this built her self-esteem and motivation. In addition, throughout lessons I modeled by thinking aloud what I do as I read. I could also see my own growth with using this procedure. In the beginning of instruction, I had a difficult time modeling what I would do by thinking aloud. As time went on, engaging in think alouds became much more natural and comfortable for me [to use as an instructional tool].
>
> [Eileen Ludwig, reflective memo, May 2000]

Think alouds are a powerful tool for assessment and, as Eileen has noted above, for modeling the cognitive processes that students can use during reading instruction. Think alouds are difficult to use initially, but they quickly become an essential assessment and instructional tool.

Metacognitive Interviews

Metacognitive interviews can be constructed to examine all five constructs related to strategic processing (see Figure 2.4). They can also be used to gain insight into student perceptions, print conventions, text handling, and purposes for reading. It is important that these interviews be just that—an interview rather than a paper-and-pencil survey. Many children are unaware of their cognitive processes and need to have all of their resources available to think about how they read. If they are expected to write about how they read, they might be inhibited by their inability to spell a word, or they may not be motivated to write all of the strategic processing that they really use. It is easier for children to talk about these processes than write about them.

An example of a typical metacognitive interview (this one was developed by Beth Davey) is provided in Figure 2.4. The questions contained in this interview are intended to determine the strategies a reader uses during comprehension and decoding. In addition, answers to the questions also lend insight into a student's motivations, attitudes, and attributions related to reading.

A great deal of information can be gathered just by asking these simple questions. Take the case of Jason, a struggling second-grade reader who is nine years old. Jason's responses to the questions on the metacognitive interview are shown in Figure 2.5. These responses provide information about how he views the reading process and the manner in which he processes text. While reading his responses, think about the strategic behaviors he uses. From the outset, it is evident that Jason may not be a risk taker or may have low self-esteem. He noted on several occasions (questions 1 and 1b) that he would seek the help from an adult rather than attempting to decode unknown words on his own. He also noted in question 4 that he felt nervous when reading out loud. We know that Jason seems to value reading (question 8) and enjoys it (question 5), but he does not seem comfortable with the act of reading. This information tells us about his attributions and motivations.

We also learn about the types of strategies he possesses, his knowledge base, and his metacognitive awareness in questions 1, 1a, 1b, 7, and 9. In terms of comprehension, it seems as if Jason is not able to monitor his comprehension (question 1a). This is not an uncommon response for struggling readers. Sometimes when asked what they do when something doesn't make sense, they state, "Nothing, I just keep reading." Such responses indicate that the reader is unaware that text *should* make sense, which can also be an indicator that a student is too print-focused. This premise is supported by Jason's responses to several questions in which he focuses on sounding and blending (questions 1, 1b, 7). He also notes (question 10) that the books in school are too difficult for him to read because the words are too big. This answer reveals Jason's frustration with the reading materials in school. If a text were at your frustration level, then it would make sense that you would be focused on print and decoding rather than comprehension. You would need to use all of your cognitive resources to decode the words.

From Jason's comments we get a picture of a classroom in which this child is often

1. When you are reading, what do you do when you come to something you don't know?

   a. What do you do when you read something that doesn't make sense?

   b. What do you do when you come to a word you don't know?

2. Which do you like best, reading out loud or to yourself? Why?

3. Which do you think takes longer, reading out loud or reading silently? Why?

4. What types of things does your teacher have you do during reading time?

5. Do you like to read? Why or why not?

6. Do you read at home? How often?

   a. Where do you read?

   b. Do you read to yourself or to someone else?

   c. What types of things do you like to read?

7. Let's say the kindergarten teacher has asked you to help her during reading time. How would you teach a kindergarten child how to read?

8. Do you think it's important to know how to read? Why or why not?

9. What is a good reader? How could you be a better reader?

10. Do you ever read anything easy in school? If so, what?

FIGURE 2.4. Sample metacognitive interview, blank version. Developed by Beth Davey, University of Maryland.

1. When you are reading, what do you do when you come to something you don't know?
   "I ask my Mom or I raise my hand to ask the teacher to sound and blend. I make the sounds of the letter it makes pretty good."
   a. What do you do when you read something that doesn't make sense?
      "I never did that before. I don't know. Everything makes sense pretty much."

   b. What do you do when you come to a word you don't know?
      "Ask a grown-up what the word is. I sound and blend."

2. Which do you like best, reading out loud or to yourself? Why?
   "To myself because it doesn't interrupt people or disturb people. I like it to be quiet."
3. Which do you think takes longer, reading out loud or reading silently? Why?
   "Reading out loud. It disturbs me."

4. What types of things does your teacher have you do during reading time?
   "I have to read out loud one at a time. Then we read it again. Then we make a word. I feel nervous when I read out loud."
5. Do you like to read? Why or why not?
   "Yes, because if it doesn't have pictures I can make the pictures in my head."

6. Do you read at home? How often?
   "Fifteen minutes a day by myself."

   a. What types of things do you like to read?
      "Dr. Seuss."

   b. Do you read to yourself or to someone else?
      [not asked]

   c. What types of things do you like to read?
      [not asked]

7. Let's say the kindergarten teacher has asked you to help her during reading time. How would you teach a kindergarten child how to read?
   "Help him sound out the words. Start with easy words and go to harder words."

8. Do you think it's important to know how to read? Why or why not?
   "Yes, because then you couldn't read the newspaper and wouldn't know what was going on in the world."
9. What is a good reader? How could you be a better reader?
   "I have no idea. They write books or read a lot. I don't know."

10. Do you ever read anything easy in school? If so, what?
    "No. Never. They have bigger words than usual."

FIGURE 2.5. Jason's responses to the metacognitive interview.

reading out loud from texts that are too difficult for him. Certainly this scenario would be damaging to one's self-esteem. Jason does note (question 5) that he makes images in his head while reading. Image-making is a good comprehension strategy, and it would be worthwhile to see whether he truly uses this strategy when reading authentic text. Conducting an interview that is performance-related would be an important next step. Text interviews provide a framework for incorporating the insights gained from the metacognitive interview with performance data.

Text Interviews

Text interviews give students the opportunity to interact with texts as they think about how they read. To prepare for a text interview, select a variety of texts that represent diverse interests, genres, and ability levels. It is important to have available at least 15 different types of texts (narrative books, expository books, magazines, newspapers, CD liner notes, etc.). Display the texts in an attractive manner on a table and then begin the interview process. Figure 2.6 displays a text interview developed and used by students in a master's level course at the University at Buffalo. Several of the students had the children bring in favorite books from home, and texts used in school, to supplement their collection. Students can also talk about the books they brought from home and why they enjoy them so much, as well as talk about their classroom texts. Many of the graduate students also used the self-selected texts as a means of initiating a miscue analysis. The

---

Provide a selection of varied texts that represent diverse interests, genres, and ability levels.

INTEREST

1. What types of texts do you like to read?

2. Take a look at these texts. Have you ever read any of them before? If so, which ones? What did you think of them?

3. Do you see anything here that you would like to read? Why or why not?

4. Who are your favorite authors? What do you like about his/her books?

READING LEVEL

Frustration Level (Read Aloud)
5. Which text, or what type of text, would you like someone to read to you?

(cont.)

FIGURE 2.6. Example of a text interview. Developed by Angela Bies, Anita Brocker, Erin David, Renee Danielewicz, Sheila Ewing, AnnaMaria Figliomeni, Chastity Flynn, Keli Garas, Renee Guzak, Jill Hatfield, Bob Hirsch, Jennifer Izzo, Krista Jaekle, Eileen Ludwig, Jaime Quackenbush, Mike Rock, Kathy Sadowski, Donna Von Hendy, and Kristin Zahn (Spring 2000).

6. What types of text does your family read to you?

7. Which of these texts would be really hard for you to read? What makes it hard?

8. What do you do when you don't understand what you read?

9. What do you do when you come to a word you don't know?

Instructional Level

10. Which of these texts would you like to read, but think you might need a little help to read it on your own?

Independent Level

11. Which of these texts would be easy for you to read on your own? What makes it easy?

12. Which of these texts would you choose to read on your own for fun? Why?

13. Which of these texts would you like to read to a younger child? Why?

14. Which of these texts would you feel comfortable reading in front of your class? Why?

TEXT HANDLING/STRATEGIC AWARENESS

15. How would you go about reading this text?

16. What kinds of things do you do before you start to read?

17. What kinds of things do you do while you are reading to help you read the text?

18. What kinds of things do you do while you are reading to help you understand the text?

19. What kinds of things do you do after you read to help you understand or remember the text?

PURPOSE OF READING

20. Which of these texts would you use to find facts about _____? How would you go about reading this text?

21. [Select two texts of different genres] What is different about these texts? Which type of text do you prefer? Why?

CHARACTERISTICS OF STRATEGIC READERS

22. Do you know someone who is a good reader? If so, what makes them a good reader?

23. How do you feel about reading? Why?

24. Is it important to learn to read? Why or why not?

FIGURE 2.6. *(cont.)*

miscue analysis served as further performance-based evidence to support their emerging hypotheses about their readers' strategic processing.

Miscue Analysis

Teachers can make inferences about a reader's strategic processing by analyzing the miscues, or errors, made while reading aloud (Walker, 2000). Miscue analysis is a means by which a teacher can evaluate and interpret the significance of a reader's miscues in relation to the context of the passage being read. Walker (2000) has noted that a reader's miscues provide insight into the cues and strategies used to construct meaning from text. Some miscues are more significant than others. Those that do not alter the meaning of the text (e.g., substituting "Mom" for "Mother") are viewed as insignificant. Sometimes a reader will make an error, realize it, and go back and self-correct the error. These miscues, known as self-corrections, are also not significant for they indicate that the reader was monitoring her comprehension and using repair strategies, as needed.

Miscues that are not corrected and that change the meaning of the text are considered significant. There are five types of oral reading errors: omissions, substitutions, mispronunciations, insertions, and repetitions. *Omissions* occur when the reader skips a word, several words, parts of words, or a sentence. If an omission changes the meaning of the text, then it is considered significant. Omissions that do not alter the meaning, are not considered significant.

Substitutions occur when a word is substituted for the word in the text (e.g., substituting "begin" for "began"). Again, if the miscue alters meaning it is considered significant. Quite often readers who make numerous substitutions are attempting to bring meaning to the text; however, they are not attending closely to letter–sound cues or structural aspects of the words.

Mispronunciations are miscues that often result in a nonword (e.g., pronouncing "corner" as "*karmra*"). Such miscues are usually significant because they alter the meaning of the sentence. They are indicative of a reader who is processing words mostly by using letter–sound correspondences.

Insertions occur when an extra word (or words) is inserted in the text. Usually these miscues are not significant if done in a limited manner. Good readers will often insert a word here or there to make the text more fluent or more meaningful. However, a reader who inserts words consistently may be overrelying on background knowledge to read rather than attending to the print.

Repetitions of a word or phrase often occur to enhance fluency and comprehension. Other times they function as a "stall" tactic, in which a reader repeats a word or phrase just prior to reading an unknown word. The reader is trying to "buy time" to try to decode the unknown word and repeats the familiar words or phrase to give her- or himself a few extra seconds for decoding.

Very often teachers use miscue analysis as a means of determining a student's reading level. In those instances the teacher may use an Informal Reading Inventory (IRI) to determine the student's independent, instructional, and frustration reading level for oral and silent reading. An IRI is a series of graded reading passages that range in difficulty from emergent reading (preprimer) to eighth grade. Students read word lists to determine at which level oral reading should begin. Then they are asked to read a passage at that level orally. During the oral reading, the teacher records the student's miscues. Following oral reading, the student is told to retell the passage and then asked several comprehension questions to determine comprehension level. Based on the student's performance on oral reading and comprehension, the teacher administers other passages of either higher or lower levels to determine the student's independent (i.e., level at which the student can read fluently with good comprehension), instructional (i.e., level at which the student experiences a bit of stress while reading), and frustration (i.e., level at which the student is unsuccessful with decoding and comprehension) reading levels. Examples of commercially prepared IRIs include the Basic Reading Inventory (Johns, 1993) and the Qualitative Reading Inventory (Leslie & Caldwell, 1995).

When the teacher's goal is to gain insight into the strategies a reader is using while reading, it is not important to use an IRI. Any text that is not at the child's frustration level will suffice, because the goal is simply to determine the strategies used while reading. To determine the strategies the student uses while reading text at independent, instructional, and frustration levels, either an IRI or a series of leveled texts would be needed. An alternative to purchasing an IRI is to have the student self-select a text that is neither too difficult nor too easy for him to read and make a copy of the text on which to record the reader's miscues. Running records—a method of analyzing students' oral reading from authentic texts—would be suitable for this purpose as well (Clay, 1993). Figure 2.7 depicts one way to code oral reading miscues on a copy of a selected text.

The type of information gained from a miscue analysis gives an indication of the word identification strategies a reader is using and whether she is monitoring her comprehension as she reads, but it does not provide a complete picture of all strategic processing used while reading. Miscue analysis is better suited to providing insight regarding a reader's procedural and conditional knowledge related to word identification strategies. It is unable to provide insight related to comprehension strategies used while reading other than the reader's ability to monitor comprehension, as evidenced by self-corrected miscues. It is also unable to provide insight related to a reader's motivations, ability to analyze the task, and the degree of declarative knowledge possessed (see Table 2.1).

GROUP-ADMINISTERED INFORMAL ASSESSMENTS RELATED TO STRATEGIC PROCESSING

Several tools have been developed to assess strategic awareness and motivation: Index of Reading Awareness, Metacomprehension Strategies Index, and Motivation to Read Profile. Each of these tools provides teachers with a means of quickly assessing children's awareness and use of strategic behavior and their motivations for using strategies (see Table 2.1). Group-administered assessments provide a rapid means of assessing the entire class. All of the assessments reviewed here also have exhibited high reliability and validity. However, the multiple-choice format taps only students' self-reports of strategic behavior, not their actual performance in authentic contexts. For this reason, caution when interpreting data from these measures is advised. It is possible that a student may report using a given strategy or strategic behavior but may not actually use it while reading. Additionally, the closed-ended nature of multiple-choice questions means that the child is limited to the response options only. This limitation may invite guessing or random selection of responses that are not indicative of a reader's true processing style. Gambrell, Palmer, Codling, and Mazzoni (1996) have alleviated this problem slightly in

Type of Miscue	Code	Example
Omission	Circle omitted word.	Jill looked both ways (and) then began to cross.
Substitution	Draw a slash through the actual word and write the substitution above.	Jill looked both ways and then ~~began~~ begin to cross.
Mispronunciation	Draw a slash through the actual word and write the incorrect pronunciation.	She walked down our street to the ~~corner~~ karmra.
Insertion	Draw a carat between the words in which the insertion was made and write the inserted word above.	She ∧ ran away. quickly
Repetition	Draw an arrow under text that was repeated.	Jill saw the car and ran the rest of the way. ◄———————
Successful correction	Draw a "c" with a circle around it to indicate that a substitution was corrected.	Jill saw the car and ran the rest of the way. ©was
Attempted correction	Draw an "ac" with a circle around it to indicate that attempts to correct the miscues were unsuccessful.	The man in the car had to put on the brakes. (ac) balak / bakery

FIGURE 2.7. Key for coding oral reading miscues.

their Motivation to Read Profile by providing an additional conversational interview format to afford a more in-depth look at students' motivations.

Strategy use is flexible, varies from individual to individual, and varies depending on the context. Multiple-choice formats are scored in a manner that assumes that one response is "better" or "more correct" than others. This assumption does not take into account the flexibility of strategy use or the possibility that a particular context may warrant multiple plans. These measures provide only a quick index of strategic awareness and motivation. As with any assessment, they should be used in conjunction with other assessments and performance data to provide a more complete picture of students' strategic processing.

General Strategy Use

Index of Reading Awareness

Several researchers have developed instruments designed to assess readers' strategic awareness. Paris and Jacobs (1984) initially developed a metacognitive interview designed to assess how students evaluate reading tasks and their own abilities, how they plan to reach a specified goal, and how they use monitoring strategies. The interview data from that investigation was used to develop a 22-item multiple-choice assessment, known as the Index of Reading Awareness (Paris & Oka, 1986a), which assesses knowledge of task goals, planful use of strategies, and evaluation of comprehension (see Table 2.2). For example, the question " 'What do you do if you don't know what a whole sentence means?' " (p. 35) is followed by three multiple-choice responses, each awarded a point value of 0, 1, or 2. Scores on the index range from a low of 0 to a high of 44.

Metacomprehension Strategy Index

Schmitt (1990) developed an assessment of strategic reading processes known as the Metacomprehension Strategy Index (MSI). The MSI assesses students' awareness of strategies used before, during, and after reading narrative text. The strategies assessed include (1) predicting and verifying, (2) previewing, (3) purpose setting, (4) self-questioning, (5) drawing on background knowledge, and (6) summarizing and using fix-up strategies (see Table 2.1). The 25-item multiple-choice assessment includes four response options that are coded as either correct (1 point) or incorrect (0 points). Scores on the MSI range from a low of 0 to a high of 25.

Assessments must reliably measure the construct (in this case, strategic awareness). Reliability means that the measure consistently scores a given trait accurately. Schmitt (1990) reported a reliability of 0.87 (Kuder–Richardson Formula 20) for the MSI, which indicates a high degree of reliability. An assessment must also demonstrate that it is valid—that is, that it measures what it purports to measure (in this case, strategic awareness). Schmitt has reported the MSI to be a valid measure of strategy awareness that offers teachers a quick assessment of students' abilities. For this reason, teachers might find it most beneficial to use at the beginning of the year, administering it to the entire class to gain quick insight into each student's awareness of strategies and how to use them. However, Schmitt cautioned that the MSI provides just one measure of students' reading abilities and should be used in conjunction with multiple sources of information.

Motivational Assessments

Gambrell et al.'s (1996) Motivation to Read Profile (MRP) is an instrument designed to assess a reader's self-concept and the value of reading. These two elements are essential to motivated strategy use (Paris & Oka, 1986b). The MRP contains a Reading Survey and a Conversational Interview. The Reading Survey is a group-administered 20-item multiple-choice questionnaire with a 4-point response scale. The 10 items related to self-concept are intended to provide information about students' perceived competence and performance in reading. The other 10 items on value provide information about the value students place on various reading tasks.

The Conversational Interview is administered individually to students and consists of 14 open-ended questions that elicit information about motivation as it relates to reading narrative text, informational text, and reading in general. This interview provides information about students' motivation during authentic reading experiences that supplements the information gleaned from the Reading Survey. The Reading Survey has a moderately high reliability ($\alpha = 0.75$ for self-concept subtest; $\alpha = 0.82$ for value of reading), and the MRP as a whole has proven to be a valid measure of student motivation (Gambrell et al., 1996). The authors cautioned that the MRP is a self-report instrument and therefore subject to the same limitations as any verbal report data (i.e., metacognitive interviews). Again, teachers might consider administering the MRP to the entire class at the beginning of the school year to gain insight into each student's self-concept as a reader and the value they place on reading. Those students who exhibit low self-concept, or those students who are struggling readers, may be selected for the Conversational Interview portion of the MRP to find out more about their motivation for reading. Like the Metacomprehension Strategy Index, the authors of the MRP suggest that it be accompanied by close classroom observation to verify or reject any emerging hypotheses about student motivation.

GENERATING HYPOTHESES ABOUT STUDENTS' STRATEGY USE

Assessment is integral to the model of ongoing assessment and instruction described in Figure 2.2. Assessment and instruction provide critical information that enables us to hypothesize about a student's strengths and needs as they pertain to strategic processing. Teachers continually engage in this recursive process of generating, revising, and altering hypotheses about students. However, this is usually a very informal process. Afflerbach (1993) developed a system that formalizes this process to permit close scrutiny of the reader, textual task, and contextual factors that contribute to hypothesis formation. The STAIR system (System for Teaching and Assessing Interactively and Reflectively) consists of compiling and maintaining information based on observations, informal assessments, and instruction to plan for students' individual development. It consists of three components: (1) observing and assessing students, (2) generating, revising, and deleting hypotheses about students' needs, and (3) planning and implementing instruction to meet students' needs. Figure 2.8 depicts a sample recording sheet used to describe original hypotheses. The teacher, Eileen, began her ongoing assessment and instruction by drawing on information gleaned from a metacognitive interview, a text interview, and an instructional lesson related to activating background knowledge. She then used the information from her observations and interviews to generate an initial hypothesis about the student's needs and instructional plans. The recursiveness in the assessment/instruction process is apparent: Eileen was able to gather information from informal assessments and observations made during instruction to help her plan. Each component of the ongoing assessment model depicted in Figure 2.2 informs, and is informed by, the other (Klenk & Almasi, 1997).

Although initial hypotheses are generated, it is important to realize that these hypotheses are based on limited information in one particular context. As instruction and assessment proceed, the original hypothesis may be altered, revised, or dropped altogether, based on more information.

Figure 2.9 depicts the next phase of the STAIRs system—ongoing assessment, instruction, and reflection on hypotheses. In Eileen's reflection on the previous lesson, she realized that it was important for Maria to be able to verbalize more completely what she was thinking and doing as she read. Therefore, Eileen revised her original hypothesis slightly to reflect her new insights based on observation, assessment, and reflection. The continual refinement that comes with disciplined reflection and examination of data from

System for Teaching and Assessing Interactively and Reflectively (STAIRs)
Original Hypothesis

Teacher: ___Eileen Ludwig_____   Date: ___2/22/00_____

Student: ___Maria_____

Context: Metacognitive/text interview and initial lesson related to activating background knowledge.

Text: 13 different narrative and expository texts available for text interview. One was self-selected for use in lesson on previewing text and activating background knowledge.

Task: Maria was taught how to make predictions while reading a story. She was also taught how to use textual evidence to make predictions and why making predictions is important.

Original Hypothesis and Source(s)

Hypothesis # ___1___ :

Maria does not seem to use any comprehension strategies before, during, or after reading to help her make sense of text.

Original source/evidence supporting hypothesis:

During the metacognitive interview Maria was asked, "What do you do while you are reading to help you understand what you are reading?" Maria responded, "Nothing, I just keep reading." When asked, "What do you do after you read to help you understand and remember what you read?" Maria responded, "I don't do anything." She was also asked, "What about if you are studying for a test, do you do anything to help you remember?" Maria responded, "No, nothing." When Maria was asked if she did anything before she read something new, she said, "I just look at the words inside the book to see if they are too big or hard." Maria's Individualized Education Plan (IEP) also indicated weak comprehension when reading silently and orally. Based on discussions with Maria's classroom teacher and the resource director, it seems as if Maria does not use any comprehension strategies to help her understand text. Observations during the first instructional lesson also support this hypothesis.

Instruction to address hypothesis:

An overall plan is to introduce Maria to a variety of comprehension strategies that she can use flexibly before, during, and after reading. Instruction will need to teach Maria the declarative, procedural, and conditional knowledge associated with strategy use so that she sees the value and benefit of using strategies. Think alouds will be used to assess her emerging use and awareness of comprehension strategies while reading.

FIGURE 2.8. Example of a filled in STAIRs original hypothesis sheet. Blank STAIRs forms from Afflerbach (1993). Copyright 1993 by the International Reading Association. Used by permission.

System for Teaching and Assessing Interactively and Reflectively (STAIRs)
Ongoing Assessment, Instruction, and Reflection on Hypothesis

Teacher: Eileen Ludwig   Date: 2/22/00

Student: Maria

Context: Instructional lesson on making predictions

Text: *Ira Sleeps Over*, by Bernard Waber

Task: Maria will learn how to make predictions while reading. She will learn how to use textual evidence to help her make predictions, and she will learn why making predictions is important for comprehension.

Hypothesis # 1 :

Maria does not seem to use any comprehension strategies before, during, or after reading to help her make sense of text. It is important that she begin to verbalize more about what she is thinking and doing as she reads to help her comprehend.

Hypothesis _____ maintained x revised _____ dropped

Source of information:

Based on previous lessons, I believe that Maria will use some comprehension strategies with explicit instruction. The previous lesson involved activating prior knowledge and previewing text in order to read and understand expository text. Maria did use her background knowledge and experiences to help her understand what she was reading for this lesson. However, a great deal of time was needed to help Maria activate her background knowledge before she could use this strategy. I have also noticed that Maria will make predictions before and while reading, if she is asked to do so. However, I am not sure that she will use these comprehension strategies on her own. Based on my observations, she still needs a great deal of modeling and guided practice. In addition, I have not observed Maria using many other comprehension strategies before, during, or after reading on her own. Although Maria will sometimes use the author's pictures to help her, I do not think Maria makes her own mental images as she reads.

Detailed reflection and explanation:

After doing the lesson on making predictions and indicating what evidence was used in order to make predictions before and during reading, I realized that Maria can use this strategy if she is provided with a great deal of modeling and guided practice. I do feel that she may not use this strategy on her own, unless it is contin-

(cont.)

FIGURE 2.9. Example of a filled in STAIRs hypothesis maintenance sheet. Blank STAIRs forms from Afflerbach (1993). Copyright 1993 by the International Reading Association. Used by permission.

ually reinforced. I also realized that many times she seemed to be able to make predictions but would have trouble verbalizing why she made them. In addition, through questioning I found that Maria had a difficult time understanding the parts and structure of a story. I feel that if she could understand and organize the parts and structure of a story, she could better understand what is going on in the story. While reading *Ira Sleeps Over,* Maria was able to draw from some of her own experiences and relate it to the story. Activating background knowledge and drawing on her own experiences are skills that we worked on in our first lesson together. This is a strategy that will continually be reinforced throughout future lessons. I feel that if Maria has plenty of guided practice and feedback with this strategy in various contexts, it can become a strength for her.

Instruction to address hypothesis:

I will continue to model how to make predictions and give Maria several opportunities for guided practice. I will provide her with a lot of positive feedback in order to make her more self-confident. Furthermore, I will always tell Maria why we are learning certain strategies and why they are important. Maria will also be given opportunities to verbalize about the strategies she is using. We will start off with more concrete experiences, which can help reduce the processing demands and help her to become more confident as a reader. While reading texts, I will give her opportunities to verbalize what she is thinking and doing as she reads. I hope that by organizing the elements through a story chart, Maria will better understand the elements and, therefore, better understand the story.

FIGURE 2.9. *(cont.)*

assessments and instruction provides teachers with an effective tool for tracking students' progress and meet their individual needs more effectively. Eileen later reflected on her own learning as a teacher of strategic processing, noting:

> As a teacher and learner of reading strategies, I feel that completing these STAIRs hypotheses were extremely helpful to me. Hypothesizing about my student's needs and determining the most essential instruction to address those needs really helped me to stay focused. They allowed me to think about what I need to do as a teacher in order for instruction to be beneficial for my student.
>
> [Eileen Ludwig, process portfolio, May 2000]

SUMMARY

It is difficult to assess the covert mental operations that occur during strategic processing. Teachers must be able to assess whether students (1) possess the declarative, procedural, and conditional knowledge associated with strategy use, (2) are motivated to use strategies, (3) are metacognitive, (4) are able to analyze the task, and (5) possess a variety of strategies. Formal standardized assessment tools are unable to measure such processes. Informal classroom-based assessments, such as think aloud protocols, metacognitive interviews, text interview, and miscue analyses, are useful means of assessing this type of strategic processing. Questionnaires such as the Index of Reading Awareness, the Metacomprehension Strategy Index, and the Motivation to Read Profile also provide insights related to strategic processing. Assessment of strategic processing must be a discursive process that is intimately connected to instruction and hypothesis generation. Each element informs, and is informed by, the other to meet individual students' needs.

REFERENCES

Afflerbach, P. (1993). STAIR: A system for recording and using what we observe and know about our students. *The Reading Teacher, 47,* 260–263.

Afflerbach, P., & Johnston, P. (1984). Research methodology: On the use of verbal reports in reading research. *Journal of Reading Behavior, 16*(4), 307–322.

Bereiter, C., & Bird, M. (1985). Use of thinking aloud in identification and teaching of reading comprehension strategies. *Cognition and Instruction, 2*(2), 131–156.

Calfee, R., & Hiebert, E. (1991). Classroom assessment of reading. In R. Barr, M. L. Kamil, P. Mosenthal, & P. D. Pearson (Eds.), *Handbook of reading research* (vol. 2, pp. 281–309). New York: Longman.

Clay, M. M. (1993). *Reading recovery: A guidebook for teachers in training.* Portsmouth, NH: Heinemann.

Gambrell, L. B., Palmer, B. M., Codling, R., & Mazzoni, S. A. (1996). Assessing motivation to read. *The Reading Teacher, 49*(7), 518–533.

Garner, R. (1987). *Metacognition and reading comprehension.* Norwood, NJ: Ablex.

Gillett, J. W., & Temple, C. (1994). *Understanding reading problems: Assessment and instruction.* New York: HarperCollins.

Johns, J. (1993). *Basic reading inventory* (8th ed.). Dubuque, IA: Kendall-Hunt.

Klenk, L., & Almasi, J. F. (1997). School-based practicum in reading disabilities. *The Language and Literacy Spectrum, 7,* 73–79.

Kucan, L., & Beck, I. L. (1997). Thinking aloud and reading comprehension research: Inquiry, instruction, and social interaction. *Review of Educational Research, 67*(3), 271–299.

Leslie, L., & Caldwell, J. (1995). *Qualitative reading inventory–II.* New York: HarperCollins.

Lipson, M. Y. (1996). Conversations with children and other classroom-based assessment strategies. In L. R. Putnam (Ed.), *How to become a better reading teacher: Strategies for assessment and intervention* (pp. 167–179). Englewood Cliffs, NJ: Merrill.

Paris, S. G., & Jacobs, J. E. (1984). The benefits of informed instruction for children's reading awareness and comprehension skills. *Child Development, 55,* 2083–2093.

Paris, S. G., & Oka, E. R. (1986a). Children's reading strategies, metacognition, and motivation. *Developmental Review, 6,* 25–56.

Paris, S. G., & Oka, E. R. (1986b). Self-regulated learning among exceptional children. *Exceptional Children, 53*(2), 103–108.

Pressley, M., & Afflerbach, P. P. (1995). *Verbal protocols of reading: The nature of constructively responsive reading.* Hillsdale, NJ: Erlbaum.

Schmitt, M. C. (1990). A questionnaire to measure children's awareness of strategic reading processes. *The Reading Teacher, 43*(7), 454–461.

Wade, S. E. (1990). Using think alouds to assess comprehension. *The Reading Teacher, 43*(7), 442–451.

Walker, B. J. (2000). *Diagnostic teaching of reading: Techniques for instruction and assessment* (4th ed.). Upper Saddle River, NJ: Merrill.

CHAPTER THREE

Designing Effective Environments for Strategy Instruction

The Strategy Instruction Model

The goal of any form of strategy instruction is to help individuals become self-regulated learners. Essential to this goal is helping learners attain (1) knowledge about strategies for accomplishing tasks and goals, (2) metacognitive awareness of their progress toward such goals in relation to the demands of the task, (3) real world knowledge, and (4) motivation to employ strategies independently and flexibly (Palincsar & Brown, 1989; Palincsar, David, Winn, & Stevens, 1991; Pressley, El-Dinary, et al., 1992). Many models of strategy instruction have been proposed and nearly all meet with some form of criticism. This chapter describes several research-based models of strategy instruction and their criticisms. A Strategy Instruction Model, based on research literature and clinical practice, that teaches students to employ strategic thinking flexibly in authentic literacy contexts, is proposed and described in detail.

Some (e.g., Poplin, 1988) criticized strategy instruction for being reductionistic rather than constructivist, contending that it (1) breaks learning into parts (i.e., instruction in using isolated strategies) rather than focusing on performance of the whole reading process, (2) portrays students as passive recipients of instruction, (3) flows from the teacher to the student, (4) focuses on knowledge that can be *reproduced* rather than *produced* by the student, and (5) promotes school goals rather than goals important to the learner. In contrast, Pressley, Harris, and Marks (1992) contended that good strategy instruction *is* based on constructivist principles. They distinguish between three types of constructivism, based on Moshman's (1982) classification system: endogenous, exogenous, or dialectical constructivism. These distinctions are explained briefly in order to provide a theoretical grounding for the models of strategy instruction that follow.

Strategy instruction based on *endogenous* constructivism is focused on child-centered exploration and discovery of instructional principles rather than direct teaching. Learning occurs in a social context, and teaching and learning are inseparable from the contexts in which they occur. *Exogenous* constructivists rely more heavily on teaching than endogenous constructivists. Modeling and explanation play a large role in this type of teaching; however, learning is not simply a matter of reproducing such knowledge but of internalizing and adapting this new knowledge to meet the particulars of a given situation. *Dialectical* constructivists believe that learning is more effective if some direct teaching occurs in the form of scaffolded assistance—hints and prompts—rather than extensive explanations. Thus dialectical constructivism lies in between endogenous and exogenous constructivism and, like endogenous constructivism, is based largely on Vygotskian principles that thought develops in social contexts (Vygotsky, 1978). In such contexts readers gradually internalize instructional principles through guided discovery/ scaffolding from more knowledgeable others and through the opportunity to interact with others as they engage in the strategic processing of text.

Next, several models of strategy instruction and their criticisms are reviewed to provide readers with historical grounding for such instruction.

STRATEGY INSTRUCTION FORMATS AND THEIR CRITICISMS

Table 3.1 charts the three strategy instruction formats (exogenous, dialectical, endogenous) and specific models of strategy instruction that fit within each format. The characteristics of each model of strategy instruction are also provided.

Exogenous or Step-by-Step Models

Direct Instruction

Direct instruction of strategies involves explicit step-by-step training in particular strategies (Gersten & Carnine, 1986). Individual strategies are taught by teachers who model or demonstrate the strategy, provide ample guided practice and teacher feedback, and gradually diminish teacher-directed activities to foster independent student work. Student mastery of each step in the process is expected. Research has shown that this model is generally effective for teaching isolated comprehension strategies (see Gersten & Carnine, 1986 for a review); however, direct instruction takes on a "skills" look, in that it does not provide opportunities for students to learn about the conditions under which a given strategy might be used, nor does it provide opportunities for metacognitive awareness regarding strategy use—two critical components of strategic processing. Direct instruction also presents the problem that Whitehead (as cited in Palincsar et al., 1991) referred to as "inert knowledge." This limitation is also known as a lack of transfer. That is, knowledge of a particular strategy may be recalled when explicitly asked about it or told to employ it, but students may not use the strategy spontaneously. As a result of such instruction, students are not taught to employ strategies deliberately, independently, or flexibly. Teachers control the agenda for instruction (Palincsar et al., 1991).

TABLE 3.1. Characteristics of Various Types of Strategy Instruction

	Characteristics of Strategy Instruction													
Type of Strategy Instruction	Individual strategies taught	Explanation (declarative, procedural, conditional)	Modeling	Guided Practice	Independent Student Work	Metacognitive Awareness	Use strategies in authentic contexts	Flexible strategy use	Motivated strategy use encouraged	Teacher in control of instruction	Student in control of instruction	Shift inst. from Teacher to student instruction	Teacher feedback is corrective	Teacher feedback is suggestive
Exogenous														
Direct Instruction	■		■	■					■	■				
Direct Explanation	■	■	■	■	■				■	■				
Dialectical														
Explicit Instruction	at times	■	■	■	■	■	■					■	■	
Informed Strategies for Learning	■	■	■	■		■							■	
Reciprocal Teaching	at times	■	■	■	■	■	■	■	■			■	■	
Transactional Strategies Instruction	at times	■	■	■	■	■	■	■				■	■	
Strategy Instruction Model	at times	■	■	■	■	■	■	■				■	■	
Endogenous														
Collaborative Problem Solving		■			■	■	■	■			■		■	
Process Talk		■			■	■	■	■			■		■	

45

Direct Explanation

Similar to direct instruction models, direct explanation models (e.g., Duffy et al., 1987) include the use of modeling, guided practice, and independent practice. However, this approach differs in that it provides for teacher explanation of the declarative, procedural, and conditional knowledge associated with strategies, and it allows for a gradual shift in responsibility from teacher-directed to student self-regulation of strategy use. The focus of direct explanation is on teacher verbalization, or think alouds, of the mental processes associated with using strategies to understand text. Students taught using this approach demonstrate significantly greater awareness of the procedural and conditional knowledge of strategies, the metacognitive aspects of strategy use, and the nature of strategic reading (Duffy et al., 1987). Thus direct explanation offers a greater awareness of elements critical to strategic processing than direct instruction. Palincsar et al. (1991) noted, however, that students do not have the opportunity to influence the learning environment during direct explanation—the teacher still retains a high profile position during instruction.

Dialectical Models

Explicit Instruction

Similar to direct explanation, explicit instruction also involves teacher modeling, explanation, and think alouds of what, how, when, and why a strategy is used (i.e., declarative, procedural, and conditional knowledge); guided practice in which teachers gradually release responsibility for task completion to students; and independent practice and feedback (Fielding & Pearson, 1994; Pearson & Dole, 1987). In addition, explicit instruction features application of the strategy in authentic reading contexts. What distinguishes explicit instruction from previous models is that there is no assumption (as in direct instruction) that complex strategies should be broken down into separate, sequentially ordered subskills. Each time the reading task is performed during explicit instruction, the entire process is performed, not just practice with a particular strategy or skill. Another distinction that Pearson and Dole (1987) made is that explicit instruction does not have "correct" answers. That is, there are multiple sets of strategies and combinations of strategies that can be used to accomplish a given reading task. Such variation is encouraged, as readers develop their own strategic solutions to complex reading tasks. A final distinction is the use of suggestive rather than corrective feedback during explicit instruction. That is, teacher feedback to students does not "correct" errors but provides alternative suggestions, or multiple ways, of approaching the task. Teachers praise students for their efforts and for applying strategies appropriately, and they also encourage students to try alternative ways of attacking the same problem to compare various approaches.

Like direct explanation, explicit instruction provides students with a greater awareness of aspects related to strategic processing than direct instruction. Explicit instruction takes into account the flexibility of strategic processing and the need for variation in how individuals accomplish similar tasks. However, it does not offer students an opportunity to influence instruction.

Informed Strategies for Learning

Informed Strategies for Learning (ISL) is an approach to strategy instruction that consists of 20 modules addressing four comprehension processes: planning for reading, identifying meaning, reasoning while reading, and monitoring comprehension (Paris & Oka, 1986a). The primary goal of ISL is to help students learn to be strategic as they read. Different strategies are taught in five lessons within each module. Lessons teach children about the declarative, procedural, and conditional knowledge associated with each strategy; provide metaphors that help students remember the strategy (i.e., "Be a reading detective"); and offer opportunities for guided practice to apply the strategies with social studies and science content. ISL lessons place an emphasis on teaching reading strategies and persuading readers about their usefulness. As in explicit instruction, ISL lessons feature faded teacher support, such that strategies are first modeled and explained explicitly and then students are gradually required to generate or select strategies independently. ISL lessons also feature group discussions between teachers and students aimed at discussing students' thoughts and feelings about strategies and their usefulness.

Although ISL offers a very strong focus on strategic processing, the sequential and somewhat scripted nature of the 20 lessons means that meeting the individual needs of students is not a primary goal. Although the opportunity for student discussion and dialogue is a critical component of ISL, the teacher still remains the focal point of instruction, leaving little opportunity for students to influence instruction.

Reciprocal Teaching

Reciprocal teaching provides instruction in four strategies: generating questions from text, summarizing, clarifying portions of text, and predicting upcoming content based on content and structure of text (Palincsar & Brown, 1984, 1989). These strategies are taught as complementary sets to be used flexibly in response to the needs of the reader and the demands of the text. Instruction takes the form of dialogues between the students and the teacher, as each takes turns attempting to use the strategies to construct a meaningful interpretation of the text. The teacher may begin by taking responsibility for modeling the use of the strategies for understanding text, but students are immediately encouraged to join in the discussion by generating their own questions, summarizing, clarifying, and making additional predictions. The teacher facilitates student participation by providing feedback, explanation, and modeling. Students' use of the targeted strategies and their performance on standardized and criterion-referenced comprehension measures are significantly increased by using reciprocal teaching (Palincsar & Brown, 1984, 1989).

Although there is a much greater role for student participation in reciprocal teaching, and strategies are viewed as complementary sets rather than as isolated tools, this approach is limited by the narrow range of strategies taught and the absence of motivated strategy use as a specific goal (Pressley, El-Dinary, et al., 1992).

Transactional Strategies Instruction

Transactional Strategies Instruction (TSI) involves many of the same goals as the previous strategy models: development of (1) a repertoire of diverse reading strategies, (2) metacognition related to the appropriate use of strategies, (3) real world knowledge, and (4) motivation to use strategies to enhance reading (Pressley, El-Dinary, et al., 1992). However, it also features teachers and students jointly constructing meaning of text as they read; the "transaction" that occurs is one in which individual readers approach the text with individual interpretations and understandings (Pressley, El-Dinary, et al., 1992). However, when working collaboratively to construct meaning, their individual backgrounds, experiences, and diverse interpretations create an interpretive community in which they affect, and are affected by, one another (Rosenblatt, 1978). The transactional aspect of TSI implies that there is no single "correct" interpretation of text, nor is there a single "correct" set of strategies applicable to attain a better or more "correct" interpretation of text. TSI lessons feature three primary components: (1) direct explanation and instruction on decoding, comprehension, and interpretive strategies; (2) coordinated and flexible use of diverse strategies; and (3) cycles of teacher–student transactions in which the group works collaboratively to make sense of the text. Much of this teacher–student discourse is focused on strategic processing (Pressley, El-Dinary, et al., 1992).

When compared with low-achieving second-grade students receiving solid but traditional reading instruction, similar students receiving Transactional Strategies Instruction demonstrated greater strategy awareness and use, better comprehension of text, and superior performance on standardized tests of reading (Brown, Pressley, Van Meter, & Schuder, 1996). Transactional Strategies Instruction provides solid instruction related to strategic processing and collaborative dialogue about strategy use that enhances students' reading ability.

Endogenous Models

Collaborative Problem Solving

Collaborative Problem Solving is entirely student-centered (Palincsar et al., 1991). Students identify strategies they feel will be most useful for understanding text and for monitoring their understanding, and they evaluate the effectiveness of the selected strategies. Students are introduced to strategies via problem-solving activities that have multiple solutions to them. Each problem-solving activity features vignettes in which two fictional students trying to accomplish a reading task (i.e., studying for a test or reading to inform others) approach the task in different ways. Students discuss the strategic processing of each fictional student, then combine the list of strategies they initially identified with the strategies they learned about via the vignettes. Students then use the self-generated list of strategies to guide their reading of authentic texts, discussing which strategies would be most helpful for a particular text, then test the strategies and evaluate how well they worked. Any teacher instruction is given in response to the students' discussion.

Although Collaborative Problem Solving effectively eliminates the criticism that much strategy instruction is reductionistic (see Poplin, 1988), it introduces other challenges and limitations. Palincsar et al. (1991) noted that this approach is not easy for teachers to implement because they experience difficulty resisting the desire to plan the direction of the lessons and assessment of each student is more cumbersome. Likewise, children who are unfamiliar with instructional settings that are undefined and emergent often have difficulty adapting to such contexts. In addition, students have difficulty regulating their discourse for there to be equity between the amount of talk related to making sense of the text and talk about the strategies they used to make sense of the text.

Process Talk

Process Talk is an approach predicated on the notion that strategic action gives students a sense of agency by providing them with choices and alternatives for successfully completing a given task (Ivey, Johnston, & Cronin, 1999). *Agency* refers to the empowerment experienced as a product of making a choice in response to the particulars of a situation and in relation to the alternative courses of action available. People are *agents* because they are capable of making reflective decisions involving many alternatives (Rovane, 1998).

Johnston and his colleagues examined teacher and student talk about their literate processes and strategies, and about children's sense of agency in 28 classrooms across five states. They found that students in classrooms of effective teachers were more self-assured in their learning and had a greater sense of agency. The teaching in these effective classrooms was not focused primarily on teaching strategies but on "arranging for strategic action to occur, and socializing children's attention to it wherever possible" (Ivey et al., 1999, p. 4).

The researchers categorized these classrooms as "agency-based" and described the less effective "strategy-based" classrooms as those in which strategy instruction had a central role and learning strategies was the objective of entire lessons. However, the discourse of these classrooms was more similar to the "skills" lessons of exogenous, direct instruction models than the dialectical strategy instruction models described above. The discourse labeled as "strategy-based" did not contain any talk related to metacognition, conditional knowledge, or motivated strategy use—three critical components of authentic strategy instruction. Discussing these three components is the type of talk that creates agency. The labels that Ivey and colleagues (1999) attached to their classrooms do not appear to be consistent with those used in the research literature on strategy instruction. Instead, they appear to be contrasting strategy- (or agency-) based classrooms with direct instruction- (or skills-) based classrooms. Regardless, the model of Process Talk on which their research is based is consistent with an endogenous constructivist model in which explicit instruction of strategies is secondary to student-centered discovery of strategic principles.

STRATEGY INSTRUCTION MODEL

As noted in previous chapters, many emergent and struggling readers share five limitations: They (1) do not possess an extensive knowledge base related to strategic processing, (2) are not metacognitively aware, (3) are not motivated to use strategies, (4) are unable to analyze the task, and (5) do not possess a repertoire of strategies. When readers do not possess knowledge of a given strategy, it is difficult for them to "discover" it on their own, as might occur in endogenous models of strategy instruction.

Think again about those areas in which you are *not* an expert. My knowledge base related to knitting, bowling, and dancing is so limited that I am unable even to ask questions about those areas. It would be very difficult for me to "discover" how to knit on my own without some scaffolded support. The Strategy Instruction Model proposed in this volume is based on dialectical constructivist principles in which some explicit instruction (cf. Pearson & Dole, 1987) and scaffolded support are provided for students (see Figure 3.1). The model also provides ample opportunity for student dialogue and verbalization about strategy use as meaning is constructed, as occurs in Transactional Strategies Instruction (Pressley, El-Dinary, et al., 1992), and it recommends that teachers reduce processing demands at times during instruction so that students can focus on strategic processing. These three components affect, and are affected by, one another. In Figure 3.1 circles with semipermeable borders represent each component; the broken line represents the "seepage" that is possible: What is contained in each component "seeps" out to help create and become the safe and risk-free environment that supports and facilitates motivated strategy use. Thus this safe and risk-free environment is a recursive one that creates, and is created by, the other components.

The Strategy Instruction Model is also based on sociocultural perspectives in which learning is viewed as a "cognitive apprenticeship" that occurs "through guided participation in social activity with companions who support and stretch children's understanding of and skill in using the tools of culture" (Rogoff, 1990, p. i). In this instructional context the "tools of culture" refer to use of strategies that assist entry into the culture of literacy. As Rogoff argued, different values are placed on different types of "literacy" within a given society. That is, "school literacy" or "written literacy" is highly valued in Western societies and requires different tools and strategies to be successful than, say, "oral literacy," which places a higher demand on memory.

Gee (1992) contended that there are multiple literacies, and each individual possesses many different literacies. For example, as a white female elementary school teacher

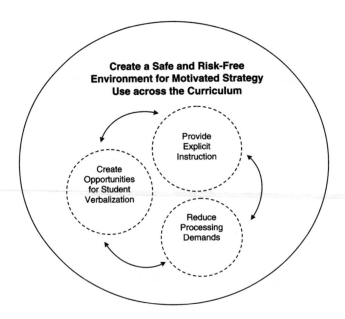

FIGURE 3.1. Strategy Instruction Model.

who speaks English as my native language, I am literate in traversing most Anglo-European cultures, female cultures, elementary school cultures, as well as the more traditional literacy associated with proficiency in reading and writing English texts. Gee suggested that individuals possess different Discourses, or identity kits, that enable them to negotiate the boundaries of various literacies. Gee distinguishes between "discourse" in the common sense of dialogue or conversation and "Discourse" (with a capital *D*) that refers not only to dialogue but to the requisite knowledge that permits us to "fit in" or be "literate" in a given culture (i.e., how to speak, how to act, how to think, how to dress).

As an example, I am writing this text in the tiny, rural, outport community of Victoria Cove, Newfoundland, and I am reminded daily of my "illiteracy." Although my mother is from a similar Newfoundland outport community, and over the years had taught me a great deal about the culture prior to my current visit, I still have to be enculturated and apprenticed into the culture. My mother could not possibly have prepared me for each of the day-to-day situations in which I find myself, for I do not possess the Discourse of a Newfoundlander. I am illiterate in the Newfoundlanders' culture, and they know it. I look different, I speak differently, and I act differently. I am an oddity—an outsider.

I was the only one unable to catch even a single smelt while ice fishing. I could not distinguish between a sculpin, a caplin, and a codfish. I had no idea what the Janeway, the ACW, or VOCM was. I did not put milk or sugar in my tea, and people often wondered how I could drink such "switchel." Young Newfoundland children taught me about the habits of the moose and seals that frequent the community. They took great delight in answering my questions and were curious as to how I could have survived all of these years without such knowledge. When asked if I "found the days long" or if "everything's narder," I found myself unable to respond. Although the language is English, the dialect and idiomatic expressions of Newfoundlanders are entirely different, as are their customs. "Dinner" is at noon and "supper" is in the evening. There is no lunch, other than a late-night snack, referred to as "lunch" or a "mug up."

My Aunt Sue, Uncle George, and Aunt Maisie, who still reside here, as well as my mother, who does not, served as my initial mentors. They served as tour guides, translators, historians, and cultural brokers while educating me, their grateful apprentice, about the nuances of life in an outport community. Joy, who is the Postmaster and who owns the variety store and the nursery, graciously endured my daily barrage of questions and willingly shared her expertise in any topic I asked about—from the nature of the moose lottery to the consequences of northeasterly versus southwesterly winds. My neighbor Lynn willingly shared her expertise about Newfoundland flora and fauna and the art of gardening in a wind-swept land with an astonishingly brief growing season and more rock than soil. Each of these individuals has served as a mentor who scaffolded my interactions with the community, and taught me how to navigate within it. When I leave the community I will be able to understand the language and the culture better as a result of their mentoring, but I will still not be fully literate, nor will I possess the Discourse of a Newfoundlander—a process that takes many years.

So it is with reading. As children learn the Discourse of written literacy, they learn how to speak the language of literacy, how to act literate, and how to use the tools of literacy. It is a process that takes many years to learn. It is also a process that requires a mentor who provides scaffolded assistance in the form of explicit instruction, opportunities to verbalize the strategies one is using, and reduced processing at some points to help create a safe environment for motivated strategy use. Each of these four components of the Strategy Instruction Model is described throughout the remainder of the chapter.

Create a Safe and Risk-Free Environment for Motivated Strategy Use

As noted in Chapter 1, motivation is critical to strategy use (Paris, Lipson, & Wixson, 1983; Pressley, Woloshyn, & Associates, 1995); students must be motivated to employ strategies. Personal attributions that support strategy use are critical to such motivation. That is, students must view themselves as active and in control of their own processing, and they must see that their efforts pay off. However, traditional classroom cultures often do not promote or support such attributions. This lack of support in this crucial area is not usually deliberate but more of an unintentional outgrowth of Western education. We assess and test a great deal—perhaps too much. Children in such environments begin to view every interaction with their teacher as a form of assessment. As discussed in Chapter 2, nearly every interaction with students provides an opportunity for assessment; however, how we package these opportunities makes the difference between a safe and an unsafe environment.

Creating a safe environment requires overhauling the conventions that govern many classroom cultures. An environment must be created in which it is okay to be wrong, okay not to know how to perform tasks, okay not to understand, and okay to take time while reading. Students in typical classrooms see the purposes of assignments differently from their teachers (Duffy, Roehler, & Rackliffe, 1986; Winne & Marx, 1982). Many students see the majority of activities and lessons in school as assessment-oriented. These students then become assessment-focused or performance-oriented, as Prawat (1989) described them, rather than learning-focused. They are concerned with end products and "getting done" (Anderson, Brubaker, Alleman-Brooks, & Duffy, 1985). They vie to be the first one to complete an assignment, or they neglect to read texts thoroughly for fear they may not complete a task. The ultimate goal of reading is often sacrificed at the expense of task completion. Students in such environments know that after reading a text, their teacher will want to determine how well they have understood what they read. Very often, unfortunately, teachers assess such understanding by asking a lot of questions. Prawat (1989) noted that assessment-focused students do not view errors as something useful from which to learn but as something to be avoided. Assessment-focused students who understand what they have read try to "perform" for the teacher, while those students who may not understand as well try to hide from the teacher. These students are often quite strategic in their efforts to "hide." They may only raise their hand to answer known-answer questions (often those that require their personal opinion). They often hope to be called on for these questions to get their "turn" over with and avoid being called on for tougher questions. These students attempt to hide their misunderstanding from the teacher. They feel that if the teacher finds out they do not understand the text, they will receive a poor grade. When these students do not understand the text or are confused, the goal becomes trying to "trick" the teacher into thinking they do understand, rather than trying to learn how to repair their comprehension. In these traditional, teacher-centered classrooms the focus is on end products, task completion, and assessment rather than strategic processing and understanding.

Imagine a different classroom in which students enjoy gathering with their peers to discuss their interpretations, confusions, misunderstandings, and misgivings about texts (cf. Almasi, 1995, 1996; Almasi, O'Flahavan, & Arya, 2001; Fall, Webb, & Chudowsky, 2000). These discussions include lots of opportunity to chat about confusions, why they occurred, and how to resolve them. Peers share various strategies they used to overcome the confusion or assist others who continue to struggle. Students can often be heard saying things like "I didn't understand that part of the story" or "I don't know why the author did that. It was very confusing to write it that way." In these classrooms students are not afraid to openly say they do not understand something, and they are eager to chat with their peers to resolve their difficulties. The teacher in this classroom is not making notes about who understood and who did not. Instead she is noting what strategic processes each student is using to make sense of the text. These notes permit her to chart each student's growth and development over time, and they also provide a blueprint for future instruction. The teacher also recognizes, in accord with reader response views of literacy (e.g., Bleich, 1978; Rosenblatt, 1978), that there may be multiple and conflicting interpretations. The teacher may occasionally scaffold such transactions but does not lead them by asking questions or determining the discussion agenda. There is no ready-made kit that can create a "safe" environment. The manner in which the teacher interacts with students and the types of learning opportunities that she arranges are key to creating such an environment.

The thinking that underlies strategic processing is often very abstract and internal. It is essential to make these thought processes as visible as possible and to assist students in learning how to become metacognitively aware of when and where strategies are used. Metacognitive awareness is the key to strategic action, but younger and less proficient readers have difficulty with this concept (Baker & Brown, 1984; Garner, 1987).

One way to make this concept more accessible for students is to introduce them to the notion of "clunks" (Almasi, 1991). Anderson (1980) explained that while reading, individuals engage in the "clicks of comprehension and the clunks of comprehension failure" (p. 497). Teachers can explain to students that reading clicks along like a train running smoothly on a track until you hit a *clunk*. There are two types of clunks: word clunks and meaning clunks. Word clunks occur when the student cannot read the word, at which point he needs to use special strategies to overcome the problem (i.e., word recognition strategies, see Table 1.1). He might also encounter a meaning clunk in which he does not understand a word, a sentence, or a larger piece of the text. To overcome a meaning clunk, he needs to use different strategies (i.e., comprehension and fix-up strategies, see Table 1.1). In our summer reading program at the University at Buffalo, we introduce children to the clunk concept by using a cartoon depiction (see Figure 3.2). The "clunk" character represents those instances in which students are unable to proceed with the reading process either because they cannot identify a word or because they do not understand some aspect of the text. The cartoon character depicts that moment of becoming metacognitively aware that something is impeding the reading process (see Almasi, 1991 for further discussion).

One of our teachers, Patty DiLaura George, created a "click" character to accompany the "clunk" character (see Figure 3.3). "Click" is a cartoon depiction of those times when the reading process is "clicking" smoothly. Many of our teachers duplicate each of these cartoon characters for their students. During read alouds, shared readings, and guided reading lessons, they encourage students to hold up a click card when the text makes sense and to hold up a clunk card when something does not make sense. Teachers then engage students in dialogues related to those aspects of the text that made sense,

FIGURE 3.2. Clunk: Something that impedes the reading process. From Almasi (1991). Copyright 1991 by the State of Maryland International Reading Association Council. Adapted by permission.

those aspects that did not make sense, and why the text was confusing or not. Discussion and verbalization about clicks and clunks is essential to student growth and development as strategic readers. "Stop" and "go" signs can be used in a similar manner. The concrete manipulatives enable teachers to assess students' metacognitive awareness and their ability to monitor the reading process. The resultant discourse also enables teachers to assess the types of comprehension and word identification difficulties students are experiencing. Such discussion facilitiates assessment of the strategies students possess for repairing reading difficulties and the conditional knowledge associated with using these strategies.

The following example depicts the type of teacher–student discourse that might initially occur as students learn about clunks. The excerpt is taken from a second-grade discussion of Stephen Mooser's (1978) *The Ghost with the Halloween Hiccups.* All students were identified as struggling readers. The teacher provided scaffolded instruction on making predictions and identifying story grammar elements (e.g., setting, character, problem, solution) to prepare students for reading the book. Students read the first half of the book and then engaged in a peer discussion of that portion (see Almasi, in press, 1996, for explanations of peer discussion). At the close of each day's discussion, the group made a chart of the questions and confusions they had about the book. On this particular day they were concerned about the author's style of writing. The author was trying to de-

FIGURE 3.3. Click: The unimpeded reading process.

scribe one character in the book who hiccupped while he talked. So the text appeared like this: "Happy HICCUP Halloween!" One of the students, Roger (a pseudonym), had noted the previous day that this confused him, and the teacher recorded his question on a discussion chart to remind students of the topics they wanted to discuss the following day.

1 CRAIG: Hey, it says, "Please bring me some hiccup water."

2 TEACHER: That's what Roger was confused by too. We can talk about that. Go ahead. What do you think about that?

3 CRAIG: It says he was drinking water, and he had hiccups.

4 CHARISE: Ooooh! Now I know! Now I know! Um, he was trying to say, "give me some water," but he said "hiccup."

5 TEACHER: What do you think of that?
   (overlapping talk)

6 CRAIG: M-maybe he got hiccups before he drank the water, like, "Please bring me some (imitates hiccup sound) water."

7 KEITH: Yeah! That's it.

8 ROGER: So, he was drinking water.

9 TEACHER: So you agree with what Craig is saying? Why did he [the author] write "hiccup" like that? What does that mean? Who thinks they might be able to start rereading this page?

10 CRAIG: "Happy (imitates a hiccup) Halloween!"

13 CHARISE: He has the hiccups, and every time he tries to say something, he hiccups and then he says it.

15 KEITH: Good, because she said that she thinks it sounded like a hiccup.

16 TEACHER: So is that what happens when you hiccup?

17 KEITH: Mmmmm hmmmm.
   (a little later)

34 TEACHER: Okay, so what happened here was great! Last Friday Roger had a clunk with that. Craig, you said that you had trouble understanding that part too. Did anybody else have trouble understanding that "HICCUP" in the middle [of the sentence]?
   (heads nod affirmatively)

35 TEACHER: Now, you did too, Keith? (Keith nods affirmatively) That's called a "clunk," but it's not a "word clunk" because you could read every word there. It's called a "meaning clunk." It means that you don't understand. Sometimes you can have a clunk where you don't understand the word because you can't read it. Sometimes you can have a clunk where you don't understand it because it doesn't make sense. It does make sense now.

36 KATHY: Yes, we figured it out.

37 TEACHER: Okay, what we did was (points to chart listing various strategies), we met a clunk [see Figure 3.5]. When you read it, you might have slowed down and re-

read it to see if you could understand it, but what we did today was, we *asked each other.* We helped each other out to help us understand that clunk. We got rid of it. So we don't really need to discuss this (*points to that question on the discussion chart*), do we?

38   ALL: Nope.

39   TEACHER: We understand that now.

40   CHARISE: What we don't understand is why did Mr. Penny gets the hiccups? (Discussion continues on this topic.)

The environment in this classroom is one in which the students are eager to share their misunderstandings and eager to help one another resolve them. Their focus is on constructing meaning and they generated their own topics for discussion. These were topics that were confusing or interesting to them; hence, their motivation was high. They were able to recognize those aspects of the text that were confusing to them, and they worked collaboratively to resolve the confusion. Students are better able to recognize and resolve comprehension difficulties when engaged in peer discussions than in more traditional teacher-led discussions, in which the teacher sets the agenda for what is discussed (Almasi, 1995).

In this vignette, the teacher functioned as a momentary scaffold for students (O'Flavahan, Stein, Wiencek, & Marks, 1992). She did not enter the discussion to initiate topics of discussion, to determine who may speak to whom, or to assess students' understanding. Instead she popped into the discussion to ask open-ended questions that fostered more student dialogue (lines 2, 5, and 9). At the end of the discussion she provided an explanation of the cognitive and strategic processes in which the students had engaged (lines 34, 35, and 37). She noted that students were able to monitor their comprehension (i.e., identifying clunks) and were able to employ a strategy to repair their comprehension failures (i.e., asking others). Her discourse in line 35 included an explanation of the declarative knowledge associated with monitoring comprehension. That is, she wanted students to know *that* when they read, they might come to places where they do not understand the meaning of the text. This explanation was not lengthy or stilted; it was an outgrowth of the processing in which students were already engaged as they were making sense of the text they had read. She attached labels to the cognitive processing in which students were engaged. In line 37 she explained the conditional knowledge associated with monitoring comprehension. That is, she noted that *when* students realize something does not make sense, they can fix up or repair the misunderstanding by trying three different strategies: slowing down and reading ahead carefully, rereading, or asking someone. The charts she used in line 35 are reproduced in Figures 3.4 and 3.5.

The teacher also served as an academic cheerleader of sorts, particularly in line 34. Her enthusiasm was a key factor in making the environment safe for students. She celebrated their ability to identify their own clunks. In a more traditional environment the teacher might have chastised students for not understanding the text. Instead, she encouraged students to share their misunderstanding. Thus she functioned as a more knowledgeable other who provided cognitive scaffolding that enabled these novice readers to gain insights into the Discourse of written literacy. Teacher support is critical to the creation of a safe and risk-free environment. Another critical aspect is the teacher's ability to design instruction that is appropriate for students. The three remaining aspects of the

FIGURE 3.4. How to avoid clunks while reading. From Almasi (1991). Copyright 1991 by the State of Maryland International Reading Association Council. Adapted by permission.

Strategy Instruction Model work together to support and create this safe, risk-free environment.

Provide Explicit Instruction

Durkin's (1978/1979) now classic investigation revealed a paucity of actual comprehension instruction in elementary classrooms. As Pearson and Dole (1987) noted, Durkin's research found that a great amount of time was spent "mentioning" (i.e., mentioning the skill students were supposed to practice), "practicing" (i.e., practicing the skill), and "assessing" (i.e., giving directions to complete assignments and workbook pages), but little time was actually spent teaching students *how* to understand and comprehend text. With this in mind, much of the research of the 1980s was dedicated to examining the effect of

FIGURE 3.5. What to do if you meet a clunk. From Almasi (1991). Copyright 1991 by the State of Maryland International Reading Association Council. Adapted by permission.

providing comprehension instruction for students (for reviews, see Dole, Duffy, Roehler, & Pearson, 1991; Pearson & Fielding, 1991; Pearson & Dole, 1987; Pearson & Gallagher, 1983). That body of research revealed that explicit instruction (as defined and described above) enhances students' learning and their strategic and metacognitive awareness, particularly struggling readers (e.g., Dole, Brown, & Trathen, 1996; Duffy et al., 1987). Although research has shown that, with training, teachers can learn to be more explicit in their comprehension instruction (Duffy, Roehler, Meloth, et al., 1986); not much has changed since Durkin's research—little comprehension instruction still occurs in elementary classrooms (Fielding & Pearson, 1994; Pearson, & Dole, 1987; Pearson & Fielding, 1991; Pearson & Gallagher, 1983; Pressley, 2000).

Explicit instruction is an important component of effective strategy instruction. By itself it is not sufficient for developing strategic, self-regulated readers, but it is a necessary component of strategy instruction, particularly for struggling readers. The model of explicit instruction presented below is based primarily on the work of Pearson and his colleagues (e.g., Dole et al., 1991; Fielding & Pearson, 1994; Pearson & Dole, 1987; Pearson & Gallagher, 1983; Pearson & Fielding, 1991). As noted earlier, explicit instruction of strategies differs from direct instruction in several ways: (1) There is no assumption that strategies should be broken down into subskills; (2) strategies must be modeled and practiced during authentic reading tasks; and (3) there is no particular strategy or set of strategies that is "correct" in any given reading situation. Instead strategies should be applied flexibly, depending on the reader, the text, and the context (Dole et al., 1991; Pearson & Dole, 1987).

Explanation

Providing a brief explanation of the declarative, procedural, and conditional knowledge associated with using a given strategy or set of strategies is essential (Paris et al., 1983). Such explanations must go beyond "mentioning" and focus on *what* strategy is being used, *what* knowledge is associated with the strategy, *why* it is being used in a given situation, *why* it is helpful in that situation, *when* the strategy can be used, and *how* to perform the strategy. Explanation is at the heart of Duffy et al.'s (1987) notion of direct explanation, during which teachers describe the mental processes that good readers use while reading text. In essence, they make the covert thought processes that normally occur during fluent reading overt and obvious. Direct explanations often occur as teachers model the cognitive processes in which good readers engage. Teachers may also engage in think alouds, in which they report the thoughts going through their mind as they read text. In this way students are able to "see" the cognitive processing involved in reading. This visible demonstration is helpful for all readers but particularly for struggling readers who are often unaware of the cognitive processes involved in strategic reading and who are often unaware of how and when to use strategies (for reviews, see Baker & Brown, 1984; Garner, 1987).

In the earlier excerpt from the second-grade discussion of *The Ghost with the Halloween Hiccups* (Mooser, 1978), the teacher provided a brief explanation of the declarative and conditional knowledge associated with the strategy of monitoring comprehension (line 35). She did not need to discuss the procedural knowledge related to *how* to monitor comprehension, because the students had already shown her they were able to monitor their comprehension in that situation.

These explanations were not lengthy, nor were they the focus of an entire lesson. Indeed, such explanations can be brief interludes that occur during read alouds, shared reading, or as a part of guided reading. As well, teachers need not be the exclusive individuals to offer explanations. As students become more comfortable sharing the cognitive processes they engage in as they read, they should be encouraged to share with others *what* strategy they used, *why* they used it, *when* they used it, and *how* they used it (see section later in this chapter on creating opportunities for student verbalization).

Explanations should also be woven into the fabric of the entire curriculum, not just during "reading class." For example, during a science lab, the teacher might model the type of thinking that occurs as one reads directions to complete the lab. She might say something like, "The instructions say . . ., but when I read it I am confused. I have a clunk. I think I'm going back to reread that part to make sure that I understand. If I don't understand the instructions, I might ruin the experiment." During this brief think aloud, the teacher communicated the declarative knowledge *that* when reading instructions to perform a science experiment, students must monitor their comprehension to make sure the text makes sense. She also communicated the declarative knowledge *that* it is possible to have a clunk when reading science text. In addition, her think aloud conveyed conditional knowledge associated with *when* students need to monitor their comprehension and *why* it is important. When integrated throughout the entire curriculum, such brief explanations facilitate transfer of the strategy to new and diverse reading contexts. Without such integration, students often think that reading strategies are to be used only in "reading class" and fail to employ them in other contexts (Garner, 1990).

Modeling

Explanation often occurs during modeling, which involves either demonstrating a strategic process or performing a think aloud of the thoughts that occur while reading and using strategies. For example, during a read aloud of *Owl Moon* by Jane Yolen, one teacher, Eileen Ludwig, explained and modeled the cognitive processes she used to the student with whom she was working:

1 [reading from text] "Then we came to a clearing in the dark woods. The moon was high
2 above us. It seemed to fit exactly over the center of the clearing, and the snow below was
3 whiter than the milk in a bowl of cereal." I can really picture that in my mind. I see a
4 large area that is covered by a lot of newly fallen snow. I also see some light coming off
5 the snow from the reflection of the moon. I picture in my mind a very open area in the
6 middle of the forest at nighttime. I picture that it is very cold outside. When the author
7 said, "the snow below was whiter than the milk in a bowl of cereal," I thought that the
8 snow might have just fallen or that no other people or animals were around. Because
9 we live in an area where it snows, I know that snow does not stay white unless it is very new
10 or nothing else is around to make it dirty. I used the author's words, what I already
11 know, and my senses to help me make those pictures in my head. When I make pictures
12 in my head while I read, it really helps me understand.

[Eileen Ludwig, March 28, 2000]

In this example, Eileen used authentic text to model the cognitive processing that occurred while she was reading. The text was highly image-laden and evoked strong sensory images. In line 3 Eileen began her think aloud by describing the strategy she used. In lines 6–11 she explained the procedural knowledge, or *how* she actually performed the strategy, and in line 12 she explained the conditional knowledge related to *why* the strategy was helpful and important for her. Through her think aloud, Eileen was able to show her student *when* she used a given strategy, *how* she used it, and *why* she used it when she did. It is important to note that the procedural knowledge used to perform a given strategy may vary from individual to individual. For example, not all readers may use the author's words, their background knowledge, and their senses to form images, as Eileen did. She described the process *she* used to create images. Teachers and students must be encouraged to share the variety of procedures they use to enact particular strategies, so that others can see that strategy use is a flexible process rather than a rigid or fixed one. Eileen's think aloud illustrates one of many possible ways to perform a given strategy.

Eileen did not communicate declarative knowledge during the think aloud. Instead she chose to explain such information prior to reading the book: "Sometimes portions of the text help you form a picture in your mind. Some stories are better than others for making those pictures. That is because some authors use more descriptive words that help readers draw on their background knowledge to understand the text." Here she explained the declarative knowledge *that* imagery is not a helpful strategy with all texts. She also included the conditional knowledge that imagery is a helpful strategy *when* authors use descriptive language. Eileen was enculturating her student into the Discourse of literacy by sharing the types of thinking and the language that accompanies strategic processing of text. Such information provides additional information about the nature of the strategy that younger and less proficient readers may not be aware of on their own. Again, the purpose of modeling and explanation is to make visible to students the very complex and obscure nature of using strategies while reading. As Eileen noted in her remarks in Chapter 2, and as Pearson and Dole (1987) have noted, it is sometimes difficult for teachers to become accustomed to modeling strategies and incorporating think alouds into their daily instruction. It feels awkward at first to share one's thinking in public. However, in time and with practice, incorporating think alouds and modeling into all aspects of the curriculum becomes second nature.

Guided Practice

Guided practice involves multiple opportunities for teachers and students to practice using strategic processing under a wide variety of instructional circumstances. Learning to become a strategic reader is a long process that cannot be accomplished in a few lessons. Such development takes years (Pressley, 2000). Although the ultimate goal of strategy instruction is to develop independent, self-regulated readers, this is a long-term goal that is attainable only through the coordinated efforts of an entire school. It is impossible for one teacher, by herself, to attain this goal in one school year.

Guided practice also enables teachers to provide students with substantive feedback *not* by evaluating the "correctness" of strategy use but by providing opportunities for students to assess and evaluate their own strategy use. In this manner students share those strategies that work and those that do not; they discuss why particular strategies work in a given situation and why others do not.

Pearson and Gallagher (1983) suggested a model of explicit instruction in which, during guided practice, teachers gradually "release responsibility" for the task to the students (p. 337). In this model any task can be viewed as requiring different proportions of teacher and student responsibility. Put another way, any task may require differing amounts of instructional scaffolding for a given student. In Figure 3.6, the diagonal line moves from instructional contexts requiring total teacher support (upper left) to those requiring no teacher scaffolding or support (i.e., independence). The ultimate goal is for students to be able to perform particular tasks (in this case, reading) on their own.

It takes a patient and willing teacher to guide students as they learn how to process text strategically. Guided practice is part of this apprenticeship. During guided practice a more knowledgeable other within the culture (i.e., either an adult or a peer) is available to provide explanation, modeling, or scaffolded assistance so that, with the other's help, students can perform tasks that they may not be able to do independently (Vygotsky, 1978). However, such practice must be situated within authentic tasks (Brown, Collins, & Duguid, 1989; Fielding & Pearson, 1994). That is, guided practice must occur during

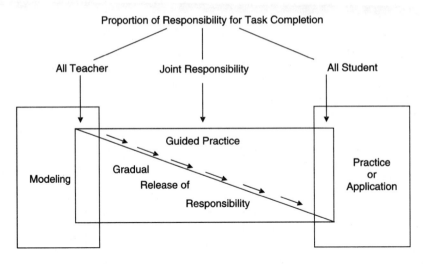

FIGURE 3.6. Pearson and Gallagher's (1983) model of explicit instruction. From Pearson and Gallagher (1983). Copyright 1983 by Academic Press, Inc. Reprinted by permission.

authentic reading of whole texts, so that authentic strategies can be modeled and used in the situations and contexts in which they will actually be used.

Reduce Processing Demands

The individuality of each student in a classroom often makes it difficult for teachers to meet each student's needs. Using many of the process-oriented assessments described in Chapter 2 helps determine students' needs, but scaffolding every student in the classroom on an individual basis is still difficult. Some students require more scaffolded support than others to achieve a similar reading goal. Therefore, it is important to consider various ways to scaffold students. Two important factors to consider when planning instruction are the amount of social support given to students from others (i.e., peers and teachers) and the nature of the instructional task and texts that are used. In Table 3.2 the amount of support from others is depicted on the vertical axis and the amount of scaffolded support from texts is depicted on the horizontal axis. The amount of scaffolded support provided by each factor occurs along a continuum ranging from "more" to "less" support. The letters A, B, and C are used to describe where example lessons later in this chapter fit.

The amount of scaffolded support provided from others should be a well thought-out decision on the teacher's part. When lessons feature the teacher and the whole class engaged in any learning event, the amount of support provided to the individual from others is high if the student is actively engaged. That is, the teacher can provide explanations, think alouds, and modeling during lessons, and the other students can provide insights regarding various ways to accomplish a given task. Of course, in this situation the teacher cannot easily monitor each individual student's thoughts. In these circumstances it is helpful to plan to use Every Pupil Response (EPR) techniques, in which all students communicate their understanding or their responses to the teacher. For example, each

TABLE 3.2. Scaffolded Instructional Support for Strategic Processing

		Amount of Scaffolded Support from Text						
		More Support Concrete (semiotic) ⟵——————⟶ Less Support Abstract (linguistic)						
		Events/ Experiences (enactive)	Movies/ Videos	Wordless Picture Books	Read Alouds	Shared Reading	Picture Books	Texts (symbolic)
Amount of Support from Others — More→Less	Teacher/ Whole Class	A		B				
	Small Group							
	Trios							
	Pairs							
	Individual							C

student might be given a replica of "click" and "clunk" signs with which to signal. As the teacher performs a read aloud or uses any type of text during the instruction, students hold up "click" to indicate they understand the content and "clunk" to indicate that something did not make sense. In this manner, all students are actively involved in the lesson, and the teacher can monitor them to determine whether they are able to use a particular strategy. The teacher can also use student responses to prompt discussion and dialogue about strategy use. This teacher–whole class scenario provides the individual student with a secure environment. Students who may be struggling are not forced to perform a given strategy or set of strategies while reading on their own. Instead they receive support from others.

Small groups provide less support in that the teacher is not directly present throughout the entire lesson, but the presence of five or six peers can provide a great deal of support for students who may not yet be able to use strategies on their own. Trios and pairs provide less support in that the burden for actually performing the task rests on fewer shoulders, increasing the cognitive burden for individual students, as they have to assume more of the responsibility for task completion. As shown in Table 3.2, the individual student receives the least amount of support from others because she is completely on her own while completing a given task. This circumstance can be an anxious time for struggling readers trying to process text strategically. Although the teacher can provide one-on-one assistance in this scenario, it is obviously difficult to provide such assistance to all students in a classroom when they are working independently.

The amount of support provided from the text is one that is not often discussed during instructional planning. For this discussion it is necessary to turn to a theory that has a lengthy past—that of concrete representation. Intuitively, we have heard and attempted to mind the maxim "to proceed from concrete to abstract," particularly in elementary instruction. However, we have not really heeded this advice in strategy instruction, and as Dewey cautioned as far back as 1910, this notion is often misunderstood.

Dewey (1910/1991) defined "concrete" as meaning that which is readily apprehended by itself. What actually is concrete, however, is relative and differs from individual to individual. To fluent readers, the notions of *prediction, summarization*, and *comprehension monitoring* are fairly concrete because they use these strategies constantly, without conscious thought or overt manipulation. However, to novice readers, understanding these terms and enacting them pose significant problems. These readers might need to relate these new, abstract concepts to things that are already known or familiar to them.

In general, what is familiar is mentally concrete. Beginning with the concrete means that we should emphasize *doing* at the outset, especially in areas that are not routine or automatic. Given that strategy use, by definition, is deliberate and planful, much of strategy instruction should initially be concrete. Concrete representations in the form of actual experiences, analogies, and metaphors crystallize concepts and procedures (Prawat, 1989). The goal is to explicitly connect, or make comparisons between, previous concepts in students' knowledge base and the new strategy or process. Verbalization and a reflective attitude help foster these connections (Prawat, 1989). Instructional activities should be arranged so that interest in them and their outcome creates a desire to attend to that which is more *indirect and remote*—the abstract.

"The abstract" refers to that which is theoretical and not closely associated with practical concerns. The entire act of reading is an abstract process—from the marks on the pages to the meaning that is constructed. We use lines and shapes to represent letters, which represent sounds, which when strung together, represent words—which represent ideas to which meaning is attached. The entire process is abstract and intangible. In Table 3.2 "text" is situated at the far right or abstract end of the continuum. Text in this sense, is linguistic text, or text that uses written language to communicate. Hartman and Hartman (1993) suggested that texts can be categorized as ranging from linguistic to semiotic. Linguistic texts include any written material—books, essays, newspapers, plays, and poems; semiotic texts include nonwritten material—movies, videos, music, photography, paintings, even facial expressions and gestures. Semiotic texts, just like linguistic texts, can be "read" and interpreted. However, the "reading" is easier because it involves images and sounds that are concrete representations rather than symbolic abstractions. It is easier for struggling readers to understand the movie version of a book than to read the text because the act of reading, per se, is removed while watching a movie. That is, without the demands of decoding the words, readers (or viewers) can focus their attention on thinking about, and using, strategies for comprehending the text—the storyline.

This is *not* a recommendation to read all texts aloud to struggling readers. It *is* a recommendation to reduce the processing demands while students are initially learning about strategies by using semiotic as well as linguistic texts. Strategy use, by itself, is a very abstract and complex process. When coupled with the very abstract process of reading linguistic texts, the task becomes an enormous cognitive burden to novice readers. Thus instruction can be scaffolded so that students learn about strategies and how to use them with "texts" that may not initially require as much cognitive energy.

Bruner's (1966) theory of cognitive development helps explain how concrete representations of material influence learning. He posited that children develop three modes of representing information: enactive, iconic, and symbolic. *Enactive* forms use actions, events, or experiences to represent information. Such knowledge does not require the use of words or imagery. The teachers in the example that follows used the enactive mode to provide their students with a concrete experience that represented the targeted strategy (comprehension monitoring). *Iconic* forms use visualization to represent information and are governed by principals of perceptual organization. In Table 3.2, semiotic texts such as movies, videos, and wordless picture books fall within the *iconic* mode. *Symbolic* forms use language or symbols to represent information, as occurs in instruction using linguistic texts.

The horizontal axis in Table 3.2 arrays the range of texts that offer more and less scaffolded support. An event or experience (i.e., an enactive form) would provide the most concrete type of "text" for students to learn about strategy use. For example, during the University at Buffalo Summer Reading Program, one pair of teachers, Liz Graffeo and Summer Sciandra, wanted to help their group of fifth-grade boys become more metacognitively aware while they read. They had noticed that each of the students was passive and cognitively aloof while reading. They had hoped to teach the students what it felt like to experience a clunk while reading. They designed an "event" to foster an actual metacognitive experience in the students. The lesson they developed would be located at "point A" in the table, because it was a lesson in which the teachers and the entire group provided scaffolded support for one another during a concrete event.

The boys had shown interest in reading texts about spiders. To heighten their interest, Liz and Summer created a very large, stuffed "spider" and attached it to the ceiling for several weeks. The day of the "event" the spider was removed from the ceiling and hidden. As the boys entered the classroom, they immediately noticed the missing spider and became alarmed. They began asking questions and tried to determine what had happened. The teachers encouraged the students to jot down their questions and develop a strategic plan for locating the missing spider. The strategic plan they developed engaged them in a search for clues around the classroom and the school. Clues were derived from physical evidence as well as interviews with the principal and the custodial staff. The boys were completely engrossed in this event and read and wrote more than they ever had done previously.

This elaborate event represented a concrete experience in which the boys became metacognitively aware, suddenly, that the spider was missing. They came into the classroom and immediately noticed that "something was wrong." This feeling was likened to the same feeling one has when one experiences a "clunk" while reading. The teachers engaged the boys in a concrete experience that would help them understand the same feeling when they were reading. They drew from the initial concrete experience to help the boys understand how to monitor their comprehension while reading linguistic text. The remainder of the initial experience required the boys to develop and enact a strategic plan to locate the missing spider. This experience is similar to what proficient readers do when they notice comprehension failures. They strategically plan ways to fix up or resolve the problem. Again the teachers drew on this initial concrete experience to make connections to the use of reading strategies to repair comprehension difficulties. In this example the goal of reduced processing is strikingly evident: to *temporarily* eliminate the processing demands of reading linguistic texts so that students can learn about and *use* strategies.

Focusing all of their cognitive effort on strategic processing during a concrete event establishing new cognitive pathways that are then available to students during reading "events."

The lesson described above, located at Point A of Table 3.2 offers students the most amount of scaffolded support from others (i.e., teacher and whole class) and in terms of using concrete (i.e., semiotic) texts. "Point C," reading linguistic texts independently, offers students the least amount of support. There is no opportunity for others to provide support, and the text to be read is abstract. Independent, self-regulated strategy use would need to occur at this point.

The scaffolded instruction depicted in Table 3.2 is not intended to move in a linear fashion from concrete to abstract. Instead, as Bruner (1966) suggested, instruction should be recursive, moving back and forth between the enactive (i.e., concrete actions, events, experiences), iconic (i.e., semiotic texts, movies, videos, wordless picture books), and symbolic (i.e., abstract or linguistic texts) modes, until the child is able to use strategic processes under all conditions (see Figure 3.7). Teaching strategic processing in this model would progress from the level of active manipulation and direct experience with the strategy to symbolic representation of the strategy while reading independently from linguistic texts. When instruction begins with formal, symbolic representations that do not permit the learner to develop enactive or iconic representations, superficial, rote learning occurs rather than deep understanding of the processes involved (Bruner, 1966). Similar to Vygotsky's (1978) notions, Bruner (1966) suggested that language is the tool that leads to internalization of these concepts. Hence, we turn our attention to the final component of the Strategy Instruction Model—verbalization.

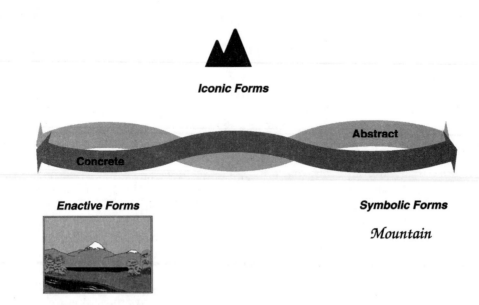

FIGURE 3.7. A recursive model of strategy instruction that reduces processing demands.

Create Opportunities for Students to Verbalize about Strategy Use

Vygotsky (1978) suggested that, as a symbolic activity, speech has an *organizing* function that penetrates the process of tool use and produces new forms of behavior. Engaging in think aloud types of discourse while performing a task plays a specific role in carrying out that task. During this process the child engages in the type of planful discourse that characterizes strategic processing. Verbalization enhances awareness by bringing subconscious thought processes to consciousness (Prawat, 1989), so that one's thoughts and processes become an object for reflection and evaluation. Such egocentric speech is the basis for inner speech, which, in its external and public form, is embedded in communicative speech. Movement from interaction with the social environment (i.e., dialogue with teachers and peers) and real objects (i.e., enactive forms and semiotic texts) to non-interactive forms of written language (i.e., reading symbolic forms of language or linguistic texts) facilitates internalization of cognitive processes. Thus language mediates experiences and helps transform them into higher-order mental operations that eventually become internalized (Vygotsky, 1978).

In its earliest stages, speech *accompanies* a child's actions and reflects the nature of the task in a disrupted and chaotic form. In later stages, speech becomes more of a planning device that *precedes* action—as in strategic processing. Once children learn to use this planning function of speech, their psychological realm is radically altered: A view of the future has become essential to the way they approach their environment and learning tasks. For teachers planning strategy instruction, this developmental step means that we must model such discourse and encourage our students to engage in it in order for them to eventually internalize such higher-order thinking.

A great deal of research and practice has emphasized the importance of verbalizing the covert thought processes that occur while reading (e.g., Bereiter & Bird, 1985; Davey, 1983; Dole et al., 1996; Duffy et al., 1987; Paris et al., 1983; Pearson & Fielding, 1991; Pressley, El-Dinary, et al., 1992). Kucan and Beck (1997) noted that think alouds focused on the strategic processes used while reading can come in the form of teacher modeling during instruction and guided practice, or as students think aloud and verbalize their own cognitive processing. Research has clearly indicated that when students are taught to verbalize and think aloud, their comprehension and achievement are significantly greater than students who do not receive these opportunities.

When such discourse is generated in social contexts (e.g., whole class discussions, small group peer discussions), students have the opportunity to hear multiple and varied ways in which teachers and peers use strategies to process text. These collaborative discussions provide students with the opportunity to assume authority and responsibility for their own thinking (Greene & Ackerman, 1995) and to observe the higher-level thought processes of their peers before trying to accomplish similar tasks on their own (Almasi, 1995; Goatley, Brock, & Raphael, 1995). Learning in these social environments can occur incidentally, as learners observe the cognitive processes of the group, or more directly, when teachers or peers scaffold the interaction so that learners become capable of engaging in more strategic processing than they would have independently (Rogoff, 1990; Vygotsky, 1978). Additionally, "when students participate in discourse environments and engage in dialogue or communication, their learning is not confined to knowledge constructed as a product in such a context, but also includes a developing understanding of and ability to use the processes by which such knowledge is constructed" (Kucan & Beck, 1997, p. 290).

We will examine a transcript of a lesson to see how teachers scaffold learning and provide opportunities for students to verbalize their cognitive processes. Patty DiLaura George, a clinician in the University at Buffalo Summer Reading Program, conducted the lesson with a group of six struggling first-grade readers. The children had all completed first grade the previous year; however, most would repeat first grade in the fall. Patty was teaching the children how to monitor their comprehension by using "stop" and "go" signs as concrete representations of the clunks of comprehension failure and the clicks of successful comprehension. In this whole group lesson she used the wordless picture book *Good Dog Carl* by Alexandra Day (1996). The lesson represents a fairly high degree of instructional scaffolding and would fall at "Point B" in Table 3.2.

Patty introduced the children to the concept of monitoring their comprehension in an earlier lesson when she explained the stop and go tags. Since *Good Dog Carl* is a wordless picture book, she encouraged the children to make up the storyline in their heads as they studied the pictures. She also encouraged them to think about whether the pictures made sense. The children were told to turn their tags to the stop side if the story did not make sense, or to the "go" side it did make sense. In the book the mother leaves Carl (the dog) to look after the baby. In this excerpt Patty turned to the page in which Carl and the baby are playing with Mother's jewelry. (Note that all children's names are pseudonyms, and the teacher is designated as PG).

52   CALEB: They're playing with the jewelry.

53   PG: Oh, my goodness.

54   CHERI: (*giggling*) Look at the dog.

55   PG: Oh, I see lots of stops, and I see some go's. That's okay, it just depends how it makes sense to you or maybe it doesn't. Stephen, why doesn't that make sense to you?

56   STEPHEN: Because, um, how could both of 'em get dressed up?

57   PG: How could they get dressed up in those things? Hmmm, that's a good question.

58   CALEB: The baby could climb on the dog's head, get up there and done that thing.

59   PG: Well, Caleb, that might be a good idea. Maybe that's how it happened. And I see lots of go's, too, so that tells me that you do understand what's happening in the story. I like how you're thinking about that and paying attention [to the pictures]. (*Turns page to reveal picture of baby at the edge of a laundry chute*) Uh-oh.

60   CALEB: Oh, no, the laundry slot!

61   PG: How did you know that was the laundry slot, Caleb?

62   CALEB: Because it says *laundry* on the top, and there was a laundry bag down there.

63   PG: Good for you.

64   STEPHEN: Uh oh he's gonna fall.

65   PG: You're a good thinker. I see Caleb has the go sign facing me because he understands what's going on now. That baby is getting ready to go down that chute.

(*Looks at Patrick*) Oops. How come your tag is not on? Can you put your tag on for me, and, Stephen, are you showing me stop or go?

66 CURTIS: I don't think it makes sense.

67 PG: Why doesn't it make sense?

68 CURTIS: Because how can a dog open a laundry thing?

Several aspects of the Strategy Instruction Model are operating in this excerpt. First, using the stop and go tags and the wordless picture book reduced the processing demands for the children, which made the environment a "safer" one in which to try using the new strategy. In line 55 the teacher facilitated the safe and risk-free environment further when she noted that she saw tags turned to both stop and go. She made it clear in this example (and throughout the lesson) that it was okay if the children turned their tags to either side, "it just depends how it makes sense to you." Throughout the lesson the children did not seem encumbered by this process, displaying their understanding, or lack of it, without hesitation. Patty continually used phrases to foster a safe environment, such as when she noted, "I like how you're thinking about that and paying attention [to the pictures]" (line 59), "Good for you" (line 63), and "You're a good thinker" (line 65). In this manner she created a safe environment by selecting safe texts and safe ways to display the strategies used, and she acted as an "academic cheerleader" by encouraging the children to take risks and by supporting their efforts.

Patty also provided frequent opportunities for students to verbalize their thoughts. Usually she accomplished this by asking an open-ended question such as, "Why doesn't this make sense to you?" or "Why does this make sense to you?" In line 55 Patty encouraged Stephen to explain why that page did not make sense to him. As in this example, the children were always anxious to share their thoughts, and the others often added explanations to help the individual understand that part of the text, such as Caleb did (line 58). Patty also encouraged Caleb to verbalize how he knew the picture was a laundry chute (line 61). In this manner she fostered a sociocultural environment in which students shared the strategies they used to construct meaning from text. Caleb's explanation may have provided another child, who did not know how to use that strategy, with a new tool for constructing meaning.

Finally, we see the students beginning to use the language of literacy (in line 66). Throughout the lesson Patty used the phrases "that does make sense" and "that doesn't make sense." In this manner she modeled the type of discourse that literate individuals use. She also modeled literate actions later in the lesson when she turned to a page that showed the baby getting into the aquarium: "Uh-oh! Looks like trouble! Think about that card. Does that make sense to you in the story? I see what's going on. I can understand when I look at it. So if I had my tag up, I would show the go side because I can see that a lot of trouble is going on there, and I can understand how that can happen. So I have the go sign showing." In effect, as Gee (1992) noted, she was mentoring the students in the Discourse of written literacy. She was teaching them how to talk and how to act during literacy events. Here (line 66) we also see that Curtis appropriated this language quickly and easily.

Patty also found opportunities to incorporate direct explanation into this lesson. When appropriate, she slipped in information about the declarative, procedural, and conditional knowledge associated with monitoring comprehension while reading:

122 PG: Get ready to turn that card. Take a look at the pictures, think about whether it makes sense or not, and then turn your card (*turns page to reveal picture of dog eating food taken from refrigerator*).

123 CALEB: How can a dog eat baby food?

124 PG: So, you're asking me that question, so what side should you have [your tag showing], Caleb?

125 CALEB: Stop.

126 PG: Right, because you don't understand how that dog could be eating that baby food or the food that the people eat, right?

127 CALEB: Oh! I got it! It's on go for me now (*turns tag from stop to go*).

128 PG: Oh, wow! (*Patty smiles broadly*)

129 CALEB: Because I got the idea figured out!

130 CHERI: Me, too!

131 PG: Good for you, Caleb. Caleb, when you looked at the pictures a little more closely, did it help you understand?

132 CALEB: Yeah, it's just that when the dog . . .

133 CURTIS: (*Interrupts*)

134 PG: Curtis, one minute. Let's listen to what Caleb is saying. Can you say that again, Caleb?

135 CALEB: Um, the dog must have been on the top and put a hole in the can, and then he started to turn his head, and it started to come out in the cup.

136 PG: You know what, Caleb? Sometimes that happens when you're reading. You don't understand something (*turns tag to stop*), and then you figure it out and you do understand it (*turns tag to go*). That's okay. Good.

Patty reiterated the procedural knowledge associated with *how* to monitor comprehension (line 122). She noted that students should read the text (in this case, look at the pictures) and think about whether it made sense. Because the lesson was fairly concrete and conducted as a whole group, she also added in the step of physically manipulating the tags. When Caleb displayed his ability not just to monitor his comprehension but also to repair it (line 127), Patty celebrated with him and then quickly explained what had occurred. Her explanation (line 136) explained the declarative knowledge associated with comprehension monitoring. She noted *that* sometimes we might not understand something while reading, but it can clear up. This declarative knowledge is something of which struggling readers are often unaware. At other points in the lesson she also communicated conditional knowledge. Whenever a learning situation presented itself, Patty took advantage of the opportunity.

These examples depict the recursive relationship of the Strategy Instruction Model. Patty began by creating a fertile environment for motivated strategy use by her text selection and the concrete nature of her lesson. As the lesson unfolded, we saw explicit instruction, reduced processing, and verbalization working in unison to nurture the safe environment. In this way the safe environment creates, and is created by, the other three components, as depicted in Figure 3.1.

SUMMARY

The Strategy Instruction Model is based on dialectical constructivist notions, in which explicit instruction and scaffolding are provided. These notions are also rooted in sociocultural theories of learning, in which learning the Discourse of written literacy is viewed as a "cognitive apprenticeship" that occurs in a social milieu. The key aspect of the Strategy Instruction Model is the creation of a safe and risk-free environment. Such an environment creates, and is created by, the recursive actions of explicit instruction, reducing processing demands, and providing opportunities for students to verbalize cognitive processes. These elements work together to create an environment for motivated strategy use.

REFERENCES

Almasi, J. F. (1991). Helping students deal effectively with comprehension failure. *Literacy: Issues and Practices, 8*, 59–66.

Almasi, J. F. (1995). The nature of fourth graders' sociocognitive conflicts in peer-led and teacher-led discussions of literature. *Reading Research Quarterly, 30*(3), 314–351.

Almasi, J. F. (1996). A new view of discussion. In L. B. Gambrell & J. F. Almasi (Eds.), *Lively discussions! Fostering engaged reading* (pp. 2–24). Newark, DE: International Reading Association.

Almasi, J. F. (in press). Peer discussion. To appear in B. Guzzetti (Ed.), *Literacy in America: An encyclopedia.* New York: ABC.

Almasi, J. F., O'Flahavan, J. F., & Arya, P. (2001). A comparative analysis of student and teacher development in more and less proficient discussions of literature. *Reading Research Quarterly, 36*(2), 96–120.

Anderson, L. M., Brubaker, N. L., Alleman-Brooks, J., & Duffy, G. (1985). A qualitative study of seatwork in first-grade classrooms. *The Elementary School Journal, 86*(2), 123–140.

Anderson, T. H. (1980). Study strategies and adjunct aids. In R. J. Spiro, B. C. Bruce, & W. F. Brewer (Eds.), *Theoretical issues in reading comprehension* (pp. 483–502). Hillsdale, NJ: Erlbaum.

Baker, L., & Brown, A. L. (1984). Metacognitive skills and reading. In P. D. Pearson, R. Barr, M. L. Kamil, and P. B. Mosenthal (Eds.), *Handbook of reading research* (vol. 1, pp. 353–394). New York: Longman.

Bereiter, C., & Bird, M. (1985). Use of thinking aloud in identification and teaching of reading comprehension strategies. *Cognition and Instruction, 2*(2), 131–156.

Bleich, D. (1978). *Subjective criticism.* Baltimore, MD: Johns Hopkins University Press.

Brown, J. S., Collins, A., & Duguid, P. (1989). Situated cognition and the culture of learning. *Educational Researcher, 18*(1), 32–42.

Brown, R., Pressley, M., Van Meter, P., & Schuder, T. (1996). A quasi-experimental validation of transactional strategies instruction with low-achieving second-grade readers. *Journal of Educational Psychology, 88*(1), 18–37.

Bruner, J. S. (1966). *Toward a theory of instruction.* Cambridge, MA: Belknap Press.

Davey, B. (1983). Think aloud: Modeling the cognitive processes of reading comprehension. *Journal of Reading, 27*(1), 44–47.

Day, A. (1996). *Good dog Carl.* NY: Little Simon.

Dewey, J. (1991). *How we think.* Buffalo, NY: Prometheus Books. (Originally published in 1910)

Dole, J. A., Brown, K. J., & Trathen, W. (1996). The effects of strategy instruction on the comprehension performance of at-risk students. *Reading Research Quarterly, 31*(1), 62–88.

Dole, J. A., Duffy, G. G., Roehler, L. R., & Pearson, P. D. (1991). Moving from the old to the new: Research on reading comprehension instruction. *Review of Educational Research, 61*(2), 239–264.

Duffy, G. G., Roehler, L. R., Meloth, M. S., Vavrus, L. G., Book, C., Putnam, J., & Wesselman, R. (1986). The relationship between explicit verbal explanations during reading instruction and student awareness and achievement: A study of reading teacher effects. *Reading Research Quarterly, 21*(3), 237–252.

Duffy, G. G., Roehler, L. R., & Rackliffe, G. (1986). How teachers' instructional talk influences students' understanding of lesson content. *The Elementary School Journal, 87*(1), 3–16.

Duffy, G. G., Roehler, L. R., Sivan, E., Rackliffe, G., Book, C., Meloth, M. S., Vavrus, L. G., Wesselman, R., Putnam, J., & Bassiri, D. (1987). Effects of explaining the reasoning associated with using reading strategies. *Reading Research Quarterly, 22*(3), 347–368.

Durkin, D. (1978/79). What classroom observations reveal about reading comprehension instruction. *Reading Research Quarterly, 14,* 481–538.

Fall, R., Webb, N. M., & Chudowsky, N. (2000). Group discussion and large-scale language arts assessment: Effects on students' comprehension. *American Educational Research Journal, 37*(4), 911–941.

Fielding, L. G., & Pearson, P. D. (1994). Reading comprehension: What works. *Educational Leadership, 51,* 62–68.

Garner, R. (1987). *Metacognition and reading comprehension.* Norwood, NJ: Ablex.

Garner, R. (1990). When children and adults do not use learning strategies: Toward a theory of settings. *Review of Educational Research, 60*(4), 517–529.

Gee, J. (1992). Socio-cultural approaches to literacy (literacies). In W. A. Grabe (Ed.), *Annual review of applied linguistics* (vol. 12, pp. 31–48). New York: Cambridge University Press.

Gersten, R., & Carnine, D. (1986). Direct instruction in reading comprehension. *Educational Leadership, 43*(7), 70–78.

Goatley, V. J., Brock, C. H., & Raphael, T. E. (1995). Diverse learners participating in regular education "book clubs." *Reading Research Quarterly, 30*(3), 352–365.

Greene, S., & Ackerman, J. M. (1995). Expanding the constructivist metaphor: A rhetorical perspective on literacy research and practice. *Review of Educational Research, 65,* 383–420.

Hartman, D. K., & Allison, J. (1996). Promoting inquiry-oriented discussions using multiple texts. In L. B. Gambrell & J. F. Almasi (Eds.), *Lively discussions! Fostering engaged reading* (pp. 106–133). Newark, DE: International Reading Association.

Hartman, D. K., & Hartman, J. A. (1993). Reading across texts: Expanding the role of the reader. *The Reading Teacher, 47*(3), 202–211.

Ivey, G., Johnston, P., & Cronin, J. (1999, April). *Process talk and children's sense of literate competence and agency.* Paper presented at the annual meeting of the American Educational Research Association, Montreal, Quebec, Canada.

Kucan, L., & Beck, I. L. (1997). Thinking aloud and reading comprehension research: Inquiry, instruction, and social interaction. *Review of Educational Research, 67*(3), 271–299.

Mooser, S. (1978). *The ghost with the Halloween hiccups.* New York: Morrow.

Moshman, D. (1982). Exogenous, endogenous, and dialectical constructivism. *Developmental Review, 2*(4), 371–384.

O'Flahavan, J. F., Stein, C., Wiencek, J., & Marks, T. (1992). *Intellectual development in peer discussions of literature: An exploration of the teacher's role* (final report). Urbana, IL: National Council of Teachers of English.

Palincsar, A. S., & Brown, A. L. (1984). Reciprocal teaching of comprehension-fostering and comprehension-monitoring activities. *Cognition and Instruction, 1*(2), 117–175.

Palincsar, A. S., & Brown, A. L. (1989). Instruction for self-regulated reading. In L. B. Resnick & L. E. Klopfer (Eds.), *Toward the thinking curriculum: Current cognitive research* (pp. 19–39). Alexandria, VA: Association for Supervision and Curriculum Development.

Palincsar, A. S., David, Y. M., Winn, J. A., & Stevens, D. (1991). Examining the context of strategy instruction. *Remedial and Special Education, 12*(3), 43–53.

Paris, S. G., Lipson, M. Y., & Wixson, K. K. (1983). Becoming a strategic reader. *Contemporary Educational Psychology, 8,* 293–316.

Pearson, P. D., & Dole, J. A. (1987). Explicit comprehension instruction: A review of research and a new conceptualization of instruction. *The Elementary School Journal, 88*(2), 151–165.

Pearson, P. D., & Fielding, L. (1991). Comprehension instruction. In R. Barr, M. L. Kamil, P. B. Mosenthal, & P. D. Pearson (Eds.), *Handbook of reading research* (vol. 2, pp. 815–860). New York: Longman.

Pearson, P. D., & Gallagher, M. C. (1983). The instruction of reading comprehension. *Contemporary Educational Psychology, 8,* 317–344.

Poplin, M. S. (1988). The reductionistic fallacy in learning disabilities: Replicating the past by reducing the present. *Journal of Learning Disabilities, 21,* 401–416.

Prawat, R. S. (1989). Promoting access to knowledge, strategy, and disposition in students: A research synthesis. *Review of Educational Research, 59*(1), 1–41.

Pressley, M. (2000). What should comprehension instruction be the instruction of? In M. L. Kamil, P. B. Mosenthal, P. D. Pearson, & R. Barr (Eds.), *Handbook of reading research* (vol. 3, pp. 545–561). Mahweh, NJ: Erlbaum.

Pressley, M., El-Dinary, P. B., Gaskins, I., Schuder, T., Bergman, J. L., Almasi, J., & Brown, R. (1992). Beyond direct explanation: Transactional instruction of reading comprehension strategies. *The Elementary School Journal, 92*(5), 513–555.

Pressley, M., Harris, K. R., & Marks, M. B. (1992). But good strategy instructors are constructivists! *Educational Psychology Review, 4*(1), 3–31.

Pressley, M., Woloshyn, V., & Associates. (1995). *Cognitive strategy instruction that really improves children's academic performance* (2nd ed.). Cambridge, MA: Brookline Books.

Rogoff, B. (1990). *Apprenticeship in thinking: Cognitive development in social context.* New York: Oxford University Press.

Rosenblatt, L. M. (1978). *The reader, the text, the poem: The transactional theory of the literary work.* Carbondale, IL: Southern Illinois University Press.

Rovane, C. A. (1998). *The bounds of agency: An essay in revisionary metaphysics.* Princeton, NJ: Princeton University Press.

Vygotsky, L. S. (1978). *Mind in society.* Cambridge, MA: Harvard University Press.

Winne, P. H., & Marx, R. W. (1982). Students' and teachers' views of thinking processes for classroom learning. *The Elementary School Journal, 82*(5), 493–518.

CHAPTER FOUR

Why Do Students Struggle with Comprehension?

This chapter provides a research-based overview of comprehension, from the perspectives of reading researchers and literary theorists, and explanations of why some students struggle to comprehend. These explanations are organized according to three types of comprehension difficulty: schema availability, schema selection, and schema maintenance. Each type of difficulty is explained using authentic classroom examples, and suggestions are included for how to alleviate each difficulty.

DEFINING COMPREHENSION

Comprehension is generally perceived as the ability to understand and construct meaning from what one reads. During the 1970s and early 1980s, reading researchers and theorists debated whether reading comprehension was a "bottom-up"—relying on incoming visual data in the form of letters, words, and sentences—or a "top-down" process—relying on the reader's background knowledge and ability to sample text to make hypotheses about meaning (see Samuels & Kamil, 1984, for a discussion). Today, however, there is general agreement that the ability to comprehend and understand what is read is an interactive process in which readers make use of both sources of information simultaneously (Rumelhart & Ortony, 1977). That is, readers use the clues from the text (i.e., letters, words, sentences) and their background knowledge to make sense of text. This process is a constructive one that requires readers to be actively engaged in their learning (Garner, 1987).

Stanovich (1980) proposed that comprehension is also a compensatory process, in which readers compensate for their deficiencies by fluidly applying both bottom-up and top-down processing. That is, if a person were reading a particularly difficult text that challenged his ability to decode, but he had a great deal of background knowledge about the topic, he could compensate for his decoding deficiencies by relying on top-down processes to successfully comprehend the text. Alternatively, if the person were reading a fairly simple text she had sufficient ability to decode but little background knowledge about the topic, she could compensate for her knowledge deficiency by relying on bottom-up processes to successfully comprehend text. Thus comprehension is viewed as an interactive–compensatory process in which readers actively adjust their processing in response to the particular demands of the text and the context.

The research of the late 1970s and 1980s highlighted the importance of background knowledge to comprehension and outlined a "schema-theoretic" view of reading comprehension (see Anderson & Pearson, 1984, for a review). From this perspective comprehension is seen as an interactive–compensatory process that involves linking "new" information derived from text to the "old" information contained in background knowledge (Rumelhart & Ortony, 1977; Wade, 1990). Such background knowledge is known as "schemata." Schema theory posits that all knowledge is packaged into units or schemata (Rumelhart, 1980) that may be likened to a series of "mental file folders" (Tompkins & McGee, 1993). As we attempt to comprehend incoming information from text, we survey our mind for schemata that will enable us to make sense of this new information. When we locate an appropriate schema, it is activated and linkages are established between the new information contained in the text and the old information contained in the schemata. As a result of these linkages, schemata are continually updated and changed in a process known as "instantiation" (Rumelhart & Ortony, 1977).

Schemata represent knowledge that is already stored in memory (Rumelhart & Ortony, 1977). Such knowledge goes far beyond the level of simple definitions, for it represents knowledge about an entire concept. Think about the word *football*. As you open your "mental file folder," or schema, for football, the sights, sounds, smells, emotions, procedures, and settings associated with it are likely to come to mind (see Figure 4.1). You may "hear" the cheers of the crowd and the sound of the referees' whistles blowing, feel the chilly air of an autumn day, or smell the scent of hot dogs grilling. You draw upon the background experiences in which you learned about or experienced football as you call to mind the word. How you understand the word is dependent on these background experiences, for it is these experiences that create schemata. Thus your schema for "football" goes beyond a mere definition, as is typically held in one's lexicon; it includes all of the interrelations associated with the word (Rumelhart, 1980).

As shown in Figure 4.1, schemata have variables. In this example the associated variables include sights, sounds, setting, odors, emotions, and procedures. These variables can also be embedded within one another (Rumelhart & Ortony, 1977). Schemata may be likened to an interrelated network of ideas and concepts. Hence, as you call to mind some of the variables associated with football, they may remind you of other schemata. Figure 4.2 depicts this process. As you think about the word *football*, you may focus on the setting associated with the game, bringing to mind the chilly autumn air that often accompanies football games. As you recall this setting, the thought of chilly autumn air might also remind you of other autumn-related experiences, such as the sight of multicolored leaves, the sound of rustling leaves, the sound of raking leaves, or the smell of wood burning in a fireplace. Each thought calls to mind another schema. In effect, we could let our minds wander infinitely far along this interrelated network of embedded schemata.

Of course, the information depicted in Figures 4.1 and 4.2 is limited. There are a number of variables not included. Variables and the degree to which one's schemata are instantiated depend on one's background experiences. I grew up in the northeastern part

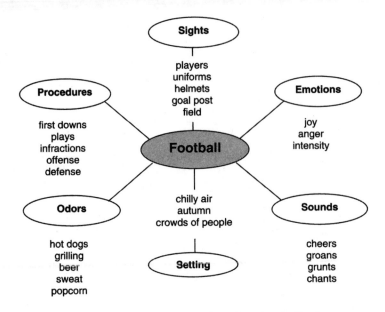

FIGURE 4.1. Variables associated with a football schema.

of the United States, in Pittsburgh, Pennsylvania, during a time when the Pittsburgh Steelers football team won four Super Bowls in a span of 6 years. My schema for *football* and *autumn* might therefore be quite different from someone who does not live in the northeastern part of the United States, or someone who does not enjoy football. Individuals living in the southern or western parts of the United States, where it is much warmer in the autumn, will likely have vastly different experiences related to football and autumn. Individuals living somewhere other than the United States, where soccer is called "football," will also have vastly different schemata for *football*. No two individuals can experience something in the same manner. Therefore, schemata and their associated variables are highly unique and individualized. These highly individualized networks of sche-

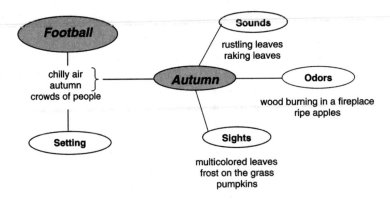

FIGURE 4.2. Variables associated with a given schema can be embedded within one another.

mata determine how new information is interpreted (Anderson, Reynolds, Schallert, & Goetz, 1977).

Literary theorists have approached comprehension from a different perspective. Rather than focusing on those social and cognitive aspects that affect comprehension, they have examined the relationship between the reader, the text, and the context. Some literary theorists (e.g., the New Critics—I. A. Richards, 1929, is one), believe that comprehension and meaning can or should be acquired from the text alone. That is, they believe text has a single, correct meaning "within" it that is independent of the reader. From this perspective a reader's job is to attempt to find the "correct" meaning in the text. When comprehension difficulties occur, they are attributed to a deficit in an individual's reading skills. From this perspective all readers would need to have identical schemata in order to "accurately" understand a given text. This perspective stands in contrast to that of the schema theorists presented above.

In contrast, other literary theorists (i.e., reader-response theorists) have maintained that meaning is not contained in the *text* but is the result of a transaction between the reader, the text, and context (cf. Beach & Hynds, 1991; Bleich, 1978; Marshall, 2000; Rosenblatt, 1978). Figure 4.3 depicts the manner in which reader factors, textual factors,

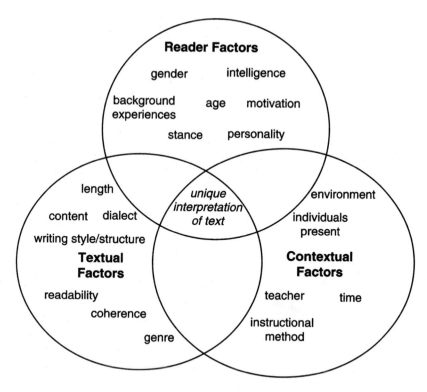

FIGURE 4.3. The impact of reader factors, textual factors, and contextual factors on a reader's understanding.

and contextual factors work as readers construct meaning from text. Reader factors include those aspects of an individual that make him or her unique (e.g., gender, intelligence, personality, age). Each reader factor has an impact on how an individual responds to, and interprets, text (Beach & Hynds, 1991; Marshall, 2000). For example, gender alone can influence the manner in which one understands text. As well, the impact of an individual's background knowledge and experiences on comprehension has been articulated in the reading research (see Anderson & Pearson, 1984, for a review).

A reader's stance, or her orientation toward the text, also plays an important part in comprehension. Rosenblatt (1978) described two primary stances: aesthetic and efferent. When a reader adopts a primarily *aesthetic* stance, he is focused on the reading experience; that is, he is primarily interested in the enjoyment of the reading experience. When a primarily *efferent* stance is adopted, the reader is focused more on what information can be gleaned or taken away from the text. Rosenblatt (1991) explained that readers never assume a completely aesthetic or efferent stance. As Figure 4.4 illustrates, even a reader with a predominately aesthetic stance (point A) adopts an efferent stance at some point during the reading. Likewise a reader at point E, although reading primarily to take information away from the text, adopts an aesthetic stance at some point. However, a reader with a primarily aesthetic stance would not read and understand a text in the same manner as he would if he adopted a primarily efferent stance.

Textual factors also influence the manner in which a reader understands text (Beach & Hynds, 1991; Marshall, 2000). Factors such as the length of the text, its readability, the author's style of writing, the text's genre, and the content of the text affect the way a reader reads and understands it. Younger and less proficient readers often have difficulty reading longer texts, and all readers tend to have greater difficulty reading informational (i.e., expository) text than narrative text. The manner in which the author writes is also critical. A text lacking cohesion or organization will severely impact the manner in which a reader understands it.

Context also plays an important role in determining how an individual comprehends text (Beach & Hynds, 1991; Marshall, 2000). The instructional decisions a teacher makes in the classroom provide the context for young readers. Whether a text is read in

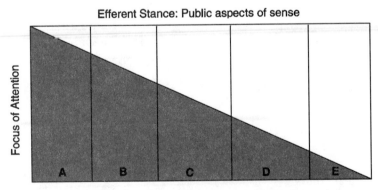

FIGURE 4.4. The focus of a reader's attention while reading. Adapted from Rosenblatt (1991). Copyright 1991 by the National Council of Teachers of English. Adapted by permission.

school or out of school, alone or with a partner, silently or aloud, or with preparation or without preparation—each factor has the potential to alter crucially the reading experience. For struggling readers who have low self-esteem, the emotional burden of having to read aloud in front of peers in school can be a traumatic experience. Even proficient readers' comprehension is often negatively impacted when reading in this context. Teaching students strategies such as tapping background knowledge, setting purposes for reading, or making predictions prior to, and during, the reading process enhances comprehension. Conversely, when such instruction is not provided, and students are merely told to "read chapter 2" without any preparation or instruction, comprehension is profoundly impacted, particularly for younger and less proficient readers.

From a reader-response perspective, meaning resides in the reading *event* and emerges as the reader, the text, and the context transact. In contrast with schema theorists, Rosenblatt (1978) used the term *transaction* rather than *interaction* to describe this organic process. The analogy of billiard balls striking one another, although not perfect, has been used to describe one aspect of the differences between a transaction and an interaction. In a game of pool, the balls strike and bounce off one another. Although the direction the billiard ball moves may be altered, the billiard ball itself remains unchanged as a result of this *interaction*. In contrast, during a *transaction*, one must envision the billiard balls being made of clay. Thus, when one ball strikes another, not only will the direction the ball moves be altered, but the ball itself is also altered permanently as a result of the experience. So, too, during reading transactions, the individuals who read the text, the text, and the context are altered by the experience. From a transactional perspective, meaning is contingent not only on the text but also on the reader, the reader's background experiences (i.e., schemata), and the context in which the text is read. Changes to any of these factors will alter the meaning that is constructed. Thus, in contrast to the New Critical perspective, the transactional perspective maintains that it is possible to have multiple and even conflicting but valid interpretations of a given text. It is at this point that the ideas of schema theory begin to complement those in reader-response theory. If one accepts the notion that each individual's background knowledge, or schema, influence the manner in which one reads and comprehends text, then one must also accept the reader-response notion that multiple and conflicting meanings can coexist validly.

If we integrate schema and literary theories, we can begin to understand the root of many comprehension difficulties. As the child reads, she selects an appropriate schema (or schemata) that will enable her to make sense of the information based on the clues provided in the text (assuming there is enough information in the text) (Wade, 1990). As new information presents itself, she evaluates how useful the selected schema is for processing the text. In this manner she continually hypothesizes and evaluates her hypotheses as she reads. At times, however, a given schema does not "fit" or does not enable her to make sense of the information in the text. At this point she must abandon the selected schema and search for a more appropriate one. This strategic process requires that she monitor her comprehension continually (Baker & Brown, 1984; Garner, 1987; Paris, Lipson, & Wixson, 1983; Wade, 1990). To restate: If a reader is able to select an appropriate schema and make a connection between it and the message of the text, within a given context, then comprehension occurs. However, if the reader does not have an appropriate schema available, is unable to select an appropriate schema, or is unable to monitor and maintain schema selection, then comprehension may be impaired. The remainder of the chapter explains and describes these three schema-related comprehension difficulties: schema availability, schema selection/retrieval, and schema maintenance.

COMPREHENSION DIFFICULTIES

Spiro (1980) identified several schema-related comprehension problems: schema avail-ability/acquisition, schema selection, and schema change/maintenance.

Schema Availability

Schema availability becomes a problem for readers who do not have the appropriate schema in their conceptual framework that would enable them to make sense of the text (Rumelhart & Ortony, 1977). Read the following text and think about how well you un-derstand it.

> "Listen, men," said Az, "you'd better start dipping the fish in right away, and make sure the cuts are wrapped tightly around the pins. Don't let the boat get too far away from the door-ways. Hey," he yelled from the top of the engine house, "tie up that span line and don't let her go out any further. Hold everything fast; I'll watch the swells." (Pilgrim, 2000, pp. 172–173)

A reader may have very little background knowledge or only partially instantiated schemata for the topic under consideration in this example. If one knows little about fish-ing—in particular, cod fishing off the coast of Newfoundland in the early 1900s—then this paragraph might prove difficult to understand. Comprehension may be partially im-paired, and the text may require a great deal of effort to understand as a result. Gee (1992) would explain the dilemma in terms of the reader not possessing the appropriate Discourse that would enable her to understand the text. Even though I was immersed in the culture while learning the Discourse of a Newfoundlander, as I read Earl Pilgrim's *Curse of the Red Cross Ring*, I found this paragraph to be particularly difficult to under-stand. In fact, my Uncle George spent nearly an hour drawing a diagram and explaining the requisite terminology related to cod traps, punts, and fishing to help me understand it.

In school these problems may become obvious from students' written and oral re-sponses to text. In the following example a fourth-grade student was reading *The Patch-work Quilt* by Valerie Flournoy (1985). After reading the book, he wrote the following in his response journal:

> "I dont [don't] like this story Because I don't have cny [any] quilts at home and I dont [don't] now [know] what they look like so I would now [know] what one looks like so I would understand it better."

Although the child is clearly having difficulty with written expression, he is meta-cognitively aware that his comprehension was hindered because he did not have the ap-propriate schema available to understand the story. After reading this student's journal entry, the teacher is now aware that she must teach this child strategies to repair compre-hension when he realizes that he does not have sufficient background knowledge to un-derstand the text. Additionally, the teacher might consider providing a bit more of an in-troduction prior to reading the text that would provide more background knowledge about quilts and quilting.

In another example of schema availability difficulties, a group of fourth graders had just read the story *Soup's New Shoes* by Robert Newton Peck. In the story a young boy (Soup) purchases a new pair of shoes for three dollars, then took advantage of a warm March day to try them out on his walk to school. The setting of this realistic fiction story (i.e., March, in Vermont, in the 1930s) was particularly troublesome for these students living in the 1990s in a part of the United States that does not typically see snow or cold temperatures in March. After reading the story, the group engaged in a peer discussion of the text that revealed their struggle to understand the setting. Although the students clearly have a schema available for "March," the notion of "snow in March" was not a part of their schema (all names are pseudonyms):

1 BRIAN: I think they wore a lot of clothes for March because it said (*reading from text*), "Soup unbuttoned his coat and took off his hat, the one with the red earlappers, then slowly unbuckled his left shoe." He's got lots of stuff on. It's in March.

2 HENNA: It was snowing out.

3 DEREK: It's usually just cold in March.

4 BRIAN: I know, it's not *that* cold in March, is it? But they said on page . . .

5 HENNA: I don't think it's cold in March.

6 BRIAN: (*Reading from text*) "A warm March day took away most of the snow."

(from Almasi, 1995)

The students also had difficulty understanding the manner in which shoes were fitted and sold in the 1930s, when X-ray machines were used to determine the appropriate size shoe to purchase:

1 TRACY: I wonder why, um, um, Soup said that in the shoe store the guy had an X-ray machine?

2 BRIAN: I don't know why, because why would the shoe man buy, a shoe salesman buy, that kind of equipment just to sell shoes?

3 DEREK: They usually have just the shoe, the foot measuring thing. You take off your shoe and stick your foot on there.

4 HENNA: Not a machine, they don't have them back . . .

5 AARON: An X-ray machine—he's probably like a doctor and a shoe salesman in one.

6 ALL: Yeah.

7 TRACY: That's what I thought.

8 DEREK: Did they have X-ray machines back then?

9 BRIAN: They said it was 1930.

10 TRACY: What he said, he said it was for to see if the foot fit in the shoe.

11 HENNA: Like how big your bones were and how much you had to grow.

12 AARON: Pretty clever.

13 DEREK: But your skin is over your bones. You can't see your skin in an X-ray.

14   BRIAN: If you want to see your skin in an X-ray machine, what's an X-ray machine for?

15   HENNA: That's true. You can see your skin outside the X-ray machine.

16   JARED: That's why they call it an X-ray machine.

17   DEREK: 'Cause just to see if the foot could fit in the shoe, then why'd they do that for? 'Cause your skin's gonna be over the bone when it goes into the shoe.

18   AARON: You could probably see right through the shoe.

19   BRIAN: Well, actually, the X-ray machine is just so you can see how big your foot really is.

20   HENNA: And how much you'll grow.

21   BRIAN: . . . and the skin will just cover it up, the foot, not really a big part of it.

22   AARON: He's probably like a doctor and like . . . I don't know what you call it but it's a doctor, but they check your feet just in case you, like, broke it or something.

23   TRACY: If he only wants it for feet, why don't he make a little small one for feet?

24   ALL: Probably is.

25   BRIAN: 'Cause how could a shoe salesman afford that big thing?

26   AARON: But why would they want an X-ray machine unless so somebody would help see what happens?

27   DEREK: He don't buy it, the store has it.

28   BRIAN: They don't sell 'em in stores do they?

29   DEREK: No! No! The store can get one. He don't have to buy it—the store guy.

30   JIGUAO: I want to know why the shoe salesman just buy a X-ray machine just for the feet?

31   BRIAN: Well, that's a question we've been on for a pretty long time. Probably just to be fancy.

(from Almasi, 1995)

In both of these events we see the impact of schema availability on students' comprehension. In the second excerpt (lines 1 and 2), Tracy and Brian struggle to understand why a shoe store would have an X-ray machine. Derek drew on his available schema for buying shoes (line 3) to explain the type of equipment that he has seen in a shoe store. Aaron attempted to make a link between his schema for buying shoes and X-ray machines (line 5). His schema for X-ray machines suggested that only doctors used such equipment. In making this connection, he thought about what kind of doctor might be associated with feet. Although he does not use the term *podiatrist,* he is aware of some type of doctor that specializes in foot care and suggested that perhaps the shoe salesman is also a podiatrist. This is a fascinating attempt at integrating information across text to make sense of it. It shows Aaron's ability to engage in critical thinking, and it also shows that he is focused on making sense of the text. Tracy directed the group back to the information in the text (line 10) by noting the purpose of using an X-ray machine to sell shoes. The ensuing discourse (lines 11–21) displays the group's collaborative effort to understand how an X-ray machine might be used to measure feet, in spite of the fact that their available schema for buying shoes did not include such information.

Many teachers who have watched this video excerpt and are familiar with the story have suggested that the students' focus on setting was trivial. The theme of the story centered on friendship, and the setting was not critical to this theme. These teachers believe that the students' discussion would have exhibited a higher cognitive level if they had examined the theme. However, for these students the theme of friendship was very obvious, and their schema for friendship was well instantiated. Because they understood the theme so well, they gave it very little attention in their discussion. Instead they spent time working collaboratively on those aspects of the text they found confusing. Hence, they focused much of their attention on examining the setting and engaged a repair strategy (i.e., asking one another) to help them understand the text better.

Strategy Instruction That Enhances Schema Availability

The strategies recommended here for helping students overcome schema-related comprehension problems should be taught using the Strategy Instruction Model described in Chapter 3, in which students were taught to use the strategies independently. To reiterate its central components: Provide (1) a safe environment for strategy use; (2) explicit instruction that includes explanation, modeling, and guided practice of the declarative, procedural, and conditional knowledge of strategy use; (3) instruction that reduces processing demands; and (4) opportunities for student verbalization about strategy use. Figure 3.4 provides an overview of relevant strategies for enhancing comprehension. Note the similarity between the strategies identified in Figure 3.4 and those listed in Table 4.1, which provides an overview of each schema-related comprehension problem, the causes of the problem, strategies to help students overcome such problems, and instructional activities to support strategy instruction. As indicated in Table 4.1 two strategies, "looking at pictures, titles, and headings" and "think about what is already known about the topic" are appropriate for students who have schema availability problems. Previewing the text by glancing at the pictures, titles, and headings and by activating relevant schema enables the reader to anticipate the content of the text.

Wade (1990) suggested that some students have difficulty activating background knowledge and using it to make predictions from relevant textual cues. These readers generally are bottom-up processors or "non-risk takers" (Wade, 1990, p. 446). That is, they view reading primarily as a task in which they decode the words on the page and are so focused on decoding that meaning is secondary. Such readers are often called "word callers." These readers, in particular, benefit from learning how to use previewing strategies such as looking at the titles, pictures, and headings and thinking about what they already know about the topic, to help them learn how to anticipate the types of words that might appear in a given text. For example, by activating prior knowledge about "buying shoes" (their schema) before reading "Soup's New Shoes," readers might call to mind several words that will appear later in the text. By activating such background knowledge prior to reading, the reader facilitates later word recognition. Readers who do not use previewing strategies approach each word in the text "cold." They read without any expectations or any form of active processing. They simply "call out" the words, as if they were unconnected to one another. Comprehension is usually negatively impacted during this type of reading.

TABLE 4.1. Overview of Schema-Related Comprehension Problems and Instruction to Facilitate Resolution

Schema-Related Comprehension Problem	Why Is It a Problem?	Comprehension Strategies[a]	Instructional Activities Supporting Strategy Instruction	Useful Graphic Organizers
Schema availability	• Appropriate schema to understand text is not in conceptual framework. • Reader may be a "bottom-up" processor focused more on decoding print than on constructing meaning.	Teach strategies that help students anticipate what text will be about: • Preview text by looking at titles, pictures, and headings. • Think about what is already known about the topic before reading.	• Provide hands-on experiences to familiarize readers with topic of text. • Provide rich semantic descriptions and discussions of concepts. • Use films, videos, and pictures to help students understand necessary concepts. • Engage students in Language Experience Approach • K-W-L	• Semantic webs and maps to organize ideas • The "K" portion of K-W-L charts
Schema selection/retrieval	• Reader's cognitive capacity may be limited due to processing demands. • Reader may have difficulty monitoring comprehension. • Text is incoherent or poorly organized.	Teach strategies that help students prepare for reading and organize thoughts while reading: • Set purposes while reading. • Generate predictions prior to and during reading and update based on textual information. • Identify text structure.	• Vocabulary–Language Prediction Activities • Directed Reading–Thinking Activities • Maintain journal/logs while reading. • Complete graphic organizers while reading.	• Prediction logs • Story maps • The "W" portion of K-W-L charts • Informational text graphic organizers (i.e., cause-effect, sequence chains, problem-solution, time lines, compare/contrast)
Schema maintenance	• Text is incoherent or poorly organized. • Reader's attention wanes while reading. • Reader's motivation wanes while reading • Reader may be a "top-down" processor who overrelies on prior knowledge.	Teach strategies that help students maintain and focus attention while reading: • Use visualization/imagery to vivify text. • Question oneself while reading to ensure that text makes sense (monitor for comprehension). • Identify text structure.	• "Sketch and share" pictures to represent mental images and engage in rich discussion of how text led to a particular mental image. • "Stop and go" or "click and clunk" activities to foster comprehension monitoring. • Promote rich discussion of episodes in which text did/did not make sense. • Complete graphic organizers while reading.	• Story maps • Informational text graphic organizers (i.e., cause-effect, sequence chains, problem-solution, time lines, compare/contrast)

[a]Strategies should be taught using the Strategy Instruction Model described in Chapter 3.

In the examples above, students could have activated their schema for "buying shoes" by glancing at the title, "Soup's New Shoes." However, the pictures in the story do not provide any clues indicating that the setting is that much different from the present day. In this situation there is little that the students, on their own, could do to prepare them for the setting-related difficulties they encountered. The teacher could have provided background information about buying shoes in the 1930s and about Vermont in the spring, which would have alleviated the schema availability problems. However, in this instance the teacher did not anticipate the possible confusion over the time period and the setting. It is impossible to anticipate every comprehension clunk that students may encounter and provide background knowledge to instantiate every schemata. Thus it is important to teach students to monitor their own comprehension and enact repair strategies when clunks of this nature are encountered. The type of peer discussion featured in the examples above, in which students bring their own questions to the discussion about which they truly are confused (rather than focusing on teacher-posed questions), fosters the ability to recognize and resolve comprehension problems and leads to higher-level thinking (Almasi, 1995). These examples illustrate that even when schema availability problems are not anticipated, students can still learn how to resolve comprehension problems if the instructional context fosters independence and strategic processing.

Activities That Support Strategy Instruction

Chapter 1 distinguished between the terms *strategies* and *activities*. This distinction is reviewed here to reinforce that the activities that follow are not used in isolation. These activities must accompany solid strategy instruction that follows the Strategy Instruction Model described in Chapter 3.

Cognitive strategies are actions that are selected deliberately by an individual to attain a goal. Thus only people can enact strategies. Activities are teaching tools that can be used to support strategy instruction; but by themselves are not *strategies* because an activity is an inanimate object and is incapable of deliberate action.

The instructional activities that support strategy instruction for schema availability problems are those that help students anticipate the content of the text. Table 4.1 identifies a number of such instructional activities. Enhancing schema availability is similar to "deep processing" as it relates to vocabulary development. Many of the instructional activities that reduce schema availability problems are similar to the types of research-based activities that facilitate deep processing of vocabulary and vocabulary development. Beck and McKeown (1991) explained that when vocabulary instruction requires the learner to actively process information (i.e., elaborating and discussing words, using words in realistic contexts), "it helps to build schematic network connections between new and prior information, and students retain words better" (p. 806). Active processing is also the key to enhancing comprehension. As Beck and McKeown (1991) noted, deep processing involves moving beyond simply memorizing and recalling new information/vocabulary from memory (i.e., looking up words in the dictionary, memorizing definitions of words). It involves linking the new information/vocabulary to known information—the same process that leads to comprehension.

Each of the activities described below requires students to engage in the same type of active processing that jointly facilitates schema availability and vocabulary development.

Drawing on the notion of making learning as concrete as possible, the first instructional suggestion is to provide *hands-on experiences*: Wherever possible, provide students with realistic experiences to instantiate their schemata. The point at which the student read and reacted to Valerie Flournoy's *The Patchwork Quilt* (1985) would be an ideal time to use hands-on experiences. The teacher and students might bring in quilts from home, especially those that are family heirlooms. With actual quilts available to touch, examine, and study, students can engage in a discussion of what quilts are used for, how they are made, why people might attach sentimental value to a quilt, or why a person would make one by hand rather than simply purchasing one. As the discussion progresses, the ideas can be captured on a semantic web (see Figure 4.5). Had the teacher provided such hands-on experience with authentic quilts prior to reading the story, the student, by his own account, would have understood the story better. This process is similar to that used in the Language Experience Approach (Stauffer, 1970), in which students first engage in an authentic experience (e.g., a field trip, an observation, a tour, a science experiment), after which they generate verbal descriptions of the experience that is recorded on paper (usually by the teacher or other adult). The recorded language is often in the form of connected prose that tells a story or describes the event, but it may also be recorded in the form of a web. The student-generated text is then used for instruction that focuses on word recognition, comprehension, and fluency.

All discussions of new concepts or ideas should involve *rich semantic descriptions*, including physical descriptions of the concept, its features, and comparisons to both related and unrelated concepts. For example, a quilt might be described as a colorful, handmade covering to keep one warm. It might be compared to, and distinguished from, bedspreads, comforters, and blankets. In this way, a network of related schemata are activated so that students' schema for quilts is linked to existing schemata and instantiated with new information as well. Such semantic descriptions and discussions should also involve active processing, as recommended by Beck and McKeown (1991). Students could be asked to discuss questions such as "Could you use a quilt in the summer?" or "Could use a quilt outside?" Such discussions require students to think beyond the definition of

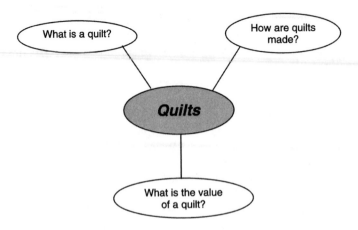

FIGURE 4.5. Semantic web for displaying ideas related to quilts.

the word, to activate their schema for the word and facilitate development of the features, attributes, and variables associated with that schema.

Films, videos, and pictures are also helpful in that they provide additional information that helps students instantiate their schemata. It is not necessary to show an entire film or video for such purposes; preview the medium and use those portions that are most salient for instantiating students' schemata.

The *K-W-L procedure* (Ogle, 1986) is helpful for facilitating active processing of expository (i.e., informational) text. The procedure involves three steps: (a) accessing what students *know*, (b) identifying what students *want* to learn, and (c) noting what students *learned* after reading the text (see Figure 4.6). The first step, accessing what students know, is relevant to facilitating schema availability in that it involves tapping into background knowledge and experiences. Ogle described two aspects of the process of accessing prior knowledge. The first step is simply to brainstorm information to see what students know about the topic. For example, if students were about to read the text *All About Deer*, by Jim Arnosky (1996) the brainstorming session might focus on accessing information that students have about "deer." As students share information about the topic, record it in the "K" column of the K-W-L chart (see Figure 4.6).

Ogle (1986) noted that the second part of accessing background knowledge is to think about general categories of information that might be encountered about the topic when reading. Using the information recorded in the "K" column, see whether there are clusters or groups of information that form more general categories. For example, some of the information shared by students about deer might involve physical characteristics, descriptions of habitat, eating habits, or survival skills. Each set of related ideas could be grouped together and given a superordinate label. Ogle noted that students often find it difficult at first to group information they have brainstormed and identify a superordinate label. This step might require teacher modeling and guidance initially; it is a crucial step because it involves the type of active and deep processing that Beck and McKeown (1991) recommended. Brainstorming information is helpful for accessing relevant schemata; the process of grouping such information together helps students learn how to make connections and comparisons between information.

Most of the activities described above require teacher involvement or guidance of some form. One must exercise caution in this regard. Strategy instruction as a whole is contingent upon teaching students to deliberately enact strategies *on their own*. If the teacher continually taps background knowledge for students and guides activities, such as those just described, without fostering students' independent use of the underlying cognitive strategies, then students will not transfer strategy use to independent reading. Many teachers engage in the good practice of introducing new stories by tapping students' background knowledge, but if this practice is not accompanied by explicit instruction aimed at teaching students how, when, where, and why they should tap their own background knowledge *independently*, they will remain reliant on the teacher's assistance.

Schema Selection–Retrieval

Suppose you plan to read a text about a *christening*. Think about what you know about christenings (i.e., tap into your available schema for christenings). When asked to do this in my university courses, my students usually generate information similar to that depicted in Figure 4.7. As noted earlier, activating prior knowledge about a topic helps alle-

K—what we know	W—what we want to find out	L—what we learned and still need to learn

Categories of information we expect to use:

A.   E.

B.   F.

C.   G.

D.   H.

FIGURE 4.6. K-W-L chart. From Ogle (1986). Copyright 1986 by the International Reading Association. Adapted by permission.

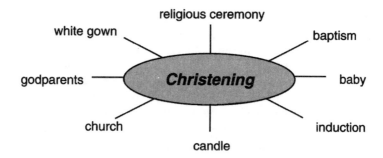

FIGURE 4.7. Web of information recalled about christenings.

viate comprehension problems in that the reader *anticipates* the types of content contained in the text. Read the following text about a christening taken from Anderson and Pearson (1984):

> Queen Elizabeth participated in a long-delayed christening ceremony in Clydebank, Scotland yesterday. While there is still bitterness here following the protracted strike, on this occasion a crowd of shipyard workers numbering in the hundreds joined dignitaries in cheering as the HMS *Pinafore* slipped into the water.

Think about how well the strategy of activating background knowledge worked to alleviate comprehension problems. In this instance, let's say you had the schema *available* for "christening," as it is used in this text, but you had difficulty *selecting* the appropriate schema. Thus, during a schema selection problem, the correct schema is available, but the reader accesses an inappropriate one. If, as you were reading, you were able quickly to realize that the text is not about a baby's baptism but about the christening of a ship, then your comprehension was affected only momentarily. You initially accessed a schema for a baby's baptism, but as you monitored your understanding, you realized that the word "christening" could also pertain to the launching of a new ship.

For less proficient readers, however, the process of monitoring and recognizing that an inappropriate schema has been selected or retrieved is difficult. Often these readers become wedded to the schema they selected initially and have difficulty adjusting their initial ideas. Wade (1990) described these top-down processors as "schema imposers" (p. 448). These readers often make the text "fit" the schema they initially selected, regardless of the incoming textual data. In the example above, these readers would continue to believe that the text was about a baptism. They might justify their understanding in the following manner. After reading the first sentence, they might think, "Wow, Queen Elizabeth attended this child's baptism. Maybe the child is of royal lineage." After reading the second sentence, they would probably disregard the information about the strike and hold onto the information about the shipyard workers, thinking, "Okay, the queen attended this event and so did all of these shipyard workers. Maybe one of the child's parents is royalty, and the other parent is the captain of a ship, and all of the shipyard workers were invited to the baptism." The last segment of the second sentence, about the HMS *Pinafore* slipping into the water, might be pondered, "I guess the child's initials were

HMS, or maybe the last name was Pinafore. Anyway, all of the people cheered as the baby was dipped into the water."

In this example the readers held onto the activated schema after it no longer fit, forcing the incoming information from the text to fit the selected schema. Schema-imposers often ignore information that conflicts or challenges the meaning they have constructed. These readers overrely on prior knowledge at the expense of textual information.

One cause of this problem may be cognitive overload. That is, the text may be so difficult to decode that readers guess at the general meaning of the text and fill in the details from their prior knowledge (which is often very well developed). One obvious solution to this problem is to provide text that is at an appropriate level of difficulty for the readers. Lacking strategies for monitoring their comprehension could be another cause of this problem. Readers' inability to monitor comprehension may still be caused by cognitive overload, or it may be that they lack the ability to monitor comprehension.

Consider the dilemma of schema retrieval as illustrated in the following example. Read the text with the goal of determining what it is about.

> The procedure is actually quite simple. First you arrange things into different groups. Of course, one pile may be sufficient depending on how much there is to do. If you have to go somewhere else due to lack of facilities, that is the next step, otherwise you are pretty well set. It is important not to overdo things. That is, it is better to do too few things at once than too many. In the short run this may be expensive as well. At first the whole procedure will seem complicated. Soon, however, it will become just another facet of life. It is difficult to foresee any end to the necessity for this task in the immediate future, but then one can never tell. After the procedure is completed, one arranges the materials into different groups again. Then they can be put into their appropriate places. Eventually they will be used once more and the whole cycle will have to be repeated. However, that is part of life. (Bransford & Johnson, 1973, p. 400)

Think about how well you understand this passage. On a scale from 1 to 5, with 1 being low and 5 being high, how would you rate your comprehension? Most readers find this to be a difficult passage to comprehend fully. Very few individuals rate themselves at 5. Although many readers have a vague notion that this passage describes some procedure for doing something, they are not confident of what that process is. Most readers activate a schema or several schemata and try to see how each fits with the textual information. This process quickly becomes frustrating because the text itself is very ambiguous. Comprehending this text presents a *schema retrieval* difficulty. I am certain that nearly everyone has this particular schema available; however, it is difficult to access or retrieve it because the text is so ambiguous. If the text had been given a title, such as "How to do Laundry," comprehension would be vastly improved. Thus the cause of this comprehension dilemma is not a reader-based problem but a textual problem. As evidenced in this example, text that is incoherent, poorly organized, or ambiguous can impair comprehension.

Strategy Instruction That Enhances Schema Selection–Retrieval

Strategies that help students prepare for reading and organize their thoughts while reading facilitate schema selection and retrieval. Table 4.1 lists three strategies for facilitating schema selection/retrieval: setting purposes, making predictions, and identifying text structure. These strategies facilitate students' ability to allocate attention while reading. When students are focused while reading, they are better able to monitor their comprehension, which helps them select and retrieve relevant schemata.

Setting purposes is a strategy that is often misunderstood. Teachers typically set purposes for students' reading (e.g., "Read to find out why the main character reacted as he did" or "Read to find out where deer live"). Although these teacher-designated purposes facilitate student comprehension, they do not promote students' independent strategy use. The goal of independent strategy use is to teach the students *how*, *when*, and *why* they should set their own purposes for reading. When the teacher formulates and enacts the strategies, rather than teaching the students how to use the strategy independently, students are removed from the decision-making process regarding what strategies to use and when to use them. As a result, they do not become planful, self-regulated readers who possess a repertoire of strategies to assist them as they read. Struggling readers, in particular, are at a disadvantage in this scenario. Students must be taught how to set their own purposes before reading and update them as they continue to read text. As we read, we are engaged continually in the process of setting purposes, seeking information that satisfies those purposes, and setting new purposes. Students must be given the opportunity to participate fully in this recursive process so that it meets *their* goals and purposes for reading rather than those of the teacher.

Like setting purposes, *prediction* is a recursive process that occurs throughout reading. We might begin reading by glancing at information from the title, pictures, headings, and the back of the book. This initial information enables an active reader to tap into available schemata and begin to generate predictions about the text. These predictions serve a similar function as purposes for reading: They become an impetus to continue reading. We want to read on to determine whether our prediction is affirmed or refuted by the text. New predictions then emerge, based on the incoming information as we continue reading. Setting purposes while reading and making predictions facilitate schema selection/retrieval because they compel readers to actively monitor comprehension. This active processing focuses a reader's attention so that relevant schema are selected and retrieved. In the christening example, you may have been expecting to read about a baby's baptism after activating your schema for "christening." Based on your prior knowledge, you were predicting, or anticipating, seeing information in the text to confirm this hypothesis. When reading the ensuing passage about a ship's christening, good comprehenders are able to monitor their comprehension and note the conflict between their hypothesis and the information in the text (e.g., presence of Queen Elizabeth, presence of shipyard workers, presence of a ship). In noting the conflicting information, good comprehenders search their schemata for an alternate one that incorporates the textual information. In this case, the original prediction would be rejected and a new one selected to reflect the incoming information. Once the prediction is altered or rejected, the reader can make new predictions and set new purposes based on this revision.

Identifying text structure while reading also facilitates active engagement. When readers are able to recognize the manner in which a text is organized, they are able to activate their schemata for that text structure. Text is generally either narrative or expository (i.e., informational). Narrative text contains story grammar elements (i.e., setting, character, goals, efforts to attain goals, and resolution). Expository text is generally organized according to one of five patterns: cause–effect, comparison–contrast, description–definition, problem–solution, or sequential. When readers are familiar with these text structures, they can anticipate how the text will be arranged and organized. The ability to anticipate text structure helps readers select and retrieve relevant schemata. For example, as you read the laundry passage above, you may have been able to determine by the structure of the text that it was describing how to perform some process. Most likely you recognized words that cued you that it was a sequential text structure (e.g., *first, next step, after, then*). Reading these words enabled you to activate your schema for texts that describe how to perform a procedure. Although you were unaware of the topic of the passage, you may have had some minimal degree of comprehension, because you knew at least that the text described a procedure of some form.

Activities That Support Strategy Instruction

When students have difficulty selecting or retrieving schemata, the activities chosen to support strategy instruction should be designed to help focus their attention on the text while they read or help them organize the incoming information contained in the text. Journals and prediction logs provide students with a place to record their purposes, predictions, and reactions to text and can be used during *Directed Reading-Thinking Activities* (DRTA) (Stauffer, 1970). During DRTA activities, students predict what they think will happen in the text and read to confirm or revise their predictions. As students read the text, they use a journal or prediction log to record their purposes and predictions (see Figure 4.8). Information that fulfills a purpose or verifies/rejects a prediction is recorded in the log in the second column, and the pages on which this information is found are recorded in the third column. Many teachers also encourage their students to use "sticky notes" in a similar manner. As students read, they record their purposes, predictions, and thoughts about the text on a sticky note and place it on the page about which they had the thought. In this manner students focus their attention on text and are encouraged to think actively about the text while reading.

The *Vocabulary-Language Prediction Activity* (VLP) serves two primary purposes: (1) to preteach vocabulary, using oral language activities that reinforce the word's structural and semantic characteristics, and (2) to use vocabulary as a basis for predicting what might occur in the text (Wood & Robinson, 1983). First the teacher studies the text to determine which words are important to understanding the text and which may cause students difficulty. Usually 10–15 total words are identified—but *most* of the words should be familiar to students so that they can draw upon their prior knowledge to make predictions. It is preferable to introduce no more than *three* or *four* new or unfamiliar words before reading. Make note of any structural aspects of the words that could be pointed out to facilitate word recognition (i.e., root words, word endings, prefixes). Place each word on a card and place the cards in front of the students. Explain to the students that these words will all appear in the text they are about to read. During the language portion of the activity, discussion focuses on developing rich semantic descriptions of new words, making connections among the words, and looking for patterns in words. The key to the language portion is to help students activate appropriate schemata for making relevant predictions. Once students understand the terms, they are taught how to make predictions about what might happen in the text based on these "starter" words. These predictions can be recorded in journals or logs if students are working in pairs or small groups, or they can be recorded on chart paper if the whole class is engaged in the activity.

The "W" column of the *K-W-L procedure* (see Figure 4.6) also serves a similar purpose for expository text (Ogle, 1986). After considering what they *know* about the topic and recording that information in the "K" column, students think about what they *want*

Title of Text: _____

Purpose (What do I want to find out?)	What I Found Out	Where I Found It (page number)

Prediction (What I think will happen)	Did It Happen?	Where Did I Find It? (page number)

FIGURE 4.8. Sample journal for recording purposes and predictions.

to know about the topic (i.e., set purposes for reading). Similar to setting purposes and making predictions in a journal or log, the "W" column of the K-W-L procedure serves to focus students' attention so that reading becomes a purposeful, active process.

   Graphic organizers serve a similar purpose in that they help focus students' attention to the manner in which text is organized while they read. Indeed, a critical aspect in the use of graphic organizers is to teach students that they can be used as a tool to facilitate awareness of text structure *while* reading. Often graphic organizers are completed as a post-reading activity. When used in this manner, they act more as an assessment than a tool to facilitate the comprehension process. Graphic organizers are particularly useful for helping students recognize and identify text structure. Story maps help students recognize the structure of narrative text (see Figures 4.9 and 4.10). As students encounter the various story grammar elements while reading, they record them on the story map. This visual aid helps students anticipate the type of information they will encounter while reading, and it helps them organize the incoming information as they read. Such organization facilitates easy access, which enhances recall and comprehension.

   Graphic organizers for informational text structures serve a similar purpose (see Figures 4.11, 4.12, 4.13, and 4.14). Students have a much more difficult time recognizing expository text structures because they are less familiar with them. That is, they do not have a schema internalized for the manner in which authors organize informational material. As well, many authors do not provide cues that help readers identify the structure of the text. Thus it is essential for students to begin to recognize how informational text can be organized. As mentioned previously, informational text generally fits into one of five patterns: descriptive–definitional, cause–effect, comparison–contrast, sequential, and problem–solution. Often informational text uses combinations of these patterns, making it even more difficult to recognize the manner in which the author has chosen to communicate information. Again, the organizers serve as a means of helping students anticipate the type of information they will encounter as they read, which helps them set reasonable purposes. While reading the text, students can record information as it is encountered. Although some students find it difficult to read and record information simultaneously, this process helps reduce schema selection–retrieval problems by focusing attention to the text. For students who are "schema imposers" (Wade, 1990)—those students who overrely on their prior knowledge and do not attend to the text—teaching strategies such as setting purposes, making predictions, and identifying text structure helps focus their attention on the text rather than on prior knowledge. The activities described above support such strategy instruction.

Schema Maintenance

In the case of schema maintenance difficulties, students have appropriate schema available to understand the text, and they have been able to select/retrieve it; however, they are unable to maintain the schema while reading. There are several possible causes of this problem. A text that is lengthy, too difficult, or poorly organized may place readers in a situation in which they are cognitively overloaded. In the midst of the reading process the reader begins to shut down and can no longer continue decoding text, comprehending it, and synthesizing information across the entire text.

   Contextual circumstances help explain other causes of schema maintenance difficulties. A reader's attention or motivation may wane while reading. Attention and motivation may wane because the text is not interesting to the reader or because the reader is not motivated to read that particular text. Alternatively, the reader himself may have other problems

Title: _____

Author: _____

WHO is in the story? | WHERE does the story take place?

WHAT is the problem? | HOW is the problem solved?

FIGURE 4.9. Story map for use with emergent readers.

Title: _____

Author: _____

Setting	Characters	Problem or Goal	Attempts to Solve Problem or Attain Goal	Solution
	Character Traits			

FIGURE 4.10. Story map for use with upper elementary readers.

Title: _____

Author: _____

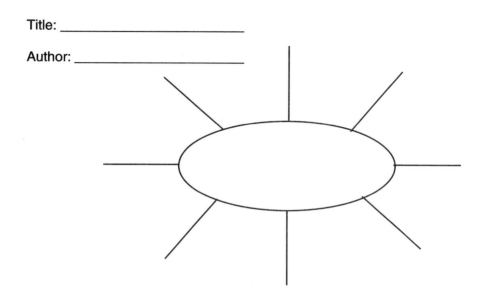

FIGURE 4.11. Graphic organizer for use in recognizing descriptive–definitional text.

Title: _____

Author: _____

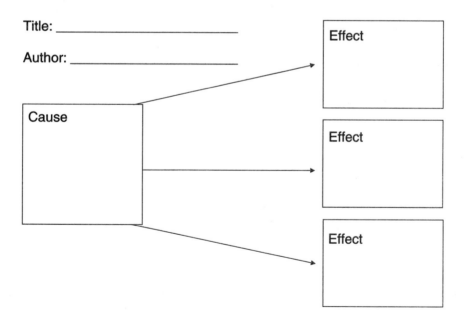

FIGURE 4.12. Graphic organizer for cause–effect structure.

Comparison between:

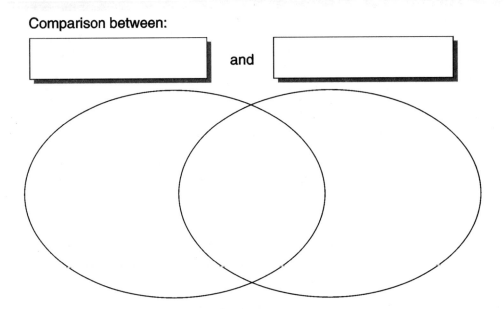

FIGURE 4.13. Graphic organizer for comparison–contrast text structure.

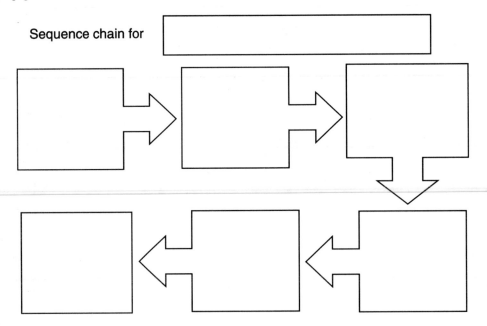

FIGURE 4.14. Graphic organizer for sequencing text structure.

(i.e., social, familial) that cause him to be distracted or unmotivated while reading. The result is a passive reader who does not monitor comprehension while reading and who often processes text in a piecemeal fashion. That is, as each new segment of text is encountered, a new schema or new idea is generated. Wade (1990) referred to these readers as "non-integrators" (p. 447). Such readers never develop a connected, integrated understanding of the text. To gain a better understanding of how these readers experience text, consider the following passage taken from Rumelhart (1980) and the subsequent analysis:

> Business had been slow since the oil crisis. Nobody seemed to want anything really elegant anymore. Suddenly the door opened and a well-dressed man entered the showroom floor. John put on his friendliest and most sincere expression and walked toward the man. (p. 43)

Generally, as people read this text, they begin by making a hypothesis about the text's topic. After reading the first sentence, people often activate schema related to gas stations, oil businesses, or other businesses that depend on the oil industry. As the second sentence is read, they refine and alter their schema selection to include the notion of "elegant." Often, good comprehenders think of businesses that rely on the oil industry but that also have something to do with elegance. Readers consider schema related to large cars or even the fur industry at this point. As they read on, they continue to modify and refine their hypotheses based on the new information contained in the text. After reading the entire passage, readers generally agree that John sells some type of large, luxury car, and that his business has been affected by the oil crisis. The process of activating schemata, generating hypotheses, determining if the incoming data "fits" with the selected schema, and refining or altering schemata based on the incoming data is ongoing and cumulative. However, readers with schema maintenance problems generate new notions about the text's meaning with each bit of new information. For example, after reading the first sentence, they may activate their schema for gas stations. After reading the second sentence, they may activate their schema for mink coats. After reading the third sentence, they may activate their schema for buying furniture. While reading each sentence, no attempt is made to link it to preceding and succeeding sentences. Instead, new schemata are activated with the introduction of each piece of new information, leaving the reader with a very disjointed interpretation of the text.

Strategy Instruction That Enhances Schema Maintenance

The goal for readers experiencing this difficulty is, again, to help them maintain and focus their attention while reading by enhancing their ability to monitor their comprehension. Table 4.1 identifies three helpful strategies that facilitate schema maintenance: imagery/visualization, questioning oneself, and identifying text structure. *Fostering imagery* is a strategy in which students are taught to visualize the text as they read. Many struggling readers are unaware that this simple process can facilitate comprehension. Making mental images while reading enhances recall and retention of text. In the example above, visualization might help a reader who has activated disparate information from each sentence form a unified picture of the event described.

Questioning oneself is another strategy that teaches students to monitor their comprehension while reading. This strategy involves teaching students simply to ask themselves "Does this make sense?" as they are reading. The strategy does *not* involve having students (or the teacher) generate comprehension questions to ask themselves. It is simply an effort to teach students to monitor their understanding as they read. Patty George's "stop and go" lesson (see Chapter 3) is an example of teaching very young readers how to stop and think after reading each page to see if the text made sense or not. *Identifying text structure*, as described earlier, is also an excellent strategy that helps readers maintain their focus while reading.

Activities That Support Strategy Instruction

One way to help children visualize as they read is to *"sketch and share."* Children are encouraged to visualize and sketch as they read the text. After students sketch, they can gather in pairs or small groups to share their images and discuss the text that evoked them. In this manner children can see others' concrete representations of the text and their interpretations. These images can elicit lively discussion of one another's interpretations of the text and of the author's style that evoked the images.

"Stop and go" or *"click and clunk"* signs, as described in Chapter 3, are excellent for helping children learn how to monitor their comprehension. The goal during these activities is to provide children with a concrete representation of comprehension monitoring. These signs can be used during teacher read alouds, shared reading, guided reading, or independent reading. It is important to provide ample opportunity for children to discuss why portions of text did or did not make sense to them. As well, it is important for students to see that different people understand text in different ways. Readers who are able to monitor their comprehension are able to maintain schema.

Graphic organizers for both narrative and expository text, as described above, provide an excellent means of helping students maintain their focus while reading. Again, using graphic organizers should accompany the reading process rather than follow it, for it is while reading that students have difficulty maintaining their schemata.

SUMMARY

Comprehension is an interactive–compensatory process in which readers attempt to make connections between their prior knowledge (i.e., schema) and the new information contained in the text. This process is a constructive one that requires an active reader. Meaning is constructed as the reader, the text, and the context transact. At times, however, meaning construction is inhibited or impaired. Schema availability poses problems for those readers who do not have an appropriate or a fully developed schema available to make connections to the new information contained in the text. Teaching students how to preview text and tap their background knowledge helps reduce schema availability problems. Schema selection/retrieval is a problem for those readers who tend to overrely on their prior knowledge to understand text. Such readers have difficulty recognizing when the text does not support the schema they have selected to help understand it. Teaching students to (1) set purposes, (2) generate, confirm, and revise predictions, and (3) identify text structure helps focus students' attention so that they can anticipate and organize textual information. Schema maintenance problems occur when readers have difficulty focusing their attention throughout the entire reading process: monitoring their comprehension as a result, they often are unable to integrate textual information and create a coherent meaning. Strategies that help focus attention, such as visualization, monitoring comprehension, and identifying text structure, help with this difficulty.

REFERENCES

Almasi, J. F. (1995). The nature of fourth graders' sociocognitive conflicts in peer-led and teacher-led discussions of literature. *Reading Research Quarterly, 30*(3), 314–351.

Anderson, R. C., & Pearson, P. D. (1984). A schema-theoretic view of basic processes in reading comprehension. In P. D. Pearson, R. Barr, M. L. Kamil, & P. B. Mosenthal (Eds.), *Handbook of reading research* (vol. 1, pp. 255–291). New York: Longman.

Anderson, R. C., Reynolds, R. E., Schallert, D. L., & Goetz, E. T. (1977). Frameworks for comprehending discourse. *American Educational Research Journal, 14*(4), 367–381.

Baker, L., & Brown, A. L. (1984). Metacognitive skills and reading. In P. D. Pearson, R. Barr, M. L. Kamil, and P. B. Mosenthal (Eds.), *Handbook of reading research* (vol. 1, pp. 353–394). New York: Longman.

Beach, R., & Hynds, S. (1991). Research on response to literature. In R. Barr, M. L. Kamil, P. B. Mosenthal, & P. D. Pearson (Eds.), *Handbook of reading research* (vol. 2, pp. 453–489). New York: Longman.

Beck, I. L., & McKeown, M. G. (1991). Conditions of vocabulary acquisition. In R. Barr, M. L. Kamil, P. B. Mosenthal, & P. D. Pearson (Eds.), *Handbook of reading research* (vol. 2, pp. 789–814). New York: Longman.

Bleich, D. (1978). *Subjective criticism.* Baltimore, MD: Johns Hopkins University Press.

Bransford, J. D., & Johnson, M. K. (1973). Considerations of some problems of comprehension. In W. Chase (Ed.), *Visual information processing* (pp. 383–438). New York: Academic Press.

Garner, R. (1987). *Metacognition and reading comprehension.* Norwood, NJ: Ablex.

Gee, J. (1992). Socio-cultural approaches to literacy (literacies). In W. A. Grabe (Ed.), *Annual review of applied linguistics* (vol. 12, pp. 31–48). New York: Cambridge University Press.

Hynds, S. (1991). Research on response to literature. In R. Barr, M. L. Kamil, P. B. Mosenthal, & P. D. Pearson (Eds.), *Handbook of reading research* (vol. 2, pp. 453–489). New York: Longman.

Marshall, J. (2000). Research on response to literature. In M. L. Kamil, P. B. Mosenthal, P. D. Pearson, & R. Barr (Eds.), *Handbook of reading research* (vol. 3, pp. 381–402). Mahweh, NJ: Erlbaum.

Ogle, D. M. (1986). K-W-L: A teaching model that develops active reading of expository text. *The Reading Teacher, 39*(6), 564–570.

Paris, S. G., Lipson, M. Y., & Wixson, K. K. (1983). Becoming a strategic reader. *Contemporary Educational Psychology, 8,* 293–316.

Pilgrim, E. B. (2000). *Curse of the Red Cross ring.* St. John's, Newfoundland: Flanker Press.

Richards, I. A. (1929). *Practical criticism.* New York: Harcourt, Brace, and World.

Rosenblatt, L. M. (1978). *The reader, the text, the poem: The transactional theory of the literary work.* Carbondale, IL: Southern Illinois University Press.

Rosenblatt, L. M. (1991). Literature—S.O.S! *Language Arts, 68,* 444–448.

Rumelhart, D. E. (1980). Schemata: The building blocks of cognition. In R. J. Spiro, B. C. Bruce, & W. F. Brewer (Eds.), *Theoretical issues in reading comprehension* (pp. 33–58). Hillsdale, NJ: Erlbaum.

Rumelhart, D. E., & Ortony, A. (1977). The representation of knowledge in memory. In R. C. Anderson, R. J. Spiro, & W. E. Montague (Eds.), *Schooling and the acquisition of knowledge* (pp. 99–135). Hillsdale, NJ: Erlbaum.

Samuels, S. J., & Kamil, M. L. (1984). Models of the reading process. In P. D. Pearson, R. Barr, M. L. Kamil, & P. B. Mosenthal (Eds.), *Handbook of reading research* (vol. 1, pp. 185–224). New York: Longman.

Spiro, R. J. (1980). Constructive processes in prose comprehension and recall. In R. J. Spiro, B. C. Bruce, & W. F. Brewer (Eds.), *Theoretical issues in reading comprehension* (pp. 245–278). Hillsdale, NJ: Erlbaum.

Stanovich, K. E. (1980). Toward an interactive–compensatory model of individual differences in the development of reading fluency. *Reading Research Quarterly, 16,* 32–71.

Stauffer, R. G. (1970). *The language experiences approach to the teaching of reading.* New York: Harper & Row.

Tompkins, G., & McGee, L. (1993). *Teaching reading with literature: Case studies to action plans.* New York: Merrill.

Wade, S. E. (1990). Using think alouds to assess comprehension. *The Reading Teacher, 43*(7), 442–451.

Wood, K. D., & Robinson, N. (1983). Vocabulary, language, and prediction: A prereading strategy. *The Reading Teacher,* 392–395.

Strategy Instruction That Enhances Comprehension

As noted in Chapter 3, the Strategy Instruction Model is a recursive one in which a safe environment for motivated strategy use creates, and is created by, opportunities for students to receive explicit instruction, verbalize strategic processing, and experience reduced processing to foster awareness and understanding of strategic processes. This model provides the instructional framework for the ideas contained in this and the next chapter. The purpose of this chapter is to provide teachers with hands-on tools and resources—sample lessons, texts, teaching ideas—that will make beginning strategy instruction less cumbersome.

IMPLICIT INSTRUCTION OF COMPREHENSION STRATEGIES

Implicit instruction provides an instructional context in which readers gradually internalize instructional principles through guided discovery and scaffolding from more knowledgeable others (Vygotsky, 1978). Two models of such instruction (e.g., Collaborative Problem Solving and Process Talk) were described in Chapter 2. Ideally such strategy instruction should occur seamlessly. As children read and discuss texts, the reading event itself (i.e., the reader, the text, the context) provides the materials of instruction. During implicit strategy instruction, students have the opportunity to interact with others as they strategically process text. The teacher plans the learning event by carefully selecting texts that require readers to use specific strategies. For example, some texts have an obvious structure that facilitates comprehension; others are written with image-laden language that fosters use of visualization as a comprehension strategy. As students read these texts, they may automatically use these strategies to understand the text without consciously understanding the principles underlying their use (Walker, 2000). Following the reading, students might engage in peer discussions of text in which they initiate the topics of discussion and work collaboratively to construct an understanding of the text (Almasi, in press; Almasi, 1995; Almasi, O'Flahavan, & Arya, 2001; Gambrell & Almasi, 1996). During these discussions, students use a variety of strategies as they make sense of the text.

As an example of this type of instruction, read the following text (Bartlett, 1932, p. 65) and think about the strategies you use to process, or make sense of, the excerpts. In other words, engage yourself in a think aloud of sorts, in which, as you read, you identify and label the strategic processes you use to make sense of the text.

The War of the Ghosts

1   One night two young men from Egulac went down to the river to hunt seals, and
2   while they were there it became foggy and calm. Then they heard war-cries, and
3   they thought: "Maybe this is a war party." They escaped to the shore and hid
4   behind a log. Now canoes came up, and they heard the noise of the paddles, and
5   saw one canoe coming up to them. There were five men in the canoe, and they said:
6   "What do you think? We wish to take you along. We are going up the river to
7   make war on the people."
8   One of the young men said, "I have no arrows."
9   "Arrows are in the canoe," they said.
10   "I will not go along. I might be killed. My relatives do not know where I have
11 gone. But you," he said, turning to the other, "may go with them."
12   So one of the young men went, but the other returned home.
13   And the warriors went on up the river to a town on the other side of Kalama.
14 The people came down to the water, and they began to fight, and many were killed.
15 But presently the young man heard one of the warriors say: "Quick let us go home:
16 that Indian has been hit." Now he thought: "Oh, they are ghosts." He did not feel
17 sick, but they said he had been shot.
18   So the canoes went back to Egulac, and the young man went ashore to his house,
19 and made a fire. And he told everybody and said: "Behold I accompanied the
20 ghosts, and we went to fight. Many of our fellows were killed, and many of those
21 who attacked us were killed. They said I was hit, and I did not feel sick."
22   He told it all, and then he became quiet. When the sun rose he fell down.
23 Something black came out of his mouth. His face became contorted. The people
24 jumped up and cried.
25   He was dead.

For most people of Anglo-European backgrounds, this text is somewhat difficult to understand. There is no "correct" way to read this passage. That is, there is no single set of strategies, or pattern of strategy use, that will produce a "better" interpretation. Each individual approaches the text differently and uses different strategies to process it. After reading it for the first time, many students in my graduate courses often break out into spontaneous conversation with one another as they try to make sense of the text. These conversations are lively and focused. Often the discourse includes discussion of the *way* in which one arrived at his or her interpretation. I often hear questions such as, "What made you think that?" Sometimes people share places in the text in which they had vivid images, such as in lines 2–5 or 22–24. Sometimes they share places in which they recognized that their comprehension was suffering, "I thought I understood it until he said, 'Oh, they are ghosts' " (line 16). The entire focus of the discussion is an effort to construct meaning collaboratively. This type of reading event is an example of implicit instruction that is based on endogenous constructivist principles (as discussed in Chapter 3), in which learning occurs in a social context that gradually permits learners to internalize instructional principles through guided discovery and interaction with more knowledgeable others rather than through explicit instruction (Pressley, Harris, & Marks, 1992). In these reading events, students who may not be familiar with a particular strategy (e.g., imagery) hear the others discussing the vivid images in lines 2–5 and lines 22–24, and, although they may not have known about using imagery previously, they incidentally learn some *declarative* knowledge about its existence, and from the discussion they learn *conditional* knowledge about how others used it. Over time readers accumulate knowledge about a strategy like imagery, and they may try using it in the future while reading independently. This is the type of learning environment that is depicted in the fourth-graders' discussion of the setting in *Soup's New Shoes* by Robert Newton Peck (Chapter 4).

The strategy instruction based on dialectical constructivist principles, in which the teacher takes a more active role in the discussion by providing hints and prompts to facilitate student scaffolding and learning (Pressley, Harris, et al., 1992), is exemplified in Chapter 3's sample discussion of Stephen Mooser's (1978) *The Ghost with the Halloween Hiccups*. This type of discourse occurs during transactional strategies instruction (Pressley, El-Dinary, et al., 1992). The teacher serves as a more knowledgeable other who scaffolds the instruction by providing labels and explanations for the strategic processing, as it occurs. Teachers might also initiate discourse about strategic processing by prompting students with open-ended probes such as, "How did you figure that out?" or "Why do you think that?"

Such discussions might also focus on the manner in which students processed the text to arrive at a particular interpretation. During this type of "strategy talk," students learn how others were able to make sense of the text. Over time, with accumulated experiences of such incidental learning, students gradually internalize the requisite declarative, procedural, and conditional knowledge associated with proficient strategy use. However, communicating such information is never the explicit goal of an implicit instructional lesson.

Kucan and Beck (1997) suggested that these implicit learning environments may be sufficient to help students learn about the process of constructing meaning. One concern, however, is the fact that the efficacy of implicit instruction is contingent upon readers who are able to engage actively in the process—a problem for struggling readers who are passive and unaware of, and unable to use, strategic processes. Can we provide the boundless amounts of time that might be required for all readers to discover and internalize these principles? Another concern is more global: readers who may be completely unaware of particular features of strategic processing that would help them. For example, there is a wealth of research indicating that readers of varying abilities have difficulty comprehending expository text structures. How can readers who have no schema available for expository text structure include it in their discussion?

Instructional practice need not be an either/or situation. It is possible to provide *all* readers, proficient and less proficient, with both implicit and explicit strategy instruction so that they reap the benefits of both environments. Suppose, as students engaged in a peer discussion similar to that described in the commentary following the "War of the Ghosts," the teacher took anecdotal notes. These notes would describe the strategies that were used to construct meaning, the manner in which students used strategies (i.e., where, when, and how), which students used particular strategies, and how successful their strategic actions were for constructing meaning. From these notes the teacher would formulate hypotheses about the type of explicit instruction needed to help her students develop even more facility for comprehending similar text in the future. These hypotheses might pertain to any aspect of the Good Strategy User Model described in Chapters 1 and 2. The teacher would then plan an explicit instruction lesson, or series of lessons, designed to introduce new strategic knowledge, and refine or expand existing knowledge. During these lessons the teacher would provide explanation and modeling of the new ideas and then ample opportunity for students to engage in guided practice in a variety of authentic reading contexts. Ideally, these guided practice events would take on the character of implicit instruction so that responsibility for selecting and using strategies is ceded back to the students. The teacher would then continue to involve all students in implicit instructional contexts to see how and whether they were using the new information taught via explicit instruction. This is the nature of ongoing assessment and instruction of strategic processes that is described in Chapter 2. It is a dynamic and recursive process, but the instructional aspect of it need not, and should not, solely reflect one ideological perspective.

EXPLICIT INSTRUCTION OF COMPREHENSION STRATEGIES

As described in Chapter 3, explicit instruction provides opportunity for more teacher influence over the learning environment and the nature of the instruction. The teacher identifies the objectives and goals for the lesson and provides explanation, modeling, and guided practice to help students attain them. Over time the teacher gradually releases responsibility for directing the instruction to the students, until they are capable of engaging in the process entirely on their own. As Pearson and Dole (1987) noted, it is essential that explicit instruction be provided using authentic texts in which the reading process is performed. That is, explicit instruction of strategies should not occur in isolation, without connected text, or as a distinct and separate activity. It must be embedded within, and linked to, authentic reading events. During explicit instruction, teachers must be attuned to the learning environment so that they are able to identify opportune moments in which to insert strategy-related language and provide opportunities for students to engage in similar practice. These opportunities for student verbalization and dialogue about strategy use enable them to "try out," or appropriate, strategy language for their own use.

With this overview in mind, the remainder of the chapter focuses on the background research and teaching tools related to those research-based comprehension strategies that are used most often by good readers. It should be noted that although each strategy is presented in isolation and the sample lessons focus on teaching only one strategy at a time, strategies should not be taught in a series of step-like lessons. Strategy use is a dynamic, fluid process that varies from individual to individual and from context to context. Strategy instruction should reflect this fluidity. Ideally, the ideas presented here can be used by teachers as an initial guide, to be adapted and altered to fit the needs of particular students in particular contexts. The ideas that follow are presented in a linear fashion because they are bounded by the limitations of publishing them in a two-dimensional format. This would make the uninformed reader think that each strategy is mutually exclusive and could be taught apart from other strategies. Many of the "single" strategies presented below, in a linear fashion, overlap and are essential components of other strategies; the strategies are mutually dependent on, and continually inform, one another. However, for the sake of clarity, I have divided them into three categories: (1) text anticipation strategies, (2) text maintenance strategies, and (3) fix-up strategies.

Text Anticipation Strategies

Text anticipation strategies are a family of strategies that includes (1) previewing the text by looking at the title, pictures, and headings; (2) activating prior knowledge; (3) setting purposes; (4) generating, verifying, and updating predictions; and (5) identifying text structure (see Figure 3.4 for a chart of all strategies). Readers use these strategies flexibly and in combination with one another as they read. As noted in Chapter 4, these strategies help readers avert difficulties with schema availability and schema selection and retrieval. The key element of each of these strategies is prior knowledge, which includes general world knowledge, specific knowledge related to the content of text, and knowledge about the way text is organized (Dole, Duffy, Roehler, & Pearson, 1991).

Readers use previewing strategies to sample aspects of the text. The cues gathered during this sampling process may be derived from (1) any semiotic or linguistic feature of the text (i.e., title, pictures, headings, or the text itself) as well as (2) the manner in which the author has organized the text (i.e., text structure). These cues help readers activate and make links to relevant background knowledge (i.e., schemata). These same cues, coupled with the activated background knowledge, enable readers to make predictions about what might happen (Afflerbach, 1990; Anderson & Pearson, 1984). These predictions often become a reason (i.e., a purpose) for continued reading and help readers anticipate the meaning of the text. That is, readers are motivated to continue reading to determine whether their prediction is accurate. Predictions are monitored and checked against textual information as more text is read (Collins, Brown, & Larkin, 1980). That is, predictions are verified, rejected, or altered as a result of the newly encountered textual information. This process means that new purposes for continued reading also are set. This entire process is a cyclical and recursive one that is repeated over and over while one reads, and at any given point a reader may have multiple predictions and purposes for reading.

Previewing Text and Activating Prior Knowledge

Based on their review of the research, Pressley, Johnson, Symons, McGoldrick, and Kurita (1989) identified prior knowledge activation as an effective research-based strategy to teach children. They contended that prior knowledge affects comprehension by creating expectations that direct attention to relevant aspects of text, permitting inferential elaboration of text, facilitating recall of text, and affecting interpretation. Research has shown that the knowledge readers possess affects the manner in which they see the world and the manner in which they understand text (Anderson & Pearson, 1984). Prior knowledge affects what is recalled from text (Anderson, Pichert, & Shirey, 1983; Bransford & Johnson, 1972; Pearson, Hansen, & Gordon, 1979; Recht & Leslie, 1988; Taft & Leslie, 1985) and one's interpretation of text (Anderson, Reynolds, Schallert, & Goetz, 1977). The results of these findings suggest that strategic readers activate their background knowledge in all three domains (general world knowledge, textual content, and text structure) prior to, and while, reading (Pearson & Fielding, 1991; Pressley, Johnson, et al., 1989).

However, prior knowledge may interfere with reading comprehension if existing knowledge conflicts with textual information. Lipson (1983) found that when children in grades 4, 5, and 6 read passages that were congruent with their religious backgrounds their ability to recall and make inferences was greater and included fewer distortions than when they read passages that were incongruent with their religious background. Similarly, Alvermann, Smith, and Readence (1985) found that sixth-grade students were wary of believing a science text when it conflicted with their previous knowledge. Because readers often ignore or dismiss incongruent information on their own, it is essential for them to participate in social environments that provide the opportunity to share their thoughts with others as meaning is constructed: Peers do not permit incongruities to be ignored or dismissed as readily as occurs during independent reading. The group holds readers accountable for their interpretations and facilitates meaning construction. Almasi's (1995) research found that fourth graders were better able to recognize and resolve such incongruities when in peer discussion than teacher-led discussion environments. Thus social environments such as peer discussion are essential for alleviating the comprehension difficulties associated with prior knowledge that conflicts with textual information.

When teaching students how to activate their prior knowledge, it is important to remember that the goal is to teach them how to use the strategy on their own. Helping students learn to use strategies independently means that lessons should communicate the declarative, procedural, and conditional knowledge associated with activating prior knowledge (see Table 5.1), and they should enable students to perform the strategy on their own while scaffolded by the teacher. As noted in column 4 of Table 5.1, activating prior knowledge is a strategy that should be used when reading all texts. Hence, selecting texts for such lessons should pose no problem in the classroom. Figure 5.1 displays a sample lesson plan adapted from Angela Bies's work with a struggling fourth grader. The lesson contains marginal glosses to indicate where each element of the Strategy Instruction Model occurs. (All sample lessons are presented to facilitate insight into how explicit strategy instruction is enacted in the preparatory stage. Teachers must modify and make adjustments while teaching to meet the needs of individual students.)

The sample lesson has only two goals: to teach students how to activate prior knowledge, and to teach them how to organize activated prior knowledge when new information is encountered while reading. Explicit strategy instruction should not be overwhelming. The lessons should be clearly focused so that students can easily grasp the concept. In this sample lesson activating prior knowledge was compared to taking a trip. This analogy was intended to make the strategy more concrete for students, so that they could liken it to something they have already done. Processing is slightly reduced in this manner but the lesson as a whole is fairly abstract because it requires students to use linguistic text. Table 3.2 is reproduced in Table 5.2 to illustrate the types of scaffolded support of-

TABLE 5.1. Rationale for Developing Declarative, Procedural, and Conditional Knowledge Associated with Comprehension Strategies

Comprehension Strategy	Associated Declarative Knowledge[a]	Associated Procedural Knowledge[a]	Associated Conditional Knowledge[a]	Teaching Methods
Previewing text	Readers need to know *that*: • Before reading any text, it is helpful to preview it. • Previewing involves looking at the title, pictures, table of contents, headings, chapter titles, subheadings or any other textual feature to gain an idea of what the text will be about.	*How* to preview text: • Look at the cover of the text. • Study the title and the pictures. • Think about what clues are given to see what the text might be about. • Open the text and look at the table of contents, chapter titles, and headings to gain more clues about what the text will be about. • Flip through the book and glance at the pictures, charts, or graphs to gain more clues about what the text might be about. • Read the back cover or introductory statements to gain more clues about what the text might be about.	*Where* is it helpful to preview text? • As you read all types of text. *When* is it helpful to preview text? • Previewing is helpful *before* you read. • Previewing is often helpful *while* setting purposes. • Previewing is often helpful *while* making predictions *Why* is it helpful to preview text? • Previewing helps prepare you for reading (reduces schema availability problems). • Previewing helps you anticipate what the text will be about so that you can activate relevant prior knowledge, set purposes, and make predictions as you read.	• Picture walks. • Rich discussion.
Activating prior knowledge	Readers need to know *that*: • Activating prior knowledge means thinking about what you know about the topic of the text. • What you already know about the world can help you understand what you read. • As you read you should continually try to make connections between what you know and the new ideas in the text.	*How* to activate prior knowledge: • Look at the title, pictures, headings, or chapter titles in the text to gain an idea of what it is about. • Think about what you already know about the topic. • Sometimes it helps to write down what you already know about the topic. • As you read, try to make connections between what you know about the topic and the new ideas in the text.	*Where* is it helpful to activate prior knowledge? • As you read all types of text *When* is it helpful to activate prior knowledge? • If done *before* you read it will help you anticipate what the text will be about. • Anticipating what the text is about will help you set purposes for reading and make predictions. • If done *while* you read it will help you update and revise your predictions, and it will help you set new purposes. • If done *after* reading it will help you evaluate and monitor how well you understood the text *Why* is it helpful to activate prior knowledge? • It helps you prepare for reading (reduces schema availability problems). • It helps you to focus your attention while reading (reduces schema selection and retrievability problems).	• Semantic webs and semantic maps to organize ideas. • The "K" portion of K-W-L procedure (see Figure 4.6). • Vocabulary Language Prediction Activities.

	Readers need to know *that:*	How to set purposes / predict:	Where/When/Why	Activities
Setting purposes	You can read for different purposes. Purposes are plans you make that tell what you want to find out as you read text. Setting purposes guides the reading process. Setting purposes helps focus attention while reading. You read differently when you have different purposes in mind. You can set purposes to learn new information, confirm predictions, identify text structure, or perform a task.	*How* to set purposes: • Look at the title, pictures, headings, or chapter titles in the text to gain an idea of what it is about. • Think about what you already know about the topic. • Think about what you would like to find out about the topic or about the story. • Sometimes it helps to write down your purposes. • As you read, think about whether the information in the text answers your purpose. • Revise your purpose or generate new purposes based on the information in the text.	*Where* is it helpful to set purposes? • As you read all types of texts *When* is it helpful to set purposes? • Setting purposes *before* reading helps focus your thinking while you read. • Setting purposes *while* reading helps guide your reading *Why* is it helpful to set purposes? • It helps you prepare for reading (reduces schema availability problems). • It helps you to focus your attention while reading (reduces schema selection and retrievability problems).	• Directed Reading-Thinking Activities. • The "W" portion of K-W-L procedures (see Figure 4.6). • Maintain journal/log while reading (see Figure 4.8). • Complete story maps while reading (see Figures 4.9 and 4.10). • Complete graphic organizers that indicate expository text structure while reading (see Figures 4.11–4.14).
Generating, verifying, and updating predictions	Predictions are guesses or hypotheses about what you think will happen in the text. Predictions are good guesses based on your prior knowledge and clues from the text. Making predictions helps focus your attention and guides your reading.	*How* to predict: • Look at the title, pictures, headings, chapter titles or any other clues in the text to gain an idea of what it is about. • Think about what you already know about the topic. • Think about the clues in the text and try to make links between those clues and what you already know about the topic. • Based on these clues and what you already know, make a guess about what you think is going to happen in the text. As you read, look for information in the text that tells you whether your prediction was on target, slightly off, or completely off.	*Where* is it helpful to predict? • As you read all types of texts *When* is it helpful to predict? • Predicting *before* reading helps focus your thinking while you read. • Predicting *while* reading helps guide your reading *Why* is it helpful to set purposes? • It helps you prepare for reading (reduces schema availability problems). • It helps you to focus your attention while reading (reduces schema selection and retrievability problems).	• Directed Reading-Thinking Activities. • Maintain journal/log while reading (see Figure 4.8). • Vocabulary Language Prediction and Story Map Activities.

(cont.)

TABLE 5.1. *(cont.)*

Comprehension Strategy	Associated Declarative Knowledge[a]	Associated Procedural Knowledge[a]	Associated Conditional Knowledge[a]	Teaching Methods
		• As you read, you may make adjustments to your predictions and make new predictions as you gather information from the text. • Making predictions sometimes helps you determine your purposes for reading.		
Identifying text structure	Readers need to know *that:* • Authors organize writing in different ways. • There are two types of text: narrative and expository. • Narrative text contains story grammar elements: setting, characters, problem, attempts to solve problem, resolution. • There are five types of expository text structures: cause–effect, comparison–contrast, sequential, problem–solution, description–definition. • Authors use cue words to signal text structures. • Some texts are poorly organized or do not use cue words, making them difficult to understand.	*How* to identify text structure: • Look at the title, pictures, headings, chapter titles or any other clues in the text to gain an idea of how it is organized. • Skim through the text. • Look for cue words. • Decide on type of text.	*Where* is it helpful to identify text structure? • As you read all types of texts *When* is it helpful to identify text structure? • Identifying text structure *before* you read gives you an idea of how the text is organized so you can anticipate what types of information will be forthcoming. • Identifying text structure *while* you read helps focus your attention and enhances comprehension and recall of text *Why* is it helpful to identify text structure? • It helps you prepare for reading (reduces schema availability problems). • It helps you to focus your attention while reading (reduces schema selection and retrievability problems). • It helps you maintain your attention while reading (reduces schema maintenance problems).	• Story map activities (see Figures 4.9 and 4.10). • Expository text graphic organizers (see Figures 4.11–4.14).

	Readers need to know *that*:	*How* to make mental images:	*Where* is it helpful to image?	
Imagery/visual-ization	• Authors use very descriptive language when they write. • Making a picture of the text in your mind as you read will help your comprehension.	• As you read, think about the author's words. • Think about what you already know about the topic. • Use your five senses to draw a picture of those words in your mind. • Change your picture as the text changes.	• As you read all types of texts, but especially image-laden text and text that is not ambiguous. *When* is it helpful to image? • Making mental images is helpful to do while you are reading. *Why* is it helpful to image? • It helps you understand and remember what you read better. • It helps you maintain your attention while reading (reduces schema maintenance problems).	• "Sketch and share" activities
Comprehension monitoring	*Readers need to know that:* • Sometimes text does not make sense as you read it. • You should stop regularly and check to make sure that you understand what you are reading.	*How* to monitor comprehension: • While reading stop periodically. • Ask yourself whether you understand what you are reading. • If you do understand, keep reading. • If you do not understand, use a fix-up strategy (reread, read ahead, ask someone) to help you understand the text better.	*Where* is it helpful to monitor comprehension? • As you read all types of text. *When* is it helpful to monitor comprehension? • Continually as you read *Why* is it helpful to monitor comprehension? • It helps you maintain your attention while reading (reduces schema maintenance problems). • It helps you know when you need to use strategies to enhance your understanding.	• "Stop and go" or "click and clunk" activities

[a]Note that the declarative, procedural, and conditional knowledge associated with each strategy is not detailed comprehensively and most certainly varies from individual to individual. These features should not be taught in a lock-step manner as if they were static.

Teacher: Adapted from a lesson by Angela Bies.

Topic: Identifying and organizing prior knowledge using semantic maps.

Grade level: 2–4

STAIRS hypothesis being addressed:
                Students are unmotivated to read informational texts and fail to apply comprehension strategies when the text is not of interest.

Goals of Lesson

Students will learn to:
• Identify and organize prior knowledge using a graphic organizer
• Organize new information from text using a graphic organizer

Materials

• *Cats* by Gail Gibbons
• Paper for making semantic maps
• At least 2 different colored markers
• Student self-assessment forms

Introduction

Create a safe environment

The lesson will begin by trying to relate the process and purposes of activating prior knowledge to other tasks in everyday life. Engage students in a conversation about what we might do if we were preparing to go on a trip. Students will share various things they do to prepare for trips. This information might include packing, purchasing some means of transportation, buying maps, etc. After students share, relate this process to reading by noting, "Before we go on a trip, we have to do lots of things to get ready. We have to do similar things before we read. We have to get our minds ready to take a trip to another place. In a sense we have to get our minds ready by 'packing' information that we might need for the journey. What kinds of things do you do to get ready to read?" Students share various strategies they use before they read. As students share strategies, record them on a chart and note that the purpose of this lesson is to teach students a strategy that will help them prepare for reading—thinking about what they already know about the text.

Reduce processing demands

Explanation: conditional knowledge

Verbalization about strategy use

Explanation: declarative knowledge

Description of Instructional Experience

Verbalization explanation: procedural knowledge

Explain that good readers think about what they already know about the subject before they start reading to help them better understand. Ask students to think about how they might do this. Try to elicit the procedural knowledge about how various students activate their prior knowledge. If students have difficulty verbalizing, display a variety of texts about cats, including *Cats* by Gail Gibbons.

Modeling that communicates procedural knowledge

Using a think aloud procedure, model how you would go about activating your prior knowledge before reading any of these texts. "Before I start to read, I look at the cover of this book and I notice that the title is *Cats*. Hmmm, I know a lot about cats because I have a cat. I guess this book is going to tell me about cats. As I look at the cover and the pictures, I

FIGURE 5.1. Sample lesson teaching students how to activate prior knowledge.

notice lots of pictures of cats. I'm pretty sure this book is going to be about cats. I'm going to stop and think for a moment about what I already know about cats. Sometimes it helps me prepare for my reading if I write down what I already know about the topic. So I'm going to take a few minutes to do that."

Explanation: conditional knowledge

At this point explain that by organizing what we already know about the topic on paper, it helps us organize what we know in our heads. This internal organization helps make learning the new information easier to understand because we can link it to what we already know.

Modeling

Model how to use a graphic organizer to record thoughts about what you know about cats. Think aloud as you record the information. "A web is one way to organize what we know about the topic of cats. We draw a circle and in the middle put the topic of the text. Since we are reading about cats, I'm going to put 'cat' in the middle of our circle. Now, I'm going to think about what I know about cats." Record the information and ask students to share information they know about cats as well. At this point you might ask pairs of students (depending on how much scaffolding you want) to work together to create a web of information about cats.

Guided practice

After recording this information, perhaps model how to group or categorize similar information. For example, group all information about characteristics, habits, or habitat together and model how to provide a superordinate label for this information. Pairs of students might try doing this with the information they recorded on their webs.

Explanation: declarative knowledge

Think Aloud

Modeling

Explain that once they have thought about and reviewed what they know about the topic, they might think about things they would like to find out about it—this is called "setting a purpose." Model and demonstrate how to quickly look at the pictures and the text of *Cats* and compare them to what they have recorded on their web for generating a purpose. "I know a lot about cats, but when I look at the pictures in this book, they make me wonder about how cats can jump so high. I also wonder why they sleep so much." As you model how to set purposes, record them on spokes of the web and explain to students that "as we read we might find information that matches what we already know, we might find information that is different than what we already know, and we might find new information. Our purposes serve as a guide for our reading so we know what we would like to find out." Have students think about what they might like to find out about cats, add spokes onto their webs, and record their purposes.

Explanation: declarative knowledge

Modeling

After preparing the web by noting known information about cats and things that students would like to find out about cats, model the thought processes that occur as you begin to read the text. You might use language like, "Hmmm, this says that cats _____. I already knew that. See, I have it on my web. I'm going to place a check beside that information on my web to show that what I already knew matched what the book says." As you read information that is consistent with the known information on

(cont.)

FIGURE 5.1. *(cont.)*

the web, place a check mark beside it to note congruence between prior knowledge and textual information. You might choose to use a different color marker once reading begins, so students can see the difference between information generated prior to reading and as a result of reading. As you encounter information that is new or that answers one of your purposes, add that information onto the web using the different colored marker. "Wow, the book says that cats _____. I didn't know that. That's something new that I learned. I'm going to add that onto my web." If information in the text conflicts with known information then you can place a question mark beside that information on the web and put a page number to indicate where the conflicting information was found. "Oh my, the book says _____. That is different from what I thought. I thought that cats _____. I'd better check on that information."

Guided practice

After reading several pages in this manner, begin to relinquish some of the responsibility to students. You might have pairs of students read the text together, and using a different colored marker, display how the textual information compares to the information contained on their webs. If students need more scaffolding, then you might read the text aloud one page at a time and ask them to look at their webs and update them based on the new information contained on each page. The goal, however, is to enable students to do this on their own, without such guided support.

Conclusion

Verbalization

Have students complete a self-assessment form. Then, after reading the entire text, engage students in a discussion in which they talk about how activating prior knowledge as they read helped them. Students can share information about how they used the strategies of previewing text, activating prior knowledge, and setting purposes while they read.

Assessment

- You will know whether students can identify and organize prior knowledge using a graphic organizer if they are able to add their prior knowledge onto the web initially, by their responses to questions 1–3 on the self-assessment, and by their concluding discussion.
- You will know whether students are able to organize new information from text using a graphic organizer if they are able to update their webs while reading, by their responses to question 4 on the self-assessment, and by their concluding discussion.

STUDENT SELF-ASSESSMENT OF STRATEGY USE

1. Thinking about what I already knew about cats was:
   very easy   easy   a little hard   very hard

2. Setting purposes before reading was:
   very easy   easy   a little hard   very hard

3. Putting my thoughts on a web was:
   very easy   easy   a little hard   very hard

FIGURE 5.1. *(cont.)*

4. Adding onto my web while I read was:

    very easy   easy   a little hard   very hard

5. Thinking about what I already know before reading

_____

_____

_____

FIGURE 5.1. *(cont.)*

fered in each lesson. In this sample lesson the portions in which the teacher was modeling occur at point 4 in Table 5.2. That is, the teacher was reading the text aloud to the students and engaging in a think aloud of the strategic processes she was using. During the guided practice portion of the lesson, the students were paired to read the text (i.e., shared reading) as they used the strategy. The guided practice portion of the lesson is located at point 26 in the table. The distance between points 4 and 26 represents a fairly large "jump" in terms of the level of scaffolded support provided between instruction and

TABLE 5.2. Scaffolded Instructional Support for Strategic Processing

		Amount of Scaffolded Support from Text						
		More Support Concrete (semiotic) ←				→	Less Support Abstract (linguistic)	
		Events/ Experiences (enactive)	Movies/ Videos	Wordless Picture Books	Read Alouds	Shared Reading	Picture Books	Texts (symbolic)
Amount of Support from Others — More ↑ Less ↓	Teacher/ Whole Class	1	2	3	4	5	6	7
	Small Group	8	9	10	11	12	13	14
	Trios	15	16	17	18	19	20	21
	Pairs	22	23	24	25	26	27	28
	Individual	29	30	31	32	33	34	35

guided practice. Some students may need more scaffolded support during guided practice. Careful analysis of each student's assessments (i.e., completed graphic organizers, completed self-assessments, and responses during discussion) will determine whether students require more or less scaffolding during future instruction.

Angela introduced her student to a semantic web as a means of organizing this information. The K-W-L organizer depicted in Figure 4.6 is another tool that many teachers and students find useful. The key is to teach students how to use and enact the strategy. The type of graphic organizer used is unimportant. Students should be encouraged to use whatever means best suit them. Some students find that simply making a list is sufficient and prefer not to use graphic organizers at all. Many students find completing such organizers burdensome, even though they enhance comprehension. As Angela reflected on her lesson, she noted:

> When I explained to her [the student] that it might be helpful if she sketched her own organizer each and every time she began reading a new text until she was used to organizing knowledge mentally, she gave me a shocked look and said, "EVERY TIME???" I explained that she didn't *have* to do it every time, but that practicing it with fun reading like *Cats* or her books at home will help her know how to do it when it will be especially useful, such as when she needs to read for science or social studies.
>
> [Angela Bies, reflective memo, March 23, 2000]

When other teachers taught similar lessons they found that their students also benefited considerably. Eileen Ludwig taught her student how to activate prior knowledge, set purposes, and use the K-W-L chart as an organizer. She noted:

> In previous lessons, I had a hard time knowing whether [the student] was using her own prior knowledge in order to help her understand. After showing [the student] pictures of animals, talking about different animals, and previewing the text, [the student] seemed to be able to talk a lot more about what she already knew about animals. She even talked about some of her own experiences that related to animals. . . . Since [the student] rarely talks about her own experiences, I was thrilled when she started telling me everything she already knew about animals and how it related to her own life. After our classroom discussion I thought of several more ways in which I could have helped [the student] activate her prior knowledge. If I had more time I would have also used a video, a computer program, or other visual aids dealing with animals. Since [the student] seems to be a very visual person, I think that this would have helped her understand the text even more. . . . I feel that [the student] definitely benefited from using the K-W-L chart. I feel that writing down everything she knew allowed her to see how much she did actually know. When I asked her about everything she knew she responded, "I don't really know that much." In reality she did know quite a bit about polar bears—the animal she chose to read about. She was actually able to see this by looking at the chart.
>
> [Eileen Ludwig, reflective memo, March 29, 2000]

Setting Purposes

Good readers are aware of their purposes for reading and use them while reading to guide, monitor, and evaluate their progress (Blanton, Wood, & Moorman, 1990; Garner

& Reis, 1981). The purpose, or plan, a reader has for reading focuses their attention while reading and guides the selection of textual information to retain in memory. As readers process text, their purposes for reading (1) determine what they will recall, (2) influence their interpretation of text, and (3) provide readers with a plan for reading and sense of security as to where they are going (Anderson et al., 1983; Anderson, Blanton, et al., 1990).

In their now classic study, Anderson and colleagues (1983) asked high school sophomores and juniors to take the perspective of either a home buyer or a burglar while reading a passage about what two boys did at one of the boy's homes while skipping school. Their findings suggested that the perspective taken selectively influenced the type of information recalled from the text. The implication for instruction is that teaching students how to set sound purposes while reading will enhance their recall and retrieval of textual information.

Rowe and Rayford (1987) found that (1) purposes serve as cues for activating relevant background knowledge to make predictions about passage content, and (2) purposes that focus on familiar topics evoke more elaborated schemata. Without solid purposes in mind, students may have difficulty activating and selecting appropriate schemata. Classroom teachers often either set purposes for their students or assign reading without encouraging students to set their own purposes. Blanton and colleagues (1990) suggested that teacher-directed purposes are often superficial and aimed at having students locate and recall literal information. Poorly defined purposes can misdirect students by leading them away from information that would help them develop a deep understanding of the text. Purposes also can be either too narrow or too broad in scope. Overly narrow purposes are too specific (e.g., "Read to find out what the main character did after breakfast"). Overly broad purposes do not pique or sustain interest throughout the duration of the reading event (e.g., "Read to find out what the story is about").

Generally readers set purposes that serve to update or enhance their knowledge about a topic, to confirm or disconfirm predictions, to learn about the structure of the text, or to perform a task (Blanton et al., 1990). Strategy instruction must focus on teaching students how to generate meaningful purposes that are motivating for them. This instruction also must include explanation of the declarative, procedural, and conditional knowledge associated with setting purposes (see Table 5.1). Figure 5.2 displays a sample lesson in which students learn how to set purposes. The explicit instruction portions of the lesson would be located at point 2 of Table 5.2: In terms of the amount of scaffolded support provided, the instruction occurs with the teacher and whole class as they watch a video. Guided practice occurring with pairs of students as they watch the video would be located at point 23.

Note that the lesson began by using an analogy to connect the process of setting purposes while reading to something with which students would be familiar—grocery shopping. Such analogies help reduce processing and create a safe environment by linking an unfamiliar process to a more familiar process. This analogy works because it shows that, just as different people have different reasons for going to a store, different readers have different reasons for reading. Likewise the link to shopping is helpful in that, just as shoppers often make lists to help them remember their reasons for going to the store, so can readers make a "list" of reasons, or purposes, that describe what they would like to find out.

Teacher: Adapted from a lesson by Eileen Ludwig.

Topic: Activating prior knowledge and setting purposes for read-
                ing.

Grade level: Can be adapted to any grade

STAIRS hypothesis being addressed:

                Students use background knowledge at times to help them
                understand text, but they require a great deal of modeling,
                guided practice, and reinforcement. Students are unable to
                set purposes for reading to enhance comprehension.

Goal of Lesson

Students will learn to:
- Preview text in order to help activate prior knowledge
- Set purposes for reading

Materials

- Informational video related to a topic being studied in social studies or
  science
- Multiple informational texts related to similar social studies or science
  topic
- K-W-L chart
- Student self-assessment sheets

Introduction

Reduce processing demands by relating strategy to concrete task

Begin by having students share reasons for going grocery shopping. Draw
a web on the board to record students' ideas. Explain that grocery stores
are full of all kinds of items and that when people go to grocery stores,
they go for many different reasons. Use the list the students generated to
reiterate some of the different items people might buy at a grocery store.
Explain that when we go grocery shopping, we have a "purpose" or a reason for going. We might have to buy meat products or dairy products or
snacks. Each person that enters the store will have different things to purchase. Explain that it is often helpful when we go grocery shopping to
make a list of the items we would like to purchase so we do not forget
anything.

Explanation: declarative knowledge

Explain that reading is similar to going shopping in that when we read, we
should have a reason, or purpose for reading. Just like when we shop, our
purpose may be different from someone else's purpose. Explain that we
might read to learn new information or to learn how to do something.
Explain that just as it is helpful to make a list for shopping, it is also helpful to jot down purposes for reading so we do not forget why we are reading. Setting purposes helps guide our reading so we do not get "lost" amid
all of the information in the text. Explain that in this lesson, we are going
to learn how to set purposes while we read.

Description of Instructional Experience

Explain that we are going to learn how to set purposes first by watching a
video and afterward we will use the same process while we read.

FIGURE 5.2. Sample lesson teaching students how to set purposes for reading.

Reduce processing demands by using semiotic text (video)

Model/ think aloud

Explanation: declarative knowledge

Explain that before we read or watch a television program we usually have a reason for doing so. We select what we watch or read based on what interests us. Explain that we are going to watch a video about _____ (whatever science or social studies topic is being studied). Model and demonstrate how to preview the video before watching it. You might engage in a think aloud of the thought processes that occur to you as you glance at the title and the pictures on the front of the case and as you read the text on the back of the case. During the think aloud note that when previewing the text it is important to preview the video (or book) before watching it because it will give you an idea of what it is about. Explain that when previewing it is helpful to look for clues that might give an indication of what the video (or book) is about. "As I look at the front I notice the title. This gives me an idea that it might be about _____. I also see pictures of _____. The title and pictures make me think that this video is going to be about _____. Does anyone notice anything else about the front cover that might give us ideas of what it might be about?" Have students share what they notice and what they think the video will be about.

Model/ think aloud

Remind students that in addition to previewing text before reading (or viewing) it is also important to think about what you already know about the subject to get your mind ready. "Remember that before we read or watch anything it is always a good idea to think about what we already know about the subject. I'm going to use the "K" column of a K-W-L chart to record everything I know about _____. First I'm going to think about what I know and then I'm going to list it in the "K" column." Engage in a think aloud as you share information that you know about the topic.

Guided practice

After modeling students can then pair with one another to share other information they know about the topic and record that information on a K-W-L chart. For increased scaffolding students can jointly record their information in "K" column of one chart rather than each having to complete their own.

Explanation: declarative and conditional knowledge

Explain that, just like when we go shopping, when we read or view a video we should also have reasons for reading/viewing. This helps guide our reading/viewing and helps us remember the information. Explain that this is called "setting a purpose" for reading or viewing.

Modeling

Explanation: procedural knowledge

Explain how to set a purpose by modeling. "Purposes are our reasons for reading or watching a video. When I set purposes I start by looking at the title and pictures as I already did. This gives me an idea of what the book or the video will be about. So, after looking at the cover of this video I think this video is going to be about _____. As I looked at the cover I then thought about what I already know about the subject and recorded it on my K-W-L chart. This will help me make connections as I watch the video. Now that I have made some guesses about what the video will be about and have thought about what I already know about the subject I

(cont.)

FIGURE 5.2. *(cont.)*

Explanation: conditional knowledge

can begin to think about what I would like to learn or find out as I watch the video. This will help me think about and remember the new information as I watch." Then begin to generate some questions about the subject or issues that you are wondering about. Demonstrate how to record your purposes in the "W" column of the K-W-L chart. Explain that the "W" column is kind of like a "shopping list." Just like in a grocery store a shopping list helps us remember what to buy, the "W" column of the K-W-L chart helps us remember what to look for as we read or watch a video.

Guided practice

Verbalization

With their partners have students think about what they might like to find out as they watch the video and record that information in the "W" columns of their charts. After recording this information, have students share the procedures they used to set purposes. This provides students with the opportunity to see how others accomplished the same task but perhaps used a different procedure.

Model/ think aloud

Explain that you are now ready to begin viewing the video and that it is important to keep your purposes in mind as you watch. Begin watching the video. As you come to places in which your background knowledge was affirmed then stop the video and model your thought processes. "Wow, I'm going to stop the video here for a moment because I just realized that they are talking about the same thing that I wrote in the "K" column of my chart. I really do understand that information. I'm going to place a check beside that information just so I can tell that what I knew was similar to what the video said." Continue watching the video and stopping at various places in which your prior knowledge was affirmed, purposes were answered, or new information was learned. Each time stop briefly, engage in a think aloud and then jot the relevant information on the K-W-L chart. When purposes are answered record the relevant information beside the purpose in the "W" column. There may also be times when you think of new purposes to add to the "W" column. Be sure to model how to generate and add new purposes as they occur to you. New information that is learned that is not related to a purpose can be recorded in the "L" column.

Guided practice

Encourage students to record similar information on their charts. It might be helpful to ask them to raise their hands to stop the video as they notice information that either affirms prior knowledge, answers a purpose, or is new information. Although this process is time consuming it will provide students with a supportive environment in which to learn the strategy.

Verbalization

After viewing portions of the video, the whole class, or small groups of peers, can engage in a discussion in which they discuss how the information in the video compared to the prior knowledge recorded in the "K" column, whether the purposes recorded in the "W" column were answered, and any new information that was learned that was recorded in the "L" column.

FIGURE 5.2. *(cont.)*

Verbalization

Transfer to new contexts

Conclusion

Have students complete a student self-assessment form and then use that information to engage them in a discussion of their experiences with setting purposes in this lesson. Be sure to have students explain what purposes are, how to set them, and why it is important to set purposes.

Explain that the same process of setting purposes that was used to watch a video is also helpful to do as we read books. Display the other books on the topic being studied and explain that sometimes some of our purposes are not answered by one source of information. It is the same as going to a grocery store for a particular item and finding out that they do not have it. You have to go to another store to find it. It is the same with reading. Sometimes we can't get all the information we'd like to get from one video or one book. We have to look at other sources. Explain that in the next lesson we will use these other sources to help us find information to answer those purposes that were not answered by the video we watched today.

Assessment

- You will know that students can preview text in order to help activate prior knowledge by looking at the "K" column of their K-W-L charts, their self-assessments, and their comments during discussion.
- You will know that students can set purposes for reading by looking at the "W" column of their K-W-L charts, their self-assessments, and their discussion.

STUDENT SELF-ASSESSMENT

1. Thinking about what I know before watching the video _____

_____

2. Setting purposes before watching the video _____

_____

FIGURE 5.2. *(cont.)*

Eileen Ludwig, the student who designed the lesson on which this sample is based, found that her student had difficulty noticing whether her purposes were answered:

> When comparing what she learned to questions that she wanted to learn, [the student] did seem to have difficulty. For instance, some of her questions were answered, but she said that they weren't answered. When we looked at our chart again I had to help her realize that she did answer some of the questions.
>
> [Eileen Ludwig, reflective memo, March 29, 2000]

During Eileen's initial lesson, she waited for a postreading discussion to identify and record the information that was learned. For this reason the sample lesson was altered from the original to include the component in which the teacher modeled how to stop the video and place checks beside information from prior knowledge that was affirmed while watching the video, how to record answers to purposes as the information was learned, and how to add new information to the "L" column *as* it was being learned rather than waiting until afterward. Although this procedure inevitably lengthens the lesson, the discourse and thought processes that are shared are invaluable. Such discourse enables students to see that setting purposes is an ongoing process in which initial purposes are set, information is encountered that answers those purposes, and then new purposes are set.

Generating, Verifying, and Updating Predictions

Good readers are able to generate predictions on their own and monitor those predictions for accuracy as they read (Brown, 1980; Collins et al., 1980; Palincsar & Brown, 1984). They use prior knowledge of the content of the text, the structure of the text, and the textual cues to generate predictions and construct meaning (Afflerbach, 1990). Prior knowledge enables them to select relevant cues from the text, which, in combination, helps them generate textually appropriate predictions.

As noted in Table 5.1, readers make predictions using any type of text, and they do so continually while reading. Predicting helps focus our attention while reading and gives us a purpose for reading. Thus prediction is intimately linked to each of the other text anticipation strategies. Our procedural knowledge about the process of prediction directs us to sample, or preview, the text to gain cues. As we sample the text, our background knowledge is activated and, ideally, we make linkages between that background knowledge and the cues in the text to generate textually appropriate predictions.

Younger and less proficient readers are often unable to generate textually appropriate predictions. At times their predictions seem to be "off the wall" or have nothing to do with the text. One teacher, Chastity Flynn, noticed this problem with one of her first graders:

> I had difficulty in the beginning because some of her predictions were off the wall. When I began probing to find out how she was thinking, it suddenly hit me that she did not fully understand the process of predicting. [The student] seemed to think that you could say whatever you wanted because there would be no penalty. So I explained that she was right, but we still want to make sure we look for clues from the title and illustrations.
>
> [Chastity Flynn, reflective memo, March 7, 2000]

Irrelevant or off-the-wall predictions usually occur when readers do not use the cues in the text to guide the prediction process but rely solely on their background knowledge to generate predictions. As with any other strategy, explicit instruction focused on prediction must communicate the associated declarative, procedural, and conditional knowledge. However, additional challenges occur in that competent prediction requires all of the text anticipation strategies and clues from the text. Thus instruction must be aimed at teaching students how to recognize and use cues from text to generate, verify, and revise their predictions.

As simple as generating predictions may seem, many readers of all ages and abilities are surprisingly unfamiliar with the process. One teacher, Jill Hatfield, noted this problem after teaching a lesson on prediction to a struggling fifth-grade reader. Although her lesson was on prediction, it was geared at a less concrete level (point 7 in Table 5.2). Jill thought that because the student was in fifth grade, she would already be somewhat familiar with prediction:

> One problem that I ran into in this lesson was assuming that [the student] had a lot of the background knowledge about what a prediction is. . . . I assumed that she knew or had some prior experience with predictions. Apparently this is not the case. When I asked her what a prediction was she said, "I don't know." I asked her what she thought it might be, and she remained quiet. I then gave her an example, and we talked about it. This lesson taught me to be more prepared when dealing with my student. I assumed that she had more background information [about predicting] than she did. Because of this I had to adjust my lesson by adding support for her so she could understand and take part in what we were going to do.
>
> [Jill Hatfield, reflective memo, May, 2000]

After this lesson Jill adjusted her future plans by making the concept of prediction more concrete. She used games (such as Clue) and jigsaw puzzles to explain and model the prediction process used while reading. She transferred these notions to linguistic text later in the same lesson. These lessons were much more successful in that they taught her student the process of how to predict without the processing demands (and frustration) that often accompany reading:

> For most of my lessons on prediction I have been trying to explain to [the student] that prediction is like making a guess by using the clues that you see or read about in the story. When I told her that we were going to be playing a game for today's lesson, she laughed and seemed to visually relax. She loves to play games, and as we played I had her talk about what she was thinking as she guessed who she thought did it. When I was trying to think of what "common things" I could use in my lessons with [the student to make prediction less abstract], it never occurred to me to think outside the idea of books. I felt like if I just found the right book to use with her, that she would "get" prediction. Instead it was a simple board game that made her understand the idea of gathering clues and thinking about what might happen.
>
> [Jill Hatfield, reflective memo, May, 2000]

The key to Jill's lesson was her ability to transfer the concrete process of predicting while playing Clue or building a puzzle to the reading process. Simply playing games and building puzzles without all of the metacognitive verbalization and thinking aloud that she included would not have yielded the same successful results. Her lessons were tailored in the same way as any other explicit instruction lesson, except that her "text" was not a book but a board game. Such lessons provide the most amount of scaffolded support and are located at point 1 of Table 5.2. An example of a similarly concrete lesson is displayed in Figure 5.3.

In this lesson Eileen used an overnight bag as her "text" to introduce the concept of prediction. In this manner she was able to teach her students the declarative, procedural, and conditional knowledge associated with prediction, free of the cognitive burden of having to make predictions while decoding the text. She then transferred the same process to authentic text; however, she continued to provide a highly scaffolded environment

Teacher: Eileen Ludwig

Topic: Generating predictions while reading

Grade level: 2–4

STAIRS hypothesis being addressed:

Students are unaware of strategies that can facilitate their comprehension and recall of text.

Goal of Lesson

Students will learn to:
- Make appropriate predictions while reading
- Indicate the evidence used to make predictions
- Monitor their predictions as they read

Materials
- *Ira Sleeps Over* by Bernard Waber
- Overnight bag filled with various items needed for a sleep over (e.g., toothbrush, pajamas, blanket, teddy bear)
- Chart with 3 columns (What I Predict, Clues I used to Make Predictions, What Happened)
- Writing supplies
- Response journal

Introduction

Explanation: declarative knowledge

Begin lesson by telling students that there are certain things that readers can do to help them understand a story. One of these things is making predictions. Predictions are guesses about what you think will happen in the story. Explain that today you will be learning how to make predictions while reading.

Procedural knowledge

Explain that you can use the evidence, or clues, in the story and your background knowledge to help make predictions.

Conditional knowledge

Explain that people make predictions before reading and while reading a story. Making predictions can help you understand text because it gives you a reason to keep reading. You read on to find out if your prediction is correct or incorrect. You can also change your predictions as you begin to read and gather more clues.

Reduce processing demands by using concrete "text"

Verbalization

Display the overnight bag filled with items that someone might take to a sleepover. Keep the bag shut and ask students to carefully observe the bag and, using their prior knowledge, think about what this type of bag might be used for. As students share their predictions record them in the "What I Predict" column of the prediction chart. Be sure to have students share the clues and background knowledge they used to generate each prediction. These clues should be recorded in the "Clues I used to Make Predictions" column of the chart.

FIGURE 5.3. Sample lesson teaching students how to predict using a concrete event.

Verbalization

After making predictions with the bag shut reach in and pull out one item. Have students carefully observe this "clue" and think about whether the clue supports any of their predictions. Have students share their thinking aloud either with a partner or with the whole class about how they arrived at their prediction so that everyone can hear the strategic processing being used to observe the clue, link it to relevant background knowledge, and decide whether it supports or refutes predictions. Ask students whether they would like to change their predictions based on this first clue. Be sure to explain that it is always okay to change your predictions based on the evidence. This is a sign of a good reader. Continue taking out one item at a time and engaging students in a discussion in which they observe the clue, link it to relevant background knowledge, and decide whether their prediction is supported or refuted.

Declarative Knowledge

Procedural knowledge

Declarative knowledge

At the conclusion of the activity reiterate the process used to make predictions: observe clues, think about what you know about such evidence, make a link between the clues and your background knowledge, and make a prediction. Be sure to also emphasize that when you are predicting there are no right or wrong answers. Predictions are good guesses based on the evidence and information you already know about.

Description of Instructional Experience

Explain that you are going to use this prediction process as you read the book *Ira Sleeps Over* by Bernard Waber. Introduce the book by showing the cover and reading the title. Explain to students that, just like making predictions with the overnight bag, when you read books you look for "clues." But the clues in a book are available by looking at the title, the pictures, and the words.

Explanation: declarative/ procedural knowledge

Modeling/ think aloud

Model how to make predictions by looking at the cover and the title. You might say something like, "When I read the title it makes me think this story may be about someone who sleeps over somewhere. I don't know anyone named Ira but that maybe that is the name of the boy in the picture on the cover. It looks like he really likes that green blanket." After predicting explain how you came to those predictions. "I think it is about a boy named Ira who sleeps over somewhere based on the clues I gathered from the title. I thought he probably liked that green blanket because in the picture he is wrapped in it." Write your prediction in the "What I Predict" column of your chart and write the clues that helped you make that prediction in the "Clues I use to Make Predictions" column.

Verbalization

Have students observe the title and pictures more closely and generate ideas about what they think will happen. Be sure to elicit language in which students have the opportunity to share how they arrived at the predictions they made. Depending on the level of scaffolded support required you may either record students' predictions and clues on a class chart, or students may work in pairs to share their predictions and clues with one another and record them on a chart.

(cont.)

FIGURE 5.3. *(cont.)*

Explanation: *procedural* *knowledge* *Conditional* *knowledge*	Explain that we will be able to check to see how accurate our predictions are as we read the story. Emphasize that there are several ways to gather clues to make predictions: what we read, the pictures, and what we already know about something. Reiterate that it is important to make predictions and check them while reading because it helps us understand and remember better. Also, we may find more clues in one part of the story than in another part. Therefore, sometimes we can alter our predictions to make better ones based on the new clues.
Modeling/ *think aloud* *Conditional* *knowledge*	Read the first three pages or so of the story aloud to the students. Stop and model your thought processes as you encounter information that either confirms or rejects your initial predictions. Also stop and model your thought processes as you encounter information that enables you to make new predictions about what will happen next. Be sure to share not only your predictions but also how you arrived at those predictions (i.e., what textual evidence and background knowledge helped you make that prediction). List your predictions and clues on the chart.
Guided *practice and* *Verbalization*	After modeling and thinking aloud have students share with a partner any predictions they may have and the clues that helped them arrive at that prediction. Students can record their predictions and evidence on their charts.
Modeling *Guided* *practice* *Declarative* *knowledge*	Continue on in this manner throughout the text reading aloud a few pages at a time and stopping at various points to model your own thought processes and then handing the same task over to each pair of students. As information is encountered that confirms, rejects, or causes you to alter your prediction be sure to stop and record the outcome in the "What Happened" column of the chart. If student predictions are not confirmed be sure to emphasize that predictions are good guesses based on what we already know and any other evidence we gather. They are not always "correct" and that is okay.
Verbalization	*Conclusion* Once story is finished engage students in a discussion in which they talk about how their predictions measured up to what actually occurred in the text. Have students share different ways in which they predicted and how the text influenced their predictions. Have students write a journal entry in which they explain their thoughts about the prediction process and how it affected their understanding of the story. *Assessment* • You will know whether students can make appropriate predictions while reading by their contributions to discussion and the information recorded in the "What I Predict" column • You will know whether students can indicate what evidence they used to make predictions by their contributions to the discussion and the information recorded in the "Clues I Used to Make Predictions Column."

FIGURE 5.3. *(cont.)*

- You will know whether students are able to monitor their predictions as they read by their contributions to discussion and the information recorded in the "What Happened" column.

Prediction Chart		
What I Predict	Clues I Used to Make Prediction	What Happened

FIGURE 5.3. *(cont.)*

in which she read the text to the students so that they could focus their cognitive efforts on using the pictures and words to make textually appropriate predictions and monitor their prediction process. The degree of movement related to scaffolded support was very slight in her lesson. She began the lesson at point 1 in Table 5.2, with the overnight bag as text, and moved to point 4 when she read *Ira Sleeps Over* (Waber, 1975) to the students. This highly scaffolded environment enabled students to experience success in a safe environment. Other teachers have found that using videos, movies, or sitcoms as "text" (point 2 in Table 5.2) and wordless picture books, such as Tomie DePaola's *Pancakes for Breakfast* (1978) (point 3 in Table 5.2), provide an equally safe and risk-free environment for students to generate and monitor their predictions.

Learning how to generate predictions is clearly important; however, without the ability to monitor whether one's predictions are confirmed or disconfirmed, students are left without the tools to become active readers. This aspect of prediction is really more of a comprehension monitoring strategy (i.e., a text maintenance strategy that facilitates schema maintenance). However, it is included in this section because it is inherently linked to the generation of predictions. One way to help students learn how to monitor their predictions in a concrete manner is to engage them in an activity that integrates elements inherent to Vocabulary–Language Prediction Activities (VLP) (Wood & Robinson, 1983) and story grammar instruction (i.e., setting, character, problem, solution) (Whaley,

1984). By combining these two activities, students not only prelearn vocabulary and predict story events, but they also use the organizational scheme of a story map (see Figures 4.9 and 4.10) to guide, structure, and monitor their predictions (King, 1990). The process is similar to that used in Directed Reading-Thinking Activities (DR-TA) (Stauffer, 1969). Students are encouraged to use the clues from the text to generate predictions prior to reading and then read to confirm or revise those predictions. The distinction is that predictions in the VLP/story grammar activity are initially based on vocabulary, include a great deal of language surrounding strategy use, and are organized by using a story map.

Teachers prepare for this activity by choosing a narrative story with a well-defined and explicit story grammar. In the lesson displayed in Figure 5.4, Stephen Mooser's (1978) *The Ghost with the Halloween Hiccups* is used because it contains a clearly identified problem (Mr. Penny has hiccups), explicit attempts to solve the problem, and a clear solution. Students will need to be familiar with story grammar elements to engage in this lesson. Providing story grammar instruction while trying to teach students how to predict may place an unnecessary cognitive burden on them.

Next, it is important to study the text to determine which words are important to understanding the text and which words may cause students difficulty. In the lesson displayed in Figure 5.4, 15 words were selected. Most of these words (12) would be familiar to the second-grade students for whom the lesson was planned. These 12 words provide clues to help students make predictions prior to reading. Three words with which students might be unfamiliar were included (*mayor, worried, hiccups*) to prepare them for encountering them while reading. The majority of words selected should (1) be within students' spoken, listening, and reading vocabularies, and (2) provide clues to story grammar elements. Figure 5.4's lesson would be located at points 6 (demonstration phase) and 27 (guided practice phase) of Table 5.2.

This lesson displays the type of scaffolding that facilitates successful initial attempts at using prediction while reading independently from linguistic text. Students of all ages and abilities have found the VLP/story map activity highly motivating and are eager to read to determine the accuracy of their initial predictions. This activity also provides a visual means of assessing a covert thought process—that of monitoring and updating predictions while reading. Normally this process occurs without any evidence. However, manipulating the word cards and making photocopies of the story map's evolution throughout the reading process provides a tangible means of assessing students' abilities to monitor and update their predictions. The manipulatives also serve as a concrete reminder to students that their predictions can (and should) be altered as warranted by text. This approach is particularly helpful for readers who tend to overrely on background knowledge or who have difficulty focusing their attention on meaning while reading. One teacher, Jaime Quackenbush, noted that teaching prediction served this exact purpose for her student:

> Using the strategy of prediction helped [the student] to become more involved in what he was reading. It was not difficult for him, and it made the reading task more meaningful. I could easily observe his prior knowledge, interest, and experiences at work as he suggested all kinds of possible scenarios and outcomes. He took the strategy and elaborated on everything we read, making me think that this was *really* something he might use in other reading situations. For the first time since I began working with him, [the student] seemed to be really actively reading. He frequently

Teacher: Janice F. Almasi

Topic: Generating predictions while reading

Grade level: 1–3

STAIRS hypothesis being addressed:

> Students are unaware of strategies that can facilitate their comprehension and recall of text. Students do not read for meaning or monitor comprehension.

Goal of Lesson

Students will learn to:

- Use new and target vocabulary to make relevant predictions about the setting, characters, problems, attempts to solve problems, and resolution of a story
- Indicate the evidence used to make predictions
- Monitor their predictions as they read

Materials

- *The Ghost with the Halloween Hiccups* by Stephen Mooser
- Blank story maps (see Figure 4.10)
- Packets of miniature vocabulary word cards
- Large vocabulary word cards with the following words on them: (*Bert, ghost, Halloween, hiccups, hopping, Laura, major, Mr. Penny, play, scare, sing, tickle, town, water, worried*)
- Chart paper and markers

Introduction

Explanation: declarative knowledge

Begin lesson by telling students that there are certain strategies readers can use to help them understand a story. One of these strategies is making predictions. Predictions are guesses about what you think will happen in the story. Explain that today we will be learning how to make predictions while reading.

Conditional knowledge

Explain that people make predictions before reading and while reading a story. Making predictions can help you understand text because it gives you a reason to keep reading. You read on to find out if your prediction is correct or incorrect. You can also change your predictions as you begin to read and gather more clues.

Procedural knowledge

Explain that you can use the evidence, or clues, in the story and your background knowledge to help make predictions. Today we are going to use some of the words in the story and our understanding of how stories are organized to help us make good predictions.

Description of Instructional Experience

Declarative knowledge

Explain that just as the title, pictures, chapter titles, and headings are clues that help us make predictions, the words in the text help us also.

(cont.)

FIGURE 5.4. Sample lesson teaching students how to predict using a picture book.

Vocabulary development

Conditional knowledge

Display the 15 large word cards on the board. Explain that you have selected 15 words from the story to help us make predictions about what might happen. Discuss the words in a rich, semantic context. Since the word "hiccups" is central to the story you might begin by drawing a web on the board and placing the word "hiccups" in the center. Explain that it is always a good idea to think about what we already know about the topic of a story before reading and that the story we are going to read today is about "hiccups." Have students brainstorm what they know about hiccups and record their ideas on the web. Have students look for ways in which this information might be grouped together. That is, look for superordinate categories such as: description, causes of hiccups, or cures for hiccups. Once background knowledge for hiccups has been activated explain that by talking about "hiccups" this helps us get ready to read the story.

Vocabulary development

Try to make connections between some of the other 14 words and "hiccups." For example, you might ask students to think about whether you might be "worried" if you had the hiccups. Have students discuss with a partner what it means to be worried and why they would/would not be worried if they had hiccups. Then have a brief whole group discussion of the issue. Other questions to elicit semantic development of concepts might include, "Could a *mayor* get the hiccups? Why or why not?" "Would you be *scared* if you had the hiccups? Why or why not?" "What would happen if you *tickled* someone who had the hiccups?" Each question should foster conversation about, and foster connections between, concepts. This might also be a time to highlight any structural aspects of the words such as the endings on *worried* and *hopping* or any other word recognition strategy that would benefit students prior to reading.

Declarative knowledge

Explain that now that we have seen some clues from the story we can begin to think about those clues and make predictions. Explain that we are going to use a story map as a way of organizing our predictions. Briefly review story grammar elements (i.e., setting, characters, problem, attempts to solve the problem, and solution). Prior to embarking on this lesson students should already be familiar with these elements otherwise the lesson may require too much explicit instruction and place students in a position in which they are cognitively overloaded.

Model/ think aloud

Select a word and model how you would make a prediction about where that word might belong on a story map. "I see the word *town*. I know that a town is like a small city. It's a place. Based on this clue and what I already know about towns, I think that maybe the setting of the story might be a town. I'm going to place my word card under the 'setting' column of my story map. Is there any other place that *town* might fit?" Encourage students to think divergently and consider that it is possible, for example, that the town might be the problem in the story. Be sure to encourage students to share the thinking they used to arrive at a particular prediction and why they think it is legitimate based on the clues and

FIGURE 5.4. *(cont.)*

Verbalization

*Model/
think aloud*

*Procedural
knowledge*

their prior knowledge. You might also have students look to see if there are other words that might be a clue about the setting of the story. Model and demonstrate your thinking with another word or so. Explain that we are going to use these words clues and our background knowledge to help us predict where the words might belong on a story map.

Once you are certain that students understand how to make predictions using the word cards, their prior knowledge, and the story map, pass out packets of miniature word cards and blank story maps. Have students work in pairs to make predictions about where the words might belong on the story map. Encourage students to talk to one another and verbalize their reasons for placing words in certain columns. As students work together listen carefully to their discussions and take anecdotal notes. It is important that the word cards are not glued onto the story maps. Instead students might gently tape each word to the story map. This will permit students to physically manipulate the word cards later as they read the story and gather further clues that will enable them to update, revise, and alter their predictions.

*Guided
practice*

Verbalization

After students have placed all of the words on their story maps, engage them in a whole class discussion. The discussion can focus on where various pairs of students placed cards and why they placed them as they did. The discussion should foster the notions that predictions can vary from individual to individual and that there are multiple ways to make predictions. You might have one pair of students come to the board, select a word, read it aloud, place it on the story map where they predict it belongs, and then explain why they placed it there. Follow up by asking whether any pairs placed the same word in a different column and have them explain why they placed it as such.

Assessment

Often this portion of the lesson is sufficient for one day's lesson. At this point pairs of students might use their story maps to write a "prediction story" in which they communicate their version of the story before reading Stephen Mooser's version. Pairs of students can then compare their versions with one another. For assessment purposes it is helpful to make a duplicate copy of the students' completed story maps and prediction stories at this point to show what their initial predictions were. This can be compared to their story map versions at later points as they update and revise their predictions based on textual information.

Before beginning to read the story have students review their story maps. Introduce the story by displaying the book, *The Ghost with the Halloween Hiccups*. Explain that now we finally know the title of the story. This is an additional clue that can help us predict. Often at this point students show outward displays that they are monitoring their predictions. They either begin to move their word cards or begin to discuss with their partner. Capitalize on these moments by encouraging students to share their strategic thinking. "I notice that you are moving your word cards. This is wonderful.

(cont.)

FIGURE 5.4. *(cont.)*

<table>
<tr><td>

Explanation:
declarative and
conditional
knowledge

</td><td>

This is exactly what good readers do when they read. They make predictions and as they gather new clues they sometimes have to change or alter their predictions. What did this new clue tell you? What kind of adjustments are you making to your story map predictions? Why?" Encourage students to verbalize their reasons for making changes or for keeping their predictions the same. If students do not begin to make adjustments on their own model and engage in a think aloud of your own.

</td></tr>
<tr><td>

Modeling/
think aloud

</td><td></td></tr>
<tr><td>

Declarative
knowledge

</td><td>

Remind students that it is always a good idea to set purposes before reading. Setting purposes helps focus our thinking as we read. At this point students should be primed to read the story and should be anxious to find out what happens. Students usually have little difficulty generating relevant purposes at this point. Have students record their purposes on their story maps.

</td></tr>
<tr><td>

Guided
practice

Assessment

</td><td>

Have students share some of their purposes and remind them that as they read they should look for clues that might either confirm their story map predictions or cause them to have to change their story map predictions. Encourage students to talk with their partners about these clues as they read. Ask students to begin reading to page 5 of the text. As students read, walk among them and take anecdotal notes to determine whether are able to use the clues in the text to update and revise predictions when necessary. After reading the first 5 pages, engage students in a brief discussion that focuses on the clues in the text and how those clues either confirmed their predictions or caused them to alter their story maps. Reiterate that this is what good readers do as they read. They continually monitor and update their predictions.

Have students continue to read further in the story and engage in the recursive process of setting purposes, making new predictions, gathering textual clues, and altering story maps based on the new information. Engage students in a discussion of such processes after completing the story.

Conclusion

Have students complete a student self-assessment in which they respond to the open-ended statements such as, "The word cards _____," "The story map _____," and "My predictions _____."

Engage students in a follow-up discussion in which they share how using the word cards and the story map affected their ability to make predictions. Have students share different ways in which they were able to make predictions and whether making the predictions helped them as they read.

Assessment
• You will know that students are able to use new and target vocabulary to make relevant predictions about the setting, characters, problems, attempts to solve problems, and resolution of a story by their contributions

</td></tr>
</table>

FIGURE 5.4. *(cont.)*

to discussion and by photocopying their initial story maps.
- You will know that students can indicate the evidence used to make predictions by their contributions to class discussion and their discourse with
  their partner.
- You will know whether students can monitor their predictions as they read
  by comparing the location of the word cards on their initial story maps to
  the position of the word cards while reading.

FIGURE 5.4. *(cont.)*

interrupted the reading at points I hadn't intended to stop, saying things such as,
"Maybe he's going to . . . " or "I think I know what's going to happen."

[Jaime Quackenbush, reflective memo, March, 2000]

Identifying Text Structure

Text structure refers to the manner in which ideas in a text are interrelated to communicate a message to the reader (Meyer & Rice, 1984). These structures specify the logical
connections among ideas as well as the subordination of some ideas to others. Just as
readers have schemata for general world knowledge and content knowledge, they also
have textual schemata (Anderson et al., 1977). Textual schemata are mental representations of the ways authors organize different types of text. Text generally has either a narrative or an expository structure. Narrative text is often referred to as "stories" or "fiction." Text that has an expository structure is informational in nature. Students of
varying ages are able to distinguish how both genres are organized and are able to use
these structures as they read, retell, and write (Langer, 1985).

Narrative text structure has a relatively predictable pattern, or story grammar, that
readers can sense and use to comprehend the material while reading (Mandler & Johnson, 1977; Stein & Glenn, 1979). Stories generally consist of a beginning in which the
protagonist is introduced in a setting, followed by an initiating event to which the protagonist responds by establishing a problem or goal; the protagonist then attempts to
achieve the goal, which ultimately brings the series of events to an end (Mandler & Johnson, 1977; Stein & Glenn, 1979). Having a schema for narrative structure directs attention to particular aspects of incoming information, helps readers keep track of what they
have read, and indicates when a given part of a story is complete or incomplete so that it
can be stored or held until more material is encountered (Mandler & Johnson, 1977).
Learning about narrative structure enhances students' memory and recall of text (Short
& Ryan, 1984) and helps them organize and write stories (Fitzgerald & Teasley, 1986).
Like instruction in story grammar, story maps (see Figures 4.9 and 4.10) are teaching
tools to help readers develop a sense of story and to assist retrieval and retention of information. Research has shown that when proficient and less proficient readers are taught to
record story grammar elements on a story map while reading, their comprehension is enhanced (Idol, 1987; Idol & Croll, 1987). Good strategy users are not only adept at using
their prior knowledge of content, but also at using their understanding of the way text is
organized to help them understand what they are reading.

The instructional implications are straightforward. Students need to learn how to
recognize narrative text structure and use this knowledge strategically to facilitate com-

prehension. Story grammar can also be used to assist students when writing narrative texts. When teaching about story grammar, use terms young readers can understand. For example, rather than using the terms "initiating event" and "protagonist," use words and phrases such as *setting, characters, problems, goals, attempts to solve,* and *solution.* Story grammar can be simplified even further for emergent readers, as in the story map depicted in Figure 4.9. Story maps used as a graphic organizer should be employed either *before* reading, to enhance students' ability to predict and set purposes for reading, or *while* reading, to be applied as a cognitive tool that focuses attention and enhances ability to monitor incoming information and compare it to earlier predictions (see the lesson in Figure 5.4).

Unfortunately, in practice many teachers use story maps *after* reading. This use serves only to *assess* students' memory and recall of text. It in no way facilitates strategic processing of text. In the lesson described in Figure 5.5, the teacher, Jaime Quackenbush, teaches her third grader to identify and use story grammar elements to enhance comprehension and recall of narrative text. She begins the lesson by making an analogy between the necessary ingredients for making a pizza and the necessary ingredients authors use to make a story. In this manner Jaime tried to make the notion of text structure more tangible for her student, so he would be able to relate to it better. Other teachers have used the analogy of road maps to help students relate to the concept of story maps. Jaime designed her lesson as a read aloud so that her student could focus all of his cognitive resources on identifying and using story grammar elements to help him understand the text. The lesson was also conducted in a teacher/whole class environment. Her lesson would be located at point 4 of Table 5.2.

There are many similarities between Jaime's lesson and the VLP/story map activity lesson depicted in Figure 5.4. The critical difference is that Jaime's lesson is focused primarily on identifying the structure of the text, whereas the previous lesson was focused more on teaching students to generate, revise, and update predictions. Both lessons incorporate similar strategies because the strategies are not easily disentangled during the fluid process that characterizes authentic reading. The difference is in a matter of emphasis. The teacher focuses more of her explicit instruction and explanation (i.e., declarative, procedural, and conditional knowledge) on identifying story grammar elements in the lesson in Figure 5.5, whereas instruction is focused on prediction in Figure 5.4.

Jaime found that her student was actively engaged and responded well to her lesson:

> I definitely think that knowing the story elements helped [the student] to monitor his reading. Throughout the book we read . . . [the student] was very conscious of the story elements. He acknowledged and considered the different story parts without my prompting; it was an intentional (strategic) thought on his part. He was very much able to complete a story map on his own while listening [to the read aloud]. This helps him to focus on the various aspects of the story instead of breezing through it. [The student] needs a purpose for reading in order to bring meaning to the text. If he is unsure of the task, he tends to "word call" and understand [nearly] nothing.
>
> [Jaime Quackenbush, reflective memo, April, 8, 2000]

Providing instruction that helps readers recognize the underlying structure of narrative text while they read is a beneficial strategy for enhancing comprehension. Similar instruction is necessary to help students recognize expository text structure as well.

Teacher: Adapted from a lesson by Jaime Quackenbush

Topic: Identifying Narrative Text Structure

Grade level: 2–4

STAIRS hypothesis being addressed:

> Students have the ability to comprehend but do not bring meaning to the text unless engaged in a strategy that elicits active thinking while reading.

Goal of Lesson

Students will learn:

- That most stories have a similar structure
- Clues to help identify story grammar elements: setting, characters, goal/problem, action, and outcome

Materials

- *Sylvester and the Magic Pebble* by William Stieg
- Blank story maps (see Figure 4.10)
- Story Parts Chart (see Table 5.3, p. 139)
- Miniature vocabulary word cards with words from story that indicate story grammar elements
- Construction paper pizza parts (dough, sauce, cheese, toppings)
- Pictures of various settings and people

Introduction

Explanation: declarative knowledge

Explain that when people write or tell stories there are certain parts of the story that are almost always there. We need to have all of these parts in order to make a good story.

Reduce processing demands

Create an analogy between needing certain ingredients to make a pizza and needing certain ingredients to make a story. Explain that to create a pizza you need to have dough, sauce, cheese, and toppings. Explain that to create a story, you also need certain ingredients.

Conditional knowledge

Explain that in this lesson students are going to learn how to identify these story "ingredients" as they read. Explain that being able to identify story parts will help them to remember and understand what they read. Explain that any time they hear or read a fiction story, they should think about and look for these story parts.

Description of Instructional Experience

Explanation: declarative knowledge

Explain that to make a story you need to have a place where the story happens (the setting). Show several pictures of various settings and explain that the setting involves where the story happens and when it happens. Engage students in discussion of each setting and describe the location and time. During discussion co-construct the Story Parts Chart (see Table 5.3, p. 139) with students by filling in information that defines each element, provides clues to help identify each element in a story, and

(cont.)

FIGURE 5.5. Sample lesson teaching students how to identify narrative text structure.

Procedural and conditional knowledge

where to find such information in a story. Use the discussion with the pictures of the setting to elicit the information for the Story Parts Chart. Elicit information that explains that the setting can be determined by looking for clues such as the names of cities or countries, the places people go, time of day, year, and the seasons. Explain that usually the setting is established at the beginning of the story.

Declarative knowledge

Explain that there are also characters in stories. The characters are the people or animals who are in the story (add this onto Story Parts Chart). These characters are placed in the setting. Examine the pictures of characters and describe what types of traits these individuals might have. Engage students in a discussion about how various characters depicted in the pictures might act in a given setting. Explain that characters are recognized by looking for clues such as names, descriptions of people/animals, words such as boy/girl, ages of characters, and words that describe the way they think or act. Explain that characters are usually introduced at the beginning of the story.

Procedural and conditional knowledge

Declarative, procedural, and conditional knowledge

Explain that these characters always have a problem or a goal. Explain that it is found by looking for an important event that happens, or by looking for words that tell us something the character is trying to do or get. Explain that the problem or goal is usually presented in the beginning and continues through the middle of the story. Have students select a setting and a main character from the pictures. Engage students in a discussion about what types of problems or goals the character might face in the selected setting.

Declarative, procedural, and conditional knowledge

Explain that the next part of a story occurs as the main character tries to solve the problem or attain the goal. Explain that clues are found by looking for things the characters say or do as they try to solve their problem or attain their goal. Often characters have to try several different ways to solve a problem or attain their goal. Explain that these events usually happen in the middle of the story. Have students brainstorm various ways the character might go about solving the problem.

Declarative, procedural, and conditional knowledge

Explain that in the end the problem is either solved or unsolved, or the goal is either attained or not attained. Explain that clues indicate that the character either no longer has the problem or has accomplished what they were trying to do. Explain that the solution is almost always at the end of the story. Have students think about how the characters in the pictures might solve the problem in their story.

Conditional knowledge

Explain that it is often helpful to use a map when we listen or read stories to help us focus our attention on the story elements as we read. This helps us understand and remember the story better. Hand out blank story maps to the students. Reiterate each of the story grammar elements and remind students to refer to the Story Parts Chart to help them remember what each element is.

FIGURE 5.5. *(cont.)*

Explain that it is also helpful before we read to make predictions about what we think might happen. Engage students in a VLP/Story Map Activity (see Figure 5.4). Present miniature word cards containing words that indicate characters' names, important places, the problem, items and events that happen throughout the book *Sylvester and the Magic Pebble*. Explain that we are going to use these clue words from the text, and what we know about story elements, to make predictions about where the words might belong on our story map.

Model/ think loud

Verbalization

Select a word and model how you would make a prediction about where that word might belong on a story map. "I see the word *hill*. I know that a *hill* is a type of landform. It's a place. Based on this clue (refer to Story Parts Chart) and what I already know about *hills*, I think that the setting of the story might be on a *hill*. I'm going to place my word card under the 'setting' column of my story map. Is there any other place that *hill* might fit?" Encourage students to think divergently and consider that it is possible, "Could a *hill* be a character? Why or why not?" "Could a *hill* be a problem? Why or why not?" Be sure to encourage students to share the thinking they used to arrive at a particular prediction and why they think it is legitimate based on the clues and their prior knowledge. You might also have students look to see if there are other words that might be a clue about the setting of the story. Model and demonstrate your thinking with another word or so. Explain that we are going to use these words clues and our background knowledge to help us predict where the words might belong on a story map.

Model/ think aloud

Guided practice

Verbalization

Have students work in pairs to make predictions about where the words might belong on the story map. Encourage students to talk to one another and verbalize their reasons for placing words in certain columns. As students work together, listen carefully to their discussions and take anecdotal notes. It is important that the word cards are not glued onto the story maps. Instead students might gently tape each word to the story map. This will permit students to physically manipulate the word cards later as the story is read and gather further clues that will enable them to update, revise, and alter their predictions.

Verbalization

After students have placed all of the words on their story maps, engage them in a whole class discussion. The discussion can focus on where various pairs of students placed cards and why they placed them as they did. The discussion should focus on the clues students used to help them place the word cards and how they were able to make strategic placements.

Verbalization

Have one pair of students come to the board, select a word, read it aloud, place it on the story map where they predict it belongs, and then explain why they placed it there. Follow up by asking whether any pairs placed the same word in a different column and have them explain why they placed it as such.

(cont.)

FIGURE 5.5. *(cont.)*

*Create a
safe
environment*

After students have completed their story maps, introduce the story by displaying the book, *Sylvester and the Magic Pebble* by William Stieg. Explain that the title of the story provides an additional clue that can help us predict. Often at this point students show outward displays that they are monitoring their predictions. They either begin to move their word cards or begin to discuss with their partner. Capitalize on these moments by encouraging students to share their strategic thinking. "I notice that you are moving your word cards. This is wonderful. This is exactly what good readers do when they read. They make predictions, and as they gather new clues they sometimes have to change or alter their predictions. What did this new clue tell you? What kind of adjustments are you making to your story map predictions? Why?" Encourage students to verbalize their reasons for making changes or for keeping their predictions the same. If students do not begin to make adjustments on their own, model and engage in a think aloud of your own.

Verbalization

Model

*Explanation:
declarative
knowledge*

Remind students that it is always a good idea to set purposes before reading. Setting purposes helps focus our thinking as we read. Have students record their purposes on their story maps.

Verbalization

*Reduce
processing by
reading
aloud so
students can
focus on
using the
strategy*

Have students share some of their purposes and remind them that, as the text is read aloud, they should look for clues that helped them identify various story grammar parts. Encourage students to talk with their partners about these clues as they read. Begin reading the first few pages of the text aloud. Stop periodically and take anecdotal notes to determine whether they are able to use the clues in the text to update and revise predictions when necessary. After reading the first few pages engage students in a brief discussion that focuses on the clues in the text and how those clues helped them identify story grammar elements and what part of the story they heard them in. Refer to the Story Parts Chart, where appropriate, to reinforce and add to each column. Reiterate that this is what good readers do as they read. They use the clues in the text to help them identify story grammar elements.

Continue the read aloud stopping at various points in the story to engage in the recursive process of setting purposes, making new predictions, gathering textual clues, and altering story maps based on the new information. Engage students in a discussion of such processes after completing the story.

Conclusion

Bring out the paper pieces of the pizza again and reiterate that, just like a pizza is not really a pizza without all of its parts, neither is a story complete unless it has all of its parts. Reiterate each of the story grammar elements and engage students in a discussion in which they share ways in which using the story map helped them as they listened to the story and aspects that were difficult (or cumbersome) about the process.

FIGURE 5.5. *(cont.)*

Assessment

- You will know whether students know that most stories have a similar structure by their contributions to the discussion.
- You will know whether students can use clues to help them identify story grammar elements (setting, characters, goal/problem, events, and solution) by their ability to place the word cards in the appropriate column of the story map before reading, and by their ability to make appropriate adjustments while reading.

FIGURE 5.5. *(cont.)*

Meyer (1975) identified five types of logical relations that operate within expository texts: (1) description (attributes, explanations, definition/example), (2) collection (sequence, enumeration, time order), (3) comparison (similarity/difference), (4) antecedence–consequence (cause–effect relationships), and (5) response rhetorical (problem–solution, question–answer, remark–reply). Authors signal text structure in a variety of ways. One way is to use introductory headings sentences, or paragraphs to explicitly tell

TABLE 5.3. Story Parts Chart. Developed by Jaime Quackenbush, 2000

	Story Parts				
	Setting	Characters	Goal/Problem	Attempt to Attain Goal/ Solve Problem	Solution
What it means	The place and time in which the story occurs	People or animals who are in the story	• What the character(s) is trying to do or get • The problems the character(s) faces	What happens as the character(s) tries to reach the goal or solve the problem	• What happens in the end • How the goal is reached • How the problem is solved
Clues to look for	• Names of cities • Names of countries • Places characters go • Time of day • Year • Season	• Names • Descriptions • Ages • Boy/girl • Thoughts • Feelings • Actions	• An important event that affects the character(s) • What the character(s) wants to do (or has to do) about it	• The things that happen during the story • What the character(s) do/say	• The goal is attained • The problem is solved • The character(s) has done or gotten what he/she/it was trying to do/get
Where to find it	Beginning of story	Beginning of story	Beginning/ middle of story	Middle of story	End of story

the reader how the text is organized. Another way is to use explicit connectives that signal text structure via various semantic and syntactic means (e.g., cue words) that link two sentences. When authors use explicit connectives, the underlying text structure becomes more obvious to readers. Table 5.4 displays six types of connectives. Table 5.5 contains the five types of expository text structures, their associated cue words/connectives, and the graphic organizers that visually depict their underlying structure.

Englert and Hiebert (1984) found that collection text structures (i.e., sequence and time order) are the most obvious and well-defined for young readers to recognize; description and comparison text structures are the most difficult. To explain this difficulty, they hypothesized that, although many elementary school content-related textbooks contain extensive descriptive text, it often occurs in short segments within other structures. Rarely is descriptive text the single organizing framework for an entire text. Text structures embedded within one another make it difficult for readers of any age to easily identify and use the structure of the text to enhance their comprehension.

Text containing ample signals or cues about the underlying structure is said to be "reader friendly." Unfortunately, many authors do not use explicit text structure signals, and their writing is so poorly organized and incoherent that the text is "unfriendly" to readers. At times publishing companies exacerbate the problem. Although the limitations of readability formulas are well known (see Weaver & Kintsch, 1991), publishing companies often rely on them to determine the level at which text is written. Such formulas (e.g., Fry Readability) often use the number of syllables and sentences in 100-word passages taken from the beginning, middle, and end of a text to determine its readability. Texts that have a large number of syllables have higher readability levels, and texts that have fewer sentences have higher readability levels. A text that has many polysyllabic words and complex or compound sentence structures rather than simple sentence structures will have a higher readability. In general, readability levels for expository texts are often far above the grade level for which they are intended. Much of the language within expository text contains polysyllabic content-related words. Typically, these polysyllabic words are repeated over and over within a given passage, thereby artificially increasing its readability. For example, a text on democracy might use the word repeatedly within a 100-word passage. In a text teaching about democracy, the word *democracy* cannot easily be

TABLE 5.4. Types of Connectives

Type of Connective	Examples	Sample Sentence
Conjunctions	and, in addition to, also, along with	John went to the store. Sally went *also*.
Disjunctions	or, either _____ or _____, neither _____ nor _____	Either John went to the store, *or* he went home.
Causality	because, so, consequently	John went home *because* he was sick.
Concession (adversative)	but, although, however, yet	John left for home, *but* he hasn't arrived there yet.
Contrast	in contrast, similarly, as, like, on the other hand	John was very sick. *In contrast*, I feel fine.
Time (temporal)	before, after, when, always, while, from now on	*Before* John got sick he went to the store.

TABLE 5.5. Expository Text Structures. *Source:* **Tompkins and McGee (1993).**

Pattern	Description	Cue Words	Graphic Organizer
Description/ Definition/ Example	The author describes a topic by listing characteristics and features or giving examples.	*for example, characteristics are*	
Sequence/ Time Order	The author lists items or events in numerical or chronological order.	Time/temporal connectives: *first, second, third next, then, finally after, before, noon, midnight, when, always, and specific times of day*	first → next →
Comparison	The author explains how two or more things are alike and/or how they are different.	Contrast connectives: *different, in contrast, alike, same as, on the other hand*	
Cause–Effect	The author lists one or more causes and the resulting effect or effects.	Causality connectives: *reasons why, if . . . then, as a result, therefore, because, consequently, so*	Cause → Effect #1 / Effect #2 / Effect #3
Problem– Solution	The author states a problem and lists one or more solutions for the problem. A variation of this pattern is the question-and-answer format in which the author poses a question and then answers it.	Concession/adversative connectives: *but, although, however, yet, problem is/dilemma is/puzzle is solved, question posed and answered*	Problem → Solution

substituted. Hence editors seek other ways to reduce the readability. They often accomplish the task by simplifying complex sentences and eliminating polysyllabic words (such as connectives) that signal text structure. For example, in the text *Spiders Are Not Insects* by Allan Fowler (1996), the author compares arachnids and insects at the beginning of the text. However, there are no explicit comparison connectives to indicate this text structure:

> Spiders are not insects. They belong to a group of animals called arachnids. Arachnids have eight legs. Insects have only six. Arachnids do not have wings. Insects do. Spiders use hairs on their bodies to sense the world around them. Insects sense things with feelers, called antennae, that grow on their heads. (pp. 6–10)

To signal the comparison text structure more explicitly, the passage could be edited, as follows:

Many people think spiders are insects. *However,* they are not. They belong to a group of animals called arachnids. Spiders *differ* from insects in many ways. Spiders have eight legs, *whereas* insects have only six. Spiders do not have wings. *However,* insects do. Spiders use hairs on their bodies to sense the world around them. *In contrast,* insects sense things with feelers, called antennae, that grow on their heads.

The original text contained 52 words comprised of 73 syllables in nine sentences. The more "reader friendly" text contained 69 words comprised of 100 syllables across nine sentences. The revised text would have a higher readability level because it has more words and more syllables across the same number of sentences. However, it uses comparison connectives (e.g., *however, in contrast, differ, whereas*) to clearly indicate the manner in which the text is structured. Each connective is a polysyllabic word, adding 13 syllables to the text. The addition of the sentence "Spiders differ from insects in many ways" signals that a list of comparisons is forthcoming. Readers should almost be able to visualize a bulleted list of those differences. The original text required readers to infer the underlying text structure—a difficult task for the beginning readers for which this text was intended. Although the revised text would be easier for young readers because it signals the comparison text structure, publishing companies would not use it because the readability would be inflated by the additional numbers of words and syllables.

Schema selection–retrieval problems and schema maintenance problems are often caused by text that is incoherent, poorly organized, or unsignaled. These problems are further compounded in expository texts (i.e., any informational or nonfiction text) for several reasons. First, students are generally less familiar with the structure of expository text. Narrative is the primary genre to which children are exposed at home and at school. Before even arriving at school, children are often able to internalize the story grammar structure inherent to the narrative genre. Their internalized schema for narrative structure helps them anticipate textual events and enhances comprehension. Pappas (1991) identified three linguistic features of expository texts for children that differ from narrative texts. First, expository texts usually contain present-tense verbs, whereas narratives are primarily written in the past tense. Second, in narrative text characters are introduced in the beginning and referred to using various referents (e.g., *he, his, him*) throughout the text. This process is known as "co-reference." Although expository texts do not refer to an animal, place, or object throughout the entire text, the same *class* of animals, places, or objects is continually referred to using referents (e.g., *them, their*). This process is known as "co-classification." Thus the ways in which common aspects of the text are linked across the text differ. Finally, expository texts use relational processes to indicate text structure, whereas narrative text does not (e.g., *in contrast, however, consequently*).

These linguistic differences make reading expository text a very different experience. Lacking exposure to expository text structure from the time they are very young, children are at a disadvantage. Young students typically are not exposed to expository text until third or fourth grade, when they are reading more fluently. Many students who were previously reading adequately begin to falter with reading at this time. The increased amount of reading from unfamiliar expository text structures becomes overwhelming for these readers, and their comprehension suffers. Much of the early research on text structure found that older and more proficient readers were able to use their knowledge of text structure as an organizational strategy for encoding and storing information gleaned from text. Such knowledge of text structure helps readers better retrieve new information from memory (Englert, & Hiebert, 1984; Hiebert, Englert, & Brennan, 1983; Meyer, Brandt, & Bluth, 1980; Ohlhausen & Roller, 1988; Spivey & King, 1989; Taylor, 1980). In their review of research, Pearson and Fielding (1991) noted that nearly any form of instruction aimed at teaching students to recognize and use text structure (e.g., visual representations of text structure, networking, flowcharting, conceptual frames, mapping, graphic organizers, hierarchical summaries) enhances comprehension and short- and long-term memory of text.

Students are so unfamiliar with expository text structure that any type of instruction will help. For decades researchers have implored classroom teachers to include more expository text in their instruction from kindergarten on; nevertheless, expository text is still a rarity in elementary classrooms. Teachers may ask students to complete a graphic organizer after they read, but such tasks are merely assessment activities unless they are accompanied by the explicit instruction that enables readers to understand and recognize the underlying structure of the text *while* they are reading. The sample lesson depicted in Figure 5.6 teaches students how to recognize comparison text structure. Such instruction provides natural links to writing as well. If students are able to recognize how authors structure text, they can use similar structures to organize their own writing. Armbruster, Anderson, and Ostertag (1987, 1989) suggested that sound instruction about expository text structure should teach students (1) to use format cues such as cue words, headings, subheadings, and paragraphs; (2) to make concrete visual representations of how ideas are organized; (3) common text structures; and (4) how to write using these structures. Each of these elements, in addition to those of the Strategy Instruction Model, is present in the lesson in Figure 5.6.

This lengthy comparison lesson might take place over the course of two days. The notion of comparison is initially made using a concrete means. Comparing diagrams of how grocery stores and department stores are organized provided a way of teaching students how to look for similarity and difference in a semiotic text. Comparing two tangible objects is also a way of achieving the same concrete experience (point 1 of Table 5.2). The notion of stores and the way they are organized was appealing because of the link that could be made to studying the way various text structures are organized.

Armbruster and colleagues (1987, 1989) suggested that sound text structure instruction should teach students how to record information by using a concrete visual representation of the underlying structure. In this lesson the T-chart was used; however, many teachers often find the overlapping circles of the Venn diagram (depicted in Table 5.5) helpful. Young students often find it difficult to understand the notion of similarity that is represented by the overlapping portions of the circles; when permitted to design their own comparison organizers, they often prefer to simply use the T-chart. Cue words were emphasized by highlighting those in the text *Frogs and Toads* (Kalman & Everts, 1994) and by using cue words in the comparison text that was composed. In this way readers were able to understand how authors construct texts by examining published text, and by creating their own. This dual learning exercise emphasizes the connections between reading and writing.

Many teachers have found it difficult to incorporate authentic expository text into their classrooms. This may be because good literature in this genre has not been readily available. However, since the 1990s publishers have been producing a wealth of good, visually stimulating expository text. The additional time it takes to identify and find such

Teacher: Adapted from a lesson by Mike Rock

Topic: Identifying Comparison/Contrast Text Structure

Grade level: 1–3 (for higher grades use age-appropriate texts)

STAIRS hypothesis being addressed:

> Students are unaware of strategies for identifying expository text structures. Their focus of attention wanes while reading exposition, and they have difficulty recalling what was read.

Goal of Lesson

Students will learn:

- To identify comparison text structure
- To compose comparison text structure
- That awareness of text structure can enhance comprehension

Materials

- *Frog and Toad Are Friends* by Arnold Lobel
- *Frogs and Toads* by Bobbie Kalman and Tammy Everts
- Copies of the store directory for a grocery store
- Copies of the store directory for a department store
- Shopping bags from grocery store/department store
- Word cards containing the phrases (*different, on the other hand, in contrast, unlike, similar, same as, alike, both*)
- Chart paper and markers

Introduction

Reduce processing demands by using maps as text

The lesson will begin by creating an analogy between the manner in which stores are organized and the manner in which texts are organized. Display shopping bags from two different stores (one from a grocery store and one from a department store). Explain that in this lesson, we are going to be thinking about how things are the same and different. "First we are going to think about and describe the types of items we might buy at a grocery store." Draw a T-chart on the board and record students' ideas as they brainstorm things to purchase at a grocery store. Have students think about what type of label this superordinate category might have. Then display the shopping bag from the department store. On the other side of the T-chart, record the information students brainstorm about the types of things they might buy at a department store and label the superordinate category. Explain that although you can buy things at both stores, the types of things within each store are quite different.

Description of Instructional Experience

Explanation: declarative knowledge

Explain that this is similar to when we read books. There are different types of books, and each type of book contains different information. Some tell stories and some tell information.

Explain that stores are also organized in different ways. Pass out copies of the directory for the grocery store. Have students work in pairs or small

FIGURE 5.6. Sample lesson teaching students how to identify expository text structure.

Reduce processing demands by working in small groups

groups to study the directory and describe the way the store is organized. Have students brainstorm why the store is organized as it is. Have students record the organizational features on the directory and the reasons why they are organized in that manner. After students have finished have them share their observations and reasons. Record students' ideas on the T-chart on the board.

Follow the same procedure for the directory of the department store. If you do not have a directory for one of the stores, have students draw their own. In this manner you are engaging them in the process of constructing a visual representation of how a store is organized. This same process can be transferred to text by having students draw their own representations of how texts are organized rather than having them use a pre-made graphic organizer. After students have identified how the department store is organized, engage them in a discussion in which they consider the notion of why it might be important to know how different stores are organized. Gather student responses, leading them toward the conditional knowledge that knowing how a store is organized helps us navigate through the store more easily than if they were to wander around the store aimlessly.

Explanation: conditional knowledge

Explain that just like stores are organized in different ways, so too are the texts we read. Grocery stores are organized in a manner that enables you to move quickly up and down aisles as you gather needed food items. Department stores are organized in a different way. They are organized in clusters that permit you to browse, and lead you from one department to the next. Explain that stores are organized in different ways depending on what they sell and what their purpose is. Texts are also organized in different ways depending on their purpose. Some texts tell a *story*. Display the *Frog and Toad Are Friends* book. Explain that these texts have settings, characters, problems, and solutions. If students are already familiar with these story grammar elements make that link. Explain that other texts tell *information*. Display the book *Frogs and Toads*. They are arranged in a completely different way. Explain that there are 5 different ways that authors organize texts to tell you information. Knowing how an author organizes a text helps you know what kind of information to expect, and that will help you remember what you read better. Explain that today we are learning about one of the ways authors organize information—by comparison. Explain that the information in the book *Frogs and Toads* tells how frogs and toads are the same and different.

Explanation: declarative knowledge

Procedural knowledge

One effective technique is to gradually create the chart depicted in Table 5.5 over the course of the year as different text structures are studied. The information in each cell can be added as students learn about it. For example, as you explain what comparison text is, add that information into the "Description" column of the chart so students can refer to it. As you introduce, or as students encounter, various cue words that indicate comparison, add them to the chart as well. Students can also add in various ways of organizing comparison information under the "graphic organizer" column.

(cont.)

FIGURE 5.6. *(cont.)*

Explanation: declarative knowledge

Procedural knowledge

Define comparison text as text in which the author explains how two or more things are alike and/or different. Add this description to the chart. Begin by asking the students to think about how they might go about comparing the two stores. "What would you do to see how the stores are the same and different from one another?" Record students' responses on chart paper. Generally the procedural steps for comparing include some variation of: (1) Observe both objects. (2) Describe the characteristics of each, (3) Carefully study the descriptions and think about how they the same, (4) Organize the similar ideas, (5) Carefully study the descriptions and think about how they are different, (6) Organize the different ideas. These steps might be written on sentence strips so they can be kept, or transferred onto the class chart of expository text structures (Table 5.5).

Model/ think aloud

Guided practice

Model and think aloud about how you might identify similarities between the two stores by looking at the lists of information gathered on each web. You might circle information on each web that is similar. Your discourse might sound something like, "Hmmm, as I look at the T-chart I notice that in both stores we can buy things. That is a similarity. I'm going to circle that on both webs." Have students work with a partner to identify other similarities and share with the larger group. Follow the same procedure to identify differences.

Model/ think Aloud

Reduce processing demands

Model/ think Aloud

Guided practice

Explain that we have now compared the two different types of stores. If we were authors, and we wanted to explain how the stores were the same and different, we could use the notes on our T-charts to help us write about those similarities and differences. Explain that before we write we are going to see how Bobbie Kalman and Tammy Everts organized their writing when they compared *Frogs and Toads*. Explain that as students listen to the text they should make a T-chart and label one side "frogs" and the other "toads." Model using chart paper. Begin reading the first paragraph from p. 7, "Frogs and toads look similar, but they are different in some ways." Engage in a think aloud, "That is a good introductory sentence. It lets me know that the authors are going to tell me how frogs and toads are similar and different. I expect they will tell me about this in the next few sentences." Continue reading, "A frog has smooth, moist skin . . ." Model how to take notes on the "frog" side of the T-chart, "They are telling me that frogs have smooth moist skin. I don't need to write that exact sentence. I'll just write *smooth, moist skin* under the 'frog' column." Continue modeling in this manner for several sentences, gradually scaffolding the responsibility to students by asking them to discuss with their partners what they should record in their charts and then sharing that with the whole group. Use this process while reading pp. 7-8 aloud.

Verbalization

After taking the notes on the T-chart, examine the structure used by the authors to create the text. It might be helpful to have a transparency copy of both pages so that cue words can be circled. Engage students in a discussion about what the authors did well to signal the comparison text structure and what they would change or alter to make the information even more clear to readers.

FIGURE 5.6. (*cont.*)

*Model/
think aloud*

Explain that students are now going to think about how they might organize this information about the two different stores to communicate it to others. You might model how to write a paragraph describing the similarities. "First let's think about words we might use to show how two things are the same." Have students brainstorm for cue words (e.g., *same, like, as, similar, both, alike*). As student generate words create word cards. Begin modeling the writing process. "Just like Bobbie Kalman and Tammy Everts did, it's always good for writers to let their audience know what they are writing about. So, I'm going to begin by letting my readers know that I'm going to be telling them about how the stores are similar. I guess I could say something like, *Grocery stores and department stores are alike in many ways.* Then I can list the circled items from the T-charts to show how they are similar to one another." Record your topic sentence on chart paper. Use the *alike* word card so students can easily see where the cue words are used. "I see on the web that you can buy things in both stores. So that will be one of the ways they are the same. It says, *Grocery stores and department stores are alike in many ways.* I want to add another sentence that tells one way in which they are the same. I could say, *You can buy things in both stores.* I am using the cue word *both* there, so as I write I'll put that word card in." Continue in this manner until the similarity paragraph is written. Students may be able to work in pairs to construct the remaining sentences.

*Guided
practice*

After modeling, ask students to work in pairs to write a paragraph that describes how the two stores are different. Have students share their paragraphs with one another and explain how they went about writing them.

Conclusion

Students write a self-assessment reflection in their journals with the sentence starter, "Comparison texts _____" and "Using the T-chart _____." After students complete their self-assessment, engage in a whole class discussion of how to recognize comparison texts and why it is important to be able to do so.

Assessment

- You will know that students are able to identify comparison text structure by observing the manner in which they complete their T-charts while listening to the *Frogs and Toads* text.
- You will know that students are able to compose comparison text structure by the structure of the "difference" paragraphs they write with their partners.
- You will know that students are aware that text structure can enhance comprehension by their contributions to the concluding discussion.

(cont.)

FIGURE 5.6. *(cont.)*

SAMPLE T-CHART	
Grocery Stores	Department Stores

FIGURE 5.6. *(cont.)*

texts is also cumbersome. Table 5.6 identifies expository texts that the teachers in the University at Buffalo School-Based Practicum have found useful. The text structures that appear within each, the type of cue words, and any signaling devices (i.e., table of contents, index, headings) are also identified.

Text Maintenance Strategies

Text maintenance strategies include (1) creating mental images, (2) monitoring comprehension by questioning oneself, (3) identifying text structure, and (4) updating and revising predictions. Like text anticipation strategies, good readers use these strategies flexibly and in combination with one another. As noted in Chapter 4, these strategies help readers avert schema maintenance difficulties. The key benefit of these strategies is their ability to help focus students' attention while reading. Monitoring is the critical factor in the reading process. If readers are unable, or unwilling, to monitor the incoming information and evaluate whether it matches their mental image, supports or refutes a prediction, provides information about a purpose, or looks like the type of information they would expect to see in a particular genre, then they will not be able to maintain focused attention, and their comprehension will be affected.

Good readers use several strategies while reading to make sure their attention is focused on meaning construction. When the text is particularly image-laden, good readers often visualize it. They update and revise these mental images, as warranted by the text. Good readers are also able to monitor their understanding throughout the entire reading process. When they notice their comprehension is failing they enact a fix-up strategy to repair their understanding. As mentioned in the previous section, good readers use their textual schema to identify the way in which the text is structured. In addition to fostering schema selection and retrieval, this strategy facilitates schema maintenance as well. Readers use the structure of the text as a guide for anticipating and recording upcoming information as they read. When readers are able to organize and store incoming informa-

TABLE 5.6. Sample Texts That Exhibit Clear Expository Text Structures

Expository Text Structure Type	Sample Texts
Description/ Definition/ Example	Implicit Cues and Signaling Arnosky, J. (1996). *All about deer.* New York: Scholastic. [Uses descriptive text and labeled illustrations to describe deer and their habitat] Asch, F. (1995). *Water.* New York: Harcourt. [Beautiful illustrations and descriptive text describe water] DePaola, T. (1975). *The cloud book.* New York: Holiday House. [Includes index, descriptive text, and some explicit definitions to describe types of clouds] Dussling, J. (1998). *Bugs! Bugs! Bugs!* New York: Scholastic. [Uses descriptive text and vivid photographs to describe insects for elementary readers] Fowler, A. (1995). *The best way to see a shark.* Chicago: Children's Press. [Includes index and descriptive text to describe shark life for young readers] Maynard, C. (1994). *Incredible dinosaurs.* New York: Snapshot. [Includes table of contents, index, and descriptive text to describe dinosaurs]
Sequence/ Time Order	Explicit Cues and Signaling Aliki. (1992). *Milk: From cow to carton.* New York: HarperCollins. [Uses cue words (e.g., spring, summer, winter, later, then, after) to indicate passage of time and explain how milk is produced from field to farm to dairy] Gibbons, G. (1999). *The pumpkin book.* New York: Holiday House. [Uses temporal cue words (e.g., spring, fall, after, when) to explain how pumpkins grow] Gibbons, G. (1991). *From seed to plant.* New York: Holiday House. [Uses descriptive text and temporal cue words (e.g., before, then, when, later) to explain how plants grow.] Jordan, H. J. (1992). *How a seed grows.* New York: HarperCollins. [Uses temporal cue words (e.g., now, after, soon) to indicate time order structure] Kalman, B., & Langille, J. (1998). *What is a life cycle?* New York: Crabtree. [Includes table of contents and index. Uses steps of a cycle that are explicitly numbered to explain various life cycles] Showers, S. (2001). *What happens to a hamburger.* New York: HarperCollins
Comparison	Explicit Cues and Signaling Kalman, B., Everts, Y. (1994). *Frogs and toads.* New York: Crabtree. [Includes table of contents, index, uses comparison cue words] Implicit Cues and Signaling Fowler, A. (1996). *Gator or croc?* New York: Children's Press. [Includes descriptive text, but primarily comparison text that describes the difference between alligators and crocodiles. Explicit cueing of the comparison structure is not apparent]
Cause–Effect	Explicit Cues and Signaling Berger, M. (1983). *Why I cough, sneeze, shiver, hiccup, and yawn.* New York: Thomas Y. Crowell. [Uses question/answer format and descriptive text to explain common reflex actions of the body] Gallant, R. A. (2001). *Rocks.* New York: Marshall Canvendish. [Includes descriptive and cause-effect text structures. Explicit descriptive and causality connectives are used to explain types of rocks and how they were formed] Gibbons, G. (1995). *Planet earth/inside out.* New York: Mulberry. [Includes descriptive, cause-effect, and time/order structures. Explicit causality connectives are used to indicate cause-effect structure]

(cont.)

TABLE 5.6. *(cont.)*

Expository Text Structure Type	Sample Texts
Problem–Solution	**Explicit Cues and Signaling**
	Berger, M., & Berger, S. (1999). *Why do flies walk upside down? Questions and answers about insects*. New York: Scholastic. [Includes table of contents, index, and uses question/answer format to explain various questions about insects]
	Prager, E. J. (2000). *Sand*. Washington D.C.: National Geographic Society. [Uses question/ answer format to describe sand]
	Whitfield, P. (1989). *Can the whales be saved? Questions about the natural world and the threats to its survival answered by the Natural History Museum*. New York: Viking. [Uses question/ answer format to explain questions about the living world]
Mixed	**Explicit Cues and Signaling**
	Gibbons, G. (1995). *Sea turtles*. New York: Holiday House. [Includes descriptive text and sequence text that uses explicit temporal connectives. Also includes a diagram comparing sea turtles and regular turtles]
	Kalman, B. (1997). *How a plant grows*. New York Crabtree. [Includes table of contents; index; and uses descriptive (pp. 4-7), sequence (pp. 8-11), cause-effect (pp. 13-27) text structures to explain how plants grow]
	Lauber, P. (1995). *Who eats what? Food chains and food webs*. New York: HarperCollins [Includes some descriptive text, mostly cause-effect structure with some explicit causality cue words, authors also use adversative cue words that gives the impression of problem/solution structure]
	Zoehfeld, K. W. (1995). *How mountains are made*. New York: HarperCollins. [Includes some descriptive text, mostly cause-effect structure with explicit causality cue words]
	Implicit Cues and Signaling
	Branley, F. M. (1988). *Tornado alert*. New York: HarperCollins. [Includes implicit descriptive, problem/solution, and sequence text structures that are implicit.]
	Fowler, A. (1996). *Spiders are not insects*. New York: Children's Press. [Primarily descriptive structure except pp. 6-10 which are comparison; includes index]

tion, memory and recall of text are facilitated. Like identifying text structure, updating and revising their predictions while reading helps students anticipate and focus their attention on the incoming information.

Making Mental Images

In their review of salient comprehension strategies, Pressley, Johnson, et al. (1989) identified mental imagery as a strategy that is easy to teach. They distinguished between two types of imagery: representational and mnemonic. *Representational images* represent and depict the content of the text. That is, readers create pictures of the author's words in their minds as they read. Gambrell's research (e.g., Gambrell & Bales, 1986; Gambrell & Jawitz, 1993) showed that comprehension is enhanced when students are taught to create mental images while reading. Gambrell and Bales (1986) taught fourth- and fifth-grade poor readers to induce mental images as they read. They found that students who were taught to form images as they read were able to identify textual inconsistencies better than their untrained peers. These results suggest that imagery fosters the ability to monitor comprehension while reading that is essential for schema maintenance. Sadoski's work (e.g., Sadoski, 1983, 1985; Sadoski, Goetz, & Kangiser, 1988) examined the impact of imagery and affect on recall. His findings suggest that all three variables are interrelated. That is, when readers have an enjoyable experience with the text, they image more, which affects the amount they are able to recall. Sadoski's findings support Paivio's (1986) dual-coding theory, which contends that "there is a parallel, nonverbal dimension to discourse processing which can be analyzed, and which contributes to the overall comprehension, integration, and appreciation of text" (Sadoski et al., 1988, p. 335).

Mnemonic images help readers learn and remember information about unfamiliar concepts. This form of imagery is often used while studying. Readers impose an artificial image onto the textual information to enable them to recall it. Pressley, Johnson, et al. (1989) use an example in which a reader, trying to remember the major exports of a particular country, might create an image of an individual trying to sell particular products in that country. This image is not in the text, nor is it suggested by the text. The reader imposes the image to help him remember the information contained in the text. Pressley, Johnson, et al. (1989) suggested that, although the research on mnemonic imagery has shown that its use produces significant gains in recall, the research has not been clear regarding whether readers are able to apply the strategy on their own, without mnemonic cues provided by researchers.

As shown in Table 5.1, good readers use imagery as a strategy to enhance comprehension with nearly any type of text (see column 4). Most narrative text contains a great deal of descriptive language that evokes sensory images of the setting and representational images of the characters and their actions. Many expository texts, particularly descriptive/definition/example text, contain similar features that evoke strong images.

The lesson in Figure 5.7 teaches students how to generate representational images as they read. Note that the teacher, Eileen Ludwig, has chosen to begin this lesson by using concrete text (listening to an audiotape) (point 2 of Table 5.2) to facilitate transfer and reduce processing demands.

During this lesson Eileen provided a great deal of modeling and thought aloud about the procedures she used to create mental images. She also provided opportunity for students to try out the process for themselves as they listened to her read the text. In this manner she reduced processing and created a safe environment for students to experiment with a new strategy. They were able to focus all of their cognitive resources on using the strategy. She also provided ample opportunity for students to sketch and share their images and describe the procedures they used to create images. In her reflective memo, Eileen noted how well the concrete text she used to begin the lesson helped her student:

When reading this text [the student] was able to use her own prior knowledge and her senses in order to form images and to understand what she read. Instead of jumping right into written text we started the lesson off by listening to nature sounds. As we listened to these sounds we tried to create pictures in our heads and tell what we were seeing. I also believe using a more concrete experience helped [the student] to learn this strategy. After our classroom discussions I realize the importance [of] starting lessons off with concrete events or experiences. . . . I believe this is

Teacher: Eileen Ludwig

Topic: Creating mental images while reading

Grade level: 1–4

STAIRS hypothesis being addressed:

        Students use some comprehension strategies (e.g., activating prior knowledge, generating predictions) when prompted to do so. However, they do not use other strategies to enhance comprehension.

Goal of Lesson

Students will learn:

- To use the author's language, prior knowledge, and senses to make mental images and increase comprehension of text
- Why it is important to make mental images while reading

Materials

- *Owl Moon* by Jane Yolen
- Tape player
- Tape of outdoor sounds including bird and animal sounds
- Modeling clay
- Drawing paper

Introduction

Explanation: declarative, procedural, conditional knowledge

The lesson will begin by explaining to students that when we read we can make images in our heads. We can use the author's words, what we already know, and our senses to make these images. Just as we use the illustrator's pictures to help us understand what we are reading, we can make our own pictures to help us understand. Good readers paint pictures in their minds as they read to understand what the author is saying. When we read we can think about what we may see, hear, smell, feel, or taste.

Reduce processing demands

Have students close their eyes and listen to a tape of different nature and bird sounds. Ask students to listen very carefully and try to think about what the sounds remind them of. Ask students to try and make pictures in their minds about what they "see" as they listen to the tape.

Verbalization

After playing a portion of the tape have students draw or depict what they imagined or pictured in their minds as they listened. Then have students share what they imaged with a partner and how they were able to arrive at that image. Engage class in a whole class discussion of these same topics focusing on the procedural knowledge of *how* students created their mental images.

Share the image that you pictured in your mind as you listened to the tape.

Modeling/ think aloud

Explain how you got your images by thinking aloud, "On the one part of the tape I could hear the birds chirping and the leaves on the tree rust-

FIGURE 5.7. Sample lesson teaching students to use mental imagery.

ling. So, I saw birds and a lot of trees in my mind. I also thought that it might be a spring day because the music was very happy and the birds chirped happily. There usually seems to be a lot of birds chirping outside my house during spring. That's why I thought it might be spring. I used my prior knowledge and a few clues from the tape."

Declarative knowledge

Conditional knowledge

Explain that this was the way that *you* pictured the sounds on the tape. Although everyone listened to the same tape, everyone has slightly different images because we all have different background experiences. When we make images while we read we become more involved in the text and it helps us remember what we read. Emphasize that there is no right or wrong way to make mental images.

Description of Instructional Experience

Conditional knowledge

After introducing the text *Owl Moon* by Jane Yolen activate prior knowledge, make predictions, and set purposes for reading. Explain that this is a text that is well suited for making mental images because the author uses lots of descriptive language that helps us get a good picture in our minds. Explain that some parts of the text may be easier to make images with than others. Further explain that some stories are better for making images than others because some authors use lots of descriptive language and others use less. Explain that these images help a reader activate their prior knowledge in order to understand text. Refer back to the introductory activity to remind students of how we were able to create images based on the sounds we heard.

Reduce processing demands

Model/ think aloud

Model how to use imagery by thinking aloud as you begin to read *Owl Moon* aloud. For example, one part of the text reads, "Then we came to a clearing in the dark woods. The moon was high above us. It seemed to fit exactly over the center of the clearing and the snow below it was whiter than the milk in a bowl of cereal." After reading engage in a think aloud that might go something like, "I picture in my mind a large area that is covered by a lot of newly fallen snow. I also see some light coming off the snow from the reflection of the moon. I picture a very open area in the middle of a forest at night. I picture that it is very cold outside." Explain how you arrived at such images as well. "The author said the snow was whiter than milk in a cereal bowl. I could really picture that in my mind. I think that it might have just fallen or that no other people or animals might have been around because we live in an area where it snows, and I know that the snow does not stay white unless it is very new or nothing else is around to make it dirty. I also know that it is night time because the moon comes out at night. I think it might be giving off a reflection because the author says it seems to fit perfectly over the center of the clearing. I also picture that it is a very cold area because I know that it gets very cold out when it snows." Explain how you are able to use the author's words, your own prior knowledge, and some of your senses to make those images in your mind. Explain that these images help you understand what is happening in the story and help you remember because it is easier to remember a picture.

Procedural knowledge

Procedural knowledge

Conditional knowledge

(cont.)

FIGURE 5.7. *(cont.)*

Model/
Think Aloud

Guided
practice

Verbalization

Continue to model and think aloud as you read more of the story aloud. Stop at those places where you naturally image and be sure to communicate what you are imaging and how you were able to create that image. Gradually relinquish the responsibility for imaging to the students. After modeling in several places, ask students to share their images with a partner and how they arrived at their images, or have some students share their images and how they arrived at them with the whole group. Another option is to have students quickly sketch their images as you are reading. Have students share their images/drawings with a partner and discuss where they imaged, what they imaged, and how they arrived at their images. A whole class discussion can focus on similar aspects: where students used imagery, what words evoked the most imagery, and how they arrived at their images.

Conclusion

Have students record their feelings about the lesson by having them complete the journal starters, "Creating mental images _____" "While listening to *Owl Moon* _____" or "Listening to the nature tape _____." Engage students in a whole class discussion of what they learned about imagery, whether it helped them as the story was read, and how they were able to image.

Assessment

- You will know that students are able to use the author's language, prior knowledge, and senses to make mental images and increase comprehension of text by their contributions during class discussion, by their drawings, and their discussion with their partners.
- You will know that students know why it is important to make mental images while reading by their journal entries at the conclusion of the lesson and the concluding discussion.

FIGURE 5.7. *(cont.)*

especially crucial for students . . . who have never had explicit instruction in reading strategies before.

[Eileen Ludwig, reflective memo, April 4, 2000]

Students are able to quickly learn how to create mental images while reading. The challenge is finding ways to transfer such learning to independent use.

Monitoring Comprehension/Questioning Oneself

The ability to monitor one's comprehension is linked to metacognition (Flavell, 1979). To reiterate: Metacognitive awareness consists of knowledge about *ourselves*, the *tasks* we face, and the *strategies* we use (Garner, 1987; Wagoner, 1983). Metacognition makes use of a series of mechanisms aimed at checking, planning, monitoring, testing, revising, and evaluating the strategies employed (Baker & Brown, 1984). Instruction or comprehension monitoring focuses on the reader's ability to oversee her own reading process and to note how well or how poorly her understanding of the text is progressing. Successful readers have an awareness of, and control over, such metacognitive skills, and they actively engage them before, during, and after reading (Brown, 1980). At times during the reading process, readers encounter discrepancies between their schemata and the text. As noted in Chapter 3, Anderson (1980) described this metacognitive awareness that something does not make sense or is hindering comprehension as a "clunk." If the reader is adequately monitoring his comprehension, he will notice the incongruity and attempt to resolve the problem (typically by applying fix-up strategies). Unfortunately, younger and less proficient readers have difficulty monitoring their comprehension (August, Flavell, & Clift, 1984; Garner, 1980, 1987; Markman, 1977; Myers & Paris, 1978; Paris & Myers, 1981). Successful readers, on the other hand, are more apt to detect inconsistencies in text and routinely readjust their reading strategies and schemata to accommodate such changes (Baker, 1984; Baker & Anderson, 1982; Garner & Kraus, 1981; Garner & Reis, 1981; Winograd & Johnston, 1982). This metacognitive awareness enables readers to comprehend better, particularly if they are able to apply appropriate fix-up strategies for mending comprehension when difficulties are encountered. Good readers purposefully and deliberately apply an array of strategies to maximize their understanding (Paris & Jacobs, 1984).

The ability to monitor one's comprehension is at the heart of strategy instruction. It is an abstract concept that younger and less proficient readers, in particular, have a difficult time learning. However, the research is clear that such readers can be successfully taught to monitor their comprehension. Patty George's lesson (introduced in Chapter 3) is a good example of how to teach emergent readers the concept of monitoring. Portions of the text of her lesson appeared in Chapter 3; however, the actual lesson plan is presented in Figure 5.8. Note that she introduced the students to the idea of monitoring by using stop and go signs to indicate whether or not they understood the text. She has also used the click and clunk characters (depicted in Figures 3.2 and 3.3) for similar lessons.

Patty's lesson enabled students to learn how to monitor their understanding, first, by listening and then by using a wordless picture book. She also provided a very safe environment for new learning (point 3 of Table 5.2). As noted in Chapter 3, other teachers created events to simulate the "aha" experience of recognizing when something does not make sense (e.g., Liz Graffeo and Summer Sciandra's Missing Spider Lesson). Once students learn to use a manipulative such as the stop and go or click and clunk tags to monitor their comprehension, the tags can be used as they view videos, during teacher read alouds, during shared reading, guided reading, and independent reading across the curriculum. By altering the amount of scaffolded support (i.e., the vertical dimension of Table 5.2) and the textual conditions, the amount of scaffolded support students need to competently monitor their comprehension is gradually reduced. Continued practice under a variety of textual conditions will foster transfer to independence.

Jaime Quackenbush noted that her third-grade student was able to monitor his comprehension on his own after she had focused several of her lessons on comprehension monitoring:

During our concluding [lesson] I had hoped that [the student] would be able to consciously stop while reading and monitor his understanding. He did so with more focus and intentionality than I'd even imagined! He was not simply following my ex-

Teacher: Patty George

Topic: Monitoring Comprehension while Reading

Grade level: K–2

STAIRS hypothesis being addressed:

> Students are unaware that reading is a meaning-getting process. They are unable to recognize when they do not understand what they read.

Goal of Lesson

Students will learn:
- That sometimes when we read the text might not make sense
- To stop and ask yourself whether the text makes sense or not

Materials
- *Good Dog Carl* by Alexandra Day
- "Stop" and "Go" tags
- Student self-assessments

Introduction

Explanation: declarative knowledge

Begin lesson by asking students to think of a time when somebody said something to you that didn't make sense. Have students share their experiences. Explain that sometimes when we read, the text might not make sense. Explain that today we are going to learn how to recognize when the text we are reading does not make sense.

Procedural and conditional knowledge

Display a sample "Stop" and "Go" tag. Explain that sometimes when we are reading things might not make sense. When that happens we should "stop" and think about why it does not make sense. As we are reading today when something does not make sense to us we are going to turn our tags to the "stop" side to show that something does not make sense. Explain that at other times the text makes perfect sense. During those times we "go" right ahead. Today as we are reading, when everything makes sense to us we will put our tags on the "go" side. Pass out tags to each student. Ask students to turn their tags to the side that will show that they do not understand something. Be sure that students are aware that the "stop" side means they do not understand. Ask students to turn their tags to the side they will show to represent that everything makes sense to them.

Explain that we are going to practice using the tags first by listening to some statements. Some of the statements might make sense to you and some may not. Read a statement to the students. Ask students whether the statement makes sense to them or not. Remind them that if it makes sense they should turn their tags to "go" and if it does not make sense, they should turn their tags to "stop."

Sample statements include:
- I made my husband an ice cream sundae, and I put spaghetti sauce on top of it.

FIGURE 5.8. Sample lesson teaching students how to monitor their comprehension.

- Last night I dusted and vacuumed my living room.
- I washed my car because it was dirty.
- The flowers in my garden needed a drink so I gave them some lemon-ade.
- I watched my favorite television show on the radio.

Model/ think aloud

Guided practice

Verbalization

Model and think aloud after reading the first sentence. You might say something like, "Hmmm, that doesn't make any sense to me. When I stop and think about what you might put on top of an ice cream sundae I think that I might put hot fudge or strawberry, but I wouldn't put spaghetti sauce. That doesn't make sense to me. I'll turn my sign to the 'stop' side." After reading each sentence remind students to stop and think about whether it makes sense to them and to turn their tags to either the "stop" or the "go" side. Ask students to share the reasons why a particular sentence made sense to them or not. Be sure to be accepting of all responses. Continue in this manner for all sentences.

Explain and remind students that this is the same thing that we do when we read. As we read we have to stop and think about whether the text makes sense to us or not. If it does not make sense, we need to think about why it does not make sense and use a strategy to help us understand it better.

Description of Instructional Experience

Explain that we are going to use this same procedure as we read the book *Good Dog Carl* by Alexandra Day. Introduce the story and have students activate prior knowledge, set purposes, and make predictions.

Declarative knowledge

Procedural knowledge

Explain that as we read, it is important to stop and think about whether the words and pictures make sense to us. Explain that we will use the "stop" and "go" tags today to indicate whether the words and pictures in this story make sense to us. Explain that this is a unique book because there are very few words. The author has chosen to use pictures to tell the story. Explain that we are going to study those pictures, make the story up in our mind as we read, and stop and think about whether the story they tell makes sense to us or not.

Model/ think aloud

Model and think aloud as you read and display the first pages. "That must be Carl the Dog. It looks like the mother is going away and leaving the dog to watch over the baby. When I stop and think about that, it doesn't really make sense to me that a mother would leave a dog to watch the baby. So, when I stop and think about the story those pictures tell me I am a little confused. I'll turn my sign to 'stop.' That doesn't make sense to me. But that must be what she's doing. I'll just read ahead and see what happens. Maybe I'll understand better as I read more."

Guided practice

Display the next set of pages, encouraging students to study the pictures carefully and to stop and think about whether they make sense or not. Observe and take anecdotal notes on how students respond using their

(cont.)

FIGURE 5.8. *(cont.)*

Verbalization

*Safe
environment*

tags. Ask students to share reasons why those pages make sense or do not make sense to them. Remind students that there are no right or wrong answers. It only matters that you honestly show whether you understand the text or not.

*Guided
practice*

Continue on in this manner reminding students at the end of each set of pages to stop and think about whether they understand or not. Ask them to turn their tags to the appropriate side for them and have various students share their thoughts about why a particular page made sense to them or not.

Conclusion

Verbalization

After reading the entire text have students complete a student self-assessment about using the tags to monitor their comprehension. After completing the self-assessment, engage students in a discussion of the usefulness of the strategy and how they used it. Conclude the lesson by reminding students that we must stop and think about whether the text makes sense while we read all kinds of text. As a follow-up you might continue to use the "stop" and "go" tags during read alouds, shared reading, guided reading, and independent reading across the curriculum.

Assessment

- You will know whether students understand that text might not make sense when we read, by their discourse during class discussion and their self-assessments.
- You will know that students can stop and ask themselves whether the text makes sense or not by observing their ability to manipulate the "stop" and "go" tags and listening to their rationales for why they manipulated the tag in the manner they did.

STUDENT SELF-ASSESSMENT

1. While reading *Good Dog Carl*, stopping and thinking about whether it made sense was:

   very easy   easy   a little hard   very hard

2. While reading *Good Dog Carl*, using the tag to show whether it made sense or not was:

   very easy   easy   a little hard   very hard

3. I think I can use the "stop" and "go" tag to show that I understand what I read:

   all the time   sometimes   never

FIGURE 5.8. *(cont.)*

ample or mechanically going through the motions. He was able to explain why he had stopped, where he did, and what he was thinking. I couldn't stop grinning!

[Jaime Quackenbush, reflective memo, April 13, 2000]

As students become more adept at monitoring under varying conditions, the manipulative stop and go tags can be removed as a scaffold and students taught to use sticky notes or a chart to note those places in the text that were confusing to them. Many teachers find that it is easy to teach students to draw a question mark on a sticky note and place it in the text where they were confused. Students can also jot down what they do not understand on the sticky note. Students can then pair off or form small groups to discuss where they had comprehension difficulties, what caused the problem, and seek help from their peers to understand the text better. These sticky notes serve as an excellent source of agenda items during peer discussions of the text. That is, students can use the sticky notes as a source for discussion topics. Students often begin such peer discussions by saying things like, "On page 37 I was really confused when _____. Can you help me understand that better?" In this manner students show that they are able to monitor their comprehension and actively seek resolution to any problems that arise while they are reading. *Resolution* is the focus of the next section.

Fix-up Strategies

Fix-up, or repair, strategies are general strategies that good readers deliberately employ after they realize they do not understand what they are reading. These strategies include (1) rereading, (2) slowing down and reading ahead for clarification, and (3) asking or discussing it with someone (see Figure 3.5 for a chart of these strategies). *Rereading* involves going back and rereading a word, phrase, sentence, or any portion of text; *slowing down and reading ahead for clarification* is often used when readers encounter new vocabulary or new ideas and they hope that the author will define or explain the unfamiliar or confusing idea in the text that lies ahead; *Asking* or *discussing* it with *someone* involves engaging another individual in a conversation in which the goal is to help each other understand the confusing aspect of the text. Readers also might consult an outside source such as another text, a video, or a television program to help them better understand what they read. Such consultation clearly takes the reader away from the current reading event; it is often used when a comprehension difficulty exceeds the text's capacity to clarify it. Consulting outside sources is not something that young readers normally do.

The difficult aspect of teaching students to use fix-up strategies is that, like any strategy, they require an expenditure of time. Many readers, particularly struggling ones, are not eager to reread text. Very often their goal is to "get done" rather than "to understand"; stopping to reread text or slowing down to read ahead carefully only delays them in achieving their goal. These are the circumstances when creating a safe environment for strategy use becomes essential. When students feel as if they must hurry to complete a reading task, there is a reason. They either do not enjoy reading or feel some sort of "assessment burden"—that is, students feel pressure to complete an assessment. If they do not "get done" on time, they may be punished by receiving a poor grade, losing their recess, or having to stay in at recess to complete the assignment. Clearly, there is little reward for slowing down and taking their time to make sure they understand text. In Chapter 3 the notion of overhauling traditional forms of comprehension assessment was discussed as one means of creating a safer environment for strategy use. This notion is of prime importance here. The lessons described throughout this chapter use authentic and alternative means of assessing students' comprehension and strategy use. These assessment forms do not elicit the same urgency to "get done" because they are linked to the reading process rather than used as postreading assessments of comprehension. The lessons were also designed to show students that there is a "payoff" for expending the cognitive effort required to use strategies. Through the student self-assessments and strategy discussions, the teachers in these lessons attempted to show students that their efforts paid off by enhancing their comprehension. As noted earlier in Chapter 1, experiencing the benefit is essential to creating motivated strategy use.

The best lessons for teaching students how, when, and why they should use fix-up strategies occur during the context of authentic reading experiences. Each strategy can be modeled using think aloud procedures and practiced during any of the lessons that appear in this chapter. As you are engaged in a teacher read aloud or modeling, you can "slip in" discourse about using fix-up strategies. For example, as you encounter text that does not make sense, you might say, "Hmmm, that doesn't make sense to me. I think I have to reread to see what the author was talking about. Maybe that will help me understand it better." It is helpful during these think alouds to refer to a classroom chart, such as the one depicted in Figure 3.5, so students can see and remember the strategies they can use to repair comprehension. It is also helpful to encourage and praise students who engage in a similar process as they read.

One difficulty with teaching students to ask or discuss the comprehension problem with someone is that students may use that strategy at the expense of employing a strategy they can use on their own. It is important to communicate the conditional knowledge that this is a strategy to be used once they have read ahead for clarification or reread. If either of those strategies did not help, then they can consider asking someone else or engaging in a discussion. Peer discussions are recommended over teacher-led discussions primarily because teacher-led discussions often become question–answer periods in which the teacher dominates the discourse by asking a series of questions. Cazden (1986) and Mehan (1979) described these interactions as I-R-E (Initiate-Respond-Evaluate) sequences, in which the teacher initiates the discussion by asking a question, students respond to the question, and the teacher follows by evaluating their responses. In her comparison of peer discussion and teacher-led discussion environments, Almasi (1995) found that 85% of the talk during teacher-led discussions were sustained by such I-R-E sequences. Additionally, these discussions were dominated by the teacher, who was responsible for asking 93% of the questions and for talking 62% of the time. Such environments do not foster student independence and self-regulation—the key to strategic processing.

Peer discussions, in contrast, provide students with the opportunity to set their own agenda for discussion; they explore and discuss questions of interest to them. If students are taught how to set a discussion agenda well, the content of their discussions will likely focus on topics that will help them understand the text better. This requires that students be able to recognize when text does not make sense (i.e., monitor their comprehension) and actively seek resolution to their comprehension dilemma. Almasi (1995) found that students who engaged in peer discussion were better able to recognize and resolve incongruities on their own than comparable students who had engaged in teacher-led discussion. Peer discussion becomes a means for peers to help one another understand the text better (i.e., a fix-up strategy) as well as a catalyst for cognitive, metacognitive, and sociocognitive growth and development.

SUMMARY

This chapter provides teachers with relevant background research, hands-on tools, and resources to streamline and facilitate beginning strategy instruction. The sample lessons were based on the Strategy Instruction Model and depict how to create a safe environment by reducing processing demands, providing opportunities for student verbalization, and providing explicit instruction. The explicit instruction depicted in the sample lessons included explanation, modeling, and guided practice to help students learn particular strategies. Teaching resources are presented for (1) text anticipation strategies (i.e., previewing text, activating prior knowledge, generating predictions, setting purposes, and identifying text structure); (2) text maintenance strategies (i.e., creating mental images, monitoring comprehension, identifying text structure, and updating/revising predictions); and (3) fix-up strategies (i.e., rereading, reading ahead for clarification, asking or discussing it with someone).

REFERENCES

Afflerbach, P. (1990). The influence of prior knowledge and text genre on readers' prediction strategies. *Journal of Reading Behavior, 22*(2), 131–148.

Almasi, J. F. (1995). The nature of fourth graders' sociocognitive conflicts in peer-led and teacher-led discussions of literature. *Reading Research Quarterly, 30*(3), 314–351.

Almasi, J. F. (1996). A new view of discussion. In L. B. Gambrell & J. F. Almasi (Eds.), *Lively discussions! Fostering engaged reading* (pp. 2–24). Newark, DE: International Reading Association.

Almasi, J. F. (in press). Peer discussion. To appear in B. Guzzetti (Ed.), *Literacy in America: An encyclopedia*. New York: ABC.

Almasi, J. F., O'Flahavan, J. F., & Arya, P. (2001). A comparative analysis of student and teacher development in more and less proficient discussions of literature. *Reading Research Quarterly, 36*(2), 96–120.

Alvermann, D. E., Smith, L. C., & Readence, J. E. (1987). Prior knowledge activation and the comprehension of compatible and incompatible text. *Reading Research Quarterly, 20*, 420–435.

Anderson, R. C., & Pearson, P. D. (1984). A schema-theoretic view of basic processes in reading comprehension. In P. D. Pearson, R. Barr, M. L. Kamil, & P. B. Mosenthal (Eds.), *Handbook of reading research* (vol. 1, pp. 255–291). New York: Longman.

Anderson, R. C., Pichert, J. W., & Shirey, L. L. (1983). Effects of the reader's schema at different points in time. *Journal of Educational Psychology, 75*(2), 271–279.

Anderson, R. C., Reynolds, R. E., Schallert, D. L., & Goetz, E. T. (1977). Frameworks for comprehending discourse. *American Educational Research Journal, 14*(4), 367–381.

Anderson, T. H. (1980). Study strategies and adjunct aids. In R. J. Spiro, B. C. Bruce, & W. F. Brewer (Eds.), *Theoretical issues in reading comprehension* (pp. 483–502). Hillsdale, NJ: Erlbaum.

Armbruster, B. B., Anderson, T. H., & Ostertag, J. (1987). Does text structure/summarization instruction facilitate learning from expository text? *Reading Research Quarterly, 22*, 449–457.

Armbruster, B. B., Anderson, T. H., & Ostertag, J. (1989). Teaching text structure to improve reading and writing. *The Reading Teacher, 43*(2), 130–137.

August, D. L., Flavell, J. H., & Clift, R. (1984). Comparison of comprehension monitoring of skilled and less skilled readers. *Reading Research Quarterly, 20*, 39–53.

Baker, L. (1984). Spontaneous vs. instructed use of multiple standards for evaluating comprehension: Effects of age, reading proficiency, and type of standard. *Journal of Experimental Psychology, 38,* 289–311.

Baker, L., & Anderson, R. I. (1982). Effects of inconsistent information on text processing: Evidence for comprehension monitoring. *Reading Research Quarterly, 17,* 281–294.

Baker, L., & Brown, A. L. (1984). Metacognitive skills and reading. In P. D. Pearson, R. Barr, M. L. Kamil, and P. B. Mosenthal (Eds.), *Handbook of reading research* (vol. 1, pp. 353–394). New York: Longman.

Bartlett, F. C. (1932). *Remembering.* London: Cambridge University Press.

Blanton, W. E., Wood, K. D., & Moorman, G. B. (1990). The role of purpose in reading instruction. *The Reading Teacher, 43*(7), 486–493.

Bransford, J. D., & Johnson, M. K. (1972). Contextual prerequisites for understanding: Some investigations of comprehension and recall. *Journal of Verbal Learning and Verbal Behavior, 11,* 717–726.

Brown, A. L. (1980). Metacognitive development and reading. In R. Spiro, B. Bruce, & W. Brewer (Eds.), *Theoretical issues in reading comprehension* (pp. 453–481). Hillsdale, NJ: Erlbaum.

Cazden, C. (1986). Classroom discourse. In M. C. Wittrock (Ed.), *Handbook of research on teaching* (3rd ed., pp. 432–463). New York: Macmillan.

Collins, A., Brown, J., & Larkin, J. (1980). Inference in text understanding. In R. Spiro, B. Bruce, & W. Brewer (Eds.), *Theoretical issues in reading comprehension* (pp. 385–407). Hillsdale, NJ: Erlbaum.

DePaola, T. (1978). *Pancakes for breakfast.* New York: Harcourt.

Dole, J. A., Duffy, G. G., Roehler, L. R., & Pearson, P. D. (1991). Moving from the old to the new: Research on reading comprehension instruction. *Review of Educational Research, 61*(2), 239–264.

Englert, C. S., & Hiebert, E. H. (1984). Children's developing awareness of text structures in expository materials. *Journal of Educational Psychology, 76,* 65–74.

Fitzgerald, J., & Teasley, A. B. (1986). Effects of instruction in narrative structure on children's writing. *Journal of Educational Psychology, 78*(6), 424–432.

Flavell, J. H. (1979). Metacognition and cognitive monitoring: A new area of cognitive-developmental inquiry. *American Psychologist, 34,* 906–911.

Fowler, A. (1996). *Spiders are not insects.* New York: Children's Press.

Gambrell, L. B., & Almasi, J. F. (1996). (Eds.), *Lively discussions! Fostering engaged reading.* Newark, DE: International Reading Association.

Gambrell, L. B., & Bales, R. J. (1986). Mental imagery and the comprehension-monitoring performance of fourth- and fifth-grade poor readers. *Reading Research Quarterly, 21*(4), 454–464.

Gambrell, L. B., & Jawitz, P. (1993). Mental imagery, text illustrations, and children's story comprehension and recall. *Reading Research Quarterly, 28,* 264–276.

Garner, R. (1980). Monitoring of understanding: An investigation of good and poor readers' awareness of induced miscomprehension of text. *Journal of Reading Behavior, 12,* 55–63.

Garner, R. (1987). *Metacognition and reading comprehension.* Norwood, NJ: Ablex.

Garner, R., & Kraus, C. (1981). Good and poor comprehender differences in knowing and regulating reading behaviors. *Educational Research Quarterly, 6*(4), 5–12.

Garner, R., & Reis, R. (1981). Monitoring and resolving comprehension obstacles: An investigation of spontaneous text lookbacks among upper-grade good and poor comprehenders. *Reading Research Quarterly, 16,* 569–582.

Hiebert, E. H., Englert, C. S., & Brennan, S. (1983). Awareness of text structure in recognition and production of expository discourse. *Journal of Reading Behavior, 15*(4), 63–79.

Idol, L. (1987). Group story mapping: A comprehension strategy for both skilled and unskilled readers. *Journal of Learning Disabilities, 20*(4), 196–205.

Idol, L., & Croll, V. J. (1987). Story-mapping training as a means of improving reading comprehension. *Learning Disability Quarterly, 10,* 214–229.

Kalman, B., & Everts, T. (1994). *Frogs and toads.* New York: Crabtree.

King, S. D. (1990). Combining a story structure strategy with the vocabulary language prediction strategy. Unpublished manuscript.

Kucan, L., & Beck, I. L. (1997). Thinking aloud and reading comprehension research: Inquiry, instruction, and social interaction. *Review of Educational Research, 67*(3), 271–299.

Langer, J. A. (1985). Children's sense of genre: A study of performance on parallel reading and writing tasks. *Written Communication, 2*(2), 157–187.

Lipson, M. Y. (1983). The influence of religious affiliation on children's memory for text information. *Reading Research Quarterly, 18*, 448–457.

Mandler, J. M., & Johnson, N. S. (1977). Remembrance of things parsed: Story structure and recall. *Cognitive Psychology, 9*, 111–151.

Markman, E. M. (1977). Realizing that you don't understand: A preliminary investigation. *Child Development, 48*, 986–999.

Mehan, H. (1979). *Learning lessons.* Cambridge, MA: Harvard University Press.

Meyer, B. J. F. (1975). Identification of the structure of prose and its implications for the study of reading and memory. *Journal of Reading Behavior, 7*, 7–48.

Meyer, B. J. F., Brandt, D. M., & Bluth, G. J. (1980). Use of top-level structure in text: Key for reading comprehension of ninth-grade students. *Reading Research Quarterly, 16*, 72–103.

Meyer, B. J. F., & Rice, G. E. (1984). The structure of text. In P. D. Pearson, R. Barr, M. L. Kamil, & P. B. Mosenthal (Eds.), *Handbook of reading research* (vol. 1, pp. 319–351). New York: Longman.

Mooser, S. (1978). *The ghost with the Halloween hiccups.* New York: William Morrow.

Myers, M., & Paris, S. G. (1978). Children's metacognitive knowledge about reading. *Journal of Educational Psychology, 70*, 680–690.

Ohlhausen, M. M., & Roller, C. M. (1988). The operation of text structure and content schemata in isolation and in interaction. *Reading Research Quarterly, 23*(1), 70–88.

Paivio, A. (1986). *Mental representations: A dual coding approach.* New York: Oxford University Press.

Palincsar, A. S., & Brown, A. L. (1984). Reciprocal teaching of comprehension-fostering and comprehension-monitoring activities. *Cognition and Instruction, 1*(2), 117–175.

Pappas, C. C. (1991). Young children's strategies in learning the "book language" of information books. *Discourse Processes, 14*, 203–225.

Paris, S. G., & Jacobs, J. E. (1984). The benefits of informed instruction for children's reading awareness and comprehension skills. *Child Development, 55*, 2083–2093.

Paris, S. G., & Myers, M. (1981). Comprehension monitoring, memory, and study strategies of good and poor readers. *Journal of Reading Behavior, 13*, 5–22.

Pearson, P. D., & Dole, J. A. (1987). Explicit comprehension instruction: A review of research and a new conceptualization of instruction. *The Elementary School Journal, 88*(2), 151–165.

Pearson, P. D., & Fielding, L. (1991). Comprehension instruction. In R. Barr, M. L. Kamil, P. B. Mosenthal, & P. D. Pearson (Eds.), *Handbook of reading research* (vol. 2, pp. 815–860). New York: Longman.

Pearson, P. D., Hansen, J., & Gordon, C. (1979). The effect of background knowledge on young children's comprehension of explicit and implicit information. *Journal of Reading Behavior, 11*(3), 201–209.

Pressley, M., El-Dinary, P. B., Gaskins, I., Schuder, T., Bergman, J. L., Almasi, J., & Brown, R. (1992). Beyond direct explanation: Transactional instruction of reading comprehension strategies. *The Elementary School Journal, 92*(5), 513–555.

Pressley, M., Harris, K. R., & Marks, M. B. (1992). But good strategy instructors are constructivists! *Educational Psychology Review, 4*(1), 3–31.

Pressley, M., Johnson, C. J., Symons, S., McGoldrick, J. A., & Kurita, J. A. (1989). Strategies that improve children's memory and comprehension of text. *The Elementary School Journal, 90*(1), 3–32.

Recht, D. R., & Leslie, L. (1988). Effect of prior knowledge on good and poor readers' memory of text. *Journal of Educational Psychology, 80*(1), 16–20.

Rowe, D. W., & Rayford, L. (1987). Activating background knowledge in reading comprehension assessment. *Reading Research Quarterly, 22*(2), 160–176.

Sadoski, M. (1983). An exploratory study of the relationships between reported imagery and the comprehension and recall of a story. *Reading Research Quarterly, 19*, 110–123.

Sadoski, M. (1985). The natural use of imagery in story comprehension and recall: Replication and extension. *Reading Research Quarterly, 20*, 658–667.

Sadoski, M., Goetz, E. T., & Kangiser, S. (1988). Imagination in story response: Relationships between imagery, affect, and structural importance. *Reading Research Quarterly, 23*(3), 320–336.

Short, E. J., & Ryan, E. B. (1984). Metacognitive differences between skilled and less skilled readers: Remediating deficits through story grammar and attribution training. *Journal of Educational Psychology, 76*, 225–235.

Spivey, N. N., & King, J. R. (1989). Readers as writers composing from sources. *Reading Research Quarterly, 24,* 7–26.

Stauffer, R. G. (1969). *Directing reading maturity as a cognitive process.* New York: Harper & Row.

Stein, N. L., & Glenn, C. G. (1979). An analysis of story comprehension in elementary school children. In R. Freedle (Ed.), *New directions in discourse processing* (pp. 53–120). Norwood, NJ: Ablex.

Taft, M. L., & Leslie, L. (1985). The effects of prior knowledge and oral reading accuracy on miscues and comprehension. *Journal of Reading Behavior, 17*(2), 163–179.

Taylor, B. M. (1980). Children's memory for expository text after reading. *Reading Research Quarterly, 15*(3), 399–411.

Tompkins, G., & McGee, L. (1993). *Teaching reading with literature: Case studies to action plans.* New York: Merrill.

Vygotsky, L. S. (1978). *Mind in society.* Cambridge, MA: Harvard University Press.

Waber, B. (1975). *Ira sleeps over.* New York: Houghton Mifflin.

Wagoner, S. A. (1983). Comprehension monitoring: What it is and what we know about it. *Reading Research Quarterly, 18*(3), 328–346.

Walker, B. J. (2000). *Diagnostic teaching of reading: Techniques for instruction and assessment* (4th ed.). Upper Saddle River, NJ: Merrill.

Weaver, C. A., & Kintsch, W. (1991). Expository text. In R. Barr, M. L. Kamil, P. B. Mosenthal, & P. D. Pearson (Eds.), *Handbook of reading research* (vol. 2, pp. 230–245). New York: Longman.

Whaley, J. F. (1984). Story grammars and reading instruction. *The Reading Teacher, 34,* 762–771.

Winograd, P., & Johnston, P. (1982). Comprehension monitoring and the error-detection paradigm. *Journal of Reading Behavior, 14,* 61–74.

Wood, K. D., & Robinson, N. (1983). Vocabulary, language, and prediction: A prereading strategy. *The Reading Teacher,* 392–395.

CHAPTER SIX

Strategy Instruction That Enhances Word Recognition

Constructing meaning from text is the primary goal of all reading instruction. However, achieving this goal means that readers also must be able to recognize and process words fluently (Pressley, 2000). Like comprehension, word recognition is a strategic process. For proficient readers, word recognition is almost always skillful and automatic. These readers rarely need to use word recognition strategies because they are able to recognize automatically nearly all words they encounter. That is, nearly all words are sight words for proficient readers and do not require analysis or decoding them.

Proficient readers use word recognition strategies only on those rare occasions when they encounter an unfamiliar word. At such times, these readers use one of the following four strategies (or in combination) to recognize the unfamiliar word: (1) analogizing to known words, (2) using letter–sound cues, (3) using orthographic features, or (4) using context cues (Ehri, 1991). Each of these strategies, and related instructional ideas, is explained in greater detail later in this chapter. First, the theoretical background related to how readers learn to recognize words is presented. Teachers who understand this developmental process are able to engage in more responsive teaching. That is, they can plan more effective instruction that meets the developmental needs of their students.

HOW DO READERS LEARN TO RECOGNIZE WORDS?

Not surprisingly, there are varying perspectives on how readers learn to read words. Juel (1991) described two paradigms that explain models of reading acquisition. *Nonstage models* view the reading process as progressing similarly for experienced and inexperienced readers alike. According to this perspective, the search for meaning from text is accomplished by using knowledge of language and knowledge of the world (i.e., syntactic and semantic knowledge) rather than orthographic knowledge (i.e., written system of language that includes the letters and patterns of letters) about the printed word.

In contrast, Juel (1991) noted that proponents of *stage models* contend that there are inherent differences between experienced and inexperienced readers. These differences are developmental and emerge over time as a reader learns new and more efficient ways of processing text. These differences are more related to a reader's knowledge of the printed word than to their knowledge of language and the world.

Both perspectives consider the construction of meaning to be the ultimate goal of reading (Juel, 1991). However, nonstage models suggest that comprehension is more successful when minimal orthographic knowledge is used. Stage models propose the opposite: that a reader's rapid and efficient use of orthographic knowledge leads to better comprehension.

The research evidence supports the existence of developmental phases of word recognition (Blachman, 2000; Ehri, 1991; Juel, 1991; Pressley, 2000). It is these phases that help us understand how and why readers use particular word recognition strategies over others. Five phases of word recognition development are described below. Ehri's (1998) terminology is used to denote each phase: (1) pre-alphabetic phase, (2) partial alphabetic phase, (3) alphabetic phase, (4) consolidated alphabetic phase, and (5) fluent recognition phase.

Pre-Alphabetic Phase

The pre-alphabetic phase has also been named the "logographic stage" (Frith, 1985), the "selective-cue stage" (Juel, 1991), and the "emergent stage" (Bear, Invernizzi, Templeton, & Johnston, 2000). Most children are pre-alphabetic readers prior to entering kindergarten. Readers in this phase of development make use of visual characteristics, rather than letters and their sounds, to recognize words (Ehri, 1998). Success in reading at this phase is largely contingent on the reader's ability to memorize words and the incidental features associated with them. These readers are not systematic in their use of any particular cue (Bear et al., 2000) and rely mostly on contextual or environmental information, rather than graphic information, to identify words (Juel, 1991). For example, pre-alphabetic readers may be able to recognize a word such as *McDonald's* not because they can read the word or recognize the letters but because they recognize an environmental cue surrounding the word: the yellow letters on a red background, the golden arches, or the familiar smell as they drive by the restaurant.

Fox (2000) noted that readers in the pre-alphabetic phase of development often use three types of cues: environmental, picture, and incidental cues to recognize words. *Environmental cues* include any salient visual cue in the environment that serves as a clue and helps the reader identify a word or phrase. Masonheimer, Drum, and Ehri (1984) found that preschoolers who used environmental cues did not usually notice when words were misspelled. They also were unable to recognize words when they were removed from their environmental context. That is, a child who is able to recognize the word *McDonald's* when it appeared in its normal environmental context (i.e., white lettering on a red background, with a large yellow "M" in the background) would not be able to recognize the same configuration of letters when printed outside of that context. These readers are able to bring meaning to words only when they are within their normal environmental context.

These readers also use picture cues (illustrations in texts) to help them recognize words and often are able to read the text based solely on the pictures. The story they read may bear little resemblance to that contained in the printed words on the pages, for these readers are relying on the pictures to guide their reading. Using picture cues is a good strategy to help bring meaning to text and can often help readers identify unfamiliar words. However, it is not always the most reliable strategy, particularly when text contains few or no pictures.

Fox (2000) described incidental cues as unreliable cues that are subordinate to alphabetic writing. Such cues might include smudges, dog-eared pages, colored inks, the shape of a word, or the shape of a letter. Readers who use these cues to recognize words do not pay attention to the specific letters or sequences of letters in a word to identify it. Instead they might be able to recognize certain words on flash cards because of incidental cues. They might know the word *happen* because it appears on a word card that is bent in the upper right corner, for example, or they might know the word *that* because it appears on a word card that has a fingerprint smudge in the lower left corner. When the same word appears in a different context, the reader would not be able to recognize it without the incidental cue. Adult readers are often impressed when emergent readers are able to read "big" words such as *dinosaur, hippopotamus,* or *Halloween.* Very often these young readers are able to recognize these words by their length or their configuration rather than by using letter–sound cues. Configuration cues include the length of the word and the shape, or configuration, its letters make (see Figure 6.1).

Because configuration cues are based on the shape of the letters within a word, they are not reliable with regard to sound. However, they do help readers narrow down the field of word choices, except when words have similar patterns of letters. For example, the words *boat, look,* and *toad* in Figure 6.1 all have a similar configuration. In these instances, using configuration cues is not a reliable strategy for identifying words.

Readers also use letter shapes or a salient graphic cue to help identify words. For example, they may recognize the "oo" in "look" and imagine a pair of eyeballs to help them recognize the word. This cue is helpful only for recognizing the word *look,* however.

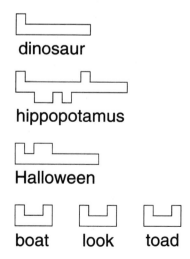

FIGURE 6.1. Using configuration cues to identify words.

Encountering the words *book, cook, hook,* and *took* may confuse them because they all have the same letter feature.

Pre-alphabetic readers have difficulty recognizing words outside of their environmental context. These readers encounter difficulties because the associations they form are unsystematic and arbitrary—and therefore hard to remember. Readers in the pre-alphabetic phase become confused and frustrated because their use of environmental, pictorial, and incidental cues is not consistent or reliable in all contexts. During oral reading, these readers often mistake visually similar words (e.g., *book, look, took*), substituting synonyms or semantically similar words. Readers in the pre-alphabetic phase must learn to recognize letters and their sounds so they can rely on cues that are consistent. As these children begin to develop letter–sound awareness, they move into the partial alphabetic phase.

We can also recognize pre-alphabetic readers by examining their writing. These readers have difficulty reading their own writing after a day because their writing is not systematic. Their writing consists of drawings, scribbles, letter-like forms, and random marks on the page (see Figure 6.2). Bear et al. (2000) refer to this as the "emergent spelling" stage. These children may be aware of the convention of directionality, or the notion that writing moves from left to right and top to bottom in English, but they are unaware of letters and their sounds.

Partial Alphabetic Phase

Readers in Ehri's (1998) partial alphabetic phase are beginning to read words by processing letter–sound relationships, but these relationships are only partial at this point. Bear and colleagues (2000) refer to readers in this phase as "beginning readers." These readers understand that letters are constant symbols that represent sounds, and they are able to use one or two letters to help them identify words. They are aware of the features that distinguish one letter from another, can identify most individual letters consistently, and know the sounds associated with some letters. These readers often use the initial and/or final letter–sounds in words and make a "guess" at the medial portion of the word. For example, the sentence "I went down the *hall*" might be read "I went down the *heal.*" These readers typically rely on context, as well, to identify words. For example, they might read "We ate *pretzels*" as "We ate *pizza.*" They notice a /p/ and a /z/ and use the context to think of a word that is a food that begins with a /p/ and has a /z/ somewhere near the end. They then think of a word that fits those criteria, and guess based on those cues. The medial portion of the word is disregarded.

Readers in the partial alphabetic phase have an awareness of print conventions (e.g., writing in English proceeds from left to right and top to bottom). They have a concept of "word," in that they know that white spaces separate words in writing, and they have the ability to match speech to printed words by pointing to words as they are read (Roberts, 1992). They also use the context, the pictures, and beginning and/or ending letter sounds to recognize unfamiliar words. These readers are able to read many single syllable words and can reread books with predictable patterns, but they are likely to confuse words that begin and end alike, and they may guess at the medial portions of words. Their oral reading is fairly disfluent, and they often subvocalize (i.e., read aloud in a low, mumbling tone) while they read and "track" the text with their fingers (i.e., fingerprinting). The next step for these readers is to begin to look at

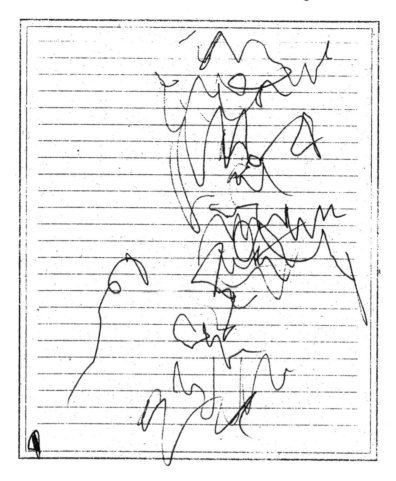

FIGURE 6.2. Example of emergent spelling.

the letters and patterns of letters in the medial portions of the words to recognize them with greater accuracy.

Readers in the partial alphabetic phase are usually semiphonetic spellers (Gentry, 1987) or letter name–alphabetic spellers. Bear and colleagues (2000) explain that writers early in this stage use one or two letters (usually consonants) to represent an entire word. These writers can usually reread what they have written after a day, but their writing is fairly disfluent. For example, "ISAK" might represent "I saw a cat." Later these writers consistently use beginning and ending consonant sounds to represent words and may even use some medial vowel sounds. Figure 6.3 illustrates a first grader's writing at this stage. The child wrote a riddle in which the reader is supposed to use each clue to guess what the object might be. Notice that the child recognizes the need for white spaces between words, indicating that he or she has a concept of *word*. The child also represents the initial and final consonant sounds in the words and is beginning to represent medial portions. The riddle says: "It is hard. It is hard. It is steel. It has a speaker."

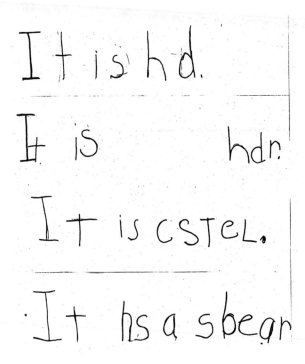

FIGURE 6.3. Example of letter name–alphabetic spelling.

Alphabetic Phase

Readers in the alphabetic phase of development are able to make maximum use of graphic information and use letter–sound relationships to recognize unfamiliar words (Ehri, 1998; Frith, 1985). Juel (1991) referred to these readers as being in the "spelling–sound" stage of development. These readers have a good understanding of letters and the sounds they make and use them to identify words. They also are able to "sound and blend": to recognize individual letters and the sounds they make and blend each sound together to produce the entire word. Initially the effort to sound and blend is a very overt and deliberate one (Ehri, 1991). Indeed, readers often become "glued" to print at this phase of development, and they may become overly reliant on letter–sound relationships (Juel, 1991). Many alphabetic readers overrely on letter–sound cues to identify words at the expense of context and meaning. These readers often forget that reading is a meaning-making venture. Instead they begin to view reading as "word calling." Their oral reading is often halting, disfluent, and word-by-word, as they deliberately "sound out" unknown words letter by letter. Their substitutions are often non-words. For example, when reading the sentence "She went around the *corner*," alphabetic readers might read it as "She went around the *karmra*." In their efforts to sound out every letter in an unknown word (i.e., graphic cues), these readers forget to use semantic cues to bring meaning to their reading. They may expend so much cognitive effort sounding out unknown words that they have little energy left for comprehension and self-monitoring.

These readers usually spell phonetically (Gentry, 1987). That is, they are able to represent all of the important sounds in the words they write, but these words may not be spelled conventionally. These writers are able to reread their writing fairly fluently. Figure 6.4 displays the writing of a student who is spelling phonetically. This writer is able to represent all of the important sounds in words but still has some difficulty spelling conventionally. For example, he spelled *would* as *wode*, *neat* as *neet*, and *could* as *cold*.

Consolidated Alphabetic Phase

Readers in the consolidated alphabetic phase have sufficient knowledge of the spelling patterns that recur across words and use them to recognize unfamiliar words (Ehri, 1991, 1998). Frith (1985) described these readers as being in an orthographic phase, in which they are able to instantly process multiletter chunks, or orthographic units, in words rather than letter by letter as in the alphabetic phase. These readers are beginning to use a variety of spelling patterns to recognize words. They use their knowledge of rimes (i.e., a vowel and any consonants that follow it within a syllable) to recognize recurring spelling patterns in words. For example, if a reader is able to recognize the rime *–est* in words like *best*, *nest*, *pest*, and *rest*, then she will be able to use that knowledge to help her decode other single syllable words, such as *chest*, *guest*, and *quest*, and larger and unfamiliar words, such as *investing*.

Readers in the consolidated alphabetic phase also are beginning to recognize and use affixes (i.e., prefixes and suffixes) as multiletter chunks. In the previous example a reader might quickly notice the *–ing* ending in *investing* and then notice the *–est* rime. In essence, these readers are "consolidating" the reading process by having to process less information. Instead of having to sound and blend each of the nine letters in the word *investing*, these readers would only have to process three multiletter chunks: *in*, *vest*, and *–ing*. Ehri (1991) noted that this process helps readers (1) decode polysyllabic words (i.e., words with more than one syllable), (2) set up access routes in memory for recognizing words by sight, and (3) speeds up the process of accessing these sight words. Consolidated alpha-

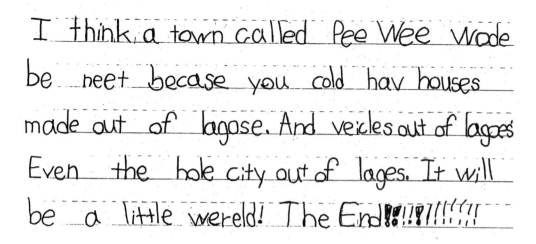

FIGURE 6.4. Example of phonetic writing.

betic readers are able to recognize many words by sight, their reading is fluent, and they are able to read silently (Bear et al., 2000). These readers are able to recognize most words but they may have difficulty decoding polysyllabic words. These readers are usually transitional (Gentry, 1987) or within-word (Bear et al., 2000) spellers. These writers are able to spell most words conventionally; however, they may use variants or alternate spellings. For example, they may spell *awake* as *awaik* or *driving* as *driveing*.

Fluent Recognition Phase

Readers who are able to recognize all of the words they normally encounter in everyday reading fluently and automatically, and who proficiently use the orthographic patterns in words to read the occasionally unfamiliar word, are said to be in the fluent recognition phase (Ehri, 1998). These readers are able to read fluently nearly any form of text at any level. When these readers do encounter a technical word in a high school or college content area textbook, or a professional journal, they are able to use a variety of word recognition strategies to fluidly decode the new word.

These readers are usually conventional spellers (Gentry, 1987) who spell most regular and irregular words correctly, and use their knowledge of letter–sound relationships and orthographic patterns to spell unfamiliar words.

WHAT STRATEGIES DO READERS USE TO RECOGNIZE WORDS?

The primary goals of word recognition instruction are to teach readers how to recognize unfamiliar words rapidly and independently, and how to use multiple strategies for dealing with unknown words. Awareness of the developmental phases involved in learning to recognize words helps teachers understand why some readers use, or rely on, particular strategies. Such awareness also provides teachers with an understanding of what readers are currently able to do and where instruction should lead them. That is, recognizing that a reader is in the pre-alphabetic phase of development (1) informs the teacher about what types of strategies the child is currently able to use to recognize words (i.e., possibly environmental cues, picture cues, and incidental cues) and (2) suggests a focus on those particular strategies that will best help the reader begin to recognize words more reliably. In the section that follows, connections are drawn between the developmental phases of word recognition and their impact on strategy use. Five word recognition strategies are described in detail: (1) recognizing words by sight, (2) analogizing, (3) using letter–sound cues, (4) using orthographic features, and (5) using context cues. Each description is accompanied by instructional suggestions and sample lesson plans.

Recognizing Words by Sight

Ehri (1991) noted that speakers of any language possess a lexicon, which stores words that are held in memory. When people are able to read words by sight, they use information they remember from their prior experiences with those words. When reading, we notice the features of a given word and access the identity of the word from memory. A word's features include its (1) pronunciation, (2) meaning (i.e., semantic characteristics), (3) syntax (i.e., the grammatical role it plays in sentences), and (4) orthography (i.e., information about its spelling and the way it is written). Those words that are encountered frequently in our reading are more likely to be read by sight than those that occur infrequently. After repeated encounters, accessing the features of the word from our lexicon occurs with increasing speed. Eventually, after many encounters with the same word, it is recognized automatically.

Initially, emergent readers are able to recognize a small number of words by sight. These are usually the words that appear most frequently in their reading such as *I*, *and*, *the*, *a*, *to*, *was*, *in*, *it*, *on*, *my*, *is*, *not*, *go*, *an*, and *like*. Readers are often in the pre-alphabetic or partial alphabetic phases as they begin to recognize words by sight. This means that they remember the words based on incidental or configuration cues, not on orthographic or alphabetic features. This method of learning sight words works for a while, but as noted above, these readers often become confused when words have similar features. For example, they may confuse visually similar words such as *in* and *is*, *on* and *or*, or *then*, *them*, and *they*. Letter–sound correspondences are required at some point to achieve competent sight word recognition. It is this point at which readers must learn a more reliable strategy, such as using letter–sound cues or analogizing.

Individuals who read words by sight possess several characteristics that distinguish them from readers who use other strategies to recognize words. First, they recognize words automatically. If they are emergent readers, they either "know" the word or they do not, and they will tell you so. They recognize sight words as a whole unit without pauses between phonemes (i.e., the smallest unit of sound) or syllables. Words that are recognized by sight are read rapidly. Readers who have been taught to read words by sight are usually able to distinguish correct spellings of words from homophonous ones. That is, because they learned to recognize the word by its visual features rather than its phonemic features, they are able to recognize that *wait*, rather than *wate*, is the conventional spelling. When these readers encounter unconventional spellings, they often say, "That doesn't *look* right." These readers also are able to pronounce irregularly spelled words correctly rather than phonetically. For example, sight–word readers would be able to pronounce *cough* as /kōf/ rather than /kouf/, /koug/, /kō/, or /kōg/.

Learning words by sight is not really a strategic process. When one encounters an unknown word, one would not think, "Hmmm, I think I'll try to read this word by sight." Sight words are either known or not known. It is not a strategic or deliberate choice to employ recognizing sight words as a strategy. Sight–word recognition is skillful and automatic. It is the ultimate goal for every reader to be able to recognize by sight nearly every word encountered. Thus the instructional recommendations that follow are not presented in terms of how to teach sight word recognition as a strategy, for it is not a strategy. The recommendations are presented as tips for enhancing sight word recognition in a safe environment.

Because recognizing words by sight requires many exposures to the words, text selection is critical to instruction. Texts that have a predictable or repetitious pattern are ideal. One type of predictable text has predictable words. Often these texts have a rhyming pattern and repetitious phrases that permit one to predict upcoming words and text. For example, in Deming's (1993) book, *Who Is Tapping at My Window?* a little girl hears a tapping at her window and asks, "Who is there?" Various farm animals respond, "It's not I." Eventually she discovers that it is the rain tapping at her window. The repetition of the phrases throughout the text, "Who is there?" and "It's not I," is ideal for enhancing sight–word recognition. In addition, the text offers rhyme in the names of each pair of animals that respond (e.g., the loon's response is followed by the raccoon's, the dog's response is followed by the frog's). Rhyming helps children anticipate what an unfamiliar word might be by using the rhythm of the text.

Another type of predictable text features repetitious phrases. An example is Mirra Ginsburg's *The Chick and the Duckling* (1991). In this text the duckling has a busy day filled with many adventures (digging, climbing, running). The duckling uses the same phrase to tell the chick what he is doing, "I am _____ing," to which the chick always responds, "Me too." The chick follows the duckling on every adventure but soon finds, when the duckling decides to go swimming, that this is not always wise. The duckling must save the chick, and the chick learns his lesson. The next time the duckling decides to go swimming, the chick responds, "Not me." This text is well suited for sight word instruction. It tells a simple story using repetitious language. Emergent readers can easily use the language patterns to recognize the repeated words (*I, am, said, the, duck, me, too, chick*). Those words that vary are all verbs with an *–ing* ending (*digging, climbing, running, swimming*). Although these readers may have difficulty with the unfamiliar words, the pictures vividly depict the action, providing picture cues for decoding them.

Books with a cumulative pattern add one new phrase (usually a new character or a new event) as every page is turned. As the story progresses, all of the characters (or events) are repeated each time a new character is encountered. Steven Kellogg's *Chicken Little* tells the classic story of the chicken who becomes alarmed when an acorn hits her on the head, and exclaims, "The sky is falling! The sky is falling! I must tell the king!" On her way to inform the king, she meets a succession of animals who join her (Henny Penny, Ducky Lucky, Goosey Loosey, and Foxy Loxy). As each animal is encountered, Chicken Little repeats the story and that animal joins the group on their journey to the king. Other tales with cumulative patterns include Verna Aardema's (1983) *Bringing the Rain to Kapiti Plain*, Rodney Peppe's (1985) *The House That Jack Built*, and Maurice Sendak's (1962) *Chicken Soup with Rice*; however, these texts are much too difficult for pre-alphabetic and partial alphabetic readers. Table 6.1 provides a list of texts that can be used during explicit instruction to teach various word recognition strategies. Texts for use during sight word instruction can also be drawn from children's own language as they produce stories during the Language Experience Approach or from songs, chants, nursery rhymes, and poems.

In addition to selecting an appropriate text to use during instruction, there are a number of other factors that should be considered when teaching children to read by recognizing sight words. First, only a limited number of sight words (normally, between three and five) should be taught at one time. These should be the words that recur most frequently in the text selected for the lesson. In the example above, in which Ginsburg's (1991) *The Chick and the Duckling* was used, the words *I, am, said, the, me*, and *too* recur most frequently. Five of those words would be appropriate for focused sight word instruction. With pre-alphabetic and partial alphabetic readers, it is best to use the Shared Book Experience (Holdaway, 1979) to introduce text. This technique, which simulates the "lap reading" experience that occurs in many homes, has proven to be an effective means of enhancing young children's word analysis, comprehension, vocabulary, and fluency development (Eldredge, Reutzel, & Hollingsworth, 1996). The sample lesson depicted in Figure 6.5 uses this instructional method and focuses on other comprehension and word recognition strategies in addition to sight word recognition.

Notice that during this lesson, the sight words were taught using a direct teaching

TABLE 6.1. Texts for Use in Word Recognition Lessons

Strategy and Texts	Instructional Use
Recognizing Words by Sight	
Cole, J. (1989). *101 jump-rope rhymes.* New York: Scholastic.	Over 100 rhymes that use repetitious phrases and rhyme.
Cole, J., & Calmenson, S. (1990). *Miss Mary Mack and other children's street rhymes.* New York: Morrouno.	These rhymes involve hand-clapping, ball-bouncing, and counting-out rhymes that involve rhyme, repetitious phrases, and alliteration.
Deming, A. G. (1994). *Who is tapping at my window?* New York: Penguin.	A young girl hears a tapping at her window and repeatedly asks, "Who is there?" Various animals each respond, "It's not I." Each animal pair rhymes (e.g., the dog's response is followed by the frog's)
Eastman, P. D. (1960). *Are you my mother?* New York: Random House.	Tells the tale of a baby bird going on a long journey to find his mother.
Florian, D. (2000). *A pig is big.* Singapore: Greenwillow.	Rhyming text is used to explain the concept of size from pigs to cows to cars, and finally to the universe.
Galdone, P. (1968). *Henny Penny.* New York: Scholastic.	Classic cumulative tale in which an alarmed hen believes the sky is falling when an acorn hits her on the head. On her way to tell the king she meets a variety of animals that join her.
Ginsburg, M. (1999). *The chick and the duckling.* New York: Macmillan.	Uses repetitious phrases at an emergent reader level to tell the story of a chick that mimics a duckling's every move—until the duckling decides to take a swim.
Hutchins, P. (1968). *Rosie's walk.* New York: Macmillan.	Rosie the hen goes for a walk and unwittingly leads a fox, who is after her, into multiple disasters. Uses directionality words (e.g., over, around, past, through, under, into, across).
Kalan, R. (1981). *Jump, frog, jump!* New York: Greenwillow.	Cumulative tale of a frog trying to catch a fly without getting himself caught.
Langstaff, J. (1974). *Oh a-hunting we will go.* New York: Atheneum.	Uses rhyme and repetitious phrases to tell the story of a group who catches various animals (e.g., a fox is put in a box) and then lets each one go.
Martin, B. (1993). *Brown bear, brown bear.* New York: Holt, Rinehart, & Winston.	Beloved story that uses repetitious phrases (Brown Bear, Brown Bear what do you see? I see a _____ looking at me.) to describe the various animals that are seen.
Marzollo, J. (1989). *The teddy bear book.* New York: Dial.	These poems about teddy bears are adapted from songs, jump rope rhymes, cheers, and poems. Each uses repetitious phrases and rhyming.
Otto, C. (1991). *Dinosaur chase.* New York: HarperCollins	Minimal text and rhyme tell the story of a dinosaur chase that ensues after a valuable necklace is stolen.
Raffi. (1989). *Five little ducks.* New York: Crown.	Repetitious phrases and rhyme are used to tell the story of five little ducks who disappear one by one until their mother finds them.
Shaw, C. (1947). *It looked like spilt milk.* New York: Harper.	Repetitious phrases (Sometimes it looked like ____, but it wasn't _____.) are used to pique children's creative ideas about what a cloud might look like.
Silverstein, S. (1964). *A giraffe and a half.* New York: HarperCollins.	Uses rhymes and cumulative patterns to explain what happens when a giraffe is "stretched another half."
Taback, S. (1997). *There was an old lady who swallowed a fly.* New York: Penguin.	Classic cumulative tale of an old woman who swallows a series of creatures. Uses repetitious phrases and rhyme.

(cont.)

TABLE 6.1. *(cont.)*

Strategy and Texts	Instructional Use
Using Letter-Sound Cues	
Base, G. (1986). *Animalia*. New York: Harry Abrams.	Uses alliteration and fanciful illustration to provide a variety of images for each letter of the alphabet.
Brown, M. W. (1993). *Four fur feet*. New York: Doubleday.	Reader is drawn to the /f/ sound. The phrase "four fur feet" is repeated in every sentence as the furry creature walks through different places (along a river, into the country, etc.)
Ehlert, L. (1989). *Eating the alphabet: Fruits and vegetables A to Z*. Sand Diego, CA: Harcourt Brace Jovanovich.	Various fruits and vegetables are depicted for each letter of the alphabet.
Gordon, J. (1991). *Six sleepy sheep*. New York: Puffin Books.	Reader is drawn to the /s/ sound as six sheep try to fall asleep by slurping celery soup, telling spooky stories, singing songs, and sipping simmering milk.
Hague, K. (1984). *Alphabears*. New York: Henry Holt.	26 teddy bears introduce the alphabet using alliteration (e.g., Teddy Bear John loves jam and jelly).
Van Allsburg, C. (1987). *The Z was zapped*. Boston: Houghton Mifflin.	Depicts how each letter of the alphabet was engaged in an alliterative misfortune.
Analogizing	
Degan, B. (1983). *Jamberry*. New York: Harper.	Uses rhyme to share the joys of berry picking.
Fortunata. (1968). *Catch a little fox*. New York: Scholastic.	A group of children goes hunting and talks about what they will catch and where they will keep it. Each phrase rhymes (e.g., a frog will be put in a log). In the end the animals capture the children and put them in a ring to hear them sing.
Hawkins, C., & Hawkins, J. (1986). *Tog the dog*. New York: G. P. Putnam's Sons.	The use of the –og rime is prevalent in this tale of the adventures of Tog the dog who likes to jog, gets lost in the fog, etc.
Hawkins, C., & Hawkins, J. (1985). *Jen the hen*. New York: G. P. Putnam's Sons.	The use of the –en rime is prevalent in this tale.
Hawkins, C., & Hawkins, J. (1984). *Mig the pig*. New York: G. P. Putnam's Sons.	The use of the –ig rime is prevalent in this tale.
Hawkins, C., & Hawkins, J. (1993). *Pat the cat*. New York: G. P. Putnam's Sons.	The use of the –at rime is prevalent in this tale.
Hepworth, C. (1992). *Antics: An alphabetical anthology*. New York: Putnam	Uses intriguing illustrations of various ants as they engage in activities or with objects containing the –ant rime (e.g, antique).
Most, B. (1999). *There's an ant in Anthony*. New York: Econo-Clad Books.	Polysyllabic words containing the –ant rime are present throughout as Anthony tries to find "ants" in everyday objects.
Most, B. (1981). *There's an Ape Behind the Drape*. New York: Morrow/Avon.	The –ape rime is prevalent in this tale.

TABLE 6.1. *(cont.)*

Strategy and Texts	Instructional Use
Analogizing *(cont.)*	
Rosen, M. (1995). *Walking the bridge of your nose.* New York: Kingfisher.	Collection of poems, riddles, and rhymes.
Shaw, N. (1986). *Sheep in a jeep.* Boston: Houghton Mifflin.	Use of the –eep rime is prevalent in this tale.
Shaw, N. (1989). *Sheep on a ship.* Boston: Houghton Mifflin.	Rhyme and alliteration abound in this story of sheep on a deep sea voyage. Uses rimes –ip, -ap, -orm, -ail, -ide, -aft, and -ift.
Shaw, N. (1992). *Sheep out to eat.* Boston: Houghton Mifflin.	Rhyme and alliteration are used to tell the tale of sheep in a tea shop who have trouble finding something palatable to eat. Uses rimes –op, -eat, -urp, -ard, -ite, -ake, -ash, -out, -unch, -ip.
Silverstein, S. (1974). *Where the sidewalk ends.* New York: HarperCollins.	Classic collection of poems that use rhyme and alliteration.
Seuss, Dr. (1974). *There's a wocket in my pocket.* New York: Random House.	Uses manipulatives of onsets with rimes (zlock/clock) to tell the zany tale of a character who meets a variety of pleasant and unpleasant characters (yottle/bottle).
Seuss, Dr. (1957). *The cat in the hat.* New York: Random House	A variety of rimes are used to tell the story of the Cat in the Hat as he comes to entertain the children on a rainy day.
Seuss, Dr. (1960). *Green eggs and ham.* New York: Random House.	Uses (-am, -ouse, -ox, -ere) to tell the cumulative tale of Sam, who tries to convince his friend to eat green eggs and ham.
Seuss, Dr. (1963). *Hop on pop.* New York: Random House.	Uses a variety of rimes (-up, -ouse, -all, -ay, -ight, -im, -ee, -ed, -at, -ad, -ing, -ong, -alk, -op, own, -ack).
Winthrop, E. (1986). *Shoes.* New York: HarperTrophy.	Describes various types of shoes using repetitious phrases and rhyming.

method. Sight words should be introduced using a predictable method to which students become accustomed. Notice also that the teacher incorporated comprehension strategies and links to other word recognition strategies when possible. The lesson began by engaging students in the comprehension strategies of previewing the text, thinking about what they already know about chicks and ducklings, and making predictions. As the sight words were taught, the teacher pointed out some of the structural features of each word. Although these readers may be in the pre-alphabetic and partial alphabetic phases of development, this does not preclude them from being introduced to letter–sound cues or other cues that might help them distinguish one word from another. These readers may not fully understand or use these cues to identify words yet, but they should begin to hear the strategic language associated with their use. In reality, these readers may be able to recognize *me* as the small word and *chick* as the long word, but as they continue to read and reread the same text and other texts, they will notice other features of those words—which is another reason why sight word instruction should provide ample practice in a variety of strategies.

Students should use the new words they have learned in their writing, their oral language, and their reading. For example, after rereading the text over the course of several

Teacher: Janice Almasi

Topic: Recognizing words by sight

Grade level: K–2

STAIRS hypothesis being addressed:

Students are partial alphabetic readers who are just beginning to learn to read. They are able to use environmental cues and pictures cues to read words and are able to "read" text they have memorized. Students are beginning to recognize the relationship between letters and the sounds they make and use initial consonant sounds and some ending sounds to represent words in their writing. Students need to develop a bank of words they can recognize quickly and automatically by sight.

Goal of Lesson

Students will learn:

- To recognize the words *me, too, said, the, chick* by sight
- That sentences are read from left to right and end with a period

Materials

- *The Chick and the Duckling* by Mirra Ginsburg (big book version)
- Sentence strips
- Word cards with the words: *am, said, the, me,* and *too* on them
- Pocket chart
- Paper (or felt) representations of the Chick and the Duckling depicted in the text

Introduction

Declarative and conditional knowledge about comprehension strategies

Introduce the story *The Chick and the Duckling* by having the students look at the pictures on the cover. Ask students to describe what they see. Read the title to the students and have students make predictions about what the story might be about. "Today we are going to read a story. Before we read any story it is always a good idea to look at the pictures on the cover and think about what it might be about. So let's study the picture on the cover. What do you see?" Have students share their observations and predictions about what the story might be about. Then read the title to the students and have them refine their predictions and observations further.

Declarative and conditional knowledge about

Comprehension strategies

Remind students that it is always a good idea to think about what we know about the subject of a book before we read it. This helps us get ready to read. Have students think about what they know about chicks and ducklings. Try to guide their thoughts to things that chicks and ducklings do as this is the focus of the text. As students share their thoughts, record their ideas about what chicks do on one semantic web and their ideas about what ducklings do on another. Have students think about and share what they might like to find out as you read the book.

FIGURE 6.5. Sample lesson teaching students to recognize words by sight.

Begin reading the book aloud to the students. Since the text has repetitious language you might encourage the students to join in once they pick up the pattern, or after reading the lines in which the duckling says, "I am _____ing." you might ask the students, "What do you think the chick might say?" and have them join in chorally as you read the chick's response, "'Me too,' said the Chick."

After you finish reading the text aloud once engage students in a brief discussion in which they stop and share their reactions to the book with a partner. You might ask students to think and talk about whether the ideas they had about what chicks and ducklings do matched the author's ideas.

Description of Instructional Experience
Explain that the author, Mirra Ginsburg, uses many of the same words over and over throughout the story. Ask students if they remember any of the words that were used over and over again. Often students remember the phrase, "Me too, said the Chick." Place a sentence strip with that phrase written in black marker in the pocket chart. Point to each word as you reread the sentence aloud for the students. Explain that today we are going to learn to read a few new words that the author used over and over again in the story *The Chick and the Duckling*.

Direct teaching of sight word
1. *Look at word and say it*
2. *Tell the meaning*
3. *Analyze the word's structure*
4. *Discuss the the word and use in context*

Show students a word card with the word *me* written in red on it. Say the word. Point out various features of the word. "Listen to the sounds in the word *me*." Pronounce the word very deliberately emphasizing the sounds /m/ and /ē/. Have students think about other words that begin with the same /m/ sound. "The word *me* has the same sound at the beginning as lots of other words. *M-m-m-m-e*. What other words do you know that start with an /m/ sound?" Have students share those words. "Yes, all of those words (repeat the words) begin with the /m/ sound. The word *me* starts the same way. The letter that makes the /m/ sound is "m." Notice that the word *me* has an "m" at the beginning. It also has an /ē/ sound at the end. *M-e-e-e-e*. Do you know any other words that end with an /ē/ sound?" Have students share words. They may have difficulty with this concept. You may have to model and share rhyming words such as *be, see, knee, tree, pea,* and *we*. Discuss the word's meaning and how it is used in sentences. Have students use the word in sentences.

Guided practice

Pronounce the word again and have one student place it on top of the word "Me" in the sentence in the pocket chart. Pass out envelopes containing each of the five target sight words in them (me, too, said, the, Chick). Ask students to spread out their word cards and find the word "me." Follow the same procedure to teach the other four sight words. Follow the same direct teaching method for each of the remaining sight words.

Model/ think aloud

Explain that now that we know several words we can use them to build sentences. Model and demonstrate how to build the sentence from *The*

(cont.)

FIGURE 6.5. *(cont.)*

Chick and the Duckling. Engage in a think aloud as you explain that when we read in English the words always start on the left and go to the right. Place the sentence strip with the phrase, "'Me too,' said the Chick." written in black in the pocket chart. Model how to rebuild the sentence by placing the red word cards over top of the black words. Try to use strategic language to help students learn to distinguish between the sight words. "I know the sentence says, 'Me too, said the Chick.' I have to find the word *me* first. *M-m-m-m-e.* Hmmm, it starts with an /m/ sound. I know that the letter "m" makes an /m/ sound so I have to find a word that starts with 'm.' Okay, I see one." Pick up the red word card "me" and as you say it place it on top of the black "me" on the sentence strip. Continue in this manner, placing the rest of the red word cards on top of the sentence strip. Remind students that a period marks the end of this sentence. Place a period word card as the last word card in the sentence. Ignore the quotation marks for now, unless students ask about them. If they do ask, use the teachable moment to explain quotation marks.

Guided practice

Pass out a sentence strip containing the phrase, "'Me too,' said the Chick." to pairs of students. Have them work together to rebuild each sentence using their word cards. Make sure students pronounce each word as they lay it on top of the identical word in the sentence. As students engage in this activity, observe their progress by making anecdotal records. You may stop and ask each pair of students how they knew a particular word to try to gauge what strategies they are using to recognize the sight words. "How did you know that word was _____?" Record students' responses in notes. Make sure students mix up the word cards each time they rebuild the sentence. As a challenge you can have them remove the sentence strip to see if they can build the sentence without the sentence strip as a guide.

Reread

Guided practice

After students have practiced for awhile, gather them together to reread the story. Explain that you are going to reread the story and that the students can join in with the reading at any time now that they are more familiar with some of the words. Begin rereading the story and encourage students to join in chorally, reading those parts with which they feel comfortable. If students did well with the sentence rebuilding you might have them place their word cards on top of the phrase, or build it on their own, each time it is reread in the story.

Conclusion

Have students complete a self-assessment using their three faces on craft sticks. One craft stick has a circle with a smiley face on it, one has a frowning face on it, and one has a straight mouth on it. Each student should have their own set of craft sticks. Ask students the following questions. "Which face shows how you felt about the story *The Chick and the Duckling*?" Have students hold up the appropriate face and take anecdotal notes on their responses. "Which face shows how

FIGURE 6.5. *(cont.)*

well you were able to learn the new words *me, too, said, the, Chick?*" Have students hold up the appropriate face and take anecdotal notes on their responses. "Which face shows how well you were able to rebuild the sentence?" Have students hold up the appropriate face and take anecdotal notes on their responses. After each response engage students in a discussion about their responses (e.g., Why was it hard to recognize some of the words? Why was it easy to rebuild the sentence?).

An alternative is to type the questions on a piece of paper and draw the three faces after each question. Each student receives his own self-assessment to complete. As you read each question, have students think about their responses and circle the appropriate face. This procedure takes a bit more time but eliminates the need to take anecdotal notes.

Assessment

- You will know whether students are able to recognize the words *me, too, said, the, chick* by sight if they are able to pick up the appropriate word when it is read aloud and place it on the sentence strip.
- You will know whether students know that sentences are read from left to right and end with a period if they are able to rebuild the sentence using their word cards going from left to right and ending them with a period word card.

Follow up

Students can identify those sight words from the story they know automatically. These words can be added to their personal word banks for use in word hunts, concept sorts, and writing activities (see Bear, Invernizzi, Templeton, & Johnston, 2000 for many more word bank activities). Word hunts require students to search through their word banks for words that have a given feature (i.e., words that begin with a /k/ or end with /t/). Concept sorts require students to find words from their word banks that fit a particular category (i.e., words that are movements [kick, jump, fly], words that are animals). Word banks can be used to help students as they write, or students may try to generate sentences using words from their word banks.

FIGURE 6.5. *(cont.)*

days, students might work in small groups or with a partner to create an alternate version of the text. Each group or pair of students might add an adventure for the chick and the duckling. That is, they might add their own sentence about the duckling doing something and the chick responding, "Me too." You might encourage students to draw from their original list of duckling actions that was brainstormed and webbed prior to reading the story. If students noted that ducklings "jump," then they might add the adventure, " 'I am jumping,' said the Duckling. 'Me too,' said the Chick." Each pair of students can illustrate their adventure on a large piece of paper, with their adventure written on the bottom. After each pair completes their adventure, the entire new version can be bound into a book. Each pair of students can read their page of the new book. To give them practice in using the new sight words orally, students might also dramatize their new story or the original story.

Students should also be encouraged to use the new sight words in their daily journals or in Language Experience stories. You might write some of their sentences on sentence strips leaving a blank where one of the new sight words belongs. Place the sentence strip in the pocket chart and read the sentence to the students. Students can use their individual word cards to hold up the sight word they think makes sense in the blank. In this way students use their semantic and syntactic knowledge as well as their grapho–phonemic knowledge to help them determine which sight word fits in a sentence. Given that these sentences differ from those in the story, students learn to recognize words outside of their original context. Table 6.2 highlights those elements that are most essential to remember when teaching students to recognize words by sight.

Using Letter–Sound Cues

Readers who use the letter–sound strategy are able to recognize unknown words by looking at letters and groups of letters in a word, thinking about the sounds associated with those letters, and blending those sounds together to form a spoken word. Readers in the partial alphabetic phase of development are beginning to use letter–sound cues to recognize unknown words. That is, they look at the letters in a word, associate sounds with those letters, and use that knowledge of letters and sounds to read words. As noted earlier, readers in this phase of development normally use the letter–sound cues they glean from the beginning and end of the word and search their mind for a word that begins and ends similarly. They take an "educated guess" at the word, based on the letter–sound cues, the context, and their schemata. Readers who are at the alphabetic phase of development are able to use letter–sound cues to decode the entire word.

Intrinsic to the ability to recognize letter–sound correspondences is *phonological awareness*. Phonological awareness is a superordinate term referring to the ability to at-

TABLE 6.2. Teaching Readers to Recognize Words by Sight

1. Teach a limited number of sight words at a time (3–5 words).

2. Select those words that recur most frequently in the text you are using for instruction. Be sure that the text is developmentally appropriate for your students. Most texts for sight word instruction contain predictable patterns: repetitious words or phrases, cumulative patterns, or rhyme.

3. Use a direct and predictable teaching method for sight word instruction:

   a. Look at the word and say it.

   b. Explain the meaning of the word.

   c. Analyze the word structurally.

   d. Discuss the word and use it in context.

4. Provide ample practice in a variety of authentic ways in addition to flash card activities.

5. Encourage students to use the word in their oral and written work.

6. Use a pocket chart with slotted sentences from stories and other text with which children are familiar, so that students can use their background knowledge and knowledge of sentence structure (i.e., syntax) to take educated guesses about the word.

tend to, identify, and manipulate the sound segments of speech (Bear et al., 2000; Blachman, 2000). Recognizing alliteration, rhyme, and syllables requires phonological awareness, as does the ability to segment words into their constituent sounds and blend those sounds into words. *Phonemic awareness*, a subcategory of phonological awareness, refers only to the ability to identify and manipulate individual phonemes within words. For example, when the word *cat* is pronounced, a child with phonemic awareness would be able to identify each phoneme in the word *cat* (/k/, /a/, /t/) and blend the sounds together to say the word. The child would also be able to manipulate those sounds. That is, if you asked her to substitute the /k/ sound in *cat* with a /s/ sound, the child would be able to identify the phonemes /s/, /a/, /t/ and blend them together to say the word *sat*. There is convincing research evidence that phonological awareness is a predictor of future success in reading (Blachman, 2000). There also is evidence that many children develop such understanding naturally by playing rhyming games, oral language games, singing, chanting, and connecting speech to print during read alouds (Murray, Stahl, & Ivey, 1996). For these children, explicit instruction and training in phonological awareness is *not* necessary. However, those children who do not develop phonological awareness on their own by playing with oral language require more explicit instruction.

Phonological awareness and phonemic awareness refer only to the *sounds* in words and therefore are *not* equivalent to *phonics*, which refers to the relationship between *letters* and the *sounds* that make them. Blachman's (2000) review of the research noted that when instruction links phonological awareness to the letters that represent those sounds (i.e., letter–sound correspondences, phonics) word recognition is enhanced. Thus letter–sound relationships are critical to becoming a proficient reader in English.

The sounding and blending process that readers who use letter–sound cues employ to read unfamiliar words is often a slow, deliberate one (Ehri, 1991). Fox (2000) noted that as readers become facile with letter–sound cues, they begin to recognize letter–sound "neighborhoods"—a letter sequence that represents one or more sounds in a word. For example, the *c* in *cat* is a letter that represents one sound, /k/, but the *ch–* in *chat* is a letter–sound neighborhood (i.e., a consonant digraph) that represents one sound, /ch/. The *–augh* in *caught* is also a letter–sound neighborhood. It is a sequence of letters that recurs in English words to produce an /aw/ sound. As students read more, they become more familiar with these letter–sound combinations. Eventually the sounding and blending process speeds up, but it is always a slower process than recognizing words by sight or than using orthographic cues.

The success of using letter–sound cues to recognize unfamiliar words depends on the regularity of the letter–sound correspondences in a word (Ehri, 1991). For example, the sequence of letters *–ough* can have multiple pronunciations in the English language, as in the words *tough*, *bough*, *cough*, and *dough*. These inconsistencies make it difficult for emergent readers to use letter–sound cues. Those readers who have auditory difficulties are further impeded when trying to use letter–sound cues. Many struggling readers have had some form of auditory difficulty (i.e., hearing loss, tubes in ears, ear infections) at the time when they were learning to read.

Children who have learned to read using primarily letter–sound strategies (i.e., phonics) often make miscues, or reading errors, that produce nonsense words (i.e., mispronunciations). For these students, reading has become more a matter of word calling than meaning getting. It is essential for these readers to engage in "cross-checking" as they use letter–sound strategies to decode words (Fox, 2000). As shown in Table 6.3, cross-checking is one of the procedural steps necessary for learning how to use letter–sound

TABLE 6.3. Declarative, Procedural, and Conditional Knowledge Associated with Word Recognition Strategies

Word Recognition Strategy	Associated Declarative Knowledge	Associated Procedural Knowledge	Associated Conditional Knowledge
Using Letter–Sound Cues	Readers need to know *that*: • Words are comprised of letters • Letters represent sounds • Sounds can be blended together to form spoken words • Consonant sounds are more reliable than vowel sounds	*How* to use letter–sound cues: • Look at the beginning of the word. • Think about what sound the letter(s) at the beginning of the word makes. • Look at the next group of letters. • Think about what sound(s) the letter(s) makes. • Blend the sounds together. • Cross-check to make sure the sounds blended together form a real word that makes sense in the context. • If the blended word does not make sense, reblend it, trying different sounds with the same letters; and cross-check; or regroup the letters, reblend, and cross-check.	*When* is it helpful to use letter–sound cues? • Readers can recognize words that are in their spoken vocabulary but not in their reading vocabulary. *Why* is it helpful to use letter–sound cues? • Provides readers with a more reliable means of decoding unfamiliar words. • Enables readers to read sight words with increased accuracy (Ehri, 1991).
Analogizing	Readers need to know *that*: • Words share common letter patterns (e.g., rimes). • Beginning sounds can be added to those common letter patterns. • Blending beginning sounds with the common letter patterns can create new words. • Analogizing is helpful when decoding polysyllabic words.	*How* to analogize: • Look for a familiar letter pattern in the word (e.g., rimes). • Pronounce the letter pattern. • Look at the letters that come before the letter pattern (e.g., "onsets"). • Think about what sounds the letters make. • Blend the beginning sounds together with the letter pattern. • Cross-check to make sure the blended sounds form a real word that makes sense in the context. • If the blended word does not make sense, reblend it, trying different sounds with the same letters, and cross-check; or regroup the letters, reblend, and cross-check.	*When* is it helpful to use analogizing? • When reading single syllable and poly-syllabic words *Why* is it helpful to use analogizing? • Readers who use analogizing expend less mental effort in recognizing unfamiliar words than readers who decode letter by letter (Fox, 2000). • Blending onsets and rimes is easier than blending individual sounds in words. • Remembering rimes makes it easier to learn vowel variants and eliminates the need to learn exceptions to vowel rules.

	Readers need to know that:	How to use orthographic cues:	When is it helpful to use orthographic cues?
Using Structural Analysis Cues (Chunking)	• Spoken words can be divided into small and large sound units. • The same sound units, or letter patterns, recur in many words. • Some of the multiletter chunks in words are meaningful and some are not. • Recognizable multiletter chunks include prefixes, suffixes, root words, compound words, contractions, and syllables.	• Look carefully at the word. • Look at the beginning of the word for a prefix. If there is one, pronounce it. • Look at the end of the word for a suffix. If you see one, pronounce it. • Now look for a smaller word or a root word within the word. Think about its meaning. • Look for ways to divide the word into syllables. • Blend the chunks together. • Cross-check to make sure the word is pronounceable. Can I pronounce the word? Does it look right? Does it make sense? • If the word does not make sense or does not sound right, then rechunk the word by dividing it into different multiletter chunks. • Reblend the chunks. • Cross-check. • If the word still does not make sense, use the letter–sound cue or the analogy strategy.	• When reading polysyllabic words *Why* is it helpful to use orthographic cues? • These cues facilitate decoding unfamiliar words, particularly polysyllabic ones (Ehri, 1991). • Readers who use chunking expend less mental effort in recognizing unfamiliar words than readers who decode letter by letter (Fox, 2000). • Blending chunks is easier than blending individual sounds in words. • These cues enable readers to set up access routes in memory for reading words by sight (Ehri, 1991).

	Readers need to know that:	How to use context cues:	When is it helpful to use context cues?
Using Context Cues	• When they come to words they don't know, they can use the pictures and surrounding words to help them. • They must be able to read most of the surrounding words in order for context cues to be effective. • Sometimes there are not enough cues in the context to help readers figure out an unknown word.	• When an unknown word is encountered, stop and think about what word might make sense in that space. • Reread the words in that sentence and the sentences before and after it for contextual help. • Look at the clues in the pictures. • Make a list of words that might make sense in the space. • Look carefully at the letters in the word and the sounds they make to see if any of the words in the list have those letters and sounds in them.	• When an unknown word has a supportive context (i.e., pictures and words) *Why* is it helpful to use context cues? • They help bring meaning to the reading event.

cues as a strategy. Cross-checking occurs after the reader has sounded out and blended each letter–sound neighborhood. It involves stopping and thinking about whether the resulting word is a real word that the reader has heard before, and whether it fits in the context of what is being read.

Several instructional principles for teaching letter–sound cues foster a safe environment for using this strategy. First, instruction should occur within an authentic reading context rather than in isolation. "Isolation" refers to activities and instruction that are not linked in any way to text. Sometimes teachers design word recognition instruction in kindergarten and first grade around a "letter of the week." Such instruction introduces letters and sounds without relating them to authentic reading and writing contexts (Wagstaff, 1997–1998). Even when such instruction features rich language development around many different words that begin with the featured letter of the week, and even when such instruction is linked to alphabet books, readers are left with no understanding of the *strategic processes* that underlie the application of using letter–sound cues to decode unfamiliar words (Stahl, 1992). Teaching letter–sound cues outside authentic reading contexts creates greater opportunity for failure that lowers self-esteem. Without authentic contexts, readers have no other cues to rely on to help them with the word recognition process. Texts that are most appropriate for beginning reading instruction are those, as in sight word instruction, that have predictable and repetitious patterns of language. These texts—which include familiar nursery rhymes, poems, and jump-rope chants as well as books—provide a more supportive context for readers to use letters and sounds as a strategy for recognizing unknown words.

The idea of teaching word recognition more as a strategy than a skill is one that my graduate students find particularly challenging. Fluent adult reading is comprised entirely of skillful reading, which makes it very difficult to even see the need to be strategic during the word recognition process. In the sample lesson in Figure 6.6, a model of explicit instruction in using letter–sound cues as a *strategy* is presented. This lesson, like the lesson on sight word instruction, uses the shared book experience (Holdaway, 1979) as a methodological framework.

The major distinction between this lesson and those that are more skills-based is that the teacher provides explanations of the declarative, procedural, and conditional knowledge associated with using letter–sound cues as a word recognition strategy (see Table 6.3). The lesson also relates this instruction to authentic texts. Once students have been introduced to the strategy, they can be encouraged to use it in their independent reading. This usage can be modeled for students during read alouds as well as shared reading experiences. For example, during independent reading time (i.e., Drop Everything And Read, Sustained Silent Reading), students can be encouraged to jot down any words they did not recognize automatically. Some teachers find that providing students with a chart, such as the one depicted in Figure 6.7, is helpful for such tasks. As students read, they record any words they did not know automatically, then place check marks next to the strategy (or strategies) they used to try to decode the word. Students can place a star in the column of the strategy that helped them the most, and they can place a smiley face or a frown face next to the unknown word to indicate whether their strategy use was successful or not. It is important that teachers model using this chart prior to asking students to use it during their independent reading time. Modeling can be done during a read aloud. As you encounter a word that might be difficult for your students to decode, you can think aloud about the strategies

Teacher: Janice F. Almasi

Topic: Recognizing words using the letter-sound cue strategy

Grade level: 1–2

STAIRS hypothesis being addressed:

Students are partial alphabetic or alphabetic readers. They are able to identify the sounds in a spoken word and are beginning to use initial and final letters to help them recognize unfamiliar words.

Goal of Lesson

Students will learn:

• To identify words that begin with /f/, /fl/, /fr/
• To identify words that begin with /sn/, /sw/, /sl/ (if students are ready)

Materials

• *Jump, Frog, Jump!* by Robert Kalan
• Words cards with the words: *fly, frog, fish,* on them
• Pocket chart
• Chart paper

Introduction

Declarative and conditional knowledge about comprehension strategies

Introduce the story *Jump, Frog, Jump!* by Robert Kalan by having students look at the pictures on the cover. Ask students to describe what they see. Read the title to the students and have students make predictions about what the story might be about. "Today we are going to read a story. Before we read any story it is always a good idea to look at the pictures on the cover and think about what it might be about. So let's study the picture on the cover. What do you see?" Students might notice the fly, fish, frog, snake, and turtle on the cover and make predictions about how those characters might be related to the title. Have students share their observations and their predictions about what the story might be about. Then read the title to the students and have them refine their predictions and observations further.

Declarative and conditional knowledge about comprehension strategies

Remind students that it is always a good idea to think about what we know about the subject of a book before we read it. This helps us get ready to read. Have students gather into five small groups and ask each group to think about what they know about the habits and habitat of one of the characters. Each group can record their ideas on a web or brainstorm their ideas. As each group shares their thoughts record their ideas on a semantic web for each creature. Have students think about and share what they might like to find out as you read the book.

Declarative knowledge

Draw students' attention to the names of each character depicted on the cover. Explain that sometimes the first letter in a word is the same as in *fish, fly,* and *frog.* Explain that today we are going to be learning how to use the other letters and sounds in words to help us recognize them.

(cont.)

FIGURE 6.6. Sample lesson teaching students to use letter–sound cues as a strategy for recognizing unknown words.

Description of Instructional Experience

Explain that first we will read the book. Read the book aloud to students. Stop at various points to have students discuss their predictions with a partner to determine whether their predictions were verified or rejected. Once the book is completed, have students share their thoughts and reactions to the book with a partner and then hold a brief whole group sharing of those reactions to the text. Make links between the students' initial webs and what habits the creatures actually exhibited in the text.

Declarative and conditional knowledge

1. Draw attention to students' use of the words *fish, fly,* and *frog* and ask how we might be able to tell the difference between those words when we are reading them, since they all start with the same sound /f/. Explain that although using the beginning letter of a word is very helpful in reading words, sometimes words start with the same letter. Explain that when this happens we have to look more carefully at the rest of the word to tell them apart. Display word cards with the words *fish, fly,* and *frog* on them.

Model/ think aloud

"Hmmm, as I look at the words *fish, fly,* and *frog* I notice that they all start the same way with an 'f.' I'd better look more carefully at the next letters to see how they are different." Model and think aloud as you pronounce the individual phonemes in each word and then blend them together to pronounce the entire word. Next, model how to cross-check to make sure the blended word is a real word that makes sense. Continue in this manner, thinking aloud as you examine the graphic and phonemic differences between the three words. Have students share their insights as to how they may be able to distinguish among the three words as well. Explain that sometimes two consonants work together to make sounds. Explain that in the beginning of the word *fly* the "f" combines with the "l" and we hear two sounds. Explain that there are lots of words that begin with "fl." Share a couple of examples and have students share others. Add these words onto the class word wall under "fl." Follow same procedures for "fr."

Procedural knowledge

Verbalization

Guided practice

Explain that as we reread the story *Jump, Frog, Jump!* There will be several times when we hear words that begin with /f/, /fl/, and /fr/. Pass out word cards with *fish, fly,* and *frog* on them. As the story is reread, have students hold up a word card each time they hear a word that starts the same way as *fish, fly,* or *frog.* Reread text, stopping as students hear words with the /f/, /fl/, or /fr/ sound in them. Have students share how they could tell that the word on the card had the same beginning sound as the word in the text. Students can then engage in a word sort activity in which they sort a number of different word cards each word beginning with either /f/, /fl/, or /fr/. Students group the words into categories by comparing the similarities and differences within and across the words.

Verbalization

2. If students seem fairly successful with the previous portion of the lesson, they might be able to consider other consonant blends as well. If they are not then it would be wise to move on to step 3. Ask students if they noticed any other words that started with two consonant sounds. For example, students may notice that *swallowed* and *swam* both begin with

(cont.)

FIGURE 6.6. *(cont.)*

*Model/
think aloud*

*Guided
practice*

/sw/, that *snake* begins with /sn/, or that *slid* begins with /sl/. Write each word on a word card and engage in a think aloud in which you point out the graphic and phonemic features of the words. Explain that we can add an "sw," "sn," and an "sl" section onto our word wall. As we reread let's listen to see if we hear the words that start with /sw/, /sn/, and /sl/." Pass word cards out to students and have students continue listening, holding up either *swam*, *snake*, or *slid* each time they hear a word that starts with those sounds. Again, a word sort activity using words with initial consonant blends /sw/, /sn/, and /sl/ could be used at this point to help children compare and contrast the features of words beginning similarly.

*Guided
practice*

3. At the conclusion of the rereading, note the words that were added to the word wall. Explain that there are many other words that we might encounter as we read that begin with /f/, /fl/, and /fr/. Have pairs of students engage in a word hunt in which they look through magazines for pictures of words that start with either /f/, /fl/, or /fr/; or they can look through their word banks, writing folders, or familiar texts they have already read to find words that start with "f," "fl," and "fr." Materials should be ones with which students are familiar. As students locate words and pictures, they can add them to the sheet of paper that has the appropriate consonant or consonant blend on the top and the keyword from the story (i.e., /fl/ fly). If students cut out pictures, they should also be asked to label each picture as they paste it onto the appropriate paper.

Verbalization

4. Once students have completed their hunt, the groups can gather together to engage in a discussion, listing the words and pictures they found that represent each sound. Discussion should focus on verbalizing why particular words fit into particular categories. Words can then be added to the class word wall under "f," "fl," and "fr" columns.

Conclusion

Verbalization

Have students share what they should do when during reading they come to a word they don't know how to pronounce. Have students share whether it was easy or difficult to find words that started with /f/, /fl/, and /fr/. Have students explain how they can tell the difference between these words given that they all start with "f."

Assessment

• You will know whether students are able to identify words that begin with /f/, /fl/, /fr/ or /sn/, /sw/, /sl/ if they are able to locate pictures and/or words from familiar texts that begin with those sounds.

FIGURE 6.6. *(cont.)*

Unknown Word	Page Number	Word Recognition Strategy Used			
		Letter–Sound Cues	Analogize	Chunk	Context Cues

FIGURE 6.7. Sample sheet for recording word recognition strategies used during independent reading.

you would use to decode the word. As you use engage in the process, model how to complete the chart. As students use the chart for the first few times, you might want to circulate among them to scaffold its use. After independent reading time, students might pair with one another and discuss the book they read, the words they could not recognize automatically, and the strategies they used to try to decode them. This strategic discourse is as essential to learning how to use word recognition strategies as it is to using comprehension strategies. Students need opportunities to verbalize the strategies they use and listen to how others strategically approach words.

Again, as with any strategy instruction, it is essential that students feel safe and secure in their learning environment, if they are to be willing to share their frustrations and their attempts to resolve them. It is important during this time to praise and celebrate students' efforts, even when they are unsuccessful at actually decoding the unknown words. Taking risks by trying to use strategies is the primary goal.

Analogizing

Skilled readers do not recognize unfamiliar words letter by letter or sound them out letter by letter, as is done when using the letter–sound cue strategy (Pressley, 2000). As readers mature, they are able to recognize common letter patterns and have a store of known words that they are able to read by sight. Therefore, instead of reading words sequentially in a letter-by-letter fashion, they recognize common letter chunks and, when reading unfamiliar words, blend the chunks together. This method makes word recognition a quicker, more automatic process (Ehri, 1991; Fox, 2000).

When readers use analogizing to recognize unknown words, they are making use of familiar letter patterns to help them read unfamiliar words. These letter patterns provide readers with a stable and regular system for decoding. For example, if a reader knew the *–ust* letter pattern, he could use that knowledge to read the words *rust, trust,* and *disgust.* As noted, the *–ust* letter pattern is called a *rime* or a *phonogram.* Rimes are the vowel(s) and consonant(s) at the end of a syllable. In the example above, the vowel *u* and the consonants that follow it, *st,* comprise the *–ust* rime. The consonants that come at the beginning of a syllable are called *onsets.* In the example above, *r* is the onset in *rust* that is attached to the *–ust* rime. Onsets can consist of single consonants (e.g., *b, d, g, j, r*), consonant blends (e.g., *cr, tr, thr, scr*), or consonant digraphs (e.g., *sh, wh, ch, th*). Some refer to the words that are derived from onsets and rimes as word families. Thus the *–ust* "word family" would consist of single syllable words (e.g., *bust, crust, dust, gust, just, rust*) and polysyllabic words that contain the *–ust* rime somewhere within it (e.g., *disgust, distrust, encrust, entrust, sawdust*). When words end with similar rimes (e.g., just, trust), they usually rhyme.

Rimes can also consist of a single vowel, as in the *–y* family (e.g., *by, cry, dry, fly, my*). Some rimes consist of letter patterns (found in sight words) that can stand alone without an onset (e.g., *–an, –it, –on, –in*) or can be combined with onsets. These usually make the best rimes for beginning analogizing instruction, because they are sight words containing letter patterns that readers internalize and remember quickly.

Ehri (1991) noted that older readers are more likely than younger readers to use analogizing to read unfamiliar words. For it to help younger readers, analogizing must be taught more formally. Ehri's review of research also noted that, for younger readers to be able to use analogizing, they must be able to segment words into onsets and rimes, and they must have some ability to use letter–sound cues. Thus, for readers to successfully use analogizing, they should at least be in the partial alphabetic or alphabetic phase of development. A list of 37 high-frequency rimes in the English language is presented in Figure 6.8.

The underlying principle of analogizing is that if readers can automatically recognize a letter pattern or rime, such as *–end,* and if they are able to blend onsets onto that rime, then they should be able to read a multitude of words even if they are unfamiliar (e.g., *bend, blend, fend, lend, mend, send, amend, commend, comprehend*). Sometimes readers can use their knowledge of a familiar letter pattern in a sight word and analogize the letter pattern to an unfamiliar word. For example, suppose a reader could not recognize the word *twig* in the sentence, "There was a twig on the ground." However, the reader does know the word *big* and is able to manipulate the sounds in a word. Therefore, she can use her knowledge of the *–ig* rime and substitute a /tw/ for the /b/ to help her recognize

-ack
back, black, clack, crack, hack, lack, knack, pack, quack, rack, sack, shack, smack, snack, stack, tack, track, whack, attack, backpack, bushwhack, Cossack, cutback, drawback, haystack, hijack, horseback, knapsack, piggyback, racetrack, ransack, rickrack, setback, skyjack, tamarack, thumbtack, tieback, wisecrack, zwieback

-ail
bail, fail, grail, hail, jail, mail, nail, pail, quail, rail, sail, snail, tail, trail, airmail, assail, bewail, bobtail, coattail, contrail, curtail, derail, detail, entail, fingernail, handrail, hangnail, hobnail, monorail, ponytail, prevail, retail, toenail, topsail, travail

-ain
brain, chain, drain, gain, grain, main, plain, sprain, stain, train, abstain, appertain, ascertain, attain, complain, constrain, contain, detain, disdain, domain, entertain, eyestrain, explain, ingrain, maintain, ordain, pertain, refrain, restrain, sustain, terrain

-ake
bake, brake, cake, fake, flake, lake, make, rake, shake, snake, stake, take, wake, awake, cheesecake, clambake, cupcake, forsake, fruitcake, grubstake, handshake, keepsake, mistake, muckrake, namesake, overtake, pancake, partake, snowflake

-ale
bale, dale, gale, hale, kale, male, pale, sale, scale, shale, stale, tale, vale, wale, whale, exhale, female, impale, inhale, regale, resale, baler, azalea, salesman

-ame
blame, came, fame, flame, frame, game, lame, name, same, shame, tame, became, mainframe, nickname, overcame, surname

-an
bran, can, fan, man, pan, plan, ran, scan, span, tan, than, van, afghan, airman, bedpan, began, caravan, divan, dustpan, fireman, mailman, rattan, sampan, seaman, sedan, suntan, toucan, wingspan

-ank
bank, blank, clank, crank, dank, drank, flank, frank, lank, plank, prank, rank, sank, shank, shrank, spank, stank, swank, tank, thank, yank, gangplank, outflank, outrank, riverbank, sandbank

-ap
cap, clap, flap, gap, lap, map, nap, scrap, slap, snap, strap, tap, trap, wrap, bootstrap, burlap, catnap, entrap, firetrap, gingersnap, handicap, hubcap, kidnap, mishap, mousetrap, overlap, pinesap, stopgap, thunderclap, wiretap

-ash
bash, cash, dash, gash, hash, lash, mash, rash, sash, abash, brash, clash, crash, flash, gnash, slash, smash, stash, trash, potash, rehash, splash, thrash, cashew, cashier, fashion, dashboard

-at
bat, cat, chat, fat, flat, gnat, hat, mat, pat, rat, sat, scat, slat, spat, that, acrobat, bobcat, brickbat, bureaucrat, butterfat, chitchat, combat, copycat, democrat, diplomat, doormat, format, habitat, hemostat, muskrat, nonfat, Photostat, rheostat, wildcat

-ate
crate, date, fate, gate, late, mate, plate, rate, sate, skate, slate, state, abate, calculate, candidate, create, debate, disintegrate, dissipate, donate, elate, elevate, estimate, excavate, inmate, irate, irritate, locate, migrate, motivate, mutate, negate, notate

-aw
caw, haw, jaw, law, man, paw, raw, saw, claw, draw, flaw, gnaw, slaw, thaw, bylaw, macaw, squaw, straw, bawdy, brawl, crawl, drawl, shawl, trawl, dawn, fawn, gawk, hawk, lawn, pawn, tawny, yawn, dawdle, lawman, lawyer, tawdry, jawbone, rawhide, sawdust, sawmill

-ay
bay, clay, day, gay, gray, hay, lay, may, pay, play, ray, say, stay, stray, sway, tray, way, allay, anyway, ashtray, away, betray, birthday, castaway, dismay, doorway, foray, freeway, gateway, hearsay, holiday, mainstay, payday, portray, relay, someday, subway

-eat
beat, bleat, cheat, cleat, heat, meat, neat, peat, pleat, seat, treat, wheat, browbeat, buckwheat, defeat, downbeat, drumbeat, entreat, heartbeat, mincemeat, offbeat, overheat, repeat, retreat, upbeat

(cont.)

FIGURE 6.8. Thirty-seven high-frequency rimes in the English language. *Sources:* Wylie and Durrell (1970) and Fox (2000).

-ell

bell, cell, dell, dwell, fell, quell, sell, shell, smell, spell, swell, tell, well, yell, barbell, befell, bluebell, bombshell, doorbell, eggshell, farewell, foretell, inkwell, nutshell, oversell, stairwell

-est

best, chest, crest, guest, jest, lest, nest, pest, quest, rest, vest, west, wrest, zest, armrest, arrest, attest, bequest, congest, conquest, contest, detest, digest, divest, infest, ingest, invest, request, suggest

-ice

ice, dice, lice, mice, nice, rice, vice, price, slice, spice, trice, twice, advice, device, entice, splice, thrice

-ick

brick, chick, click, crick, flick, kick, lick, nick, pick, prick, quick, sick, slick, stick, thick, tick, trick, wick, airsick, derrick, gimmick, handpick, homesick, limerick, lipstick, maverick, sidekick, rollick, seasick, yardstick

-ide

bride, chide, hide, pride, ride, side, slide, stride, tide, wide, abide, aside, astride, bromide, chloride, collide, confide, decide, dioxide, divide, fireside, fluoride, outside, oxide, peroxide, preside, provide, reside, roadside, subside, suicide, sulfide

-ight

bright, fight, flight, fright, knight, light, might, night, plight, right, sight, slight, tight, airtight, alright, copyright, daylight, delight, firelight, fortnight, headlight, highlight, hindsight, limelight, midnight, skylight, spotlight, starlight, stoplight, tonight, twilight

-ill

bill, chill, dill, drill, fill, frill, gill, grill, hill, kill, mill, quill, sill, skill, spill, still, swill, thrill, till, twill, anthill, distill, doorsill, downhill, fiberfill, foothill, freewill, fulfill, goodwill, handbill, instill, landfill, playbill, sawmill, treadmill, windchill, windmill

-in

chin, grin, pin, skin, spin, thin, tin, twin, win, akin, begin, chagrin, doeskin, kingpin

-ine

dine, fine, line, mine, nine, pine, sine, tine, vine, wine, brine, shine, spine, swine, thine, twine, whine, alpine, bovine, byline, canine, cosine, define, devine, equine, feline, iodine, refine, recline, shrine, supine, ninety, winery, dinette, nineteen

-ing

bring, cling, ding, fling, king, ring, sing, sling, sting, string, thing, wing, wring, zing, anything, awning, bedspring, bowstring, bullring, downswing, drawstring, earring, hamstring, handspring, latchstring, offspring, plaything, shoestring, upswing, wellspring

-ink

ink, blink, brink, chink, clink, drink, fink, kink, link, mink, pink, rink, shrink, sink, slink, stink, think, wink, hoodwink

-ip

chip, clip, dip, flip, grip, hip, lip, nip, quip, rip, ship, sip, skip, slip, snip, strip, tip, trip, whip, zip, airship, catnip, equip, fingertip, flagship, kinship, outstrip

-ir

fir, sir, stir, whir, astir, nadir, tapir, birch, bird, birth, circa, dirge, dirt, dirty, firm, first, girl, girth, mirth, circle, circuit, giraffe, girdle, mirage, piranha, sirloin

-ock

block, clock, crock, dock, flock, frock, knock, lock, rock, shock, smock, sock, stock, bedrock, deadlock, gamecock, hemlock, livestock, o'clock, padlock, peacock, roadblock, shamrock

-oke

awoke, broke, choke, coke, joke, poke, smoke, spoke, stoke, stroke, woke, yoke, artichoke, backstroke, bespoke, cowpoke, evoke, heatstroke, invoke, keystroke, provoke, slowpoke, sunstroke

(cont.)

FIGURE 6.8. *(cont.)*

-op	-or	-ore
chop, crop, drop, flop, hop, mop, pop, prop, shop, stop, top, airdrop, backdrop, bellhop, blacktop, dewdrop, doorstop, gumdrop, hardtop, hilltop, lollipop, outcrop, raindrop, rooftop, tabletop, teardrop, treetop, workshop	for, nor, born, cord, cork, corn, ford, fork, form, horn, lord, morn, pork, torn, worn, acorn, adorn, chord, flora, glory, scorn, shorn, short, snort, sport, stork, story, sword, sworn, thorn, décor, abort, aorta	chore, more, score, shore, snore, spore, store, tore, wore, adore, anymore, before, bookstore, carnivore, commodore, deplore, drugstore, encore, explore, folklore, herbivore, ignore, implore, seashore, semaphore, sophomore, therefore

-uck	-ug	-ump
buck, chuck, cluck, duck, luck, pluck, snuck, struck, stuck, suck, tuck, truck, amuck, awestruck, mukluk, potluck, woodchuck	bug, chug, dug, drug, hug, jug, lug, mug, plug, pug, rug, shrug, slug, smug, snug, thug, tug, bedbug, earplug, firebug, fireplug, humbug	bump, chump, clump, dump, frump, grump, hump, jump, lump, plump, slump, stump, thump, trump, mugwump

-unk
hunk, chunk, clunk, drunk, dunk, flunk, funk, hunk, junk, plunk, punk, shrunk, skunk, slunk, spunk, stunk, sunk, trunk, debunk, chipmunk

FIGURE 6.8. *(cont.)*

the unknown word. The reader's thinking process might be: "I don't know that word, but it ends the same way that *big* does. Maybe it sounds the same as *big*. I'll substitute a /tw/ sound for the /b/." The reader then pronounces the /tw/, blends it to the *–ig* rime, and cross-checks to see whether the word she has blended sounds like a real word that makes sense in the sentence.

Analogizing places fewer cognitive demands on readers than using letter–sound cues, because readers only need to blend the onset and the rime—as opposed to sounding and blending each individual letter and sound (Fox, 2000). Fewer cognitive demands make analogizing an ideal strategy to teach younger and less experienced readers. The consonant sounds represented in onsets are usually very reliable, but vowel sounds are much less reliable. When vowel sounds are present in a rime, however, their sounds are much more reliable. This reliability provides emergent readers with more dependable cues for decoding than having to remember all of the various vowel sounds and their associated rules and exceptions when using letter–sound cues as a decoding strategy. (See Table 6.3 for the declarative, procedural, and conditional knowledge associated with using analogizing as a word recognition strategy.)

Students who benefit from learning how to use analogizing as a strategy are those who understand letter–sound relationships but who may not know that words also contain common letter patterns. One of the graduate students in the reading program at the University at Buffalo, Eileen Ludwig, described her student's reading ability in the following manner:

> In one of my sessions with [the student] I conducted a miscue analysis. I feel as though I learned quite a bit about [the student's] decoding strategies even before ana-

lyzing the data. As I observed [the student's] behaviors and decoding strategies while she read the passage, I believe I gained a greater insight to what she does or does not do when she reads. As [the student] read the passage she worked extremely hard at sounding out words that she did not recognize. Rather than chunking words or analogizing unknown words to known sight words, she sounded out each letter in order to decode a word. For example, when she came to the word *corner* she worked very hard at sounding out the word letter-by-letter. She then read the word as *cormer*. She also substituted *what* for *was*. Since *cormer* is very similar to *corner*, and *what* is somewhat similar to *was* I do feel that [the student] used visual information in order to help her figure out some words. During our lessons I noticed that [the student] would try to sound out words but would then take a guess if she thought it was taking her too much time. However, when she read this [passage], she spent much more time trying to sound out each individual letter in order to form a word. Even though she did take more time trying to sound out letters, there were some words in which she could only pronounce certain sounds. Most of these included initial consonant sounds. For example, she substituted *what* for *was*, *after* for *afraid*, and *wouldn't* for *wasn't*.

[Eileen Ludwig, reflective memo, March 22, 2000]

Eileen's insights from her observations and miscue analysis reveal a child who is relying on letter–sound cues to decode unfamiliar words because she has no other strategies to use. Eileen noted that much of the child's previous classroom instruction was focused primarily on phonics-based approaches to learning to read in which much of the instruction focused on completing phonics workbooks. Thus the strategies she employed were consistent with those to which she had been exposed. Eileen's hypotheses focused on broadening the child's repertoire of available word recognition strategies to include learning to recognize common word families and using them to facilitate decoding. Analogizing is an ideal strategy to teach these readers, who recognize the beginning and sometimes the ending sounds in a word and "guess" at the medial portion. Sometimes teachers analyze such students' miscues and determine that they should be learning vowel sounds and vowel combinations (i.e., digraphs, diphthongs, r-controlled vowels) because it is the medial portion with which they are having difficulty. However, it is more helpful, as noted above, to teach these readers about rimes and onsets than specific vowel sounds because the vowel sounds in rimes are more reliable than teaching them separately as one would when teaching them as part of the letter–sound cue strategy.

The sample lesson in Figure 6.9 was derived from Eileen Ludwig's and Keli Garas's lessons. The sample lesson provides a large amount of scaffolding for students, as teachers model and demonstrate how to sound and blend onsets with the *–ape* rime to recognize unfamiliar words in Bernard Most's *There's an Ape Behind the Drape*. Before reading the text, the students are engaged in manipulating letter tiles to build the *–ape* rime. After the reading, they add consonants to the beginning of the rime. They hunt for words containing the *–ape* rime. The teacher has the primary role during the read aloud of the text as she models and demonstrates what it would look like and sound like to use the analogizing strategy. In essence, the teacher is teaching students the Discourse of a new word recognition strategy. Internalizing this Discourse and engaging in similar actions and thoughts as they read is the long-term goal. With practice, students will be able to recognize common rimes in larger words and use their knowledge of those rimes to help them decode unfamiliar words.

Teacher: Adapted from lessons by Keli Garas and Eileen Ludwig

Topic: Recognizing words using the analogy strategy

Grade level: 2–4

STAIRS hypothesis being addressed:

Students are in the alphabetic phase of development. They are able to identify the sounds in a spoken word and are able to use initial and final letters to help them recognize unfamiliar words, but they have difficulty with medial portions of words and vowel sounds.

Goal of Lesson

Students will learn:

- To identify unknown words using onsets and rimes (long-term goal); specifically, they will learn to recognize unknown words having an *–ape* rime
- To blend onsets and rimes to recognize unknown words (long term goal); specifically, they will learn to blend onsets with the *–ape* rime to recognize unknown words
- To cross-check to make sure that identified words make sense (long term goal)

Materials

- *There's an Ape Behind the Drape* by Bernard Most
- Chart paper, markers
- Pocket chart/alphabet letters, letter tiles, or magnetic letters
- Hidden Pictures from *Highlights for Children* magazine

Introduction

Reduce processing by using concrete example

The lesson will begin by displaying a "Hidden Picture" from the *Highlights for Children* magazine. Ask students to study the large picture to see if they can find any other pictures hidden within it. Have students share the pictures they find and explain *how* they were able to locate the pictures. As students share the procedures they used for finding the "hidden" pictures within the larger picture, write them down on chart paper. Explain that sometimes when we are reading and come to a word we do not know, we can use the same process to help us figure it out. Instead of looking for small pictures within a big picture, we can look for smaller words, or letter patterns, within a bigger word. Explain that today we are going to learn how to look for these letter patterns in bigger words to help us read them.

Procedural knowledge

Declarative knowledge

Description of Instructional Experience

Model/ think aloud

Since students are familiar with compound words, the lesson will begin by showing some compound words. Explain that when you look at these words you can see smaller words inside them, just like we could see hidden pictures inside the larger picture. Model and think aloud using some examples such as *snowman*. Explain that *snowman* is one word but it has smaller words inside it. Explain that sometimes when we are trying to

FIGURE 6.9. Sample lesson teaching students to use analogizing as a strategy for recognizing unknown words.

Declarative knowledge

Conditional knowledge

Procedural knowledge

Declarative knowledge

Declarative knowledge

Model/ think aloud

Procedural knowledge

Model/ think aloud

Guided practice

Verbalization

Declarative and conditional knowledge about comprehension strategies

read big words and small words it helps to look inside the word and study it to see if there are smaller words or parts of words in it. Explain that this strategy is a good one to use for small words, but it is also very helpful in reading big words.

After reviewing a few examples note the process you used during the think aloud to locate the smaller words. Compare your process to that which the students used to locate the hidden pictures in the larger picture. The goal here is to try to verbalize the procedural knowledge associated with recognizing smaller word parts in larger words. For example, you might explain that there are certain steps we can follow to help us recognize unknown words. First, we should look carefully at the word. As we look we can look for smaller words or chunks inside the bigger word. Say each word chunk and then blend the chunks together. Finally, we need to cross-check to make sure the word makes sense. Ask yourself "Can I pronounce the word?" "Does the word look and sound right?" "Does the word make sense in the sentence?" Explain that it is important to cross-check to make sure that what you read makes sense.

Explain that just as some big words have small words within them there are also common word parts that we can look for too. Explain that these word parts are called "word families." Just like people in families have similar last names, words in word families have similar letter patterns. Explain that one word family is the −*ape* family. Build the rime −*ape* using letter tiles or magnetic letters. Pronounce the rime and then explain that we can add sounds to the beginning to make different words in the −*ape* family. Explain that all of the words will have the common letter pattern −*ape* so they will all rhyme. Add single letters (c, g, t), blends (gr, scr), and digraphs (sh) to the rime and model and demonstrate the process of blending the onsets with the rime. Be certain to think aloud and reiterate the procedural steps used above to blend the onsets and rimes. For example, if you were reading the word *grape* you might say, "I see the little word −*ape* inside that word. I see a /t/ sound at the beginning. Those letters make a *t* sound. *T* and *ape*. *Tape*. Let me think is that a word? *Tape*. Yes, I've heard of tape before. It's something you use to hold things together. If I were reading I'd want to make sure that *tape* made sense in the sentence I was reading. Yes, the word *tape* makes sense." Model using another letter tile as an onset and then have students work with a partner using their own letter tiles (or paper letters) to build the −*ape* word family and add various consonants and consonant clusters to build real and nonsense words. Have students talk about whether they were able to blend the onsets and rimes and what part of it was difficult.

Explain that we will be using this strategy and the -*ape* word family while reading the book *There's an Ape Behind the Drape* by Bernard Most. Have students look at the cover and make predictions. Ask students to describe what they see. Read the title to the students and have students make predictions about what the story might be about. "Today we are going to read a story. Before we read any story it is always a good idea to

(cont.)

FIGURE 6.9. *(cont.)*

look at the pictures on the cover and think about what it might be about. So let's study the picture on the cover. What do you see?" Have students share their observations and their predictions about what the story might be about. Then read the title to the students and have them refine their predictions and observations further. Using the −ape words that were generated prior to introducing the story, have students work with a partner to write sentences using the −ape words to predict what the story might be about. For example, students might predict that the ape is wearing a cape as he stands behind the drape. Students might choose to use a story map to help them generate predictions about the characters, their goals/ problems in the story, and how they might go about solving those problems.

Declarative and conditional knowledge about comprehension strategies

Remind students that it is always a good idea to think about what we know about the subject of a book before we read it. This helps us get ready to read. Have students think about and share what they might like to find out as you read the book.

Reduce processing

Model/ think aloud

Guided practice

Explain that as we read the book we will see if there are places where we can use the analogizing strategy to read the −ape words. Begin reading the book aloud and thinking aloud as you read. When you come to the first −ape word model and think aloud using the procedures for sounding and blending onsets and rimes. Be sure to cross-check the blended word to make certain that it makes sense in the sentence. As the reading continues, model and have students assist with this sounding and blending process when −ape words are encountered.

Verbalization

After reading the story, have students discuss how well their predictions and prediction sentences compared to Bernard Most's version. Engage students in a whole class discussion of their thoughts about the story, their predictions, and how well the analogizing strategy worked.

Guided practice

Explain that we might even find the −ape family in larger words such as landscape, skyscraper, shipshape. Have pairs of students engage in a word hunt in which they look through their word banks, writing folders, and familiar texts they have already read to find words that have −ape in them. Materials should be those with which students are familiar. As students locate words and/or pictures they can record them on a sheet of paper. Once students have completed their hunt, the group can gather together to engage in a discussion and listing of the words and pictures they found that have −ape in them. Each new −ape word can be added onto the word family wall. Students can then work with a partner to create their own −ape story using the words added to the −ape section of the word family wall.

Conclusion

Verbalization

Students will write their responses to the lesson and what they have learned about using analogizing as a strategy for recognizing unknown

FIGURE 6.9. (*cont.*)

words. Students should be encouraged to write about their understanding of *what* the analogizing strategy is, *when* they might use it, and *why* they should use it.

Assessment

- You will know whether students are able to recognize unknown words having an –*ape* rime as they use the letter tiles to build words with –*ape* in them, by their participation and discussion during the read aloud, and by their ability to locate –*ape* words as they hunt through their writing folders and familiar texts.
- You will know whether students are able to blend onsets and rimes to recognize unfamiliar words with –*ape* in them by their ability to use the letter tiles to build, sound, and blend words with –*ape* in them.
- You will know whether students are able to cross-check to make sure that identified words make sense as they assist during the cross-checking procedures of the read aloud.

FIGURE 6.9. *(cont.)*

When teaching word recognition strategies, it is important to embed and link the instruction to authentic literacy contexts, such as the text featured in this lesson, as well as authentic writing experiences. This lesson provided opportunity for students to use the –*ape* rimes in their writing before reading the text, as they wrote prediction sentences about what might happen in the story, and after reading the text, as they created their own stories using the –*ape* rimes they gathered during their word hunt. Authentic reading experiences were linked to the text *There's an Ape Behind the Drape*, which featured several opportunities for the teacher to model how to use the –*ape* rime to help decode unknown words.

After teaching this lesson, one of the teachers, Keli, noted how important the teacher modeling during the read aloud was for her student:

> I think the most important thing that I learned in this lesson is the benefit of reducing processing demands. When I was reading the book, *There's an Ape Behind the Drape*, [the student] was more focused on the –*ape* words in the story rather than trying to decode every word in the book. She also seemed more at ease during the rest of the session.
>
> [Keli Garas, reflective memo, April 3, 2000]

Keli also grappled with the question of how much to include in one lesson. In preceding lessons she had tried to teach several word families at once, hoping that her student would be able to use them all in the texts that were chosen; however, the struggling reader with whom she was working was not able to process so much material, and she was having difficulty understanding the concept of blending the onsets and rimes. Therefore, Keli focused her ensuing lessons on only one word family to make certain that her student understood the concept of blending onsets and rimes. She also selected texts that featured that particular word family. In Keli's summation:

This lesson went very well. I'm glad that I just focused on one word family. [The student's] use of the analogy strategy was more prevalent and more immediate while she was reading *Sheep in a Jeep* than in other readings she has done after instruction. I counted the number of times she correctly identified an *–eep* word. Out of 29 *–eep* words in the story [the student] correctly identified 20 of them. She often substituted *truck* for *jeep*. I am thinking that she is overrelying on the pictures, or, on a positive note, she is bringing meaning to the text.

[Keli Garas, reflective memo, March 20, 2000]

Eileen Ludwig also felt that her student responded well to similar instruction. She noted:

According to Fox (2000) readers who use analogous onsets and rimes put less mental effort into word identification than do readers who decode words letter–sound by letter–sound. Blending onsets and rimes is much easier than blending individual sounds because with onsets and rimes there are usually only two items. Since [the student] does have auditory processing difficulties, I thought that this may be a good strategy for her to use. With this strategy, [the student] did not have to concentrate so much on sounding out each letter. I did feel that this strategy did put much less stress on [the student] and did increase her learning. Walker (2000) states that a diagnostic teacher adjusts instruction incorporating what students know and what students can do. The teacher can reduce the student's stress by using a student's strengths. I feel that in this lesson I was able to use one of [the student's] strengths in order to help her read the text. Through observation during the lesson, I found that [the student] did recognize similar patterns and was able to identify words that she would not have been able to recognize without using this particular strategy. More importantly, I believe that [the student] was able to see the success she was having. She even said, "Wow, I can do this." Furthermore, with a great deal of modeling, guided practice, and feedback [the student] started to use the cross-checking strategy.

[Eileen Ludwig, reflective memo, March 15, 2000]

The students involved in these lessons were quickly able to use the strategy to help them read unfamiliar words. The texts that are selected for such lessons are critical. Texts should support the instruction so that readers can actually use what they are learning to help them read the text. Table 6.2 provides a list of texts that our teachers have used successfully in their lessons. Many of the titles indicate the rime that appears most frequently in the text. Included are books of poetry, jump-rope chants, and nursery rhymes—all of which are very appropriate for use in teaching readers how to recognize rimes and onsets while analogizing.

The sample lesson in Figure 6.9 focused more on using analogizing to recognize unknown words of one syllable. For those readers approaching the end of the alphabetic phase of development and transitioning into the consolidated alphabetic phase, lessons that focus more on using analogizing as a strategy to help read unfamiliar polysyllabic words would be appropriate. Texts such as Cathi Hepworth's *Antics: An Alphabetical Anthology* and Bernard Most's *There's an Ant in Anthony* are very appropriate because the *–ant* rime is clearly apparent in many polysyllabic words in both texts. Cathi Hepworth's alphabet book uses intriguing illustrations of various ants. For example, the first page contains the word **antique** and a picture of an old ant in a rocking chair listening to an antique record player. The limited amount of text and vivid illustrations make it an ideal way of reducing processing demands for readers who are just beginning to learn that rimes occur in polysyllabic words.

Bernard Most's text *There's an Ant in Anthony* is also a perfect accompaniment in that it features a young boy (Anthony) who discovers that the word *ant* appears in his name. He then goes on a search for *–ant*'s in other objects. He finds that there is an *–ant* in a *plant* and in many other objects. Bernard Most highlights the *–ant* in each word by using red ink, which makes the *–ant* rime very obvious and easy for readers to locate. As the story progresses, the *–ant* rime turns up in many polysyllabic words. The book is ideal for introducing students to the notion that big words are not as mysterious and difficult as they may appear, because they are comprised of familiar letter patterns and chunks.

Using Structural Analysis (Chunking)

Structural analysis involves using meaningful and nonmeaningful multiletter chunks to recognize unknown words (Fox, 2000). Using structural analysis, or chunking, is most helpful when reading polysyllabic words. Meaningful multiletter chunks provide the reader with root words, prefixes (e.g., *pre–*, *un–*, *dis–*), suffixes (e.g., *–able*, *–or*), contractions (e.g., isn't, wasn't), and compound words (e.g., houseboat), all of which may yield insight into meaning and sound. Nonmeaningful multiletter chunks only help readers with sound and may consist of syllables, accents, and other units of pronunciations such as rimes. For example, the word *table* consists of two syllables (*ta* and *ble*). These syllables do not carry any meaning. They are simply common letter patterns that recur in words.

When readers recognize or use the same multiletter chunks repeatedly, in time they internalize these letter patterns and recognize them as intact units (Fox, 2000). The ability to recognize multiletter chunks streamlines the word recognition process and greatly reduces a reader's cognitive burden. Fox noted that when readers decode words letter by letter (as in phonics), they must hold each individual letter–sound in their short-term memory. This method becomes an enormous burden when reading longer words. For example, if a reader were trying to pronounce the word *unavailable*, he would have to identify and consider 11 individual letters. This length overburdens short-term memory, which is only capable of holding between five and seven thought units at one time. When short-term memory is overburdened, some thought units are lost or forgotten. When this happens during reading, it inevitably means that the letters that were sounded out at the beginning of the word are most certainly forgotten, and by the time the entire word is sounded out comprehension is affected as well. Thought units can consist of a single letter or a group of letters. Thus recognizing a group of letters as a whole chunk makes word recognition more efficient. For example, if a reader is able to recognize automatically the prefix *un–* as one multiletter chunk, the root word *avail* as another chunk, and the suffix *–able* as a third, then the burden on short-term memory is limited to three thought units. Recognizing multiletter chunks reduces the amount of mental effort expended and accelerates the word recognition process. The reduced burden on short-term memory also means there is less disruption to comprehension.

The chunking strategy is similar to analogizing in that both methods involve recognizing and using common letter patterns in words. However, readers who use meaningful and nonmeaningful multiletter chunks to recognize unfamiliar words are at the consolidated alphabetic phase of development (Ehri, 1998). Indeed, the word *consolidated* is used to describe this phase of development because these readers are aware of letter–sound relationships to such an extent that they have consolidated various letter sequences into chunks that they recognize as intact units, rather than decoding letter by letter, as occurs with readers in the alphabetic phase of development. These readers are, therefore, proficient with alphabetic phase reading (Ehri, 1991). Readers in the consolidated alphabetic phase know that spoken words can be divided into large and small sound units, and they can separate spoken words into their constituent sounds and blend them together to form words (see Table 6.3 for the declarative, procedural, and conditional knowledge associated with this strategy). These readers also know that some multiletter chunks yield meaning and pronunciation (i.e., meaningful chunks) and some are helpful only with pronunciation (i.e., nonmeaningful chunks). For most children, much of this development begins to occur in second grade as they begin to acquire sufficient experience reading words to recognize standard spelling patterns in English (Ehri, 1991; Fox, 2000).

When using the chunking strategy, readers are likely to recognize different multiletter chunks, depending on their background knowledge (Fox, 2000). For example, one reader may not recognize the word *disappointment* while reading. He knows that it is a large word and that using the chunking strategy would be helpful, but he is not aware that *disappoint* is a root word. Instead he notices the multiletter chunk *dis–* (even though it is not a prefix), the suffix *–ment*, the smaller word *point*, and the *–ap* syllable. As he blends the chunks together, he is still able to blend a word that makes sense, even though he may not recognize the actual root word. This is part of what makes using chunking strategic. Different users approach the task in different ways. They may all accomplish the same goal of recognizing the word, but they may not all go about accomplishing the goal in the same manner.

When teaching students to use chunking as a strategy, it is helpful to focus instruction on those multiletter chunks that recur most frequently in English words. It is especially important to focus on those prefixes and suffixes that occur most frequently. White, Power, and White (1989) noted that the number of words with prefixes and suffixes encountered by students doubles from fourth to fifth grade, and doubles again by seventh grade. Four prefixes account for 58% of the prefixed words students encounter in grades 3 through 9 (White, Power, et al., 1989). These prefixes are: *un–*, *re–*, *in–* (meaning "not), and *dis–*. The prefix *un–* is the most frequently occurring, found in 26% of all words with prefixes. It is most worthwhile to focus instruction initially on these four prefixes.

According to White, Sowell, and Yangihara (1989), those suffixes that occur most frequently in English words are *–s(–es)*, *–ed*, *–ing*, *–ly*, and *–er*. The suffixes *–s(–es)*, *–ed*, and *–ing* make up 65% of the suffixes readers in grades 3 through 9 encounter. Therefore, the most beneficial instruction occurs regarding these word endings. Many readers are aware of these three word endings by the end of first grade because authors use them so much in their writing. The remaining high-frequency suffixes are usually familiar to most readers by the end of second grade (Fox, 2000). Young readers also find it easy to recognize and break compound words into meaningful chunks. Thus a reader's ability to begin to recognize multiletter chunks can occur early on; however, these young readers may not be fully able to recognize these intact multiletter chunks as quickly as older readers who are in the consolidated alphabetic phase.

A sample lesson teaching students how to use structural analysis cues, or chunking, to recognize unfamiliar words is presented in Figure 6.10. Because the lesson focuses on

Teacher:	Adapted from lessons by Kristin Zahn and Anita Brocker
Topic:	Recognizing words using structural analysis cues (chunking)
Grade level:	2–4

STAIRS hypothesis being addressed:

Students are in the consolidated alphabetic phase of development. They are able to use letter-sound correspondences to decode words, but they have difficulty decoding polysyllabic words.

Goal of Lesson

Students will learn:

- To decode unfamiliar words that are big by chunking the word into smaller pieces and blending the pieces together
- Why chunking is helpful for reading unfamiliar words
- To look for suffixes in words and use them to decode unfamiliar words
- To cross-check to make sure that identified words make sense

Materials

- "The Invitation," a poem by Shel Silverstein in *Where the Sidewalk Ends;* written on chart paper
- "Spring," a poem by Karla Kuskin; written on chart paper
- Chart paper, markers
- Sticky notes
- Word wall
- Word cards with sample root words and suffixes (-s, -es, -ed, -ing)
- Model train
- "Chunkable Words" sheets

Introduction

Reduce processing demands

Show students the model train and explain that trains are comprised of lots of different cars. Demonstrate how you can add cars on and take them away to make the size of the train bigger or smaller. Explain that words are kind of the same. Big words, like trains that are really long, are usually made up of smaller words or word parts. Explain that today we

Declarative and conditional knowledge

are going to be learning how to add and delete word parts from big words to make them easier to read.

Description of Instructional Experience

Explain that today we will be learning a strategy called "chunking" that helps readers figure out unknown words. Note that the strategy works especially for big words. Explain that chunking involves breaking a word

Declarative knowledge

into smaller pieces and then blending the pieces back together again, just like pulling some of the cars off of a train and adding others.

Declarative knowledge

Explain that today's lesson will focus on parts of words that get added to the end. Explain that a suffix is kind of like the "caboose" on the end

(cont.)

FIGURE 6.10. Sample lesson teaching students to use structural analysis cues to recognize unknown words.

of a train. These word parts are called "suffixes." Explain that a suffix is a word part that can change the meaning of a word or add information about the word. Place a word card with a root word on it (e.g., play) on one of the cars on the train.

Declarative knowledge

Model/ think aloud

Procedural knowledge

Explain that the cars of the train are kind of like the root words in a word. Explain that the suffixes would go on the caboose, or at the end, of the train. Place a word card with the suffix –s on the caboose. Model and think aloud how you blend the word parts together. "If I didn't know this word when I first saw it I'd look carefully at the whole word. Then I'd look at the beginning of the word for a prefix. I don't see one on this word. Then I look at the end of the word for a suffix. I do see an "s" added to the end of this word. So, I'm just going to 'chunk' it. That means I'm going to remove that word part to make the word smaller. This helps make the word easier to read. Now I see that the word I'm left with is *play*. Now that I've chunked the word into two parts, I have to blend it back together." Demonstrate how to blend each word part back together. "Now I have to cross-check to make sure it makes sense. *Plays*. That is a real word that makes sense." Now demonstrate how the meaning changes by adding a different suffix (-ed or –ing) to the end. Use the words in sentences to demonstrate the differences in meaning.

Conditional knowledge

Explain that we just added suffixes to the end of the root word, but when we are reading and see really long words that we can't read, we temporarily chunk off the suffixes so we can see all of the word parts. Then we blend them back together.

Model/ think aloud

Procedural knowledge

Explain that we can use this strategy as we read. Explain that we are going to try using it while reading a poem entitled "Invitation." Have students think about what they know about invitations and make predictions about what the poem might be about. Display the poem "Invitation" on chart paper. Model and think aloud while reading the poem. As you encounter "chunkable" words containing the suffixes –s, -es, -ed, or –ing, stop and model the process of how you might go about reading the big word. Model the procedural knowledge of how to chunk the word and use the sticky notes to cover up the suffix temporarily so that you can focus on the root word. During the reblending step, uncover the suffix. Be sure to also model the cross-checking procedure in which you monitor the reblended word to make sure that the word is pronounceable and makes sense in the sentence. Continue modeling and thinking aloud in this manner as the rest of the poem is read.

After reading the entire poem, have students engage in a discussion with a partner about how well their predictions matched the text. Then begin a discussion focused on the "chunkable" words. Add each new word to the word wall under the appropriate suffix (-s, -es, -ed, -ing) and reiterate how chunking helps when reading longer words.

FIGURE 6.10. (*cont.*)

Guided practice using comprehension strategies

Explain that students will now have an opportunity to use the strategy with a partner as they read a poem called "Spring" by Karla Kuskin. Have students share what good things they know to do before reading (read the title, think about what they know about Spring, make predictions about what the poem might be about). Have each pair of students brainstorm and record their background knowledge and predictions on a web.

Guided practice using chunking

Provide each pair of students with a copy of the poem, a sheet entitled "Chunkable Words," and sticky notes. Explain that as students read, they should watch for "chunkable" words and use the sticky notes to "chunk" them into readable portions before blending the word back together. Have students record their "chunkable" words on the sheet. The sheet should also serve to help students engage in all of the procedural steps involved in chunking. Explain that students can leave the sticky notes on the words that they chunked. After reading the poem, have students discuss their responses to, and predictions about, the poem.

Conclusion

Verbalization

Engage the whole group in a discussion in which they share their "chunkable" words and discuss which words they chunked, *how* they chunked the words, and *why* those particular words were chunkable. Have students explain and share whether the chunking strategy was helpful for them or not. Have students add the newly chunked words onto the word wall under the appropriate suffix.

Students can also look for chunkable words during their independent reading using this same procedure.

Assessment

- You will know whether students are able to decode unfamiliar polysyllabic words by chunking them into smaller pieces and blending the pieces together by observing their work with their partner as they read the poem and complete the "Chunkable Words" sheet.
- You will know if students know why chunking is helpful for reading unfamiliar words by their responses during the concluding discussion.
- You will know whether students are able to look for suffixes in words and use them to decode unfamiliar words by observing their work with their partner as they read the poem and complete the "Chunkable Words" sheet.
- You will know whether students are able to cross-check to make sure that identified words make sense by observing their work with their partner as they read the poem and complete the "Chunkable Words" sheet.

(cont.)

FIGURE 6.10. *(cont.)*

CHUNKABLE WORDS SHEET

Chunkable word (word and page number)	Is there a prefix?	Is there a root word?	Is there a suffix?	Cross-check	
				Can I pronounce it?	Does it make sense in the sentence?
[example] playing, 2	—	play	–ing	yes	yes

FIGURE 6.10. *(cont.)*

teaching readers to look for the most recognizable suffixes, it is probably best suited for students in the late alphabetic or early consolidated alphabetic phases of development. Similar lessons can certainly be used with prefixes, other suffixes, root words, or compound words. One of the key features to note in this lesson is how the concept of chunking is linked initially to a concrete analogy of adding and removing cars from a train, thus making the process more tangible. In addition, the lesson features brief texts (poems) that have several chunkable words in them (e.g., –s, –ed, and –ing suffixes) on which the instruction focuses. Finally, the lesson features modeling and demonstration by the teacher and affords students the opportunity to try chunking during guided practice with a partner. The "Chunkable Words" sheet that students complete as they read reiterates the procedural steps involved in chunking and provides the teacher with a means of assessing students' ability to recognize those words that are chunkable and to decode them using the strategy.

Using Context Cues

Context cues enable readers to form an expectation about the text (Ehri, 1991). These cues may come from the pictures, headings, subheadings, or text that surrounds a given word. Context cues enable readers to make a guess at what words would make sense in a given context—or at least to narrow down the range of possibilities.

In her review of research on word recognition, Juel (1991) noted that although the use of context has been shown to facilitate comprehension processes, the research supporting its use for word recognition is not substantive. Research has consistently shown that poorer readers tend to rely on context for word recognition. Both Ehri (1991) and Juel (1991) noted that when a reader's ability to use graphic information (i.e., letter–sound cues) is limited, the reader compensates by relying on background knowledge and contextual information. Thus, the use of context cues as a word recognition strategy is recommended with caution.

Instruction focusing on context cues must emphasize that in order for the strategy to be helpful, the surrounding words must be known. That is, the unknown word must be surrounded by a known meaningful context. If the student is struggling to read a large portion of the text, there will not be a sufficient number of recognizable words to make the strategy successful. Likewise, if the surrounding context is not supportive then students will have difficulty using contextual cues. For example, suppose a student came across the sentence "It was oppressive" in the course of reading. If the student has difficulty reading the word *oppressive*, and there are no other cues available to help him bring meaning to the word, then using context cues is certainly not a beneficial strategy for decoding the word. However, if the sentence were surrounded by other sentences that gave an indication of the meaning, then context cues might be more helpful: "It had been over ninety degrees every day for the past two weeks. The sun's rays were relentless, there was no trace of wind, and our air conditioner was broken. It was *oppressive*." In the second circumstance the sentences leading up to the unknown word provide the reader with meaningful cues (assuming the reader knows all of the words in those surrounding sentences). If the unknown word is not in the reader's spoken or listening vocabulary, then it is possible that not even a supportive context would help the reader decode the unknown word. That is, the reader may be able to gain a vague notion of what the word *oppressive* means by the surrounding context, but if he has never heard the word before, then even a highly descriptive context may not help him decode it. He may decide to skip over the word, having but a vague notion of the word's meaning and pronunciation.

During strategy instruction, these aspects of using context cues as a strategy for word recognition must be communicated to readers. They need to know under what conditions the strategy might and might not work (i.e., conditional knowledge) and they need to know that using context cues is not the way that readers recognize most unknown words. It is an additional strategy that comes in handy in those circumstances in which there is a very supportive context and in which most of the surrounding words are known.

Students who benefit most from instruction that focuses on using context cues are those who overrely on letter–sound cues to decode unknown words, as in the sample lesson in Figure 6.11. These students often mispronounce words when they are reading, and their miscues are nonsense words rather than real words (e.g., reading the word *corner* as

Teacher: Adapted from a lesson by AnnaMaria Figliomeni

Topic: Recognizing words using context cues

Grade level: 1–4 (for higher grades alter text accordingly)

STAIRS hypothesis being addressed:

    Students rely on letter-sound cues as their primary decoding strategy at the expense of comprehension. Students may also have difficulty monitoring their understanding while reading.

Goal of Lesson

Students will learn:

- To decode unfamiliar words by using context cues along with letter-sound cues

Materials

- *I Know an Old Woman Who Swallowed a Fly* (big book and little books)
- Sticky notes
- Puzzle
- Paper
- Markers

Reduce processing demands by using concrete experience

Verbalization

Introduction

Begin by presenting students with a puzzle that is partially completed. As students work to complete the puzzle, ask them to explain what they are thinking as they select pieces and fit them into place. The goal of this think aloud is to get students to verbalize the process they use while working on the puzzle.

Description of Instructional Experience

Explain that when we put together a puzzle, we have to use the surrounding pieces to help us determine which pieces fit in the empty spots. Explain that when we read, using context cues is similar to this process.

Declarative knowledge

"When readers come to words they don't know, they can use what they do know and what they see in the text to help them figure out the words much like you used the completed parts of the puzzle to help you fit in the missing pieces. This is called using context clues. By *context* I mean the other words in the sentence or even the pictures on the page. These other words and pictures can help you figure out what an unknown word is. So, if you see come across a "clunk word" or a word that you don't know, think about how the words fit together in the sentence to make

Procedural knowledge

sense. First it is important to get an idea of what you are reading about. Skip the word you don't know and think about what kind of word might make sense in the sentence. If the other words in the sentence don't help, the pictures might. You can even look at the letters and sounds in the word you don't know to help you. All of these things can work together to help you figure out the word."

(cont.)

FIGURE 6.11. Sample lesson teaching students how to use context cues to recognize unknown words.

Model/ think aloud	Model the process of using context cues with the book *I Know an Old Lady Who Swallowed a Fly.* Begin by glancing at the cover and reading the title. For example, you might model what you would do if you did not know the word *lady* in the title. "I know an old . . . hmmm I don't know that word. I know an old BLANK who swallowed a fly. Hmmm, what word would fit in the title and make sense?" Cover the unknown word with a sticky note so students can see how you would focus on meaning first and then use letter-sound cues to verify your context-based guesses.
Procedural knowledge	Have students generate a list of words that might possibly fit in the blank and list them on the board. "The only context I have is the rest of the words in the title and the picture. When I look at the picture I see two children and an old woman. The title 'I know an old BLANK' gives me the clue that there is something or somebody old. The only old person I see in the picture is an old woman. Let's see if that fits, or makes sense, in the title 'I know an old *woman* who swallowed a fly.' Yes, that makes sense. Let me look at the first letter of the word to see if it begins with /w/." Reveal the first letter by moving the sticky note over. "Oh, the first letter is *l*. Now I need to think if I know a word that means the same thing as 'woman' that begins with *l*. Can anyone think of a word that means 'woman' that beings with *l* ?" Have students think about words that might fit those two clues. List the words on the board or on chart paper. Then reveal the remaining letters in the word and cross-check with the words on the board to see where it occurs.
Conditional knowledge	Explain that this process is similar to the way we determined which puzzle pieces fit into the empty spaces. Explain that we can only use context cues to help us if we can read or carefully observe all of the cues in the words and pictures surrounding the unknown word.
Model/ think aloud *Guided practice Verbalization*	Before continuing with the book, have students make predictions about what might happen in the book based on the title and picture clues. After sharing their thoughts with a partner, students can write their predictions in their prediction logs. Begin reading the book aloud, stopping to model in places where there might be a word that students can not recognize. After modeling a few more words using this procedure, have students work with a partner to continue reading the story. Have students use sticky notes to cover up words they do not know and then think aloud with their partner as they work to use context cues to figure out their unknown words. As students work together carefully observe and take anecdotal notes on their ability to use the context cue strategy.
	Once students finish reading the book, have them share their thoughts and reactions about the book with their partner. Encourage students to discuss how well their original predictions matched the text.
	Conclusion
Procedural knowledge	Gather students together and have them share some of the unknown words in which they tried to use context cues to help them deduce the word.

(cont.)

FIGURE 6.11. *(cont.)*

Verbalization

> Have students explain the procedure they used and how well it worked. Students might elect to actually model the procedure they used, explaining how it worked by using the big book version of the text and a sticky note. Be sure to talk about those conditions under which using the context cues may not have worked as well as those that did. This will help students understand that sometimes the context is not always helpful for recognizing unknown words.

Verbalization

Verbalization

> Have students share what they learned about using context cues and use this discussion to review the declarative, procedural, and conditional knowledge associated with its use.
>
> ### Assessment
> - You will know whether students can decode unfamiliar words by using context cues along with letter-sound cues by observing them as they work with their partners, using sticky notes and verbalizing their thinking about context cues while completing the reading of the book.

FIGURE 6.11. *(cont.)*

karmra). Thus teaching these students to use context cues provides them with a strategy that helps them focus more on meaning than solely on graphic information to read unknown words. This is precisely the type of student that AnnaMaria Figliomeni had in mind when she designed the sample lesson in Figure 6.11. In her reflective memo she noted that although her student said that he sounded out words and used context cues when he came to unfamiliar words, her observations revealed that he relied solely on letter–sound cues and was not reading for meaning. Based on these observations, she designed lessons that would focus on teaching her student how to use context cues in conjunction with letter–sound cues to decode unknown words.

In the sample lesson the teacher began by using a concrete experience that would help her student link the use of context cues to building a puzzle. After teaching the lesson AnnaMaria noted:

> When [the student] assembled an unfinished Clifford [the dog] puzzle I asked him to explain his thinking to put it together. Such thoughts as, "I knew this piece went here because his eyes are at the top" and "I'll put this piece back for later" were shared. Unknown to me at the time of planning my lesson was that his comments would serve as a springboard to analogize this process of putting a puzzle together with using context clues. The full impact of this experience was realized in my past session with [the student] when he stated, "I didn't know that before" and began applying [the context cue strategy] as he read. For example, while reading *Harry and Willy and Carrothead* [the student] came across the word *cooed*. At first he used a [sticky] note to indicate it was a CLUNK word, a word he could not say, however he later removed the [sticky] note when he reached the end of the sentence. When asked how he got the word [the student] replied, "It looked like *cooled* but it doesn't have the *l* and it wouldn't make sense, 'He cried and *cooled* and waved his arms like any baby.' "

[AnnaMaria Figliomeni, reflective memo, March 24, 2000]

AnnaMaria's reflections show that sometimes strategy use takes a while to gel. Her first lesson on using context cues was taught in early March, but her student was not able to begin using the strategy on his own until several weeks later after consistent modeling, demonstration, and guided practice in a variety of contexts.

COORDINATING FLEXIBLE USE OF SETS OF STRATEGIES

AnnaMaria's lesson in Figure 6.11 also featured the coordinated use of context cues and letter–sound cues. This coordination is essential for all strategy use. Strategies are rarely used in isolation. They are coordinated as sets that are used flexibly and in conjunction with one another. Thus instruction must provide students with the opportunity to see how strategies are used together and how they are mutually supportive. Making this co-ordinated use of strategies visible requires a great deal of modeling, demonstration, and thinking aloud about the thought processes that occur while reading.

The chart in Figure 6.10 is useful for students to complete as they are learning how to use strategies flexibly. As they begin to make their lists of unknown words and the strategies they used to decode them, discussions can revolve around the conditions under which various strategies worked and did not work. As well, students can study the types of words that lent themselves to decoding using a particular strategy. Such study and re-flection can help students realize that polysyllabic words lend themselves better to decod-ing by chunking than by letter–sound cues. Even though our instruction might directly communicate this information, sometimes it takes extensive use of strategies, and reflec-tion on such use, before students begin to understand fully the conditional knowledge as-sociated with each strategy.

SUMMARY

This chapter provided an overview of relevant research, sample lessons, and guidelines for instruction in teaching readers to use word recognition strategies. Relevant theory pertaining to the phases of reading development was discussed and connected to authen-tic teaching contexts and sample lessons. These phases of development are the pre-alpha-betic phase, partial alphabetic phase, alphabetic phase, consolidated alphabetic phase, and fluent recognition phase. The sample lessons focused on five ways that readers learn to recognize words: using sight words, using letter–sound cues, analogizing, using struc-tural analysis (chunking), and using context cues.

REFERENCES

Aardema, V. (1983). *Bringing the rain to Kapiti plain: A Nandi tale.* New York: Penguin.

Bear, D. R., Invernizzi, M., Templeton, S., & Johnston, F. (2000). *Words their way: Word study for pho-nics, vocabulary, and spelling instruction* (2nd ed.). Upper Saddle River, NJ: Merrill.

Blachman, B. A. (2000). Phonological awareness. In M. L. Kamil, P. B. Mosenthal, P. D. Pearson, & R. Barr (Eds.), *Handbook of reading research* (vol. 3, pp. 483–502). Mahweh, NJ: Erlbaum.

Deming, A. (1993). *Who is tapping at my window?* New York: Penguin Putnam.

Ehri, L. C. (1991). Development of the ability to read words. In R. Barr, M. L. Kamil, P. B. Mosenthal, & P. D. Pearson (Eds.), *Handbook of reading research* (vol. 2, pp. 383–417). New York: Longman.

Ehri, L. C. (1998). Grapheme-phoneme knowledge is essential for learning to read words in English. In J. L. Metsala & L. C. Ehri (Eds.), *Word recognition in beginning literacy* (pp. 3–40). Mahweh, NJ: Erlbaum.

Eldredge, J. L., Reutzel, D. R., & Hollingsworth, P. M. (1996). Comparing the effectiveness of two oral reading practices: Round-robin reading and the shared book experience. *Journal of Literacy Research, 28*, 201–225.

Fox, B. J. (2000). *Word identification strategies: Phonics from a new perspective* (2nd ed.). Upper Saddle River, NJ: Merrill.

Frith, U. (1985). Beneath the surface of a developmental dyslexia. In K. Patterson, J. Marshall, & M. Coltheart (Eds.), *Surface dyslexia: Neuropsychological and cognitive studies of phonological reading* (pp. 301–330). London: Erlbaum.

Gentry, J. R. (1987). *Spel . . . is a four letter word.* Portsmouth, NH: Heinemann.

Ginsburg, M. (1991). *The chick and the duckling.* New York: Simon & Schuster.

Hepworth, C. (1996). *Antics: An alphabetical anthology.* New York: William Morrow.

Holdaway, D. (1979). *The foundations of literacy.* Sydney, Australia: Ashton-Scholastic.

Juel, C. (1991). Beginning reading. In R. Barr, M. L. Kamil, P. B. Mosenthal, & P. D. Pearson (Eds.), *Handbook of reading research* (vol. 2, pp. 759–788). New York: Longman.

Masonheimer, P. E., Drum, P. A., & Ehri, L. C. (1984). Does environmental print identification lead children into reading? *Journal of Reading Behavior, 16*, 257–271.

Murray, B. A., Stahl, S., & Ivey, G. M. (1996). Developing phonemic awareness through alphabet books. *Reading and Writing: An Interdisciplinary Journal, 8*, 307–322.

Peppe, R. (1985). *The house that Jack built.* New York: Delacourte.

Pressley, M. (2000). What should comprehension instruction be the instruction of? In M. L. Kamil, P. B. Mosenthal, P. D. Pearson, & R. Barr (Eds.), *Handbook of reading research* (vol. 3, pp. 545–561). Mahweh, NJ: Erlbaum.

Roberts, B. S. (1992). The evolution of the young child's concept of word as a unit of spoken and written language. *Reading Research Quarterly, 27*(2), 125–138.

Sendak, M. (1962). *Chicken soup with rice.* New York: Harper Collins.

Stahl, S. A. (1992). Saying the "p" word: Nine guidelines for exemplary phonics instruction. *The Reading Teacher, 45*, 618–626.

Wagstaff, J. M. (1997–1998). Building practical knowledge of letter–sound correspondences: A beginner's word wall and beyond. *The Reading Teacher, 51*(4), 298–304.

Walker, B. J. (2000). *Diagnostic teaching of reading: Techniques for instruction and assessment* (4th ed.). Upper Saddle River, NJ: Merrill.

White, T. G., Power, M. A., & White, S. (1989). Morphological analysis: Implications for teaching and understanding vocabulary growth. *Reading Research Quarterly, 24*, 283–304.

White, T. G., Sowell, J., & Yanagihara, A. (1989). Teaching elementary students to use word-part clues. *The Reading Teacher, 42*, 302–308.

Wylie, R. E., & Durrell, D. D. (1970). Teaching vowels through phonograms. *Elementary English, 47*, 787–791.

Teaching Strategic Processing Isn't Easy

Strategy Teachers' Development

"It is not easy to be a strategic teacher." These words appeared repeatedly as I read and reread my graduate students' reflective memos and portfolios. I told them that it wasn't easy at the beginning of the semester, when they began learning about teaching strategic reading processes. It is a long and difficult journey—one that many teachers do not embark upon in their careers. The intense reflection and personal growth that must accompany strategy instruction is often painful. The goal of this chapter is to explore this growth process. Research-based descriptions of teachers' growth and progress are presented, followed by an examination of my own students' difficulties, triumphs, and emotional reactions as they learned to teach strategic processing.

GROWTH AS TEACHERS OF STRATEGIC PROCESSING

Research to date has suggested conclusively that learning to become an effective teacher of strategic processing takes time (Anderson, 1992; Brown & Coy-Ogan, 1993; Duffy 1993a, 1993b; El-Dinary & Schuder, 1993; Pressley, Schuder, SAIL Faculty and Administration, Bergman, & El-Dinary, 1992). It is a lengthy process that takes years before teachers feel comfortable implementing it. Several studies of teachers learning to teach Transactional Strategies Instruction reported that this process can take up to 3 years (Pressley et al., 1992). Brown and Coy-Ogan (1993) found that becoming an effective strategy teacher was a long and difficult process and that the teacher in their case study progressed through similar phases of development as her students did, as they learned to become independent strategy users. Brown and Coy-Ogan also found that the teacher's growth and development followed a pattern similar to Hall and Hord's (1987) Concerns-

Based Adoption model of teacher change. Initially, teacher implementation of strategy instruction was mechanical and routinized. This stage was followed by one of experimentation, in which the teacher altered her procedures and tried variations of the more routinized ones with which she began. Finally she internalized and personalized her instruction. Anderson (1992) found that the teachers in her experimental study also followed a similar pattern of growth.

In their study of teachers' acceptance of Transactional Strategies Instruction, El-Dinary and Schuder (1993) found that for effective professional development, teachers must (1) experience a safe, supportive environment in which to learn, (2) be respected as professionals, (3) receive explanations and modeling of what good instruction looks like, and (4) engage in interactive coaching to help them solve instructional difficulties. Like other researchers, El-Dinary and Schuder found that it took years of development before their teachers felt comfortable implementing strategy instruction.

Duffy (1993a, 1993b) examined 11 teachers' growth and development across a 5-year period, as they became expert strategy teachers. Duffy (1993a) described strategies as "plans for solving problems encountered in constructing meaning" (p. 232). He further described a good strategy user as someone who "consciously adapts individual strategies within an overall plan for constructing meaning" and "who uses *sets* of strategies, *coordinates* those strategies, and *shifts* strategies when appropriate" (p. 232). Duffy's definitions suggest that teaching students to be strategic involves much more than teaching students individual strategies such as predicting and setting purposes. Teaching students to be strategic means teaching them a way of thinking about what it means to be strategic, and teaching them how to adapt and use individual strategies flexibly, in combination with one another, as an integrated set to construct meaning.

Duffy (1993b) conducted two interviews with each teacher each year and wrote descriptions of each teacher's experience based on these interviews. Teacher interviews and transcripts were then analyzed using qualitative methods of analytic induction, in which interviews were read and reread to identify any recurring comments and themes. These recurring comments and themes were grouped together to form categories. The teacher descriptions were rewritten, using the teachers' words as much as possible. Duffy found that the teachers in his longitudinal study experienced nine "points of progress" (p. 113) as they grew in their ability to teach strategic processing. He cautioned that these points of progress were not to be viewed as linear developmental stages but as a recursive process that was affected by social, cultural, and experiential conditions. Each point of progress is briefly described below.

Point 1: Confusion and Rejection

Duffy (1993b) noted that teachers generally experienced confusion and rejection at this point at the beginning of the project. As in other staff development projects, the teachers expected to receive a set of materials to follow; however, in this case they were expected to create their own program. Many teachers suggested that they could not create their own program because they were expected to follow their basal textbooks. It was inconceivable to them that they could create their own program, based on the needs and interests of their students.

Point 2: Teacher Controls the Strategies

At this point teachers used individual strategies in conjunction with the stories in their basal textbooks or with children's literature or content area lessons. During these lessons, the teacher engaged students in using strategies (i.e., setting purposes, making predictions, tapping into background knowledge); however, only the teacher was aware of the strategic processing. The students passively responded to the teacher's request to activate background knowledge or set purposes. The teacher was doing all of the active processing and decision making regarding *where* and *when* strategies would be used. Strategy use was implicit, and the teacher did not explain the declarative, procedural, or conditional knowledge associated with strategy use. Students were not involved in actively planning or initiating strategy use. Duffy (1993b) noted that postlesson interviews with students revealed that better readers were able to glean information about strategy use from such implicit lessons, but poorer readers were completely unaware of the strategies.

Point 3: Trying Out

Teachers at this point realized that less proficient readers needed more explicit instruction to become aware of strategies. These teachers were interested in acquiring lists of strategies recommended by experts. Their lessons often focused on explicit instruction of strategies in isolation and were taught without texts at the end of the reading period. These teachers named strategies (e.g., predicting), made generic statements about their importance, and gave specific steps to follow to perform the strategy. Teachers did not relate strategies to one another or talk about an overall strategic approach to constructing meaning. Strategies were taught individually, using worksheets, and they were taught apart from real-world literacy situations. After these lessons, students could identify the strategies they had learned and provide a generic statement about their importance, but they could not describe the conditional knowledge associated with *when* they should be used or the declarative knowledge of *what* function was served by each strategy.

Point 4: Modeling Process into Content

Teachers at this point were still concerned about teaching the "right" strategies, but they were more concerned about helping their students gain metacognitive control of the strategy process. They shifted to teaching strategies before students read texts, and they explicitly related strategy use to the text rather than teaching it in isolation or at the end of the reading period. However, teachers at this point did not embed instruction in authentic literacy tasks. They also modeled the thinking associated with the given strategy by performing think alouds. Students were much better able to express the function of strategies and the thinking that occurred when using each, but they were not aware of *why* they were learning a particular strategy or *when* to use it (i.e., conditional knowledge).

Point 5: The Wall

At this point teachers began to realize that modeling strategic thinking and providing explicit instruction was not enough. They noticed that students thought only in terms of individual strategies, rather than sets of strategies, as they read authentic texts, and the teachers felt the need to make strategy use more genuine and useful. These teachers, who were once euphoric and confident, now felt emotionally drained and guilty because they were not doing enough for their students. Duffy (1993b) noted that this was a pivotal point in teachers' progress. Many sought ways to simplify strategy teaching. They yearned for lists of strategies, commercially prepared materials, packaged programs, and directives from staff developers that would enable them to fit strategy instruction within the traditional school framework. These teachers still wanted to exert some measure of control over the curriculum.

Point 6: Over the Hump

Teachers at this point realized that strategy instruction is much more complex than teaching individual strategies. They were less concerned about a list of "approved" strategies to teach and focused instead on teaching students to approach text strategically as independent problem solvers. They realized that there is no one way to make sense of text or to approach text and sought ways to impart the flexibility inherent in this understanding to students. Teachers integrated reading and strategy use into authentic contexts in which students had a goal to achieve, problem to solve, or a product to create. These integrated units were keyed to students' interests, which further motivated them to make sense of the texts through strategy use, thereby accomplishing the task. Students in these lessons began to talk about strategy use as a means to an end rather than as the end product of a lesson.

Point 7: "I Don't Quite Get It Yet"

Teachers at this point were characterized as still holding onto the belief that there is a "right" way to teach strategies. These teachers were uncomfortable modifying strategies in relation to their students, the texts, and the contexts in which the strategies were used. They continued to seek out authorities to "approve" their methods rather than creating their own variations.

Point 8: Creative-Inventive

These teachers were comfortable and secure with their understanding of strategic processing and how to teach it and were able to create, revise, or invent strategies. They observed and listened to their students carefully to determine the direction in which instruction needed to go. There was no pre-planned agenda or curriculum, and they no longer sought out lists of "approved" strategies. Their students engaged in authentic reading and writing that centered on units of interest to them and used strategies to construct meaning. As teachers observed their students, they noticed when explicit instruction on a given strategy or set of strategies might be helpful and provided it.

Duffy (1993b) noted three conditions associated with teachers at point 8: they gave control to students, were willing to fail, and tolerated ambiguity. These teachers provided opportunities for students to direct the course of their own learning but stood alongside them to provide scaffolded support when necessary. When their efforts or their lessons failed, they viewed these failures as learning opportunities. Now comfortable with the complex nature of strategy instruction and the ambiguity that goes with such instruction, they often realized that the lessons they had planned were not needed or appropriate, and they were flexible enough to make adjustments and be responsive to their students' needs. They comprehended the dynamic, changing nature of strategy instruction and were able to communicate this process to students, as they engaged in authentic reading and writing.

Point 9: Unnamed

Duffy (1993b) did not observe Point 9, but he and the teachers with whom he worked expected to continue to grow and develop. They assumed that they were not at an endpoint in their understanding of strategy instruction.

This type of growth and development is difficult to accomplish in teacher preparation programs primarily because of the finite nature of semester-long courses that are often devoid of authentic teaching experiences. The teachers in Duffy's (1993b) study felt that teacher education about strategy instruction needed to occur in classrooms where teachers could see strategy instruction in action and use what they were learning. They felt that learning to write lessons for the professor was inauthentic, that lessons needed to be planned for real students in real contexts. Duffy's teachers also felt that professors and teacher educators needed to attend not just to the cognitive dimensions of teacher development but the affective dimensions as well.

With these thoughts in mind, I began rethinking my own graduate courses at the University at Buffalo. The course that I teach on strategic reading processes is an elective in the master's program in literacy at the University at Buffalo. Teachers entering the course have had at least two graduate courses in literacy that focus on childhood literacy methods and assessment. Some have had many more literacy courses. Teachers in the master's program in literacy education at the University at Buffalo have two options. They can pursue a 36-credit program that produces graduates who have a master's degree in education and certification as a literacy specialist in the state of New York, or they can pursue a 33-credit program that produces graduates who have a master's degree in education with an emphasis in literacy education. The latter program does not yield certification as a literacy specialist. Its goal is to provide classroom teachers with additional courses in literacy education (18 credits), but it does not include all of the clinical work that is required in the literacy specialist program. Both programs, however, require teachers to be involved in a 3-credit supervised school-based literacy practicum. The 6-week school-based practicum is held in the summer in a local school district and requires teams of graduate students (usually a literacy specialist and a literacy emphasis student) to work with small groups of struggling readers. At the conclusion of the practicum, students write case study reports of each child with whom they worked. The case study details each child's strengths and needs, describes the program of instruction that was developed based on those strengths and needs, and summarizes how the child responded to the instruction. These case study reports are given to school administrators, teachers, and parents.

The intent of the practicum is to imitate the context in which the graduate students may find themselves when they are working as teachers in schools. They learn to plan and implement instruction for struggling readers, but they also learn how to work with colleagues. In this sense, we try to imitate the "push-in" model of instruction, in which the literacy specialist works collaboratively with the classroom teacher to plan and implement instruction in the classroom (see Klenk & Almasi, 1997 for further explanation). Working in pairs enabled teachers to learn how to plan collaboratively and to serve alternately in the classroom as instructor or observer.

My course in teaching strategic reading processes is an elective that teachers often take just prior to participating in this intense school-based practicum. In the course teachers begin learning what is involved in strategic processing and how to teach and assess it. In the spring of 2000 they were required to work one-on-one with a struggling reader as a way to implement what they were learning about teaching strategic processes. The course requirements included planning at least eight one-hour lessons with a struggling reader. These lessons operated within the framework of ongoing assessment described in Chapter 2, in which observation, assessment, and instruction inform one another simultaneously. Using the STAIRS model described in Chapter 2, teachers learned to generate hypotheses based on these observations, assessments, and instruction. Teachers wrote full lesson plans similar to those presented in Chapters 5 and 6. They were expected to provide the marginal glosses on the sides of their lessons to indicate each part of the Strategy Instruction Model that was operating in their lesson. The intent of this part of the assignment was to help them become more metacognitively aware of critical elements of strategy instruction as they planned. In contrast to the lessons in Chapters 5 and 6, students' lesson plans also included a research-based rationale for their instruction, and they had a concluding section in which they tried to anticipate instructional challenges.

After each lesson, teachers wrote a reflective memo that detailed what they had learned during their observations and experiences with their case study students. The goal was to articulate and share discoveries, insights, and reflections that occurred to them about the process of teaching strategic processing to students, as they attempted to integrate the course readings with their experiences. The focus in these reflective memos was on *their* growth and development as a *teacher* of strategic processing, rather than on their students' growth.

The final course requirement was a process portfolio in which students displayed, reported, and detailed their growth as a learner and teacher of strategic processing. Their portfolios included the reflective memos from each meeting with their case study student as well as any other evidence of their progress as a learner and teacher of strategic processing (e.g., data from case study student, audiotapes, videotapes, artwork, music, narratives, articles that had had a significant impact, pictures, graphic organizers, etc.). Teachers were asked to find a creative means of collecting, organizing, and presenting their development. They wrote a metacognitive analysis of their development in terms of their strengths, areas of growth, and areas of improvement; they were encouraged to make connections to texts read, class discussions, and their work with their case study student to illustrate how their growth and development was affected by those external influences.

It is the work of these 19 former graduate students that informs the remainder of this chapter. As recommended by the research of El-Dinary and Schuder (1993), I designed the course to be taught in the same flexible manner that strategy instruction should proceed. Thus, although there was an initial syllabus, the content of the course was altered and modified continually, based on the needs of my students. I tried to model the process of good strategy instruction in which the teacher responds to students' needs on a moment-by-moment basis. This meant that, at times, what I had planned for a three-hour class needed to be altered considerably. Although we closed each weekly class by creating the following week's agenda together, the teachers found that as they read their assignments and worked with their students throughout the week, they needed assistance in areas other than what we had previously planned. Sometimes teachers requested alterations to the planned agenda even at the beginning of class. I often found myself going back to my office during their small group discussions or during a break to gather the necessary materials to quickly adjust to their needs.

I also read and reacted to their lesson plans and reflective memos as they were submitted, and I reacted to portions of their case study reports prior to their final due date. However, I did not read or react to their process portfolios until they were completed. I then analyzed all of these written documents, using analytic inductive methods. That is, I read and reread all documents (152 lesson plans, 152 reflective memos, 19 case study reports, and 19 process portfolios) and my own comments on them on multiple occasions. As I reread these documents, I made notes regarding strengths, weaknesses, and growth patterns for each student. I color-coded relevant portions of these documents to highlight various strengths and weaknesses and grouped them into categories. I then recorded the categories on a grid and mapped out each student's growth and development across the eight lessons and his or her final portfolio reflection. As I continually read and reread the documents, patterns and trends emerged regarding their difficulties and frustrations, their triumphs, and their emotional reactions as they learned to teach strategic processes. It is these patterns that I share in the remainder of the chapter.

DIFFICULTIES AND FRUSTRATIONS

Teachers' difficulties and frustrations were manifested primarily via their lesson planning. They were evidenced in their reflective memos and process portfolios. Often what initially was a difficulty or a frustration became a triumph over the course of the semester. Although a total of 20 distinct difficulties emerged from the analysis, only the five most common difficulties are presented below; the other difficulties did not occur with enough frequency to warrant any sort of generalizability. Students had difficulty with:

- Explicit instruction
- Reducing processing demands
- Unfocused lessons
- Planning coherent lessons
- Distinguishing between skills, strategies, and activities

Explicit Instruction

The teachers initially had great difficulty including explicit instruction in their lessons. The element that gave them the most difficulty was communicating the underlying declarative, procedural, and conditional knowledge associated with strategic processing. The second aspect of explicit instruction that was problematic was providing enough modeling and guided practice to facilitate students' successful implementation.

Communicating Declarative, Procedural, and Conditional Knowledge

Understanding the concepts underlying declarative, procedural, and conditional knowledge presented the greatest difficulty for my graduate students. Although 12 of the 19 teachers had taken their previous childhood literacy methods course with me, where they were introduced to the notion of strategy instruction and the importance of declarative, procedural, and conditional knowledge to such instruction, 18 of 19 students were confused about the terms and experienced difficulty including these three types of knowledge in their instruction throughout the semester. I introduced these terms by defining them and linking them to authentic contexts, similar to the manner in which the terms were introduced in Chapter 1. Throughout the semester, I continually used the terms and made connections in varied contexts whenever possible. In addition, as noted, teachers were required to make marginal glosses on their lesson plans to note where they had included each type of knowledge in their lessons. These marginal glosses were intended to help teachers remember to include the three types of knowledge in their instruction, and to serve as a way for me to assess whether they understood and could use the terms appropriately.

The type of knowledge that was most problematic for teachers was procedural knowledge. Most often teachers simply neglected to include information about how to perform a given strategy or set of strategies in their instruction. They would include information related to what the strategy was (declarative knowledge), when to use it and why it was important (conditional knowledge), but they never actually taught students the procedural knowledge related to *how* to perform the strategy. Some teachers thought they were including procedural knowledge, but were actually teaching students how to perform an *activity* rather than engage a *strategic* mental process. For example, they taught students how to complete a K-W-L chart (Ogle, 1986) but did not teach the related strategies of how to tap their background knowledge or set purposes while reading. Thus, in the early stages of the semester it was also clear that teachers had difficulty distinguishing between strategies, skills, and activities. Such confusion would obviously make it difficult to convey the relevant declarative, procedural, and conditional knowledge to their students.

It was not surprising that understanding these three types of knowledge would prove difficult for teachers to understand and include in their teaching. Good readers never consciously think about the abstract concepts involved in the *process* of reading as they read. I began to realize that the teachers were having difficulty including this knowledge in their lessons because they themselves were not really sure what declarative, procedural, and conditional knowledge was associated with particular strategies and sets of strategies. Although I had always balked at "giving" them such information, I sensed their anxiety and frustration. Thus, we decided to spend part of one class thinking about each type of knowledge in relation to particular strategies. They were elated. They worked in small groups to discuss the type of declarative, procedural, and conditional knowledge that might be associated with various strategies. Their collaborative thinking helped produce charts similar to those displayed in Tables 5.1 and 6.3. In fact, they told me that I must include these charts in this text because it was so helpful for their planning.

Duffy (1993b) would describe this type of thinking as indicative of point 3 teachers who were "trying out" strategy instruction. The focus was on specific strategies and teaching students names of strategies (declarative knowledge), how to perform strategies (procedural knowledge), and the importance of the strategy (conditional knowledge).

Such instruction often promotes use of individual strategies rather than the coordinated, flexible use of sets of strategies that typifies mature reading and mature strategy instruction. I used to worry about this; however, throughout the semester I came to realize that it is okay to be at point 3. Strategy teachers grow and develop just as readers do. Point 3 is a necessary step along the way in such growth.

In his staff development project, Duffy (1993b) did not provide such direct information to his teachers, and for years I would not provide my students with such information. I felt they needed to experience the ambiguity that accompanies authentic strategy use, and I was uncomfortable with the limitations of identifying specific declarative, procedural, and conditional knowledge for strategies. However, I also have become acutely familiar with the affective dimension that accompanies strategy instruction. It can be a very painful growth process that, when coupled with the pressure that comes from being enrolled in a graduate course, can become debilitating and demoralizing. Duffy's (1993b) teachers were volunteers involved in a 5-year staff development project. They had time to grow and develop. My teachers enrolled in the course as an elective; however, the finite nature of a 15-week course and the added pressure of grading made this learning environment more intense than a staff development project.

Although I assured the teachers repeatedly that their final grade would be based on their individual growth rather than comparisons with other students, they still had an intense desire to excel. Thus, I celebrated the teachers' insights regarding the declarative, procedural, and conditional knowledge associated with individual strategies. Their collaborative discussion helped them understand these concepts more fully, and, in turn, they began to incorporate these critical aspects of strategy instruction into their lessons. Rather than remaining paralyzed by the complexity of strategy instruction, mapping the declarative, procedural, and conditional knowledge onto specific strategies enabled them to "try out" and experiment with strategy instruction. Their experiments eventually led many of them to points far beyond point 3. One teacher commented in her final portfolio:

> I am not fully confident that I understand declarative, procedural, and conditional knowledge. I do know that I have really grown in this area. At first I never heard of these terms before and by the end of the semester I was successfully using them in my lessons. The funny thing is I now find myself thinking about these terms and using them daily in other subject areas . . . I need to help equip my students with the "know how" of what to do when reading breaks down. At first I found myself focusing on making sure my students knew each individual strategy. I now realize one must also have an overall idea of what it means to be strategic. This also proves why declarative, procedural, and conditional knowledge is crucial to strategy instruction.

Many other teachers also noted that understanding declarative, procedural, and conditional knowledge was one of their greatest areas of growth.

Modeling Strategic Processing and Providing Opportunity for Guided Practice

The teachers had difficulty modeling their own cognitive processes for students via think alouds and demonstrations, and they had difficulty understanding how to provide appropriate guided practice. Often teachers did not include modeling or thinking aloud in their lessons at all. Sometimes they merely engaged the student in an activity and did not provide any strategic instruction. They believed that simply telling students what to do or how to perform a strategy was sufficient. Some teachers initially felt uncomfortable thinking aloud, which may have inhibited them; however, in time, they began to model their cognitive thought processes while reading and using strategies for their students. Other teachers felt strongly that implicit instruction could achieve similar results with struggling readers. I encouraged these teachers to try both types of instruction and reflect on the results. In his final portfolio reflection, one of these teachers noted:

> In the process of developing these lessons, I came to the realization (after some lengthy introspection) that I am an implicit learner. This was just one of many insights I was to acquire on the path to self-discovery, but this little bit of knowledge opened my eyes to the importance of concrete scaffolding when working with a struggling reader. Many of the things that I took for granted as easily absorbed through the process of observation had to be taught in a much more explicit manner. And so, I learned a valuable lesson, the basic premise being, that you can never start out too concrete in your instruction, and that once the base knowledge has been established you can then start to remove the scaffolding.

Explicit instruction bothered this teacher. He thought of it as stifling and narrow. Once I demonstrated lessons that allowed for open-ended thinking and also included elements of explicit instruction, he began to experiment with this type of instruction and found that, while it may not suit *his* style of learning, it did suit his student's needs.

Guided practice also was difficult for the teachers to understand. They saw it as a quick opportunity for students to practice the strategy they had been taught. Once this guided practice had occurred, they felt that instruction could proceed. However, as they observed their students' independent strategy use in varied contexts, they realized that their students were not approaching text in the strategic manner that had been taught and modeled. Often, the guided practice the teachers provided was in a much less scaffolded context than the original instruction, and their students were unable to implement the instruction. For example, if the original instruction occurred in a highly scaffolded context in which the teacher modeled strategy use during an event or while reading a wordless picture book together (i.e., points 1–3 of Table 5.2), but the guided practice required them to use the same strategies while reading a text independently (i.e., point 35 of Table 5.2), the guided practice was too far removed from that explicit instruction (however excellent it may have been), and students were unable to use the strategies. Many found that their students needed a great deal of scaffolded support in order to think strategically at all. In her fifth reflective memo, one student wrote: "I also need to slow down and realize that the process is what I want [the student] to learn. I sometimes feel rushed to have him work independently. I need to provide enough support and guidance so that when I am not there, he has enough background [knowledge] to utilize the strategy independently." The teachers also found they were able to understand their student's difficulties better by comparing them to their own learning in the course. One student wrote:

> I feel that I have just made a major discovery both as a teacher and learner. As a teacher I would get very frustrated at my students when it was time for them to work independently and they could not do it. I would think to myself, "I just spent 30 minutes [teaching them], and they still do not understand it." This has become a pet

peeve of mine. Hopefully I have never let my students know how much [their failure to understand] bothers me. Unfortunately, I can remember myself saying, "I don't think you were paying attention." Now as a learner I find the same thing happening to myself. In class everything makes sense, it is not until Thursday night when I start to work independently I have difficulty . . . This has really hit home with me and made a lasting impression.

When I read this comment, I immediately identified with this teacher. I had been thinking the exact same thing about my graduate students. I knew that I had taught them a lot about strategy instruction; yet they acted as if they had never heard about it before. I even altered my teaching style and the nature of the course but still had the same feeling. I now realize, as mentioned above, that learning to teach strategic processing takes a great deal of time and must be practiced in a variety of contexts, under a variety of conditions, before various aspects of this complex process are understood, let alone integrated. My graduate students would often say, "Can't you just show us a video of someone teaching strategies?" I would think, "Yes, I could. I showed you one last semester in the Childhood Literacy Methods class. Obviously you weren't paying attention." I was ready to take them to a higher level of understanding regarding strategy instruction; however, they were not at that point. It was not that they did not pay attention in the previous class, nor was it that they did not understand it. They understood it at one level—a level appropriate for an introductory course in literacy instruction. Now that they had to put strategy instruction into practice with a real student, across a whole semester, it took on a completely different perspective. They needed to hear explanations of terms repeatedly, see demonstration lessons again, and watch videos of strategy instruction several times. Embarrassed, I often thought, "Well, I don't really have that many videos to share. They've already seen that one."

I pondered these difficulties for years but did not share them with my graduate students until the spring of 2000. When I finally shared my own instructional insecurities with the teachers, they responded unanimously: "We *want* to see the same videos again. We *want* you to do the same demonstration lessons again. Now we understand so much more. We'll view them completely differently. If you showed us different videos, then we'd be starting at square one again. This way, we have some background knowledge, and we can begin watching with a more informed eye." And so we did. We reviewed videos of Patty George's comprehension monitoring lesson, I retaught basic "how to" elements of strategy instruction, and I did demonstration lessons again. Where I had intended to begin the course on a "higher" level, in which we focused on research and theory, I found that I was focusing on many of the same basic aspects of strategy instruction that I had already taught most of them in a previous course. And they got it. What was different? The type of guided practice I expected of them. They now had a reason for understanding. Rather than writing a lesson plan only for me to read, they had to meet, face to face, with a struggling reader and plan instruction for at least one hour every week. They found they could not look into the eyes of those children and teach them without understanding the underlying concepts. One student expressed the importance of modeling and guided practice in her last reflective memo:

After working with [the student] over the course of the semester I also realize the importance in constant modeling and guided practice. I observed throughout all the lessons that [the student] was much better able to utilize strategies when [I provided] constant modeling and opportunities for guided practice along with the declarative, procedural, and conditional explanations. I believe that without the modeling and guided practice these strategies would have meant nothing to her. I have discovered that not only do students . . . need to apply what they have learned in different contexts, I also need to apply what I have learned in different contexts in order to have a much better idea about how to engage in explicit instruction because this is the way we have been taught in class. In my opinion, having the opportunities for guided practice by actually working with a student is the best way to learn how to teach reading strategies.

It is the same with children. We must provide opportunities for guided practice that are meaningful, authentic, and important to *them*. Using strategies without authentic purpose does not produce the same level of understanding. Thus, not only must guided practice be meaningful, it also must be appropriate and at the right level. After teaching her fourth lesson, one teacher was able to make links between her reading of Paris, Lipson, and Wixson's (1983) article and her student's behavior:

> As I reviewed the Paris, Lipson, and Wixson article entitled "Becoming a Strategic Reader" (1983), I came to a section that I highlighted. It said that, "If they [the students] do not judge the behavior as significant or useful, it is unlikely that they would pursue it in the absence of external directives or incentives" (p. 800). I kept flipping back, rereading my highlighted portions, and read, "Without conditional knowledge regarding why it is a useful procedure, it might only be executed in compliance with a teacher's request" (p. 798). These quotes in particular made me reflect very hard on [the student's] performance, both in our one-on-one sessions and in a small group. Although [the student] often rushes to complete her work, she always wants to please me, and does not usually complain when I ask her to complete a task. She is never resistant to scaffolding, especially using questioning to assist her in coming to her own conclusions. However, she does not appear to be ready to use these strategies independently. She still requires quite a bit of questioning and support. This leads me to believe that [the student] may be using strategies because she knows that I want her to, not because she thinks that they are important to use.

This teacher's insights are revealing and instructive. First, they show the amount of effort and reflection that she put into her instruction and planning. She read and reread course readings in an effort to try to understand the behaviors she was observing in her student. She worked diligently to make connections between theory and what she was seeing in practice. This is a dedicated teacher. Her reflections also reveal that she is beginning to see that strategy instruction must be meaningful to the student. Although this teacher was not yet at the point of designing completely authentic reading and writing events, in which students would see the need to learn and use strategies to accomplish their goals, she gave evidence of being well on her way.

Reducing Processing Demands

My graduate students also had difficulty understanding the notion of reduced processing. Given that the previous section included information about their difficulties providing appropriate levels of scaffolding, this discussion focuses on their difficulty providing con-

crete instruction. Their difficulty in this area arose from two sources: (1) they did not initially "buy in" to the notion that concrete examples and concrete texts would be necessary or make a difference in their instruction, and (2) they had difficulty thinking of ways to make strategy instruction more concrete.

The teachers seemed to understand the theory underlying the strategy of reduced processing; however, their inexperience prevented them from including it in their planning. Because they were all successful readers, they could not understand just *how* concrete instruction needed to be in order to make it possible for less proficient readers to approach text strategically. In her last reflective memo, one teacher noted:

> I have learned that so many of the little things that I take for granted are big things to struggling readers. It seems like common sense, and I thought that I knew this fact all along, but it took sitting down with a student and watching her struggle with what I had given her, for me to realize just how true everything that I have been reading over the course of this school year is concerning the absolute necessity of reducing processing demands, modeling, and repetition. While I thought I knew this, putting it into practice both with [the student] and with the students in the schools in which I substitute teach this semester has given me an entirely new perspective on how concrete I need to be in order to successfully teach.

This same teacher noted that her earlier lessons put too much pressure on her student, who withdrew in response and exhibited decreased motivation. When she reduced processing by using semiotic texts, such as pictures and photographs, to elicit strategic thinking, her student "laughed and smiled throughout the entire lesson" and was able to use strategies independently to make sense of those texts.

Another teacher noted that using concrete examples helped her as well as her student:

> While [the student] has been learning different ways to improve his comprehension, I have learned many significant lessons about both my instruction and my learning. Using a concrete example to introduce a concept is much more important than I realized. Not only did it help [the student] grasp the idea that I would be teaching him, but it also helped to solidify the abstract nature of the strategy in *my* mind. It gave me a foundation to base my instruction on, and my lessons began to flow more and build on one another.

Another teacher aptly summed up the importance of concrete instruction as follows:

> Through our readings and class discussions, I have come to see how critical concrete beginnings are to the successful introduction of reading strategies. By building our foundation upon the concrete, we allow the student to make connections to what they already know. This linkage to prior knowledge will help the student to see the applicability of the strategy being taught in relationship to a process they already understand. Therefore, the inclusion of this strategy into the student's schema for reading is more likely to occur.

As the teachers experimented with incorporating concrete events and experiences into their instruction, they began to see the value. However, one of their difficulties in getting to that point was thinking of ways to make their instruction concrete. Many of the teachers expressed their frustration about having to think so creatively. One third-grade teacher noted that it was challenging to think of ways to make her instruction concrete, but she was also struggling to accept the notion because she felt that if we reduced processing, we would not set high expectations for our students. In class I explained that we *must* set high expectations and goals for *all* of our students, but it is our job first to meet them where *they* are, take them by the hand, and lead them to those same high expectations. We cannot expect students to meet us where we are, or where the "average" student is. It is up to teachers to meet each student where he or she is. After considering these ideas, the same teacher noted:

> During these sessions with [the student] I have become increasingly aware of the importance to start off using concrete examples so that the student is able to link these to the more abstract ideas or concepts that I am trying to teach. I think that coming up with concrete ways to help [the student] understand what is being taught has been one of the biggest challenges that I had to face in planning the lessons. The chart that you introduced us to in class [Table 5.2] helped me to see how much [of] a strain I am really putting on my student when I ask her to grasp something very abstract at the beginning of a session. This also fits in with the reduction of processing demands, which I really think has been one of the main reasons for [the student's] recent progress. . . . In the past couple of weeks I have come to learn the importance of removing obstacles so that the student may tackle one problem at a time and experience success.

Other teachers expressed similar frustrations and shared how they were able to think about instruction in new ways. One experienced second-grade teacher had taken the Childhood Literacy Methods course with me previously and had already begun trying to use concrete events and experiences to teach strategies to her second graders. She noted that one of my demonstration lessons in class (a vicarious concrete experience) had created a "lasting impression":

> I could not wait to use this idea of moving from the concrete to abstract gradually through events, read alouds, wordless picture books, and texts. Implementing this model, however, would involve a new way of thinking. "How can I create an 'aha' experience linked to a particular comprehension strategy?" At first it took me awhile to think in such a way, but eventually it became easier. Rather than going to the text first, as I was accustomed to doing, I thought of ways to make such abstract concepts . . . more concrete.

This teacher tried out these new concepts in her classroom, and when I applied the same notion to word recognition strategies, she noted that she had another "aha" experience in which she now tried to think of ways to make word recognition strategies more concrete:

> With this revelation, along with considering [the student's] strengths and needs, I had to create an event for him to understand how to use context to assist with words. As noted in my previous reflective discovery memo, since verbalization serves as a key assessment component in lessons, I needed something that would captivate him along with fostering discussion. Immediately, using a puzzle came to mind. While [the student] assembled an unfinished Clifford puzzle, I asked him to explain

his thinking [as he] put it together. Such thoughts as "I knew this piece went here because his eyes are at the top" and "I'll put this piece back for later" were shared. Unknown to me at the time of planning my lesson was that his comments would serve as a springboard to analogize this process of putting a puzzle together with using context clues.

After the concrete lesson was linked to using context cues to recognize unknown words, this teacher found that her student was able to begin applying the strategy, in conjunction with other strategies, on his own while reading:

> While reading *Harry and Willy and Carrothead* (Caseley, 1991) [the student] came across the word "cooed." At first he used a Post-it note to indicate it was a CLUNK word—a word he could not say; however, he later removed the Post-it when he reached the end of the sentence. When asked how he got the word [the student] replied, "It looked like *cooled*, but it doesn't have the *l* and it wouldn't make sense, 'He cried and *cooled* and waved his arms like any baby.' "

In this example, the student demonstrated that he was able to recognize when he encountered an unfamiliar word, and he was able to verbalize the strategic processes he used to recognize it. In this case, he used a combination of letter–sound cues and context cues to decode the word strategically.

    While my class discussions and demonstration lessons helped these teachers see the importance of reduced processing and gave them an overall view of how reduced processing looks during instruction, they found that the opportunity to share ideas with one another in class stimulated their thinking and helped them as well. The professional exchange of ideas is essential for strategy teachers, who often feel alienated and alone in their planning. Teachers typically rely on manuals, textbooks, publisher's materials, and kits to gain new instructional ideas. However, strategy instruction is not, and cannot be, prepackaged, which is what makes it so difficult. In this circumstance the support that came from professional relationships and networks became especially critical for teachers.

Unfocused Lessons

It took the teachers a long time to begin to realize that "less is more." Many of their lessons were overly ambitious and included lots of objectives that I knew could never be attained within one hour of instruction. For example, one teacher's lesson had five primary objectives for her student and eight secondary objectives. All of these objectives were appropriate and would be ideal if the student could actually integrate all of these strategies; however, it was an overwhelming amount of new information to introduce at one time. Some of the primary objectives included being able to use prediction to aid comprehension, relating background knowledge to text, improving word recognition strategies, increasing self-monitoring, and being self-directed in using strategies. These are all fine objectives, but there is no viable way a student who has never heard of, or used, any of these strategies to digest all of this new information in one hour.

    In the margins next to these long lists of objectives, I would note: "These are all fine objectives, but this is a lot to do in one lesson." Some of the teachers' reflective memos that followed these "powerhouse" lessons did not acknowledge their enormity, nor did they seem to notice whether their students were able to digest all of this new information. It took about five or six lessons before the teachers noticed their students beginning to succumb to information overload. After teaching her sixth lesson, in which she focused her lesson more and reduced processing by teaching strategy use with pictures, this same teacher noted in her reflective memo: "In our previous sessions, I think the learning context that I created for [the student] was a bit overwhelming for her, and thus her motivation was just to get the 'right answers.' Today the pressure was off of her, and she seemed to enjoy herself, and as a result, performed much better." Other teachers were able to recognize that they were trying to do too much in their lessons, and they subsequently began to focus their instruction more. One teacher was able to recognize this misdirection after her third lesson:

> I think that the first mistake that I made was that I expected my student to remember and be able to use right away the prediction strategy that I taught during our last lesson. I still cannot figure out why I thought that. Most of the time when you are teaching, the student cannot remember what was taught the day before, let alone a few days before. I think that in the future, I need to keep this in mind. Since we only have to meet five more times, I need to focus on just one thing and try to keep working on that rather than doing lots of different things. I feel like I am muddling my way through and that I am trying to do too many things at once and therefore am rushing. . . . I remember thinking that an hour is a long time to be working one-on-one, but I am now finding out that it is not.

The teachers noted several reasons for their ambitious planning. One reason was that they assumed their students would be able to handle this much new information. This misconception seemed to be a product of just getting to know their students. One teacher, who had tried to teach her student how to use prefixes, suffixes, and root words to recognize unfamiliar words all in one lesson, noted:

> This lesson did not go as planned. I think I tried to give way too much information at one time. Since I still do not know the child's abilities, I assumed that he would not have a problem with this lesson. . . . By trying to give direct instruction on prefixes, suffixes, and root words the demands on cognitive processing were too demanding. This in turn did not create a safe environment. . . . During the assessment, I realized that the lesson was not a success. He could not tell me what a root word is. I also did not relate the lesson to an authentic text so it was probably meaningless to the student.

These are very painful, but necessary, lessons to learn. Although I know I explained, demonstrated, and modeled very focused lessons for these students before they embarked on their own lessons, my demonstration lessons were only that—demonstrations. Authentic contexts provide more meaningful learning. Such lessons are poignant and motivating reminders of just how complex strategy instruction is.

One of the students noted that she overplanned because she was afraid she might "run out of material to cover in our hour lesson. I thought it was better for me, and it would give me more confidence, if I was overprepared, than underprepared." This is a very reasonable and understandable explanation. This same teacher noted that she felt especially anxious because it was the first lesson in which she was on her own without any support or guidance from class to help her plan. We had spent a great deal of time preparing for their initial sessions with their students; however, after those initial sessions, each teacher had his or her own unique circumstances for which to plan, making it difficult to spend as much time helping each individually. In essence, I had done precisely what my students had difficulty with: I had provided a lot of scaffolded support in class initially and then removed most of the scaffolds too quickly, expecting my students to be able to stand on their own. Teaching people to think strategically is difficult at *all* levels.

Planning Coherent Lessons

The teachers described another common difficulty: providing coherence within and across their lessons. Particularly in the beginning, some of their lessons stated one objective, but their instruction focused on another. For example, one objective stated: "The student will learn to organize important information from a text." This statement gave me the impression that the lesson was going to focus on identifying or summarizing those ideas that are most important in a text; however, the actual lesson involved using a K-W-L chart. Clearly, this teacher selected an activity to "do" first and tried to think of an objective to match it later. Neither the objective nor the lesson was focused on the student's needs or on strategy instruction. It was just an activity.

At other times teachers' assessments did not match their instruction; they taught one area and assessed a completely different area. Usually this type of interlesson incoherence was more evident in the initial lessons with their students, when the teachers had little information on which to base their lessons. After pointing out the incoherence in their lesson plans and encouraging them to plan lessons around students' needs rather than a "neat idea" or an activity, this type of interlesson incoherence subsided quickly.

From there, however, the teachers began to have difficulty planning *across* lessons. Because they believed that one form of guided practice was sufficient to help a student understand strategy use, they expected students to understand and use strategies much more quickly than is actually possible. Perhaps because most of the teachers were at the "trying out" point on Duffy's (1993b) continuum of progress, they often taught multiple strategies in one lesson or taught a different strategy every lesson. In time, they found that their students were not retaining or transferring any of the information they had been taught. In the reflective memo after her seventh lesson, one teacher noted:

> I also think I am having a difficult time providing [the student] with opportunities to practice strategies that he is learning. As I look back, I have thrown a different strategy at him every lesson. I think I should have only done a couple of these strategies, or possibly only one and found many different ways of teaching it, which in turn would give him much more practice with the strategy. Garner (1987) states in chapter seven that guided practice is the key in teaching readers to be strategic, "Learners come to use strategies concurrently and semi-automatically through temporally distributed practice. To ensure that students practice strategies, teachers must allocate some school time to the activity. . . . This sort of practice must be guided. Teachers must intersperse practice with more direct instruction and must give substantive feedback about strategy use during practice sessions" (p. 136). I wish this were something I realized at the beginning of all these lessons because now looking back, I wonder if [the student] and myself would have been more successful in our journey

together. If we took small steps, with lots of modeling, practice, and scaffolding, the outcome might be different than what it is with one lesson left.

This teacher was not alone. Many of her peers mistakenly thought that they needed to teach as much as possible, as quickly as possible. They had difficulty understanding that strategic processing needed to be taught as an overall process that continued from one lesson to the next and from one context to the next. Many of the teachers came to this awareness near the end of their teaching experience. One teacher noted in a reflective memo after her seventh lesson: "[The student] was visibly pleased to learn that our lesson was going to be a continuation of last time! Again, I realize in hindsight that a slower pace in the beginning would have benefited him. He needs more time to let these complicated ideas settle in his head."

Distinguishing between Skills, Strategies, and Activities

Many of the teachers struggled to understand the difference between instruction that was skill-like and that which was strategic. Although they tried to incorporate the basic elements of strategy instruction into their lessons, some still designed instruction that focused on narrow skills taught apart from authentic reading and writing experiences. For example, one of the teachers knew that his student had difficulty recognizing unfamiliar words, particularly polysyllabic words. Therefore, he decided to teach his student how to recognize prefixes in words. His lesson began by presenting the student with index cards that had the prefixes *un-*, *re-*, *in-*, and *dis-* printed on them, along with their meanings. The teacher pronounced each prefix and explained its meaning, and showed the student a list of root words. The teacher pronounced each root word, then added one of the prefixes to the beginning of each word. Next the student repeated each word and recited its meaning. They read a text together that had words with prefixes in it; however, contextualized instruction regarding how to use this procedure as a strategy to help the student read unfamiliar words never occurred. The lesson was devoid of any strategic language or explicit instruction related to strategy use. It was a skills lesson on prefixes.

Another experienced teacher struggled with the same confusion. In her final portfolio reflection, she noted:

> At first, I was very confused about what strategies were. How was this different from what I already do in my classroom? I honestly thought at first that strategy instruction was just a different way of doing the same activities. For example, with my student, I worked on prediction. Of course I have my students predict in reading group on a regular basis. Of course they know how to do it. However, they did not know *why* they were doing it, nor *when* they should do it on their own. In essence, they had procedural knowledge, but not declarative or conditional knowledge. It took me most of the semester to realize that what I was teaching were specific *skills*, not *strategies*.

Some teachers found themselves providing students only with the opportunity to "do" an activity rather than teaching them how to be strategic as they read. In her sixth reflective memo, one teacher noted: "I was more caught up in the teaching of the activity than the actual strategy. For example, although I knew that I wanted [the student] to learn the importance of prediction and using what he knows to understand what he does not know, I began to focus my instruction on the K-W-L chart and how *it* is used rather than the actual strategy." This teacher was beginning to see that strategy instruction involved teaching students to approach reading as a problem-solving situation.

Several teachers did not evidence any sort of difficulty distinguishing between skills and strategies in their lesson plans but noted in their final portfolio reflections, that understanding the difference was a struggle for them. These teachers were able to mechanically design "strategy-like" lessons but did not fully understand the nature of strategy instruction even as they implemented it. One teacher wrote:

> This semester I have also learned the difference between a strategy vs. skill. I have now realized after several of our assigned classroom readings, that strategies are distinct from skills. Students perform skills the same way every time. Traditional skill instruction relies on drill and practice techniques. Duffy (1993b) states that strategies do not replace skills. Strategies are plans for solving problems. Unlike skills, these plans cannot be automatic because the uniqueness of each text requires readers to modify strategies. Pressley (1989) [Pressley, Goodchild, Fleet, Zajchowski, & Evans, 1989] states a "good strategy user" uses sets of strategies and shifts strategies when appropriate. After reading these articles and listening to class discussions I realize that a good strategy user tries something else when they are not successful. This is where my role as a teacher comes to play. I need to make sure I help equip my students with the "know how" of what to do when reading breaks down.

These self-realizations did not come easily. The teachers worked diligently to make sense of difficult readings, and they worked hard to make sense of their own instruction. Like some of the teachers at points 1 and 2 on Duffy's (1993b) continuum, these teachers wanted me to tell them what to do to make their instruction strategic rather than skill-like. One teacher, in particular, struggled with how to make word recognition a strategic process. She felt that her student would benefit from lessons on diphthongs and consonant blends. Immediately I knew that her focus was on skills rather than teaching the student to approach unknown words strategically. My comments on her lesson plans pointed out that I wanted her to try to make her lessons more strategic rather than focusing on isolated skills. She e-mailed me, noting that she felt frustrated: "At first I was defeated by reading your comments on my lessons 2 and 3. I was assessing [the student's] needs and trying to create lessons that would help her. I worked hard and thought I was on the right track, but obviously I wasn't. I'm not crying yet!" She went on to ask me to help her make her lessons more strategic rather than skill-like. I responded:

> The major point of my comments is that your lessons are seemingly focused on skills rather than strategies. Now, I can tell you what to do, but that will really defeat the purpose of the course, for this is a course on learning how to be reflective as a teacher—only you can do such reflection—not me. I think that a good place for you to begin would be to review the readings and class notes on what the differences are between a strategy and a skill, then reflect upon these readings/class notes, your lessons, and my comments. Think about questions such as:
> - What are the primary differences between strategies and skills?
> - What makes a reader strategic?

- How does [the student] fit into the Good Strategy User model described in class?
- What phase of word reading development is she in and what code cueing strategies would help her move to the next phase?
- What am I doing in my previous lessons that reflect skills-based instruction?
- What could I do to make my lessons focus more on strategies?

I know this is not the response for which you had hoped, but as a professor, my goal must be to push you to think on your own. You are a very bright and energetic woman—I *know* that you can figure this out. I will be here to support you all the way—by asking you hard questions, by pushing your thinking, and by reacting to your reflections.

This way of responding is not what any of us would hope to receive when we are seeking *answers*, not more questions. However, this teacher took the challenge. She described herself as a "mature learner" who was "not easily discouraged or overwhelmed." I knew that she possessed these traits and that I could push her with this challenge. Her lessons did indeed become more strategic, and in her final portfolio reflection, she noted, in three different places, that her "greatest single moment of growth came when Dr. Almasi would not answer my question via e-mail of how to change my lessons from being skill-based to being strategy-based instruction." Ambiguity makes strategy instruction very difficult. Learning to teach strategically requires an intense amount of reflection and effort from teachers. Often times the learning is painful. These teachers, like good strategy users, were able to see, first-hand, that their intense efforts paid off. However, they were discouraged at the end of the semester when they began thinking about who would teach their student next. One first-grade teacher was so pleased with the progress she had made with her student that she began teaching her entire class to be strategic as they read. In her final reflective memo, she noted:

> After implementing a strategic program in my own class I am 100% positive that reading strategies work. It has been so amazing to see my first grade students using these strategies and using the terms that go along with them. I have had several parents comment on some of the words that they had heard their child say. One parent mentioned to me recently that they heard their first grader tell a sibling who is older that they forgot to activate their prior knowledge before reading. I also had to take a day off from work due to my father-in-law's surgery, and when I got back there was a note from the substitute mentioning how impressed she was with their reading ability and reading terminology of my students. The substitute also mentioned how well behaved my class was. I think that goes along with the fact that the students are taking an active part in their learning. By doing so they are too busy to get into trouble. I am looking forward to next school year when I can implement these strategies right from the beginning of the school year. The only thing that bothers me is my class this year will be going to a teacher that does not use this in her classroom. I have discussed this with her, and she thinks it is way too much work.

This teacher clearly saw the value and benefit of her efforts, and she was willing to continue working hard to understand and implement strategy instruction. My response to her final comment was, "Yes, it is [too much work]. I guess it depends on whether you think the children are worth it or not." In the end, despite all of the hard work, the frustrations, and the difficulties that they endured throughout the semester, my graduate students decided that children *are* worth it. I cannot imagine any greater insight. I am proud of my students and their efforts to overcome their difficulties and frustrations.

Triumphs

Although the teachers encountered difficulties and frustrations, they also experienced their share of successes and triumphs. Many teachers found that they learned and grew the most in those areas in which they had had difficulty. In this sense they (and I) considered such growth a triumph. However, there were two areas in which they met with success from the onset: (1) creating a safe environment that fostered student motivation and self-esteem, and (2) being flexible and maintaining an open mind. Both of these triumphs are described below, using the teachers' own words whenever possible.

Creating a Safe Environment

Although the teachers had difficulty learning how to reduce processing demands and designing guided practice so that a safe environment was nurtured, from the beginning they recognized the importance of creating an environment in which students would feel comfortable taking risks. Some of the teachers immediately recognized their student's passivity, lack of motivation, or negative attitude while reading and worked diligently to gain the student's trust. They found the course readings helpful in gaining an understanding of the theoretical reasons why students have low self-esteem, low motivation, and negative attitudes. In her final portfolio reflection, one teacher noted:

> The Johnston [and Winograd] (1985) article was a real eyeopener for me. It states that less successful children are treated differently from more successful children in several ways, which make it easy for less successful children to attribute their failure to low ability (p. 285). I believe this is true especially from what I am observing in middle school. The teachers are giving me the impression that the lower achieving kids are not putting in enough effort. They may not be putting in effort because they are not being motivated the right way. The teachers seem to not even consider the affective domain. I do not see them trying to create a safe environment for the students.

The teachers often noted that, during their lessons, their students would say things like, "Wow, I can really do this." They noticed their students smiling more, exuding a relaxed posture, and verbalizing more as they gained trust in one another. One teacher, who had been working with a quiet child who viewed reading very negatively, noted in her final portfolio reflection that creating a safe and relaxed environment for her student was an area in which she had had great success by reducing processing demands, engaging the child in motivating activities that taught her how to be strategic, and sharing her own (the teacher's) difficulties while reading. One very successful incident occurred during her fourth lesson when she detected the student's fragile self-esteem through an unplanned, informal conversation and was able to gain her student's trust and respect by sharing how she struggles when she reads difficult texts:

> While talking with [the student] I was telling her what I do if I am not sure about a word or what something means. She said, "I'm sure you probably know all the words already. You probably don't have to do anything." I found this to be the per-

fect opportunity to pull out my articles and notebook from this class. I showed her how I have to underline things I think are important, how I put notes in the margins, how I constantly reread, and how I ask questions in class in order to understand what I have to read for my class. I think that she was very surprised to see how much I have to do in order to understand what I read. [The student] then began to tell me whatever she does is not good enough for her parents so she feels as though she shouldn't do anything. She made several other comments to me that revealed her negative attitudes and lack of self-confidence toward reading, especially when it comes to academics. [The student] was much more open and talkative than she had been in the past. Since I got to the school early, and it was during her snack and free time, I spent her snack time talking with her and her friends. I think that this really made her feel a lot more comfortable and attributed to her openness when it actually came time to do a lesson. In the future, I am going to try and arrive to the school a little early so that [the student] can have the opportunity to become more relaxed before working with me on the lesson. It seemed as though something as simple as this made a difference when working with her.

This teacher used skillful observation and quick thinking to make the most out of this situation. In so doing, she was able to help her student understand that good readers need to work hard to make sense of text—constructing meaning is difficult for everyone. This insight enabled her student to feel a little better about her own struggles and helped her see her teacher as someone with whom she could talk openly and candidly.

Many of the teachers in the class had never worked intensely with struggling readers in a one-on-one situation; they had never had the type of intimate contact with a struggling reader that would help them understand the frustration. One teacher shared an experience that she had with her student, in which she realized how motivation affects students' attitudes: "I think the greatest lesson I learned was that motivation is definitely an important component when working with struggling readers. When I took the book out for my student to start reading, her whole attitude changed. She became reluctant and quiet, and I felt that I was pulling responses or answers out of her." This teacher was observant and noticed the affective changes in her student as they switched gears from using strategies with more concrete (i.e., semiotic) texts to using them with more abstract (i.e., linguistic) texts. We often miss these subtle behavioral changes when working with students in a whole class atmosphere. Near the end of the semester, after the teacher had successfully captivated and motivated her student by reducing processing demands and linking strategy instruction to authentic contexts, this same teacher was able to understand her student's initial frustration and lack of motivation by comparing it to her own frustrations as she struggled to learn about strategy instruction:

I keep thinking about how I felt throughout the course of this semester and all of the emotions that I have gone through at one time or another. Then I think about [the student] and how it must feel to sit in class day after day and really struggle with reading. I think that I gained the important perspective of a student rather than a teacher over the past few months. To be an effective reading teacher I think that a person has to look past all of the best methods and ideas at times and really take a look at the student that they are dealing with. This lesson also made me rethink the effect that motivation can have on a student. [The student] went from almost not wanting to participate in this lesson to almost not wanting this lesson to come to an end. That was a huge difference in attitude than when we first started working together. I think that in the beginning her motivation was that her mom was telling her that she was going to be working with me. Now I feel like she (almost) looks forward to working with me because she wants to see what I will do next. I think that this has definitely helped her to make some of the progress that she has made.

These teachers' comments show their success at capturing their students' attention and creating a safe environment in which to try out new strategies. They were able to motivate their students and gain their trust. At the beginning of the course, I emphasized how crucial the environment was for successful strategy instruction. Without a safe environment, students do not feel comfortable exposing their inadequacies or exploring new ideas. Although the teachers struggled with many aspects of strategy instruction, they were very successful in the area that is truly the most important and fundamental aspect of the Strategy Instruction Model—creating a safe environment.

Flexibility and Open-Mindedness

The teachers in my class were also very successful at demonstrating flexibility and open-mindedness. They felt that their growth as strategy teachers was due, in large part, to their "willingness to try new things" and be "flexible enough to modify their thinking," as one teacher put it. They noted the importance of seeing themselves as lifelong learners and viewed their growth as strategy teachers to be unfinished. In short, they recognized how difficult strategy instruction is and realized that, after working diligently and reflecting deeply on their practice, they still were not quite "there" yet. They grew accustomed to the ambiguity and uncertainty that accompany strategy instruction and realized that, instead of trying to control the process, they had to be flexible and open-minded to understand it better. One teacher noted that she was used to being a passive learner who took notes and waited for information to be given to her. She found that being a strategy teacher required something different of her—there were no neat and tidy answers or solutions. To teach strategies, one had to *be* strategic—which meant taking an active part in one's own learning:

> The reason that I felt like I was muddling through the first few lessons was that that is what I was actually doing. I was teaching lessons using the pieces of knowledge that I had and not really making any connections between the two parts—the information/ideas and the actual putting it into practice. I believe that this is what led me to have the feelings of confusion and frustration that I did. I thought that the pieces were going to naturally fall into place. Once I realized that this was not going to happen, and that I had to be the one that took some initiative to make some of the pieces come together (make connections), I had to go from being a passive learner to an active one that had to try and connect the information that I had.

This is exactly what we must teach children to do as they learn to become strategic. They must be actively involved in their own learning in authentic situations, so that they learn how to solve problems in the contexts in which they encounter them. It is much easier and more comfortable to sit passively and absorb information. The class in which my graduate students were enrolled required them to be active participants in their own learning. Although difficult and different for many of them, they accepted the challenge (albeit, reluctantly for some) and this acceptance became one of their biggest triumphs.

The teachers showed that they were able to adjust their instruction flexibly, in response to their students' needs. They grew into this area of strength because of their desire to help the children with whom they worked. Many of the teachers noted this point in their final portfolio reflections. One teacher described this process in the following manner:

> As I continued to work with my student I realized that it was much more important to make sure that she understood the concept being taught than just getting through the entire planned lesson. For example, there were many times that I had to change what we were going to do when we were in the middle of a lesson. I would realize that another strategy had to be reinforced or that she just wasn't getting it. In the beginning of the semester changing plans midway flustered me; I wanted to cover as much as I could possibly cover in the plan. By the time I taught the third lesson, I realized the importance in making sure my student understood what the strategy was, how it could be utilized, and when and why it would be appropriate rather than just trying to get through a lesson because that was the initial plan. Therefore, I feel that this experience has made me much more flexible in adjusting instruction *while* I am teaching.

While working with their students, the teachers realized that they had to "be flexible, open-minded, and willing to do whatever it takes to help." Coming to this realization is another great triumph because it shows that these teachers were forming habits of mind for teaching that are not discernible from written lesson plans and are possible only because of the fabric of one's being.

Emotional Reactions

As I planned this text, I always thought this chapter would be "fun" to write. I have now read, reread, and relived my students' emotional experiences repeatedly, and it somehow does not seem fun at all. Theirs are stories of struggle filled with emotions such as confusion, pain, agony, and despair. At times their stories are hopeful, but that hope always seemed to be tinged with doubt—for they sensed that, although the semester had come to a close, they themselves were not "finished." There was much more to learn about teaching strategic processing, and although they were exhausted, they knew they were not done learning. As I analyzed their final portfolios, I found that they characterized their growth in one of four ways: (1) as a journey, (2) as a maturing process, (3) as a puzzle to be solved, or (4) as raw emotion. I describe each type of growth briefly and then share samples from their portfolio reflections.

Strategy Instruction as a Journey

Those teachers who described their growth as a journey often used the analogy of a road trip. They tried to capture the notion that roads are sometimes bumpy, sometimes smooth, and sometimes nearly impassable. Some used road signs to indicate various "road" conditions. Some used the notion of packed suitcases to represent the knowledge they brought with them on the journey, and souvenirs to represent the knowledge they gained along the way. Some used poetry, such as Robert Frost's "The Road Not Taken," or song lyrics such as "The Long and Winding Road" by the Beatles, to characterize their journeys. Being on this same journey myself, I identified with and empathized with my students and their struggles when I read these poems and lyrics. I knew from the moment they entered the course what they would face, and I tried to prepare them for it. I tried to prepare myself for it. However, when I think about how hard these teachers worked, and when I read the lyrics to "The Long and Winding Road" a teacher had written on the last page of her portfolio, I couldn't help but wonder whether these journeys should be so difficult.

This teacher struggled to digest and implement the course of information, and although she experienced successes and triumphs amid her frustrations, in the end she realized that this type of learning is a lifelong process.

Figure 7.1 depicts a similar, but more lighthearted, journey, using maps from different ages as a metaphor for the journey of personal growth and development. The teacher who created this visual display described his journey in the following manner:

> The use of maps represents my personal voyage of discovery and how at times the course and direction of which were not easily discernible. The often-used term in early navigation maps "there be monsters here" was frequently appropriate when describing the unseen perils of wading into strategy instruction, especially when dealing with struggling readers. My journey began with a map that was as incomplete as the early seafaring charts of the ancient mariners. As I was later to learn, I was not alone in my uncertainty. This approach to strategy instruction was new to most of us. We all thought we knew what strategy instruction was, but invariably we were confusing skills with strategies. Based on the often-misleading information in print, it is apparently a common mistake.

I would like to think that the "seasoned guides" and "trained navigators" to whom the student refers in the first and second maps refer to my guidance and instruction; however, I know that, in his efforts to understand strategy instruction, he went far beyond course requirements and sought experienced teachers and administrators to help him. He interviewed and sought advice from other teachers, and he requested that administrators observe and critique his teaching, even though the district in which he tutored did not employ him. Despite the heavy burdens of my course requirements, these teachers read and reread over 100 class readings, they sought additional reading from outside sources, and they often interviewed and discussed strategy instruction with other professionals. These are extraordinary teachers who undertook an extraordinary journey.

Strategy Instruction as a Maturing Process

Those teachers who viewed strategy instruction as a slow and gradual maturing process used analogies of a maturing tree or the life cycle of a butterfly to depict their growth. One teacher likened most of the semester to the long "cocoon" stage, in which she actually "hid" from strategy instruction. This is an apt analogy in that many students choose to avoid it when frustrated and confused by the complexity of strategy instruction, rather than doing the hard thinking required to understand it. It would be similar to what would happen to a caterpillar that, knowing the process of maturing into a butterfly involved considerable change, decided that it would be more comfortable to remain a caterpillar. My student described her analogy in the following manner:

Every journey begins with a plan or map, but even with a good chart we often get lost in unfamiliar waters.
Even a seasoned traveler can become disoriented without the help of a guide who knows the route.
The use of fanciful monsters to delineate the unknown areas on early seafaring charts was a way of expressing
this uncertainty. That is why I chose these maps, to symbolize the uncertain beginnings of my venture into the
daunting realm of strategy instruction. Thank God for seasoned guides who help us through these unfamiliar waters.

In the beginning, there where many monsters, and obstacles impedeing my path to becoming a teacher of stratagies.
Without the help of a trained navigator all would be lost.

FIGURE 7.1. Growth as a teacher of strategic processing depicted as a journey.

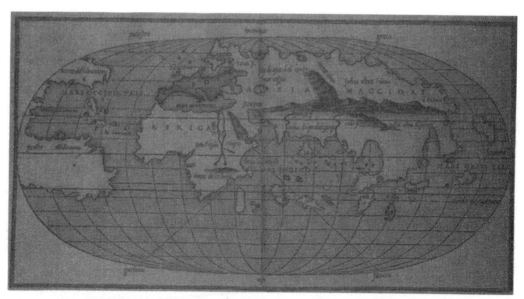

Each week the map got more complete, less uncharted reefs, less monsters, more confidence in my knowledge as an instructor of strategies. This is not ot say that I've called off the watch for unforseen obstacles, it's just that I don't have to be quite so diligent about it. Which means I now sleep a little more soundly.

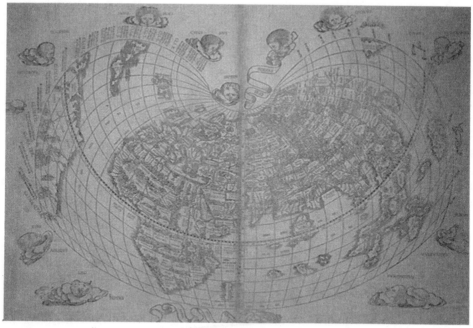

Maps like educators need to be updated if they are to remain useful. There is no branch of knowledge that is ever truly stagnant. Therefore, as educators we must be diligent in our efforts to stay abreast of the changes that will affect our students.

FIGURE 7.1. *(cont.)*

In the last few months I have learned a lot about myself as a teacher and as a person in general. I wish that I could say that throughout this process of change, everything was wonderful, but I cannot. I struggled and became frustrated with myself over instances that I was in control of and decided that I was overwhelmed. I like to compare myself to the life cycle of a butterfly. This creature in its beginning stages of life is a caterpillar, which is eager to crawl around and explore new experiences, as I was at the beginning of the course. I was excited to try new strategy instruction and learn about the student I was going to be working with. The caterpillar then makes a cocoon and hides in this cocoon until it is ready to mature. After a few lessons in implementing strategy, or sometimes by error, skill instruction, I closed myself off, just as a caterpillar is hidden within a cocoon. I was not exactly sure where to go with my instruction, but one thing I knew for sure is that I wanted to help the child I was working with become a better reader. The caterpillar then emerges from the cocoon as a beautiful butterfly after some time. This is the way I feel now. I feel that I have emerged into a better teacher with greater understanding of what strategy instruction entails. After hitting a wall and feeling that I was not succeeding, I grew into someone different.

This type of development is particularly painful to watch because the "dormant" phase, if left too long, can lead to low self-esteem, lack of motivation, and despair. I, like Duffy (1993b), feel that genuine and lasting growth and development as a teacher of strategies must come from within. However, as noted earlier, the parameters of a 15-week graduate course often meant that I had to gently prod and poke the "cocoon" to awaken it.

Strategy Instruction as a Puzzle/Mystery

While other teachers characterized the difficult aspects of strategy instruction as "road obstacles" or "monsters," some teachers saw these difficulties as puzzle pieces to be put together, or a mystery to be solved. Those who made an analogy between their growth as a strategy teacher and that of an investigator probing a mystery sought "clues" and "evidence" in their lesson plans, reflective memos, and their student's work. Those who viewed their growth as a puzzle used the analogy not just to represent the "puzzling" nature of strategy instruction but to also represent the manner in which they were able to "piece together" their understanding. Figure 7.2 depicts one teacher's experience of her growth and development. In her description she likens her growth to the declarative, procedural, and conditional knowledge she struggled so hard to understand.

Another teacher described her puzzle analogy in this manner:

This has been an interesting course. Since it was the last course in my reading specialist program, and I had already completed the clinical practicum experiences, I thought eight tutoring sessions would not hold much challenge. I soon found, however, that things I thought I had learned had pieces to them I had not before considered. The assignments, lesson plans, and readings were all pieces of a puzzle that I attempted to fit into my picture of teaching reading. Some of them fit easily, some I had to figure out, and I am still wrestling with a few. I think this is a good way to finish my program. I have learned a great deal in all of my courses, and I feel qualified to be a beginning reading teacher, but this course has reminded me how important it is to keep growing and to never think of professional development as "finished." I believed this before, but this course has given me specific questions and goals to pur-

DECLARATIVE KNOWLEDGE: PIECES OF THE PUZZLE

At first I struggled with the concept of the different types of knowledge. I now feel that coming into this class, I possessed some of the declarative pieces (individual pieces scattered about) about reading. I knew about a few strategies and reading concepts when I first started, but I had not yet started to make connections with or between them. Now I feel that my declarative knowledge has grown, and that I am starting to make connections to ideas that I have learned in the past.

PROCEDURAL KNOWLEDGE: STARTING TO KNOW HOW TO PUT THE PIECES TOGETHER

I still have a ways to go in this area. While I have learned new strategies . . . there are still questions that I have. I am beginning to understand the steps needed to do and teach the strategies, but I still want and need to learn more. I have only recently started to make the links between the major concepts and their smaller components.

CONDITIONAL KNOWLEDGE: STILL MISSING A FEW PIECES

While some of the pieces have recently started to fall into place for me, I still have a long ways to go before I will actually feel confident in knowing what I am doing. For me, the conditional piece of the puzzle is knowing why and when to teach a student a specific strategy. I still feel very unsure in this area, but I think that with time and experience, I will become better at doing it. While I feel like I am still missing some of the pieces needed to be a successful reading specialist, I do feel like I am on my way.

FIGURE 7.2. Growth as a teacher of strategic processing depicted as a puzzle.

sue. It has made me aware of more puzzle pieces that I need to fit in, and more that I need to find. Because of this, I chose a puzzle to represent my work for this course.

The puzzle/mystery analogy worked on multiple levels for these teachers. It served as a concrete depiction of their struggle to understand strategy instruction, and it served as a symbol of that same problem-solving process.

Strategy Instruction as Raw Emotion

Although each teacher had unique students with unique reading difficulties, and each teacher had his or her own way of approaching learning and depicting growth, they all experienced similar emotions: They initially approached strategy instruction with vigor and excitement; they tried out new ideas and soon became confused and frustrated; during this frustration period, they reflected deeply and sought answers by reading, rereading, discussing, observing, and taking risks. Throughout this process they authored their own learning. They grew in many ways and were able to attribute their growth to their own efforts. In the end they realized that their growth was not complete and that they still had more to learn. This humbling realization can be overwhelming. It is these raw emotions that came through in several teachers' depictions of their growth and development.

One teacher's final portfolio reflection described, in painful detail, the emotions that she experienced while trying to understand strategy instruction. Her story is a poignant one, in which she came to understand her student's struggle to learn to read by comparing it to her own struggle to learn to teach strategic processes:

> This course has been by far, the most difficult course I have ever taken. It is also one of the few more memorable ones that has left a lasting impression on me as a teacher, student, and future reading specialist. I would not say that I ever had a conflict with this class or its instructor. I would say that I had an event that lasted for the first two and a half months of class. When I enrolled in this class, I expected to learn about strategies in the form of a lecture. I thought that the information would be presented in such a way that "if the child you are working with can't do _____, then you should _____." As the semester went on (actually it wasn't until the last six weeks) I found that teaching reading is not quite that simple. I guess that it was my lack of experience or that I was one of those people who thought that a student who is struggling can be "fixed" using a certain formula. The experience that I had with [the class] and the student that I worked with, quickly changed my view of reading to it probably being the most difficult and challenging process to teach.
>
> I think that I learned more from my student than she did from me. This class forced me to take on the perspective of a struggling student. I did not handle this role very well. In the beginning and up until the very end, I had several feelings and emotions that I went through—mainly confusion, frustration, apathy, anger, despair, hopelessness, and finally persistence. Many, if not all, of these emotions are felt by a student who is struggling with reading. To hear about them is one thing, but to actually go through it is quite another. I personally do not feel that you can truly understand the students you are working with (as a reading specialist/teacher) unless you are put into a situation that mirrors their own. My lack of motivation and the feelings that I had about this class affected every aspect of this class as well as my life. I would not speak out in class; rather I took on the role of a quiet and passive learner. Rather than going and trying to talk to the instructor, I went to my advisor and tried

to find an easier way out. Her response was, "You can either change your attitude or you are going to fail." That was it. That was all she said. However, in many ways that was all she had to say. I couldn't and wasn't going to fail this class. So I took the words of the instructor on the first day of class ("If you're at the bottom, you can only go one way—up") and I picked myself up and met with the instructor. Once I realized that she was approachable and that I could actually talk to her about what I was going through (creating a safe environment) I felt a renewed hope since she seemed to understand and said I still stood a chance of passing the class.

Each time I read this reflection, I can see this teacher's face. I see the blank, emotionless, apathetic face that stared at me throughout the first two-thirds of the semester. Her face never responded, and her hands never turned in any lesson plans or reflections. At the beginning of each class, I passed out the students' name tags and usually tried to say something personal to each student. Knowing that this teacher was struggling, I always asked whether everything was "okay" or how things were going. She always nodded slightly and said "okay" through tightly pursed lips. With her (and one or two other students) in mind, I reassured the class that they could make an appointment to talk with me or meet with me at any time. She never came. Finally, after the meeting with her advisor, she met with me. I remember greeting her warmly and asking her to share what was on her mind. I listened carefully. I shared situations in which I felt the same way as a teacher and learner, and I helped her rethink some of the issues she was pondering about strategy instruction. Together we plotted a way for her to submit her lessons and reflective memos in the few remaining weeks of the semester. As a result of this meeting, I began to see a face that smiled, and I saw a face that had eyes that squinted and eyebrows that furrowed as it tried to make sense of its environment. The blank, emotionless face that had dared me to teach it was gone. Another one had made it over "the wall."

Another teacher depicted her growth simply in terms of the feelings she experienced throughout the semester. Her growth followed the familiar pattern of many of her peers—confidence, followed by confusion and frustration, culminating in a sense of renewed hope. Figure 7.3 displays the faces that she chose to depict her emotions. In these depictions she included excerpts from her reflective memos, her most recent reflections, and prose to describe her growth and development.

Many of the teachers seemed to be at points 3 and 4 on Duffy's (1993b) continuum of teacher progress. That is, they taught strategies individually, and this instruction was often the primary focus of their lessons. Because of the overwhelmingly complex nature of strategy instruction, I heeded the advice of Pressley, Woloshyn, and Associates (1995), who recommended that strategy teachers begin by selecting only a few strategies to teach at a time—perhaps even only one. Although I knew this type of instruction did not fully represent the nature of authentic strategy use, I encouraged it to reduce processing demands. Their emotional reactions show that even this form of strategy instruction initially was arduous to understand. In time, I challenged my graduate students to try to think of strategy instruction as an overall process. They read the research on teacher development described earlier in this chapter and were encouraged to reflect on their own growth in relation to that of the teachers in those research studies. One teacher described her growth in the following manner:

It is also clear just from reading my memos that my understanding of strategy instruction increased. In the beginning of the semester I was very confused about what

CONFIDENT

When I first was given this project, I felt extremely confident. I thought I knew exactly how I would teach a child to learn. In fact, my over-confidence led me to believe that I would learn new reading activities to add to my current teaching style in my classroom. What I came to realize is that I was over-confident, and I needed to change my thinking in order to become a strategic teacher!

SURPRISED

Much to my surprise, I have discovered I made a misjudgment about a student's capabilities in my classroom. Working with him on an individual level is very helpful for me to better my instruction techniques. Plus, it makes me want to take the time to work in small groups with all my other students. Prior to these last few lessons, I did not see the need to have small group reading instruction. At this point I have always taught whole group reading. I can't believe I did not see the benefits prior to this grad class! I am glad that I am struggling because I am learning about myself as a teacher.

CONFUSED

I am beginning to question myself!! What was I thinking when I thought all I needed to learn was some new reading activities to use in my classroom. I am beginning to feel VERY CONFUSED about what it means to be a strategic reading teacher. I did not understand that I need to alter my approach in teaching! BUT how do I DO that?? I hope I'll learn as I read more and teach more lessons!!

OVERWHELMED

I practiced giving directions and modeling the behavior of a good reader. This was a difficult task for me. Sometimes I feel overwhelmed trying to think about myself as a reader. Reading is always so easy for me! I ask myself, "Am I making sense? Am I doing this right?" I don't know how I can become more aware of my students' needs. In fact, I am shocked at the attitude I had when I first began this project. Boy did I have a lot to learn!

FIGURE 7.3. Growth as a teacher of strategic processing depicted through raw emotion. Created by Reneé Guzak.

FRUSTRATED	**HOPEFUL**

Feeling upset-I don't know what I'm doing! **R**eally feel like screaming **U**nderstanding this stuff is TOUGH **S**truggling to learn **T**emper is rising **R**un and HIDE **A**ttempting new teaching = STRESSED **T**rying to get past the wall **E**ncounter emotions of pain **D**oing a think aloud for the first time makes me feel awkward	It has taken me five lessons to adapt to strategy instruction, adjust my teaching, and think quickly on my feet. This implies that I am learning how to "modify my instruction in order to enhance literacy" (Walker, 2000, p. 44). I feel more comfortable modifying my instruction. I am hopeful that I will be able to share some knowledge about strategies to a group of students. I am beginning to adjust my thinking as a teacher, and I must remember that I need to model how to be a strategic reader. If I approach reading instruction this way my students will be more successful.

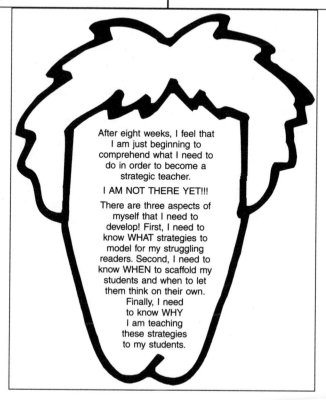

After eight weeks, I feel that I am just beginning to comprehend what I need to do in order to become a strategic teacher.

I AM NOT THERE YET!!!

There are three aspects of myself that I need to develop! First, I need to know WHAT strategies to model for my struggling readers. Second, I need to know WHEN to scaffold my students and when to let them think on their own. Finally, I need to know WHY I am teaching these strategies to my students.

FIGURE 7.3. *(cont.)*

it is we were actually expected to do with our students. By my last three memos I had developed a purpose and clarity regarding my goals as I worked with my student. I finally understood that strategic reading means more than simply knowing some strategies, and that in order to teach students to read this way, we need to encourage independence.

I still feel that I need to work on how to integrate different strategies. I have a handle on how to teach a few of them, but not on how to get kids to use all of them interchangeably. This seems to be a common problem, as Duffy (1993b) wrote; students in many instructional situations are more aware of isolated strategies than of an overall plan to be strategic. This is something I would like to pursue in my future work with students.

I do not feel badly about my progress in strategic reading instruction during this semester. Knowing that teachers who did it full time for a year still were not comfortable with strategy instruction (El-Dinary & Schuder, 1993) makes me realize that any progress I've made is impressive. Considering that I started out having never taught and knowing very little about reading instruction, I feel that just getting to Point 4: Modeling Process into Content (Duffy, 1993b) is an accomplishment. I am not positive that I fit precisely into this category, but I know that I was here to some extent. I attempted to put my student in control of his strategy use, and I tried to always use authentic texts to teach strategies. I also used think alouds to model my strategy use for my student. I do not feel that I made it over "the wall" because my student was not exhibiting totally independent strategy use, which did not happen in Duffy's (1993b) study until teachers made it over "the wall." The most significant thing I feel I have learned about strategy instruction is that it involves much more than simply teaching kids how to predict, or how to "chunk." Walker (2000) discussed the many factors that contribute to a reader's strategy use. Teachers need to encourage students to be independent, active readers and to develop a concept of themselves as good readers.

At the conclusion of the course the teachers suggested that perhaps future teachers should read about strategy teachers' development first. They felt that, had they known that all teachers experience similar feelings as they struggled to teach strategic processes, they would have felt better about themselves at various points in the process. This is an excellent suggestion—one that I plan to try myself. Each time I teach this course in teaching strategic reading processes, I struggle with the fact that although I have taught most of these same teachers in the prerequisite course on childhood literacy methods, they do not seem to retain any of the information regarding strategic processing. I often blamed my own teaching or the students for their lack of transfer. As I closely watched my own and my students' growth during the spring of 2000, I have learned that learning to teach strategic processing is a process in itself. My students helped me understand that their learning, like that of an emergent reader, is a developmental process that must be handled with care and gently nurtured.

SUMMARY

Becoming a successful teacher of strategic processing is a difficult process that takes many years. Teachers' evolution often proceeds as a pattern in which they begin by seeking routines and answers to implement rigidly. In time they begin to experiment with their instruction and eventually become flexible in their approach and feel comfortable in the process. Graduate students initially had difficulty in five areas: (1) including the basic elements of explicit instruction in their lessons (i.e., declarative/procedural/conditional knowledge, modeling, and guided practice), (2) reducing processing demands, (3) creating focused lessons, (4) planning coherently within and across lessons, and (5) distinguishing between skills, strategies, and activities. In time they were able to master these elements and were consistently successful in creating a safe environment for their students, maintaining an open mind and flexibly adjusting their instruction to meet students' needs. These teachers experienced a range of emotions as they learned how to implement strategy instruction. An initial (and brief) period of excitement was followed by confusion, frustration, and anguish. Teachers found that persistence and tenacity enabled them to reach a deeper level of insight and to feel hopeful that they would eventually become successful teachers of strategic processing.

REFERENCES

Anderson, V. (1992, November). *A teacher development project in Transactional Strategy Instruction for teachers of severely disabled adolescents.* Paper presented at the Annual Meeting of the National Reading Conference, Palm Springs, CA.

Brown, R., & Coy-Ogan, L. (1993). The evolution of Transactional Strategies Instruction in one teacher's classroom. *The Elementary School Journal, 94*(2), 221–233.

Duffy, G. G. (1993a). Rethinking strategy instruction: Four teachers' development and their low achievers' understandings. *The Elementary School Journal, 93*(3), 231–247.

Duffy, G. G. (1993b). Teachers' progress toward becoming expert strategy teachers. *The Elementary School Journal, 94*(2), 109–120.

El-Dinary, P. B., & Schuder, T. (1993). Seven teachers' acceptance of Transactional Strategies Instruction during their first year using it. *The Elementary School Journal, 94*(2), 207–219.

Garner, R. (1987). *Metacognition and reading comprehension.* Norwood, NJ: Ablex.

Hall, G. E., & Hord, S. M. (1987). *Change in schools: Facilitating the process.* Albany: State University of New York Press.

Johnston, P. H., & Winograd, P. N. (1985). Passive failure in reading. *Journal of Reading Behavior, 17*(4), 279–301.

Klenk, L., & Almasi, J. F. (1997). School-based practicum in reading disabilities. *The Language and Literacy Spectrum, 7,* 73–79.

Ogle, D. M. (1986). K-W-L: A teaching model that develops active reading of expository text. *The Reading Teacher, 39*(6), 564–570.

Paris, S. G., Lipson, M. Y., & Wixson, K. K. (1983). Becoming a strategic reader. *Contemporary Educational Psychology, 8,* 293–316.

Pressley, M., Goodchild, F., Fleet, J., Zajchowski, R., & Evans, E. D. (1989). The challenges of classroom strategy instruction. *The Elementary School Journal, 89,* 301–342.

Pressley, M., Schuder, T., SAIL Faculty and Administration, Bergman, J., & El-Dinary, P. B. (1992). A researcher–educator collaborative interview study of transactional comprehension strategies instruction. *Journal of Educational Psychology, 84,* 231–246.

Pressley, M., Woloshyn, V., & Associates. (1995). *Cognitive strategy instruction that really improves children's academic performance* (2nd ed.). Cambridge, MA: Brookline Books.

Walker, B. J. (2000). *Diagnostic teaching of reading: Techniques for instruction and assessment* (4th ed.). Upper Saddle River, NJ: Merrill.

Index

(*"i"* indicates an illustration; *"t"* indicates a table)